The Red Army and
the Great Terror

The Red Army and the Great Terror

Stalin's Purge of the Soviet Military

Peter Whitewood

University Press of Kansas

Published by the University Press of Kansas (Lawrence, Kansas 66045),
which was organized by the Kansas Board of Regents and is operated and
funded by Emporia State University, Fort Hays State University, Kansas State
University, Pittsburg State University, the University of Kansas, and Wichita
State University

Library of Congress Cataloging-in-Publication Data

Whitewood, Peter.
The Red Army and the Great Terror : Stalin's purge of the Soviet military /
Peter Whitewood.
pages cm. — (Modern war studies)
Includes bibliographical references and index.
ISBN 978-0-7006-2117-0 (cloth : alk. paper)
ISBN 978-0-7006-2169-9 (ebook)
1. Political purges—Soviet Union—History. 2. Stalin, Joseph, 1878–1953.
3. Soviet Union. Sovetskaia Armiia. 4. Vsesoiuznaia kommunisticheskaia
partiia (bolshevikov)—Purges. 5. Soviet Union—Politics and
government—1936–1953. 6. Political persecution—Soviet Union—History.
I. Title.
DK266.3.W48 2015
355.00947'09043–dc23

2015016627

British Library Cataloguing-in-Publication Data is available.

Printed in the United States of America

10 9 8 7 6 5 4 3 2 1

The paper used in this publication is recycled and contains 30 percent
postconsumer waste. It is acid free and meets the minimum requirements
of the American National Standard for Permanence of Paper for Printed
Library Materials Z39.48-1992.

Contents

Acknowledgments

This book owes a considerable debt of gratitude to many people who have contributed to its creation. I owe special thanks to James Harris, who has been a constant source of encouragement and incisive criticism from the very early stages of this research. James kindly shared archival sources and read several draft versions of this manuscript. Others who have read the whole or parts of the book and given me the benefit of valuable suggestions include Roger Reese, David R. Stone, Stephen Brown, and Steven J. Main. I owe thanks to Mark B. Smith for conversations about this research and his encouragement to think about the social history of the Red Army. Mark Harrison provided insightful advice and forced me to challenge many of my assumptions. Any errors remaining in what follows are my own.

I am grateful for a travel grant from the Royal Historical Society and funding from the School of History at the University of Leeds that allowed me to travel to Moscow to carry out archival research. I owe thanks to the staff at the Russian State Military Archive and the Russian Archive of Socio-Political History for their assistance and patience. Researching in Moscow would have been impossible without Irina and Dmitri, who showed me nothing but warm hospitality during my stay.

The second half of chapter 6 was published as "The Purge of the Red Army and the Soviet Mass Operations" in *Slavonic and East European Review*. Elements of several chapters have been published in *Europe-Asia Studies* in "Subversion in the Red Army and the Military Purge of 1937–1938."

Finally, I owe a debt of gratitude to my parents for their unwavering support throughout my PhD and beyond, without which writing this book would have been impossible. It is to them that I dedicate this book.

Introduction

On 11 June 1937, a closed military court sentenced a group of the Red Army's most talented and experienced officers to execution. Charged with membership of a supposed military-fascist plot, working with the Nazis, and planning to overthrow the Stalinist regime, all were shot immediately after the trial. The executions of Marshal Mikhail Tukhachevskii, Iona Iakir, Ieronim Uborevich, Boris Fel'dman, Robert Eideman, Avgust Kork, Vitalii Primakov, and Vitovt Putna sparked international scandal. Tukhachevskii in particular was world renowned. He was a hero of the Russian civil war and the Red Army's most capable strategist. Moreover, as soon as this supposed military conspiracy was discovered, Josef Stalin and the head of the Red Army, Kliment Voroshilov, ordered a massive purge of the armed forces. A wave of repression quickly spread throughout the officer corps and the rank and file as a growing number of fellow conspirators were connected to the military-fascist plot. This purge was not brought to a halt until November 1938, and it cost the army dearly. In addition to the execution of some of the Red Army's most talented officers, over the next two years, approximately 35,000 military leaders were discharged from the ranks. Thousands were arrested, and many were executed.[1] Indeed, this decapitation of the Red Army between 1937 and 1938 is still pointed to as contributing to its terrible performance in the months after June 1941, when the Soviet Union was caught off guard by Adolf Hitler's Operation Barbarossa.[2] Similarly, the military purge is also blamed for ruining any chance that Britain, France, and the Soviet Union might have forged an alliance against Hitler's Germany in the years before the outbreak of World War II. Stalin's attack on the Red Army made him seem like an unpredictable ally, and one with now reduced military strength.[3]

The military purge is a pivotal event in the history of the Great Terror—the name given to the surge in political violence and repression in the mid- to late 1930s, during which over one million Soviet citizens were imprisoned in labor camps and over 750,000, at the very least, were executed. During these years of repression, the military purge marked the point at which the growing political violence, formerly almost exclusively targeted at Stalin's old political opponents, began to affect those without such black marks on their records. Someone like Mikhail Tukhachevskii, for instance, had never supported the former political opposition before his arrest and execution. The military purge was thus not merely an attack on the Red Army. As we shall see, the military purge broadened the scope of the Great Terror in a number of important respects.

The reason why Stalin lashed out at his military in such an extreme manner in the summer of 1937 remains a mystery. What is certain is that there was no genuine conspiracy inside the Red Army. It has long been known that the military-fascist plot had no basis in reality. Evidence used in support of the conspiracy was obtained by the Soviet political police by forced confessions and torture. After Stalin's death in 1953, many victims of the military purge (like other prominent victims of the wider Great Terror) were posthumously rehabilitated during Nikita Khrushchev's de-Stalinization.[4] Since 1937, there have been frequent attempts to explain Stalin's attack on the Red Army, but no adequate or convincing explanation has been presented about why Stalin would gut his officer corps just years before the outbreak of world war. The most common interpretation depicts Stalin launching a carefully premeditated purge of the Red Army in 1937 as another part of his domination through terror.[5] However, this explanation has immediate and obvious flaws. If consolidation of power was the main objective of the military purge, Stalin chose a terrible time to do this. As we shall see, from the Soviet leadership's point of view, world war was on the horizon in the mid-1930s, and Soviet defense spending was rising rapidly in response. Why would Stalin build with one hand and destroy with the other? Why actively prepare for war while weakening the Red Army through a mass purge? The military purge potentially put not only Stalin's own grip on power in danger but also the existence of the entire Soviet Union, as Stalin might be forced to fight any future war with a weakened military. On the surface, the military purge appears to be an irrational act; it does not sit comfortably with an explanation focusing on Stalin's desire for greater personal power and control.

In this book, I offer an entirely new explanation for the military purge. I show why Stalin thought that such a great risk needed to be taken in 1937 and why, at least from the perspective of the Soviet leadership, this was not irrational. Stalin launched a wave of repression against the Red Army not as another part of a carefully orchestrated consolidation of power. Rather, he did this from a position of weakness and at the last moment. By mid-1937, in what was recognized as a time of looming war, Stalin misperceived a security threat from within his army. He came to incorrectly believe that it had been infiltrated by foreign agents at all levels. Moreover, not only had these spies managed to get inside the Red Army, but so-called evidence obtained by the political police sketched out a conspiracy at the very heart of the high command. On the basis of these misperceived dangers, Stalin was compelled to crack down on the Red Army. He thus sanctioned a major purge to root out the subversives he believed were hidden in the ranks. From Stalin's point of view, how could he fight the coming war with a military that had been so badly compromised? However, as an expanding wave of discharges and arrests ripped through the Red Army starting in June 1937, the military purge, like the wider Great Terror, escaped central control. This was partly re-established in early 1938, and the military purge was eventually called to a halt in November—the same time that the wider Great Terror was brought to a close—but not before it had caused massive damage to the Red Army. To explain why the military purge was launched, it is thus necessary to try to understand how the Soviet leadership could so badly misperceive the danger from the Red Amy in 1937 and come to believe that such drastic action was unavoidable. However, before doing so, a short survey of previous accounts of the military purge will show why few of these have been convincing.

The first attempts to provide a rationale for why Stalin attacked the Red Army in 1937 came from foreign observers and the contemporary press as soon as the executions of Tukhachevskii and the group of senior officers were publicly announced in June. However, with little access to reliable information, these early responses were understandably speculative. The *Manchester Guardian*, for instance, raised the possibility that Stalin had acted in response to a genuine military conspiracy within the Red Army.[6] This theory gained greater currency in later years. Commentators such as *New York Times* journalist Walter Duranty, who was based in Moscow for much of the 1930s, later argued that there had been a real conspiracy in the Red Army.[7] Even though Duranty is recognized as an apologist for the Stalinist regime, less biased figures, such as the American ambassador to the Soviet Union, Joseph E. Davies, agreed that a real military coup had been forestalled in 1937.[8] Although not all were so certain of the facts, Stalin's ambition for greater power and control over the state was also put forward as a possible motive behind the military purge.[9] A number of early historical works reached similar conclusions. In a book published outside the Soviet Union in 1938, German writer, communist, and former Red Army officer Erich Wollenberg saw the military purge as one part of Stalin's elimination of any possible challenge to his authority.[10] Taken together, certain unifying themes appear in these early accounts of the military purge: Stalin's desire for power, his willingness to take extreme measures to safeguard this power, and speculation about a possible military conspiracy.

Early interpretations of the military purge did not alter by the 1960s and 1970s; they appeared in more developed forms in general histories of the Great Terror and the Red Army. Historians and political scientists writing at the time of the Cold War typically saw the military purge in a similar light: this was just another part of Stalin's escalation of political repression in the 1930s aimed at securing his personal power and neutralizing potential threats.[11] Moreover, according to some Cold War historians, Stalin purged the military because he believed that certain officers in the high command, particularly those around Tukhachevskii, might one day block his expanding power. The Red Army was merely another institution that needed to be subjugated if Stalin was going to achieve total dominance. In this respect, the military purge was understood in the context of the growth of Stalin's cult of personality and his abuse of power.[12] Notably, alongside this common argument focusing on Stalin's desire for untrammelled power, Cold War accounts tend to examine the military purge on a narrow basis, referring to it as the Tukhachevskii Affair, after its most famous victim. However, this framing reduces any analysis of the repression in the Red Army to the relationship between Stalin and his military elite. Supposed animosities and assumed personal tensions between Stalin and his leading officers were seized on as providing the rationale behind the military purge. This focus on personalities neglected any serious consideration of the experiences of the rest of the officer corps and the wider rank and file during the years of the Great Terror. It left inadequately explained why the military purge affected the entire Red Army and not just the high command.

Common to Cold War accounts of the military purge is a story about a fabricated dossier of evidence that Stalin supposedly used to incriminate the senior officers he wanted out of the way. This dossier apparently contained falsified materials, which provided a smoking gun: a group of leading Red Army officers, with German assistance, were planning a coup. The dossier story exists in several versions; in some cases, there is no physical file of evidence, only verbal disinformation. In the most common version, Stalin personally ordered evidence to be fabricated to provide a credible pretext for eliminating the officers from the high command whom he believed stood in the way of his goal of attaining total power. The political police then had the necessary incriminating dossier put together outside of the Soviet Union (seemingly to give it more credibility) and returned to Stalin via an independent channel.[13] Alternatively, in another version of the story, Stalin is depicted as being duped by German intelligence agents who decide to fabricate the dossier and have it sent to the Soviet Union to provoke Stalin into attacking his own military.[14] In most versions of the story, the main protagonists are the president of Czechoslovakia, Eduard Beneš; the head of the German intelligence agency, Reinhard Heydrich; and the Russian White émigré and Soviet double agent, Nikolai Skoblin. Beneš's role was that of chosen intermediary; he was supposedly fooled into passing disinformation about the Red Army officers to the Soviet ambassador in Prague, which was then returned to Stalin. In different variations of the dossier story, either the Soviet political police or German intelligence agents arrange for the disinformation to be passed to Beneš. In his memoirs, Beneš claimed that he found out about plans for a Soviet military coup secondhand through Count Trauttmannsdorff, one of Hitler's high officials. Apparently Trauttmannsdorff accidently disclosed the existence of secret negotiations between Hitler and Tukhachevskii and had spoken about an "anti-Stalin clique" in the Soviet Union.[15] Reinhard Heydrich's role was working with the double agent Nikolai Skoblin to fabricate the necessary documents, which supposedly included genuine signatures from the incriminated officers.[16] In one version of the story, Skoblin is depicted as convincing Heydrich that there was talk of a military coup circulating among senior Red Army officers. Heydrich then agreed to fabricate the necessary incriminating materials for transmission to the Soviet Union, having sensed an opportunity to provoke Stalin into attacking his army.[17]

The dossier story is full of intrigue and conspiracy. Had it not been for Nikita Khrushchev's acknowledgment of its existence in the early 1960s, it probably would not have been given much credibility by historians.[18] Indeed, despite how often the story appears in books on the military purge, whichever way it is presented, there is no reason to believe it. The story derives from unreliable memoir accounts, often those of political police defectors who have long been discredited.[19] Other key pieces of evidence, such as Beneš's own memoir account, have also been proven to be inaccurate.[20] There is nothing to suggest that the dossier story has any basis in reality. Aside from the problems with the existing sources, there is also a complete absence of any other reliable evidence. After the opening of the Russian archives in the early 1990s, no piece of documentary evidence has been found to support the story. Moreover, the archival materials that are now accessible do not point toward the existence of a fabricated dossier either. For example, one week before the closed military trial in June 1937 that sentenced the Tukhachevskii group to execution, Stalin met with the Red Army's most senior officers to discuss the recently exposed military-fascist plot. The transcript of this meeting is now available, and throughout the entire four-day session, there is not a single mention of any dossier of incriminating evidence. Nor was it used during the June military trial itself.[21] This is remarkable if the fabricated dossier was really the central piece of evidence against Tukhachevskii and the other officers incriminated in the military conspiracy. Why would Stalin go to such lengths to have evidence fabricated with the chief aim of giving the planned executions in the high command credibility if he never publicized it or seemingly even used it? The same can be said for the version of the dossier story where Stalin is duped by German intelligence. If the German evidence was so convincing, why were the rest of the Red Army elite not told about it in June? It also seems unnecessary that Stalin would choose to have the dossier fabricated abroad, then sent back to the Soviet Union. It would have been far easier to have the group of officers incriminated on groundless charges inside the Soviet Union, like all the other prominent political victims of the Great Terror. In short, the poor source base and lack of evidence mean few historians take the dossier story seriously today.

Cold War accounts of the military purge were also shaped by dominant trends in the historiography of the Great Terror. In the 1960s and 1970s, the Great Terror was depicted by historians as little more than a brutal consolidation of power, with Stalin portrayed as the master planner who methodically executed anyone who stood in his way.[22] By extension, the military purge was viewed merely as another stage in this consolidation of power into another area of the Soviet state. However, as we have already seen, there are problems with this view of the military purge. At a time when the regime believed war was approaching, would Stalin really endanger the security of the Soviet Union by executing some of his most talented military leaders and arresting thousands of officers just to achieve personal dominance over the armed forces? How did Stalin find himself in such a position if he was such a meticulous and careful planner of promoting to the highest ranks people whom he did not fully trust? If Stalin's aim was absolute control, why was Tukhachevskii given so much authority in the Red Army in the first place? Why did he remove Tukhachevskii in 1937, and not at any time before?

Serious questions were raised against established accounts of the military purge as part of wider reassessments of the Great Terror published in the 1980s and early 1990s. Notably, a group of "revisionist" historians questioned the level of premeditation that lay behind the military purge. For instance, in examining the events leading up to the military trial in June 1937, some argued that these were not as expected if Stalin had meticulously arranged the execution of the Tukhachevskii group. Indeed, despite the clouds that had begun to circle Tukhachevskii in early May, it took several weeks for Stalin to decide on a course of action. When he finally did do something, his first move was to demote Tukhachevskii from the position of deputy people's commissar of defense to command the less prestigious Volga Military District.[23] As one historian commented, this was an unusual way to treat supposedly dangerous conspirators.[24] If Stalin saw Tukhachevskii as a threat to his power, if he was a marked man, and if there was incriminating evidence against him, it makes little sense not to arrest him immediately.

With restricted access to credible primary sources, however, historians writing in the 1980s and early 1990s could do little more than point out the obvious holes in Cold War accounts of the military purge.[25] Only with the release of huge amounts of previously inaccessible documents from the Russian archives upon the collapse of the Soviet Union were more detailed studies on the impact of the Great Terror on the Red Army published. With the declassification of internal army, Communist Party, and political police materials, it was possible for the first time to gain a fuller understanding of the course of repression in the Red Army during 1937–1938. This newer work cast even more doubts about the accuracy of Cold War interpretations of the military purge, particularly the common framing of the Tukhachevskii Affair. For example, using new archival materials, Roger Reese showed that a practice of purging (*chistki*) had already been established in the Red Army during the 1920s and 1930s. Regular internal purges were designed to improve ideological conformity in the ranks by removing anyone deemed to be class aliens, socially harmful elements, or belonging to other subversive categories.[26] Reese argued that when the regime called on Soviet citizens to participate in the hunt for enemies of the people in 1937, the resulting surge in denunciations quickly spread throughout the Red Army, as the officers and soldiers were already accustomed to purging class enemies from the ranks.[27] An established practice of internal purging transformed into a vehicle of mass denunciation in 1937–1938. In this way, Reese shined important light on the responses from ordinary soldiers to the regime's calls to root out hidden enemies, showing that the military purge was much more than the Tukhachevskii Affair. The reactions from the Red Army as a whole to both the wider Great Terror and the military-fascist plot are crucial to understanding why the violence of the military purge reached such a large scale.

With access to important archival materials, other historians similarly traced the roots of the military purge before 1937, likewise taking the focus away from the narrow framing of the Tukhachevskii Affair. Oleg Suvenirov documented repression in the military from the early 1930s, showing that before the decisive year of 1937, the Red Army saw the arrests of former political oppositionists, the lower ranks had erupted in mass protest during the years of the collectivization of agriculture, and "counterrevolutionary" groups and supposed foreign agents were frequently unmasked by the political police everywhere along the army hierarchy.[28] Further, Suvenirov revealed the impact of the most important political events of the 1930s on the Red Army. After the murder of Leningrad party boss Sergei Kirov in December 1934, for instance, Suvenirov estimated that a wave of tens or hundreds of military arrests soon followed.[29] Repression in the Red Army could be shaped by domestic tensions, fueling spikes in political violence. In short, Suvenirov demonstrated there is an important prehistory to the military purge of 1937–1938 and that the Red Army was sensitive to changing political currents in the Communist Party before the outbreak of the Great Terror. Instead of a simple story of the Tukhachevskii Affair and a fabricated dossier, the military purge must be seen in the context of the broader political repression of the 1930s.

More detail about the military purge has also been gained from important recently declassified sources, such as the transcript of the meeting of the Military Soviet of June 1937, which reveals how the news of the military-fascist plot was disseminated to the wider Red Army.[30] What is striking about this meeting is that for many, this was the first time they had heard about a military plot in the high command. Many of the assembled officers reacted with shock when informed that their former comrades—people whom they had believed to be loyal officers—were apparently dangerous conspirators. Stalin and the army leadership used this opportunity to call for a purge of the ranks and encouraged officers to assist in the hunt for enemies, leading to a surge in denunciations. More ominously, some of the assembled officers discovered their own names in the interrogation transcripts circulated at the meeting and were soon arrested.[31] Partially declassified interrogation transcripts have also contributed to our knowledge by showing how the political police pieced together a military conspiracy in 1937. This was a process not without flaws or contradictions; it provides a firm rebuttal to those who maintain that there was a genuine and coherent military conspiracy in the Red Army.[32] In addition, other historians have used new archival materials to explore the connections between the Red Army and German high commands in the 1920s and 1930s.[33] This is a connection with particular significance. One of the main charges against the senior officers at the closed military trial in June 1937 was that they were agents working for Germany. The military-fascist plot certainly had no basis in reality, but an established relationship between the German and the Red Army high commands put the latter in a vulnerable position in 1937.

However, despite this new level of detail about the military purge and the new archival sources, no credible or convincing explanation has yet been offered for why Stalin would attack his army at the same time the regime believed war was approaching. Reese and Suvenirov explored the dynamic of the purge process in the army, showing that the tide of denunciations from within the ranks could not have been wholly directed by Stalin and that there is an important prehistory of repression in the military before 1937, but neither points to why Stalin ordered the military purge in the first place.[34] Similarly, other newer works do not convincingly explain why the military purge was initiated, and they instead fall back on traditional arguments focusing on Stalin's desire for loyal officers and a premeditated attack on the Red Army.[35] In the main, the majority of recent accounts either make no firm judgment about motive or merely allude to Stalin's appetite for power and his attempt to crush any possible opposition. In this sense, despite the new archival material, there has been little development from the interpretations of the Cold War on the central question about why Stalin attacked his army in such an extreme manner in 1937. The few explanations of the military purge that do differ from the traditional Cold War view remain far from complete. For example, one historian has argued that Stalin launched the military purge because an alliance of senior officers, led by Tukhachevskii, wanted to force the head of the Red Army, Kliment Voroshilov, out of his position.[36] This group of officers were apparently unhappy with the direction that the Red Army was heading and blamed Voroshilov for this, which Stalin then interpreted as a threat. In this way, tensions within the military elite are presented as evidence of a possible plot. Even though the military-fascist plot was groundless and there were no genuine plans for anything as serious as a coup, there were still some conspiratorial moves behind the scenes from a group of senior officers who wanted Voroshilov removed as head of the Red Army. However, much of this evidence is circumstantial. There is also a big difference between a group of senior officers hostile to their superior and genuine conspiratorial plans to force him out.[37] As we shall see, Tukhachevskii certainly had a poor personal relationship with Voroshilov, and he was also subject to persistent rumors about his loyalty. Yet there is nothing to suggest that there was any concerted effort to remove Voroshilov from the army leadership. Moreover, this explanation does not account for why the military purge later affected 35,000 army leaders and not just the small group of conspirators who were apparently plotting Voroshilov's downfall.

There has been little progress in explaining Stalin's purge of the Red Army because previous work has infrequently engaged with the large body of research on the Great Terror published since the opening of the Russian archives.[38] Debates about the origins of the Great Terror and the forces behind state violence in the Stalin period have been transformed over the past twenty years as a result of access to previously classified archival sources. Since the opening of the Russian archives in the early 1990s, interpretations of the Great Terror that dominated the postwar years and that directly influenced early examinations of the military purge have been shown to be narrow and incomplete. During the 1950s and 1960s, historians typically examined the Great Terror from the perspective of political history and variously depicted Stalin as using state violence in order to overcome resistance to revolutionary change; using it as a means to increase his personal control over the Soviet Union; or using it simply as a consequence of a paranoid personality. Some historians and political theorists saw state violence as inherent to the Soviet system itself, but the majority writing in these years tended to focus solely on Stalin's purported intentions and individual actions during the Great Terror at the expense of an analysis of wider Soviet society.[39]

Even before the Russian archives opened, however, this dominant Cold War narrative had already been challenged by revisionist historians examining previously neglected aspects of the Great Terror. Notably, revisionist historians took emphasis away from high politics and instead explored the role of wider society in the formation of the Stalinist system.[40] In the 1990s, a growing number of historians began to challenge how the Great Terror had previously been framed, showing that the surge in political violence during 1937–1938 was a much more complex phenomenon than simply state repression directed from above. Research from the early 1990s, for instance, highlighted a range of societal tensions that compelled ordinary Soviet citizens to actively participate in the Great Terror and denounce one another to the authorities, whether out of fear, loyalty, or malice. These social tensions were so strong that the Great Terror took on a momentum of its own, and the regime began to lose control.[41] Other historians have offered new interpretations for the primary cause of the violence, challenging the accepted view that Stalin's desire for more power and personal control is the central factor. Before the Russian archives opened, Arch Getty argued that strained relationships between the center and regional party leaders and attempts by the center to bring local elites into line in 1937 provided the spark for the Great Terror. Importantly, Getty presented the Great Terror as a reactive process caused by a loss of control, rather than being carefully premeditated.[42] Other historians have similarly argued for the importance of internal systemic pressures and pointed to a struggle between the party and state, as well as between the elite and the workers, that encouraged the regime to turn to repression to manage the system.[43]

Following the same approach, part of this book will explore how the Red Army rank and file responded to the military-fascist plot. It will show that even though the military had a stronger sense of hierarchy and discipline than existed in wider society, the response from the troops to the regime's urgent call to root out hidden enemies during 1937–1938 created a similar level of turmoil and disorientation in the ranks. Like the broader Great Terror, the military purge eventually took on a momentum of its own.[44] Moreover, the tensions between the army leadership and the officer corps will also be examined. There are many suggestions that some officers resisted the frequent calls to find enemies within their units in the years before the Great Terror. As we shall see, like the recalcitrant regional party leaders that Stalin sometimes struggled to bend to his will, some officers had a vested interest in evading orders.

However, rather than argue that Stalin initiated the military purge as part of efforts to manage a dysfunctional Soviet system (or that this was an unforeseen consequence of these efforts), this book argues that Stalin attacked the Red Army because he misperceived a serious security threat. It will explore why Stalin saw such a grave danger from his military and how he came to believe that there was no other choice but to unleash a mass purge. This examination of the military purge has relevance to newer debates concerning the influence of Bolshevik ideology on the use of state violence and how the Soviet leadership's interpretation of the world fueled a fundamental misperception of threat. In this way, this book will help reveal the motivations behind the wider Great Terror. Indeed, even though Cold War accounts of the Great Terror are now recognized as reductive, there is still little consensus about Stalin's motivations or why he turned to state violence so frequently. Although new archival documents have allowed more nuanced interpretations of the 1930s, they have also generated many unanswered questions. New strands of research into Soviet culture and society, foreign policy, and the influence of ideology and intelligence on the behavior of the regime have created new controversies without settling older arguments about why the Great Terror began, and for what purpose.

The influence of Bolshevik ideology on the regime's perception of the world is central to this examination of the military purge. New archival documents, such as private correspondence between Stalin and members of his close circle, have already shown the strength of ideology inside the upper circles of the Communist Party. Stalin frequently used Marxist language outside of his public speeches and in his private correspondence. It is now clear that he did not just cloak a base desire for power in Marxist rhetoric.[45] Stalin viewed the world through a Marxist lens and appears to have been ideologically committed.[46] Historians have already explored the influence of ideology on the regime's domestic policies, specifically as a mobilizing force behind political violence.[47] Others have examined the regime's ideological hostility to capitalism, namely the deeply held belief that the capitalist world was engaged in a vast conspiracy to destroy the Soviet Union and what effect this had in shaping state repression.[48] Similarly, James Harris has argued that the Soviet leadership's concerns about the capitalist encirclement of the Soviet Union, combined with a stream of inaccurate or misread intelligence, left them convinced that a major war was approaching for almost all of the interwar period. Stalin often expressed concerns that foreign agents were infiltrating the country and preparing acts of sabotage, a view that was only reinforced by the regular arrests carried out by the political police of supposed foreign agents and other counterrevolutionaries. A stubborn misperception of threat lay behind the violence of the Great Terror.[49]

This book further explores Bolshevik ideology and the regime's perception of threats in examining how Stalin perceived the security of the Red Army specifically. Taking the Russian Revolution as a starting point, it shows that the Bolshevik regime had an uneasy relationship with its standing army from the very beginning. Maintaining a traditional standing army (rather than a more ideologically acceptable people's militia) clashed with the Bolsheviks' revolutionary principles and made for uneasy civil–military relations. Alongside this ideological hostility, the Red Army was regarded as an obvious target of foreign agents and domestic counterrevolutionaries throughout the 1920s and 1930s. The military was judged as vulnerable to infiltration and displaying alarming security weaknesses that the regime believed would be seized on by hostile capitalist countries. Yet these threats were consistently perceived as more dangerous than their reality. The Stalinist regime saw more enemies arrayed against the Red Army than actually existed. This gulf between the perception and reality is crucial to understanding why Stalin purged the military in 1937. Indeed, by this point, this gulf had grown extensive, creating ideal conditions for a spy scare to erupt in the ranks and for the political police to simultaneously unmask a "military conspiracy" in the high command. As we shall see, there is little to suggest that Stalin did not take these threats seriously. A radical purge of the army was the only possible response. In this respect, Stalin launched the military purge from a position of vulnerability and misperception rather than from a position of confidence and strength. Even though he believed world war was increasingly likely, Stalin purged the organization he needed the most because he misperceived a threat to his own power and the security of the regime from the Red Army. Although Stalin undoubtedly wanted to preserve his own power—and this remains an important motivation in both the military purge and wider Great Terror—it is necessary to understand what he believed put this at risk.

New documents from the Russian archives have also allowed an examination of the Soviet mass operations, which ran from summer 1937 until autumn 1938 and which were responsible for over one million arrests and nearly 700,000 executions.[50] Not only were the mass operations responsible for the majority of the victims in the Great Terror but they show that it was ordinary people, rather than the political elite, who suffered the most.[51] This is in sharp contrast to Cold War works on the Great Terror, which tended to focus on the repression within the Communist Party elite and the staging of the three notorious Moscow show trials between 1936 and 1938. Indeed, ordinary peasants, workers, and non-Russians constituted the overwhelming bulk of the victims of the Great Terror. Yet even though it is undisputed that Stalin ordered the mass operations, it is still far from clear why he did this. Some historians argue that Stalin launched the mass operations because he wanted to internally secure the Soviet Union in the face of the approaching world war, and this meant removing any unreliable groups from the population.[52] However, the importance of the anticipated future war in sparking the mass operations has been questioned, primarily because in reality there was no pressing international crisis threatening the Soviet Union in the summer of 1937. Alternatively, another explanation of the mass operations emphasizes domestic factors, arguing, for instance, that the regime feared that levels of anti-Soviet opposition in the countryside had grown significantly during the first half of 1937, which was considered a threat in the context of forthcoming open elections to the new Supreme Soviet scheduled for that year. There were growing fears that anti-Soviet elements could influence the outcome of the process. In this view, having realized the danger posed by so many unreliable groups in the population, Stalin decided to launch mass operations in the summer to internally secure his regime.[53]

This book will advance a new explanation of the mass operations that reconciles these conflicting interpretations. The military purge was launched in June 1937, just weeks before the first mass operation began. As we shall see, the military purge was sparked by the regime's misperception that the Red Army had been widely infiltrated by foreign agents. The Soviet leaders believed that a "fifth column" had been discovered in the Red Army in the summer of 1937. After the launch of the military purge, Stalin subsequently moved to secure wider society by sanctioning the mass operations. If he believed that foreign agents were inside the military, could Stalin be certain that other less reliable population groups were not equally compromised or being manipulated by foreign powers? The fear of a future war thus provided an important underlying motivation to the mass operations, but it was the more immediate threat of a perceived fifth column within the Red Army that first drove the military purge in June 1937 and then became the catalyst for the mass operations just weeks later. In this respect, it is unlikely that the mass operations were planned long in advance, and they are best seen as a knee-jerk response to a sudden and mistaken fear that a fifth column potentially extended much further than the Red Army. The mass operations are a reflection of the regime's sense of insecurity rather than its high level of totalitarian control.[54] The military purge was much more than just a subplot in the Great Terror. It transformed the scale and scope of the broader political violence.

In order to understand the military purge of 1937–1938, it is necessary to begin with the Russian Revolution of 1917. The security anxieties surrounding the Red Army in 1937 did not suddenly appear; their roots stretched back nearly two decades. Identified security threats to the army shifted and evolved over a twenty-year period until they finally peaked in mid-1937. Chapter 1 thus examines the formation of the Red Army and its early years, from its creation in early 1918 and its performance during the civil war. This chapter shows that the new Red Army was immediately identified as a target of various enemies by the Bolshevik Party leadership and the political police. Moreover, it was plagued by numerous uprisings and rebellions in the lower ranks, casting doubt on the reliability of the ordinary soldiers. Chapter 2 focuses on the post–civil war period until the early 1930s, showing that even though the war was now over, with the Bolsheviks victorious, the perceived threats to the Red Army continued to generate serious concerns about its internal security. In these years in particular, the gulf between the perception and reality of threats began to widen. Chapter 3 examines a period of crisis for the Red Army when the political police claimed to have uncovered an extensive military conspiracy in the upper ranks in the early 1930s at the same time that the rank and file were protesting against the collectivization of agriculture. Chapter 4 explores the early to mid-1930s, revealing a lull in the level of repression in the Red Army but at the same time demonstrating that there were several ongoing underlying problems with its political reliability that were never solved. Chapter 5 details the long chain of events from the summer of 1936 to the start of the military purge in June 1937. Finally, chapter 6 examines the chaotic aftermath of the military purge, arguing that it accelerated the scale of the Great Terror in acting as a catalyst for the Soviet mass operations.

1 | The Red Army in Civil War

After taking power in the Russian revolution of 1917, the Bolshevik Party quickly dismantled the Imperial Army, finally destroying the institution that had been instrumental in keeping the Romanov dynasty in control. After a long decline, the demobilization of the old army was symbolic of how the Bolsheviks were attempting to reorganize Russia on revolutionary lines. A standing army would have no place in a future communist society. The Bolsheviks believed that their successful seizure of power was the first spark in a wave of revolutions that would quickly spread beyond the country's borders. A worldwide revolution would soon tear down the capitalist system and render traditional means of national defense obsolete. However, when this anticipated world revolution failed to ignite, Vladimir Lenin was put in a difficult position, and the Bolsheviks' weak grip on power was now in danger from a series of imposing crises. The first crisis was the ongoing world war, which had carried on uninterrupted throughout the revolution and left the German army still facing Russia on the eastern front. Even though the Bolsheviks had declared peace as soon as they took power, this did not immediately bring the fighting between Russia and Germany to an end. An armistice was signed in December 1917, and peace negotiations were then initiated at Brest-Litovsk in Belorussia, but these proved disastrous for Lenin. The German representatives demanded enormous territorial concessions from the Bolsheviks—so large that they were initially rejected. Moreover, when Leon Trotsky joined these protracted negotiations, he tried to extract Russia from the war in February 1918 with the position of "no war, no peace," meaning that Russia would immediately stop fighting but would refuse to agree to any kind of imperial peace, including territorial concessions. Unsurprisingly, this proved entirely unacceptable to Germany, and its forces renewed their advance on 18 February. Lenin now had no choice but to accept the German terms. He urged the party to do so, even at the large territorial cost.[1] The renewed German offensive forced the Bolsheviks to sign the Treaty of Brest-Litovsk just weeks later, on 3 March, and Russia conceded enormous expanses of territory, including Finland, Poland, Ukraine, and the Baltic states.

The Treaty of Brest-Litovsk not only caused uproar inside the Bolshevik Party but also led to the breakdown of the unsteady political coalition that had held between the Bolsheviks and their last remaining socialist allies, the Left Socialist Revolutionaries, since the seizure of power. In contrast to Lenin, the Left Socialist Revolutionaries wanted to continue the struggle against German imperialism and were dismayed by the territorial losses stemming from the Treaty of Brest-Litovsk.[2] However, there really had been no choice but to concede to German demands. Lenin did not have a suitably strong army to defend the revolution, and in the face of renewed German aggression, he was powerless. The crux of the problem was that the Bolsheviks had mistakenly placed their salvation in world revolution and could no longer draw on the Russian Imperial Army. Even before the seizure of power in October 1917, the Imperial Army had been slowly dismantled and heavily weakened by mutinies. Its final draft had been in February 1917, and by the summer, units were already in rebellion. Millions of soldiers deserted from their units between March and October.[3] The response from the then–minister of war had been to shrink the army.

In addition to its weakened military strength, the revolutionary events of 1917 sparked a similar revolution inside the Imperial Army. Shortly after the February revolution, on 1 March, the newly formed socialist Petrograd Soviet (which would soon be in direct competition with the provisional government established after the abdication of the tsar) issued its first decree: Order Number One. This called for the election of soldiers' committees on the ground level that would control access to weaponry, which soon came to act as alternative power bases in the army. The order had the effect of weakening military discipline and removed much of the leverage that officers held over their soldiers. Later, at the end of 1917, after their successful seizure of power and following the path already set down by Order Number One, the Bolsheviks democratized command posts. Committees of soldiers could now elect their officers, and a gradual demobilization decree was promulgated.[4] In short, a cumulative effect of revolutionary upheaval and military reform throughout 1917 meant that by the time the Bolsheviks had finally seized power in Russia, the Imperial Army had collapsed as a serious force.

Despite the disarray in the Imperial Army, the Bolshevik Party did have other forms of military defense it could call on for protection, although these remained no match for the German forces. Groups of volunteer workers, the Red Guard detachments, had spontaneously formed in 1917 to help defend the revolution. However, although the Red Guards were not short in enthusiasm, they did lack sufficient military skill, training, and numbers. Their first tests against the German army in early 1918 proved disastrous.[5] Moreover, even though Lenin believed that the Russian revolution would ultimately be protected by a wider world revolution, he recognized at the same time that some form of military defense might be necessary in the months after the seizure of power. Lenin was conscious (rightly, as it turned out) that armistice negotiations with Germany might break down. Thus, from December 1917, the Bolsheviks began to experiment with more substantial forms of military organization—but, importantly, only those deemed suitable for a revolutionary regime.[6] They considered, for example, the possibility of using remnants of the collapsed Imperial Army while a more ideologically suitable territorial people's militia was brought up to strength.[7] For many in the party, a people's militia was the only proper means of defense for a revolutionary state. This would see ordinary citizens complete military training in their spare time, thus removing the need for a standing army as well as the accompanying risk of counterrevolution.[8]

Yet with what remained of the old Imperial Army in such a weakened state, and lacking enough time to gradually introduce and train a people's militia, in the end, the Bolshevik leadership decided to create wholly new volunteer units for an entirely new socialist army.[9] A People's Commissariat for War was formed in December 1917, headed by Nikolai Podvoiskii, and the All-Russian Collegium for the Organization of the Workers' and Peasants' Red Army took responsibility for the creation of this new military force.[10] This army, importantly, was intended to align with the Bolsheviks' revolutionary values and was planned as a people's army. A draft decree published in early December 1917 from the Commissariat for War described the nature of the Bolsheviks' preferred type of military force: it was to be "a free army of armed citizens, an army of workers and peasants with broad self-government of elected soldiers' organizations."[11] The new military would be based on class principles and would reject hierarchy, a democratization intended to ensure that only people deemed trustworthy would be promoted into the officer corps—a clear rejection of the old tsarist officer caste.[12] From early January 1918, preliminary moves were made in forming this new socialist army, taking as its basis the existing Red Guard detachments and already established soldiers' committees. On 15 January, the establishment of the Workers' and Peasants' Red Army (RKKA) was announced by a decree of the All-Russian Central Executive Committee.[13] This was a military founded on the principles of voluntarism and "comradely respect."[14] Yet despite these efforts, the Bolsheviks' new socialist army was still no match for the power of the German army. At the very least, it lacked experience and proper training. Its units were small and irregularly organized. On 1 April 1918, the Red Army numbered just 153,679 soldiers.[15] In this respect, while Lenin had finally begun to face reality and understood that the revolution could only be defended with a regular military, he had not done enough. As soon as the Germans renewed their offensive on 18 February 1918, without a credible means of defense, the Bolsheviks were overcome and forced to sign the Treaty of Brest-Litovsk.

The large territorial concessions demanded by the Treaty of Brest-Litovsk delivered a hard lesson in reality. Without a regular standing army, the vulnerable Bolshevik regime would not last long. Therefore, almost immediately, the new Red Army needed to transform into a powerful military force. The strengthening of the Red Army and the adoption of features associated with a traditional standing army throughout 1918 was the first step in the Bolshevik Party's reluctant dependence on a large military—a fact of life that was never fully accepted. The threat from Germany, however, was not the only danger to the exposed Bolshevik regime. Even with a costly peace now agreed upon at Brest-Litovsk, the revolution faced further challenges to its survival. The first test came from the rival socialist parties the Bolsheviks had pushed aside, which were now turning against them. The Left Socialist Revolutionaries, for instance, who had maintained an uneasy relationship with the Bolsheviks since the seizure of power, took up arms in the summer of 1918. Believing that world revolution had been betrayed by the Treaty of Brest-Litovsk, and unhappy with the hard-line agricultural policies pursued by the Bolsheviks, the truce between the two parties quickly broke down. Moreover, the Mensheviks (who had also been squeezed out of power) were looking to stoke peasant rebellion.[16] However, a second and much greater threat soon emerged from the south of Russia at the end of 1918 in the form of the volunteer army. Initially created by the tsar's former chief of staff, General M. V. Alekseev, the volunteer army was the first of several arrangements of reactionary imperial officers determined to fight what they regarded as an illegitimate seizure of power. Known collectively as the Whites, these forces were the chief threat to the Bolsheviks during a civil war that broke out in the summer of 1918.

Civil War and Military Specialists

The threat from the White armies first emerged in Kuban in southern Russia with the mobilization of the volunteer army, later led by generals Piotr Krasnov and Anton Denikin. Subsequent White leaders challenging Bolshevik power included Admiral Aleksandr Kolchak, who mustered forces from Siberia; General Nikolai Iudenich, who attacked from the northeast; and Baron Piotr Wrangel, who again attacked from the south. The danger posed by these reactionary imperial generals was nothing new. Before the Bolshevik seizure of power, General Lavr Kornilov (at the time the supreme commander of the Russian Army) had attempted to launch a coup against the provisional government in August 1917 in order to roll back the gains of the February revolution and restore the position of the imperial elite. Kornilov failed because he was unable to muster sufficient military strength, but the threat from the newly assembled White forces in the civil war was more dangerous, even if they lacked unity. The Whites dwarfed the new Red Army in terms of military knowledge and experience, primarily as they had the allegiance of large numbers of former imperial officers. The early months of the civil war had already made clear the inexperience of the new Red Army. Its disorganized forces suffered serious defeats between May and July 1918 against Cossack and Czechoslovak units allied to the Socialist Revolutionaries' People's Army.[17] These early failures pressed the urgency for a serious military reform, but the chosen solutions proved highly controversial.[18]

One of the central problems for the Bolshevik Party in maintaining a regular standing army was that this clashed with its revolutionary ideals. The creation of the Red Army was one of the first of many compromises that the early Bolshevik regime was forced to make as the difficulty of holding onto power sank in. Indeed, from their point of view, traditional standing armies were anathema. They were the tools of oppressive imperialist powers and represented little more than a holdover from a doomed capitalist era. The particular Russian experience of standing armies was also no doubt at the forefront of the party leadership's minds. From the time of Peter the Great in the seventeenth century, Russian armies had a history of interference in domestic politics and lending assistance to coups.[19] In this sense, for the Bolsheviks, maintaining a standing army posed a genuine risk of counterrevolution—a danger already made clear after Kornilov's attempted military coup in August 1917. Furthermore, the Bolsheviks were conscious of history. They knew that revolutions could be derailed by the ambitions of military leaders. They were not oblivious to the fate of the French revolution and the dangers of military dictatorship. If a powerful standing army was created to defend the Russian revolution, would it eventually meet a similar fate? In this sense, it is easy to see why there was some unease in the party about relying too heavily on a regular army. However, such fears needed to be set aside if the revolution was going to survive, and Lenin understood this. He came to realize that a traditional army was indispensible for the Bolsheviks despite the risks involved. Lenin made this point when speaking at the Fifth Congress of Soviets on 5 July 1918, commenting on the impossibility of a regular army being beaten by "guerrilla detachments" (a reference to a militia force). He went so far as to describe the suggestion as laughable.[20] Lenin knew that a regular standing army was needed quickly, and any hopes placed on forming a military on a utopian basis were soon sidelined as the reality of the dangers facing the regime became clear.

Trotsky led the new Red Army as war commissar in the civil war years, having replaced Podvoiskii in March 1918. Under his leadership, a series of military reforms were introduced that fundamentally changed the character of the Red Army. However, this was not an easy process. Trotsky faced a range of practical difficulties in creating a modern army, and many of his decisions alienated party members, who were already uneasy with establishing such an army in the first place. Creating a force powerful enough to protect the Bolshevik regime in a short space of time proved to be an immensely difficult task. The first problem was finding enough suitable volunteers to turn into soldiers. The Bolsheviks expected streams of volunteers for the new army. In this, they were sorely disappointed.[21] Facing a distinct lack of enthusiasm from the Russian people to sign up to defend the revolution, the only recently abandoned imperial policy of conscription had to be reinstated. Not only was this detested by the Russian peasantry but it also ran counter to the Bolshevik Party's own revolutionary ideals. Again, there was no other option. The Red Army needed soldiers; it also needed discipline. Thus, despite the unpopularity it brought him, alongside conscription which was reintroduced in mid-1918, Trotsky also made hierarchy and discipline central features of the Red Army.[22] This meant that the practice of electing officers was officially abolished just months after it had been introduced.[23] Moreover, by May 1918, Russian territory was being carved up into military districts. In July, the formation of regular army units was sanctioned by the Fifth Congress of Soviets.[24] Military leadership had already been centralized on 1 March with the creation of a new commanding body, the Supreme Military Soviet, and on 2 September, this gave way to the Revolutionary Military Council of the Republic (RVSR), which took over the direction of the Red Army, exercising centralized control and executive power.[25] This centralization was far removed from how many Bolsheviks had viewed a workers' army. As we have seen, the first volunteer Red Army had been founded on the principle of political rather than military discipline.[26] Yet it was traditional military discipline that would come to define the Red Army.[27] However, as the Bolsheviks were experiencing a genuine military crisis in the opening stages of the civil war, ideological principles could be easily ignored. Indeed, while Trotsky was busy professionalizing the Red Army, the Bolsheviks continued to suffer disastrous military defeats—so much so that in the summer of 1918 they were on the point of collapse. The Socialist Revolutionaries' People's Army proved to be a far more effective force and scored several important military victories in the early months of the war. In August 1918, the Bolsheviks lost Kazan' to the People's Army, adding further to the Socialist Revolutionaries' captured territory, which at this point stretched the huge distance between the Volga River and the Urals.[28] The Bolsheviks did manage to recapture Kazan' a month later, but they nonetheless remained under severe pressure.

Finding enough soldiers for the Red Army was only part of the problem. There was also the question of their quality. The Bolsheviks did not have enough supporters with sufficient military experience to staff a competent officer corps. The great wealth of military knowledge lay with the Bolsheviks' enemies, the Whites, and the Red Army was poorly trained and ill-disciplined. To compensate for this, Trotsky was forced to employ former officers from the recently demobilized Imperial Army who had not gone over to the Whites and were willing to work with the Bolsheviks. The policy of using these officers (who became known as military specialists) was one of Trotsky's most important legacies to the Red Army. As we shall see, it affected how its reliability was later perceived far more than Trotsky could have anticipated at the time. Military specialists were quickly enlisted, with agreement made on their service on 31 March 1918, and because of their professional military backgrounds, they came to dominate the higher ranks.[29] This is one reason they were so controversial. In 1918, 75 percent of all Red Army officers were from the old Imperial Army.[30] By the end of the civil war, military specialists still accounted for over 30 percent of the officer corps, with many occupying the highest positions.[31] Furthermore, the Supreme Military Soviet, established in March 1918 to exercise central control over the army, was also largely staffed by military specialists, including the former tsarist general Mikhail Bonch-Bruevich in a leading role. Unsurprisingly, the employment of military specialists proved unpopular with many Red Army men, who thought that strict discipline and the traditional approach used by their new superiors were not appropriate for a revolutionary workers' army.[32] However, the Bolsheviks had few options available. Referring to the military specialists on 18 November 1919, Lenin remarked: "If we do not take them into service and they were not forced to serve us, we would not be able to create an army."[33]

Lenin's comment that military specialists needed to be forced into service demonstrates a second important reason why their employment was controversial. The recruitment of military specialists may have begun quickly, but it was not easy. Mobilizing enough ordinary soldiers for the new Red Army proved difficult, and there was significant peasant resistance to conscription. The Bolsheviks' agricultural policies, which sanctioned forced grain requisitions to supply the war effort as well as the use of violence and imprisonment against anyone who resisted, did little to encourage enlistment.[34] Attempts to recruit military specialists proved just as discouraging. Initially, relatively few came forward voluntarily to enlist in the Red Army. Only 8,000 military specialists had joined up in the early months of 1918. In response, during the summer, all former officers living in Bolshevik controlled territory were conscripted.[35] Understandably, many of these conscripts could hardly be described as enthusiastic supporters of the new regime. Tellingly, only a minority of military specialists sided with the Bolsheviks by immediately joining the party. The majority became members only when the civil war was over, suggesting that they were not ready to side with the Bolsheviks until there was absolutely no other choice.[36] Much of the hostility military specialists faced from within the party and Red Army stemmed from a view that they were outsiders not committed to the revolution. Even Trotsky acknowledged that military specialists were potentially unreliable and that not all were committed to the Bolshevik cause. Looking back at the civil war in 1923, he wrote, "Of the old officer corps there remained with us either the more idealistic men, who understood or at least sensed the meaning of the new epoch (these were, of course, a very small minority), or the pen-pushers, inert, without initiative, men who lacked the energy to go over to the Whites: finally, there were not a few active counter-revolutionaries, whom events had caught unawares."[37] Trotsky had argued of these "active counter-revolutionaries" at the outset of the civil war that they needed to be "combated and exterminated."[38]

To avoid being betrayed by unreliable military specialists, Trotsky arranged certain safeguards. For example, efforts were made to register all military specialists from mid-1918, and at the end of the year, Trotsky ordered that only military specialists who had families within Russian territory were permitted to hold senior army positions.[39] The reasoning was that if a military specialist did turn out to be a traitor, their family would face reprisal.[40] Military specialists were also required to fill out long questionnaires, which would supposedly help reveal their attitudes toward the new regime.[41] However, most importantly, each military specialist was flanked by a Bolshevik political commissar—a party member who countersigned every order given by a military specialist officer. In practice, this established a system of dual command in the Red Army. The political commissars were to keep a close watch over the military specialists for any sign of betrayal and had responsibility for the political reliability of a unit, while the military specialists controlled military affairs.[42] The political commissars were initially coordinated by the political department of the RVSR, which, in May 1919, became the Political Administration of the Red Army (PUR). The shadowing of each military specialist, however, was not foolproof. There were not enough political commissars in 1918; indeed, in 1919 some units were still reporting their complete absence.[43] Their competency was also under question. In April 1919, the commander in chief of the Red Army, military specialist Ioakhim Vatsetis, complained to Lenin that there were too few capable commissars.[44] Moreover, dual command was unpopular with military specialists, who tried to have the policy abolished on the grounds that it was impractical.[45]

It is important to emphasize, however, that as much as Trotsky appreciated the potential danger from military specialists and arranged safeguards to prevent betrayals, he also defended them from what he saw as unjustified persecution, as is evident from an article from December 1918 in which Trotsky noted, "Rejecting the services of military specialists on the grounds that individual officers have played the traitor would be like driving out all the engineers and all the higher technicians from the railways on the grounds that there are not a few artful saboteurs among them."[46] Trotsky understood that a certain number of military specialists would undoubtedly betray the Bolsheviks and that many were hardly enthusiastic about joining the Red Army, but like Lenin, he knew that the Bolsheviks could not win the civil war without their assistance. Trotsky had to balance the protection of the Red Army from internal traitors against the unjust persecution of loyal military specialists. It was clear that valuable and loyal military specialists would be subject to class prejudices, and Trotsky remained their vocal advocate for this reason.

It must also be stressed that the military specialists were not a uniform group. Those drawn from the general staff of the former Imperial Army were typically less favorable to the Bolsheviks, but a number of junior and noncommissioned officers who entered the Red Army proved to be more committed. Many had successful military careers after the civil war and went on to fully embrace the Bolshevik regime. Mikhail Tukhachevskii is the best example of this type of young officer. Born into a line of nobility in Smolensk in 1893, Tukhachevskii served in the Imperial Army as a junior officer, gaining a certain level of notoriety as a result of his frequent escapes from German prisoner of war camps during World War I.[47] After returning to his regiment after the Bolshevik seizure of power, Tukhachevskii was elected a company commander in December 1917, but his unit was later disbanded. He then joined the Red Army in April 1918 and quickly gained a reputation as a talented military leader despite the stigma of his bourgeois background. He proved his ability on the eastern front as 1st Army commander.[48] He joined the Bolshevik Party in April 1918.

Tukhachevskii represented the ideal type of military specialist: he was willing to break with the past. He had little admiration for the skills or experience of the older and more senior military specialists. For instance, in a report sent to Trotsky's deputy, Efraim Sklianskii, Tukhachevskii offered a scathing opinion of the old officer corps, commenting, "In large part, it was created from people who had received limited military training, [who] are completely cowed and devoid of any initiative."[49] Tukhachevskii argued that the younger officers were actually better prepared to understand modern military doctrine and that the older military specialists' knowledge was outdated for the demands of civil war combat.[50] Tukhachevskii also believed that the older generation of officers was ideologically unsuitable for the Red Army: "Our old officers are completely ignorant of the bases of Marxism, cannot and do not want to understand the class struggle and the need and inevitability of the dictatorship of the proletariat."[51] Tukhachevskii wanted young and revolutionary-minded officers better suited to serving the Bolshevik regime to be advanced through the Red Army. Tukhachevskii did, however, have some disagreements with the Bolsheviks' management of the Red Army, and from an early stage in his career, he showed a tendency to push boundaries. Like many other military specialists, he was a stern critic of the system of dual command and wanted the Red Army to introduce unified command (*edinonachalie*), which would allow officers to be responsible for military affairs and to conduct political work in the place of the political commissars.[52] Nonetheless, Tukhachevskii remained an asset to the Bolsheviks. He was young, energetic, and talented, and he had no desire to maintain what he believed were outdated military strategies and conventions.[53] Such qualities ensured that Tukhachevskii quickly advanced through the army hierarchy. In April 1920, aged only twenty-seven, Tukhachevskii took command of the entire western front.[54]

Yet there were few military specialists like Tukhachevskii. As we have seen, Trotsky believed that the majority were either unenthusiastic about the new regime or, more seriously, that there were genuine counterrevolutionaries among the new recruits. The civil war saw numerous damaging mutinies by military specialists and desertions to the Whites, which did little for their public image. One of the most high-profile betrayals was the mutiny of Mikhail Murav'ev, the commander of the eastern front. Murav'ev, a Left Socialist Revolutionary, already had substantial grievances against the Bolsheviks. Like other Left Socialist Revolutionaries, he was dismayed by the Treaty of Brest-Litovsk, believing that Russia should have continued its war against Germany. However, the spark for Murav'ev's mutiny in July 1918 came with his refusal to fight the Czechoslovak Legion after they themselves had mutinied. The Czechoslovak Legion, formed from Czech and Slovak prisoners of war, had fought alongside the Russian Imperial Army in World War I. The

Legion remained in Russia after the revolution. They rebelled in May 1918 after the Bolsheviks tried to disarm them as they were traveling on the Trans-Siberian Railway (this was in accordance with German demands after the Treaty of Brest-Litovsk). The Czechoslovak Legion revolted, sparking a wider uprising, and Murav'ev refused to fight for the Bolsheviks.[55] Although Murav'ev's mutiny was short-lived (he was killed the following day), it had sustained impact. Not only had the Red Army once again proved to be ill-disciplined during combat, but Murav'ev's defection was very high profile and demonstrated the dangers of employing military specialists at the apex of the Red Army. Notably, the revolt also led the Bolsheviks to lose control of the Volga city of Simbirsk to the Socialist Revolutionaries.[56] Importantly, the fact that betrayals and mutinies by military specialists continued throughout the civil war never gave the opportunity for loyal military specialists, such as Tukhachevskii, to lose the stigma attached to the prerevolutionary officers.[57]

Fear and Class Prejudices against Military Specialists

Betrayals by military specialists undermined trust in the officer corps and the wider Bolshevik war effort. Former imperial officers were in positions to cause great damage to the Red Army. For instance, they were more likely than ordinary soldiers to have the ability, resources, and opportunities to organize espionage networks in the Red Army that could then feed information to White forces.[58] However, despite the risks attached to employing military specialists, it appears that the perception of the threat they posed to the Red Army was deemed more serious than its reality. A number of factors exaggerated the military specialist threat, thus heightening a sense of vulnerability in the Red Army. First, betrayals by military specialists unquestionably had a greater impact than those of ordinary soldiers. Mutinies or desertions in the upper ranks were undeniably more serious than in the rank and file and attracted more attention. This helped cast doubts on the overall reliability of military specialists. Moreover, because former imperial officers were already objects of suspicion and were regarded as outsiders as a result of their bourgeois backgrounds, whenever they did mutiny or desert, existing prejudices about the disloyalty of military specialists as an entire cohort were reinforced and confirmed. Senior military specialists like Murav'ev dramatically betrayed the regime, but those who stayed loyal were nonetheless subjected to unwarranted suspicions about their reliability. A poisonous atmosphere developed in the Red Army, which did not go unnoticed. The commander in chief of the Red Army, Ioakhim Vatsetis, complained to Lenin about attitudes toward military specialists in a letter from April 1919. Vatsetis, himself an ex–Imperial Army colonel who became commander in chief of the Red Army in September 1918, complained about the unreasonable hostility shown toward members of the general staff from some of the more ideological political commissars:

> Both in print, and in the speeches of demagogues speaking to a huge concourse of people, phrases still appear persistently which are insulting for those working on the General Staff. From all sides accusations pour out that they have their price, that they are counterrevolutionaries or saboteurs. Former officers who are serving on our General Staff do not deserve this unjust attitude. . . . Every commissar had his secret desire to catch our staff officers out in some counterrevolutionary attitude or treachery.[59]

Vatsetis argued that such working conditions provided no protection against unfounded arrest. In this respect, he was remarkably prescient. Only three months later, in July 1919, Vatsetis was falsely incriminated as a counterrevolutionary and accused of belonging to a military conspiracy with connections to White generals Denikin and Kolchak.[60] Even though the case later collapsed when a subsequent investigation found no credible link with the Whites, Vatsetis was removed from the position of commander in chief anyway and demoted to a teaching position. Beyond Vatsetis's personal misfortune, the case would provide yet another reminder to those already suspicious of military specialists that they could not be trusted.[61] Vatsetis's arrest was another high-profile counterrevolutionary case in the army and would not help military specialists win their comrades' trust. Most importantly, the case demonstrates the ease with which baseless accusations of treachery could be leveled at former imperial officers in the Red Army. No military specialist was safe from a false incrimination—not even the most senior officers.

Of course, military specialists were not the only people in the Red Army to mutiny or desert from the ranks. Throughout the civil war, desertion from the Red Army ran at extremely high levels. Reliability was a stubborn problem, and thousands of soldiers fled the army every month. The peasant soldiers whom the Bolsheviks were forced to rely on to build up numbers posed a particular problem.[62] However, there is some evidence suggesting that military specialist officers were actually more reliable than their communist counterparts. As Orlando Figes has shown, from 3 August to 12 November 1919, there were sixty military specialist desertions from the Red Army to the enemy and another sixty who deserted from combat. The same period saw 373 nonspecialist officers desert to the enemy and 416 flee from battle.[63] This is a significant difference and suggests that military specialists were less prone to desertion than their counterparts, the communist Red commanders. Without a more complete set of figures, it cannot be ascertained whether this was a fixed trend during the civil war. Yet it is still likely that regardless of the numbers, and even if military specialists were more likely to stay with their units than communist officers and ordinary soldiers because of the deeply entrenched class prejudices against them as a group, they would always be regarded with more suspicion and judged to be less reliable. For many, military specialists were class enemies working within the Red Army and could never be trusted.

Moreover, military specialists' close association with Trotsky did little for their public image. Trotsky was, of course, a useful ally in certain respects. He could use his position as war commissar to defend the use of military specialists in the Red Army. Trotsky was a dominating force in military affairs. He held the position of war commissar, while other key positions in the RVSR were filled by his supporters.[64] However, Trotsky was not short of critics. As war commissar, Trotsky drew criticism for his leadership style during what was a crucial period of transformation in the Red Army. An issue that provoked particular hostility was his advocacy of strict disciplinary methods and harsh punishments. Trotsky's notorious order sanctioning execution for deserters was seen by some as characteristic of the tsarist era, and it was deeply unpopular in party circles. There were refusals to carry out the punishment.[65] In short, Trotsky's military reforms, while unavoidable if the Bolsheviks were going to win the civil war, were undeniably a step backward from the hopes pinned on organizing a state and society on revolutionary lines. Trotsky's public advocacy of military specialists fed into the wider discontent stemming from the direction he was taking the Red Army.

One of the most cited episodes that drew widespread criticism of Trotsky was the execution of a political commissar, a certain Panteleev, for deserting from his regiment during the battle of Kazan' in August 1918.[66] To his critics, the Panteleev case represented Trotsky's push for discipline at any cost, and it was used to defend the political commissars from what were regarded as overbearing military specialist officers.[67] The Panteleev case exacerbated the brewing discontent concerning the uneven levels of influence in the Red Army between the military specialists and political commissars. Some believed that the trustworthy political commissars were unjustly thought to be dispensable by the army leadership, whereas the military specialist outsiders were allowed to dominate the upper ranks.[68] The Panteleev case caused Trotsky significant political damage. He acquired a reputation for meting out harsh punishments, and further doubts were raised about the direction that the new Red Army was heading.[69] This was all despite the fact that execution for desertion was in reality rare; indeed, the enormous numbers of desertions from the Red Army made this punishment impossible to consistently apply. Trotsky's opponents seized on the opportunity provided by the Panteleev case and used it to launch an attack on the military specialists.[70]

Similarly, Trotsky's political rivals were able to channel the discontent against military specialists to try and weaken his position. This is best seen during the so-called Tsaritsyn Affair of 1918. Tsaritsyn, a city on the western bank of the Volga on the southern front, was a strategic position that the Bolsheviks had managed to hold against the Whites in the summer of 1918. In later years, Stalin was lauded in party propaganda for the decisive role he supposedly played in the defense of the city; however, the reality was very different.[71] When stationed in Tsaritsyn, Stalin's hostility to military specialists was undisguised. He and several of his close allies forced out their military specialist commander, Pavel Sytin, a former general from the Imperial Army, and seized control themselves. Although Stalin clearly had little faith in Sytin's ability to defend the city, he was not just acting on his prejudices against military specialists. The Tsaritsyn Affair was as much about his personal rivalry with Trotsky as it was the security of the Red Army.

Stalin arrived in Tsaritsyn in June 1918 initially on business unrelated to military affairs. His task had been to improve food supplies and manage grain shipments from the North Caucasus to Moscow.[72] However, he soon acquired full military and civilian powers. Stalin joined the RVS in the city. The RVS included Sytin and two of Stalin's close allies, Kliment Voroshilov and Sergei Minin. Voroshilov was the commander of the troops, and Minin was political commissar.[73] Stalin soon managed to take over military affairs at Tsaritsyn, and in September 1918, he convinced the RVSR to name him the commander of the southern front

RVS. None of this pleased Sytin, who no doubt understood he was being squeezed out by Stalin, Voroshilov, and Minin. However, he could do little about it. At the time, Sytin was 350 miles away in Kozlov. When he did finally arrive in Tsaritsyn to reassert his authority, Stalin, Voroshilov, and Minin decided to dismiss him. They sent a request to Moscow that Voroshilov be put in charge.[74] The dismissal of Sytin undoubtedly suited Stalin. He was surely confident in his and Voroshilov's ability to take control of the front, especially without the interference of an unreliable military specialist. Stalin's hostility toward military specialists in general is visible in a telegram he sent to Lenin in July concerning supply problems in the area:

> The railway south of Tsaritsyn has not yet been restored. I am firing or telling off all who deserve it, and I hope that we shall have it restored soon. . . . If our military "experts" (bunglers!) had not been asleep or loafing about the line would not have been cut, and if the line is restored it will not be thanks to, but in spite of, the military.[75]

Stalin had already made similar comments in a telegram to Lenin and Trotsky in June in which he argued that specialists were completely unsuitable for fighting in the civil war.[76] Moreover, Stalin often had harsher words for the military specialists, and it is clear that his criticisms were inseparable from his rivalry with Trotsky. In a separate letter to Lenin from October, he wrote, "I ask now, before it is too late, to relieve Trotsky and give him limits, for I fear that Trotsky's erratic commands, if they were repeated, would give the whole front into the hands of those deserving full distrust, the so-called military specialists from the bourgeoisie, who will cause a rift between the army and the officers and ruin the front completely."[77] For Stalin, military specialists were both incompetent and untrustworthy and Trotsky was to blame.

Stalin's behavior at Tsaritsyn, unsurprisingly, did not please Trotsky, and it was not long before the party took action. In early October, the party's Central Committee ordered that Stalin, Voroshilov, and Minin were to subordinate themselves to the orders from the center and that they needed to abide by the decisions of the RVSR. Stalin's "insubordination" was specifically noted, though the Central Committee did agree to revisit Sytin's appointment.[78] This concession, however, did little to assuage Stalin and his allies, who responded with another attack on military specialists. On 3 October, Stalin and Voroshilov sent a further letter to Lenin criticizing Sytin as "a man who not only is unneeded at the front, but who is not worthy of trust and is therefore damaging. We of course cannot approve of the front going to ruin as a result of an untrustworthy general."[79] Importantly, it is clear from this letter that the conflict at Tsaritsyn was not just about the employment of military specialists in commanding positions. It was also closely tied to Stalin's personal animosity toward Trotsky. Stalin and Voroshilov also remarked, "We, as members of the party, categorically declare that we consider the execution of Trotsky's orders criminal, and his threats unworthy."[80] A partial resolution of the Tsaritsyn conflict was reached shortly thereafter. Stalin was recalled to Moscow, and Trotsky appointed a new commander to the southern front, although Sytin remained.[81] Notably, however, even though Stalin had been recalled from Tsaritsyn, he was given a position on the RVSR, which would only ensure further clashes with Trotsky.

The Tsaritsyn Affair shows that party figures such as Stalin and Voroshilov were not merely dissatisfied with the policy of employing military specialists in the Red Army but were also using this as an opportunity to challenge Trotsky and the central line of command. The system of control that Trotsky had established for the military allowed little room for the type of local leadership that Stalin and Voroshilov wanted to wield. These two issues are closely related. Stalin did not like having to take orders from his political rival and having to support policies he did not agree with; nor was he content to take orders from a supposedly untrustworthy military specialist like Sytin. For Stalin, attacking the reliability of military specialists was an effective means of drawing criticisms of Trotsky, who was not oblivious to what was going on. In a letter to Lenin from January 1919, Trotsky complained about such local challenges to his authority: "I consider the protection given by Stalin to the Tsaritsyn trend the most dangerous sort of ulcer, worse than any act of perfidy or treachery on the part of military specialists."[82] For Trotsky, treachery by military specialist officers was dangerous, but the type of challenge to the central military authority (embodied in the "Tsaritsyn trend") was more damaging.

In this way, Stalin's real attitude toward military specialists was ambiguous and difficult to discern. It is unlikely that he had no genuine suspicions of the military specialists whatsoever and was using his opposition to them purely as a political weapon, but at the same time, it does seem that he seized on the issue as a means to weaken a political rival. Indeed, in other cases, Stalin was more than happy to have those of questionable reliability serve in the Red Army. In mid-1920, he encouraged Trotsky to promote the Ukrainian nationalist turned Bolshevik supporter, Volodimir Vinnichenko, to the RVS of Ukraine. Vinnichenko was to assist in the struggle against the forces of the Ukrainian nationalist leader Simon Petliura, even though both men had been allies just a few years earlier.[83] Vinnichenko would surely be as untrustworthy as any military specialist serving in the Red Army. He had been one of the founders of the Revolutionary Ukrainian Party in 1900, and his loyalty could just as easily be called into question. If Stalin's chief concern really was the political reliability of the officers in the military, it is difficult to see how he could have been an advocate of Vinnichenko and request for him to be given such a responsible position. Evidently Stalin could compromise on the type of people serving in the army. He was not a purist when it came to the composition of the officer corps, and he cannot be said to have lined up with the left communists who wanted a purely workers' army.[84] It is, of course, possible that as military specialists were bourgeois, and thus representatives of the class enemy, Stalin held a lower opinion of their reliability than he did a Ukrainian nationalist. Nonetheless, his advocacy of Vinnichenko—someone who had previously fought against the Bolsheviks—suggests that as much as Stalin distrusted military specialists, he focused on them specifically as a means to foment criticism of Trotsky. Stalin's negative opinion of military specialists was probably pragmatically deployed. Indeed, on other occasions, Stalin expressed more positive opinions of them.[85]

A final point on the Tsaritsyn Affair is to look more closely at Voroshilov, who, after his military service in the civil war, led the Red Army from the mid-1920s and during the military purge of 1937–1938. Voroshilov, however, was far from suitable for the role, and this was clear enough during the civil war years. Trotsky, understandably, held Voroshilov in low esteem after his behavior at Tsaritsyn, but he also doubted his competence. In a letter sent to Lenin at the end of 1918, Trotsky criticized Voroshilov and Stalin's conduct at Tsaritsyn and cuttingly commented on Voroshilov's military experience: "Voroshilov is able to command a regiment, but not an army of fifty thousand soldiers."[86] On 7 January 1919, in another letter to Lenin, Trotsky again criticized Voroshilov's military skill and made it known that he was set against promoting him to command the Ukrainian front. Citing Voroshilov's behavior at Tsaritsyn, Trotsky wrote, "Repeating the Tsaritsyn experiment in Ukrainian territory in view of a clash with serious enemies—on this course we will not go."[87] Trotsky had good reason to doubt Voroshilov's military capabilities. He had no prerevolution military background. Voroshilov's first real military experience was leading a detachment of Red Guards in early 1918. Of course, Trotsky's military record was little better, having only been a war correspondent in the Balkan wars before the revolution. Yet the civil war required experienced officers to take up key command positions if the Bolsheviks were going to survive, and Trotsky correctly understood that Voroshilov was not up to the job. Moreover, there are indications that Voroshilov agreed with this assessment and that he had little appetite for a future military career. On 2 November 1921, for instance, Voroshilov wrote to Stalin and complained about his current military role:

> I am sick of working in the war department. . . . I suppose I would be more useful in a civilian field. I expect approval and friendly support from you before the Central Committee about my new posting. I want to work in the Don Basin, where I will ask the Central Committee to send me. I will take any sort of work and I hope to shake out of it, but I have started to become ill mentally.[88]

Voroshilov doubted early on whether he was suited for a military career, and this clearly caused him some anxiety. This contrasts with someone like Tukhachevskii, who rapidly ascended the army hierarchy in the 1920s, the same time as Voroshilov. Unlike his future superior, however, from an early stage, Tukhachevskii hungered for more responsibility in the army, and in moments of inactivity, he was eager to return to the front.[89] As we shall see, the two men's personal relationship was poor throughout the 1920s and 1930s and created tension within the high command. However, Stalin's support proved decisive for Voroshilov. When Stalin became the most powerful figure in the party after Lenin's death in 1924, he placed his old comrade Voroshilov at the head of the military. In light of Voroshilov's early misgivings about a future military career, it is possible that he never wanted this. Voroshilov correctly predicted that he was not right for a military career and proved to be out of his depth.

The Tsaritsyn Affair was not the only notable flash point in the tensions surrounding the use of military specialists in the army. These came to a head at the Eighth Party Congress, which opened in Moscow on 18 March 1919. During the congress, Lenin continued to make the case that the fragile Bolshevik government needed to borrow the expertise of the former imperial bourgeoisie. He stressed that a powerful army was indispensable for the defense of the revolution, and this meant that military specialists were necessary. Lenin criticized as "childish" those who questioned the use of any specialists whatsoever in the construction of communism.[90] However, the employment of military specialists in the Red Army came under significant pressure at the congress, primarily from a group known as the military opposition. This included left communists and other party members unhappy that the Bolsheviks were relying so heavily on military specialists. Led by left communist V. M. Smirnov, and including Voroshilov, the military opposition called for more power and responsibility to be given to the political commissars and the local party organizations rather than the military specialists. They also criticized the unpopular restoration of strict disciplinary methods in the Red Army, which, as we have seen, were associated with the former imperial officers. Smirnov did not completely reject the use of military specialists in the army despite his criticisms. He did concede that they were "undoubtedly necessary," but he stressed that the military specialists were closer to the Whites than the Bolsheviks.[91] This was a question of loyalties, and evidently there was no consensus about whether the individuals the Bolsheviks were putting into command positions could be trusted.

It did not help Trotsky's case that he was absent from the congress (Admiral Kolchak's offensive had forced him to travel to the eastern front), and in his place, Grigorii Sokol'nikov spoke in defense of Trotsky's position. While not denying that military specialists could betray the Bolsheviks, Sokol'nikov wanted to highlight that many had fought bravely and many had died in the defense of the revolution: "Practically in the entire army we came to use military specialists, and in practice it has been shown that if there were cases of treachery and betrayal from the side of the military specialists, then from the other side, military specialists quite often selflessly died at their posts."[92] Sokol'nikov added further:

> The facts show that over a period of several months our army has fought successfully. The army, in which there are tens of thousands of old specialists, has shown in practice that it is an army of the proletarian revolution. The working class has managed to use military specialists not for the resurrection of the old army, but for the creation of a new Red Army.[93]

Sokol'nikov's defense of the military specialists had little effect. At a closed session devoted to military affairs, the majority of congress attendees voted in support of the military opposition's line. Not only did the group have majority support among party members with voting rights present at the military section of the congress, but also the military opposition's suggestions were undoubtedly popular. The support the group gained is testament to the negative reaction against the restoration of hierarchy and discipline in the Red Army that had been pushed through by Trotsky.[94] However, after this initial victory by the military opposition, another committee was formed to resolve any outstanding issues, which included three representatives of the Central Committee and two from the military opposition. The final outcome was a compromise resolution that in the end represented a victory for Trotsky by a slim majority. For instance, the importance of the centralization of command and the employment of professional soldiers in the Red Army were both agreed on. However, promises were made to correct the practices that had provoked the most dissatisfaction from within the party. Assurances were given, for instance, to award political commissars more authority and to make sure that power would not solely lie in the hands of the military specialists. The party would also get a greater say in the selection of commanders. In this respect, the party had increased its influence in the Red Army, but Trotsky's position on military specialists had more or less emerged intact from the congress. The employment of military specialists would not be substantially altered, though evidently a large section of the party wanted their authority curtailed.[95] In this sense, it is unlikely that, despite the concessions they had been granted, the military opposition would be entirely happy with the outcome of the congress. Military specialists would continue to occupy positions of responsibility in the Red Army, which would do little to bring an end to the suspicions that surrounded them.

It is worth noting Stalin's behavior at the Eighth Party Congress, as he again displayed an ambiguous attitude toward military specialists. Stalin did not take an overtly tough line against military specialists; in fact, he was one of the representatives for the Central Committee who met with representatives of the military opposition to hammer out a compromise resolution.[96] The position that Stalin put forward at the congress was actually similar to Sokol'nikov's. For instance, in his speech on 21 March, Stalin criticized the poor condition of the early volunteer Red Army, commenting on its lack of discipline and its disorganization. He stressed that good discipline was vital for the army, and he criticized the argument of the military opposition.[97] As one historian has argued, it seems that Stalin was trying to distance himself from the military opposition in public and wanted to be seen as a centrist in order to draw supporters away from Trotsky.[98] It is hardly likely that Stalin had suddenly become an enthusiastic supporter of military specialists, but at the same time, he probably saw no benefit in openly siding with the military opposition. This would mean going against Lenin on an issue he strongly supported. So while Stalin no doubt retained his private suspicion of military specialists, his approach toward military affairs was once again pragmatic and informed by political calculation.

In this respect, the reality of the threat posed by military specialists to the Red Army during the civil war is difficult to disentangle from how they were perceived. This was shaped by a number of factors, including entrenched class prejudices, the high-profile nature of some military specialist mutinies, political disputes within the Bolshevik Party, and personal animosities toward Trotsky as war commissar. Stalin was certainly looking to weaken Trotsky's influence, and the military opposition wanted to reduce how much the Red Army relied on military specialists. Both played on fears about the loyalty of military specialists to achieve these ends. However, this reinforced a view that military specialists were a disloyal cohort working inside the Red Army, even if there is some evidence to suggest that, as a group, they were more reliable than their nonspecialist counterparts. Some military specialists were certainly disloyal and planned to undermine the regime, but the overall threat posed by former imperial officers to the Red Army was exaggerated during the civil war. Understanding why perceived threats surrounding the Red Army could be inflated in this way is crucial for understanding Soviet civil–military relations and, as we shall see, is central to unlocking the reasons behind the military purge of 1937–1938.

The Cheka and the Struggle for the Security of the Red Army

The Cheka, the Bolsheviks' political police force, was the single organization most concerned about security threats to the Red Army, including the use of military specialists in battle. The Cheka was the main line of defense against the subversion and infiltration of the military, and its operatives had a particular impression of army vulnerability shaped by their own institutional interests. The civil war was the starting point of a long history of the political police closely monitoring the Red Army for any signs that it had been compromised. From here on, the political police regularly raised the alarm that the Red Army was under threat and that repressive counteractions needed to be applied.

Lenin created the All-Russian Extraordinary Commission to Combat Counterrevolution and Sabotage (Cheka) in December 1917 to defend the fragile Bolshevik regime from these very threats. Led by Feliks Dzerzhinskii, the Cheka was notorious for using extrajudicial repression in safeguarding Bolshevik power. Moreover, the Cheka not only focused its attentions on political opponents but also acted as an internal security service, putting down uprisings and carrying out summary executions.[99] One of the Cheka's main tasks during the civil war was to protect the Bolsheviks against White subversive organizations. This was understood to be a serious threat. Twenty-two supposed White organizations were exposed in Moscow during 1918–1920 alone.[100] However, it was not long until monitoring the Red Army specifically came under the Cheka's remit. The Cheka was used for basic security purposes, such as putting down rebellions in the Red Army, but it was soon established that the military was also a prime target of White subversives.[101] Dzerzhinskii believed that the struggle against counterrevolutionaries in the Red Army was one of the most important tasks for the Cheka.[102] This was made clear at the first conference of the Extraordinary Commission in June 1918, when I. N. Polukarov, the head of the counterrevolution department, commented on the possible subversion of the Red Army:

> The aim of the bourgeoisie is to break down our army, to use it for their own purposes, but we as an organ of political struggle need to take on surveillance of the army. The uprising of Czechoslovakians is well known, we know what happened there. We should have in mind that the newly formed units are able to go over to the other side. Methods of terror are necessary to force the counterrevolutionaries to leave the ranks of our army.[103]

The Red Army had been identified as a potential target of subversives, its reliability was under question, and repression was a chosen solution. The mutiny of the Czechoslovak Legion also seems to have left a lasting impression. Indeed, the Cheka believed that the uprising had been instigated by the Entente powers.[104] To accommodate a closer involvement with the army, however, the Cheka underwent several organizational changes from mid-1918. So-called special departments (*osobye otdely*) were established on the southern and eastern fronts to monitor the army specifically. These replaced the existing army and front Chekas, whose task had been to secure the rear of the Red Army, as well as the Military Control Agency, which was concerned with military counter-intelligence (but which had been considered unreliable for employing too many military specialists).[105] The new special departments were thus responsible for both counterintelligence and safeguarding the Red Army from subversives. They also came to control informant networks in the military. The number of special departments grew throughout the civil war, becoming the Cheka's principal means of contact with the Red Army. A central special department was created in January 1919. The importance attributed to the Cheka's task of monitoring the Red Army can be seen in the large share of its budget funneled to the special departments. In 1920, they received one third of the Cheka's entire yearly budget, and some of the most senior Chekists coordinated the special departments during the civil war.[106]

The need for specific organizations to protect the Red Army from subversion reveals how seriously the Cheka and the Bolshevik leaders estimated the threats to the military. The Chekists did frequently expose allegedly counterrevolutionary groups in the army throughout the civil war (some of which were apparently extensive), and they conducted purges of the ranks to remove any other criminals.[107] However, the threat to the Red Army from White agents specifically was identified as a particularly dangerous problem. In December 1919, for instance, at the first congress of the special departments, I. P. Pavlunovskii, the deputy head of the organization, reported that infiltrated White agents were operating not only in the Red Army but also on the railways, in supply and transport, and in a range of other institutions.[108] Between spring 1918 and autumn 1919, White agents apparently managed to gain high-ranking positions in the Red Army in Ukraine and carried out espionage.[109] Moreover, in February 1919, a report by Genrikh Iagoda, who would later head the political police, described the extent to which he believed the military had been compromised:

> The exposure of large White guard organizations—the national center[110] and others, shows to what degree counterrevolution has penetrated our military apparatus. . . . An investigation opened during the last part of 1919 on White Guard organizations showed that counterrevolution has transferred

from the stage of a conspiratorial struggle with Soviet power to a system of using our military apparatus for their purposes and thus enjoyed fully legal means available in each specialist working in a particular institution of the military department.

Iagoda's report also pointed out that White counterrevolutionaries were using their positions on the inside to harm supplies to the fronts and to the troops.[111] Similarly, in July 1919, Dzerzhinskii also reported on Whites' having infiltrated the Red Army and gained command positions.[112] In this respect, from the Cheka's point of view, the threat posed by the enemy within (notably White subversive agents) was judged to be highly serious, and the Red Army was judged to be vulnerable to this type of infiltration. As Iagoda's February 1919 report demonstrates, unreliable military specialists were seen as providing the means for the Red Army to be internally compromised because they could be secretly recruited by the Whites.[113] In this way, it is hard to imagine that the Cheka shared the pragmatic standpoint of Lenin and Trotsky toward the use of military specialists in the Red Army. The Cheka was almost entirely focused on carrying out a class war to destroy the bourgeoisie.[114]

It was not just military specialists that concerned the Cheka, however. The use of former White officers in the Red Army was understood as a similar security threat. Trotsky needed all the experienced officers he could get, and another solution to the Bolsheviks' skills shortage was to use former Whites who had deserted from their armies as military specialists. This policy, however, posed obvious additional security risks. Former White officers having only recently left their units brought with them questions about their loyalty and whether they were secret White agents. The Cheka subsequently took additional countermeasures. For example, in February 1920, the head of the special department, Viacheslav Menzhinskii (another future head of the political police), and his deputy, Iagoda, sent a telegram to the secretary of the Central Committee, Nikolai Krestinskii, about the admittance of former Whites into the Red Army, and made their concerns clear: "The Special Department of the VChK [Cheka] considers the mass admittance of Kolchak officers into command positions impermissible, especially in those places where Soviet power has not yet had time to grow strong enough."[115] In view of protecting the Red Army from any possible resulting damage, Iagoda and Menzhinskii suggested imprisoning all such officers in concentration camps and to individually check them.[116] They also suggested that the position a former White received in the Red Army should depend on the level of their past opposition to the Bolsheviks and their estimated loyalty to the new state.[117] It seems that these concerns did have some impact. In August, the RVSR ordered a registration of all White officers serving in the Red Army and requested additional assistance from the Cheka's special departments.[118] Later, in October 1920, a department was created within the Cheka for the observation and management of former White officers specifically.[119]

The employment of former White officers in the Red Army demonstrates an important point about how assessments of threats could diverge and how they were shaped by different priorities. One of the Cheka's primary roles was to unmask internal enemies within state institutions, and the employment of former White officers in the Red Army made this task all the more difficult. It raised the chances of a damaging betrayal within the ranks and forced the Cheka to direct more of its resources at the Red Army, spreading itself more thinly. In this sense, from the Cheka's point of view, the military was sabotaging itself by employing these potentially unreliable officers, even if they added valuable experience to the Bolsheviks' war effort. However, as war commissar, Trotsky had a different set of priorities and a different judgment about the nature of the threats facing the army. His primary goal was to ensure that the Bolsheviks won the civil war, and he needed to make difficult compromises to make this happen. If victory meant using potentially unreliable former White officers, then this was a risk worth taking. Although the Cheka certainly supported Bolshevik victory in the civil war, their fixation on unmasking internal enemies ran against Trotsky's willingness to make compromises over the type of person who could serve in the Red Army. This in turn gave rise to competing judgments about the nature of the threats facing the Red Army and how susceptible it was to subversion. These differing estimations of the threat—which, as we shall see, not only fell between the political police and army leadership but also included the party leadership—persisted long after the end of the civil war. However, it was the political police's particular conception of army vulnerability that eventually achieved dominance in 1937.

While trying to prevent military specialist betrayals and unmasking White counterrevolutionaries, the Cheka also looked to uncover foreign agents whom it believed posed a security threat to the Red Army. Counterintelligence services were an important part of the Bolsheviks' war effort. They studied the systems and methods of foreign intelligence agents, investigated the activity of alleged spies, and tried to prevent harm coming to Russia's military interests.[120] The Cheka frequently discovered supposed foreign agents and intelligence networks inside state institutions and the Red Army in the civil war years.[121] The Cheka viewed the problem of foreign agents, as it did the military specialists and former White officers, as one of the enemy within. Moreover, the perceived threat from spies was at times viewed as considerable. For instance, in May 1919, Stalin sent a telegram to Lenin warning that a network of spies had amassed in Petrograd and along the Petrograd front, and that a ruthless purge was necessary.[122] In June 1920, Stalin claimed that the whole of Western Ukraine was littered with Polish spies, some of whom were managing to infiltrate the Red Army.[123] And in November 1920, Iagoda, the deputy head of the special departments, sent a telegram to the field staff of the RVSR requesting that all Estonians, Latvians, Finns, and Poles who were not members of the party be dismissed from their military positions if they had access to secret materials.[124] Foreign espionage networks apparently involving military specialists were also discovered during the civil war, showing how these two security threats could intertwine.[125]

It must be emphasized that not all the foreign agents exposed by the Cheka were genuine. The Cheka's primary role was to search for internal enemies, and it did not matter how these were found. The use of torture or violence was acceptable as long as a confession was secured. This was often the only evidence necessary. In this way, many people arrested by the Cheka on charges of espionage were innocent. At the same time, several foreign countries, including Britain, France, Poland, Japan, Italy, and Finland, lent assistance to the White movement in the civil war. Approximately one and a quarter million foreign troops were sent to Russian territory.[126] Although these foreign troops did little more than play a supporting role and were often concerned with safeguarding military equipment left over from World War I, the Bolsheviks were aware that ties did exist between the Whites and foreign governments. These were put in a more sinister light when the Cheka exposed what it believed were foreign intelligence networks apparently giving financial aid to the Whites and other anti-Bolshevik groups.[127] Whether genuine or not, such discoveries only reinforced the deeply held belief among the Bolshevik leaders that capitalist states were doing all they could to bring down the revolution and would never reconcile to its existence. Indeed, the Bolsheviks highlighted what they saw as an alliance of foreign powers with the old imperial elite early on.[128] Moreover, in an interview given in July 1919, Stalin made it clear that foreign powers were not only financing the Whites but also carrying out espionage for them. Foreign powers were apparently "bribing anyone that could be bribed" in the Red Army for espionage.[129] Yet both the Bolshevik leadership and the Cheka tended to overestimate their enemies' coherence and strength. Rather than see the divisions and conflicts that existed between the different Whites armies, rival socialist parties, and foreign powers, they instead saw a united and determined conspiracy against the Bolshevik regime.[130] The Bolshevik leadership thought that it was under siege from all quarters; this made it far easier to accept the cases of foreign espionage regularly discovered by the Cheka, however weak the evidence. In this respect, the Bolsheviks' deeply entrenched fear of capitalist encirclement was sustained by the arrests of supposed foreign-backed enemies across different state organizations. The perceived threat of capitalist encirclement made key institutions such as the Red Army appear more vulnerable to subversion than it really was. Facing what they took as a vast conspiracy of capitalist powers, it is understandable that the Bolsheviks believed that their means of defense would be targeted.

However, the Cheka's tendency of making arrests without adequate evidence did not escape criticism. Even Dzerzhinskii knew that his operatives were working up too many groundless cases against former bourgeois specialists. In an order from December 1919, he noted that some specialists were being arrested on insufficient grounds and that it was necessary to establish more clearly in the future whether an individual belonged to a White organization or was actually engaged in sabotage.[131] Dzerzhinskii was an unlikely person to be pushing for mistakes to be corrected by the Cheka. He showed nothing short of absolute and ruthless devotion to the defense of the revolution. His criticisms probably stemmed from the fact that unfounded arrests of valuable and experienced specialists could harm the war effort. Even if this was obvious, there were strong incentives for Chekists to continue to act in this way. The more "enemies" the Cheka exposed, the more resources the organization was likely to receive. Moreover, there was also some resistance within the party against awarding the Cheka too much power. Limits had been placed on the organization as early as February 1918, and although these were quickly removed when the German army relaunched its offensive after the failure of the negotiations at Brest-Litovsk, this did not bring an end to attempts to curb the Cheka's authority.[132] From late 1918, moderate Bolsheviks began to criticize its lawlessness and were starting to push for reform. The use of repression in marginalizing rival socialist parties was criticized specifically, and some party moderates called for curbs on the Cheka's power. Senior Bolsheviks such as Lev Kamenev wanted the organization abolished outright.[133] Understandably, such criticism gave the Cheka a strong incentive to prove that it remained essential to the survival of the Bolshevik regime. As long as streams of dangerous enemies were discovered on Russian soil, this case could continue to be made and would find support among the many Bolsheviks who did genuinely believe that large numbers of counterrevolutionaries were being unmasked by the Cheka.[134]

Peasant Rebellions and War with Poland

The civil war was more than a clash between the Red and White armies. Both forces also had to contend with huge numbers of rebellious peasants, the so-called Greens. These peasant bands outnumbered the Reds and Whites and were most active in the early 1920s after the Bolsheviks had largely overcome the White armies. Despite their lack of organization, the threat posed by the Greens to the regime cannot be underestimated. Their bands could number into the tens of thousands.[135] This proved a problem for the Red Army in particular. Indeed, the Red Army may have been officially titled the Workers' and Peasants' Red Army, but as three-quarters of the Russian population were peasants, the balance was certainly in their favor. By the autumn of 1920, 75 percent of the Red Army was composed of peasant soldiers. This was especially important because a major factor to victory in the civil war hinged on which side could control and manage the vast peasant population.[136] Green activity encouraged mutinies and rebellions of peasant soldiers in the Red Army and undermined its stability. The frequency and scale of these rebellions posed a genuine military threat to the Bolsheviks throughout much of the civil war and hampered the war effort.[137] Moreover, this upheaval in the lower ranks was a stark indication that problems with reliability existed at all levels of the Red Army, further reinforcing the perception that it was open to internal subversion.

Peasant soldiers in the Red Army rebelled for a variety of reasons, but like the Greens outside of the military, this was often in response to social and political grievances. In particular, the Bolsheviks' harsh agricultural policies were a source of significant discontent. Since the spring of 1918, the Bolsheviks had increasingly used forced grain requisitions to support the war effort, which meant seizing grain from the peasants to feed the cities and the Red Army. Any peasants who refused to give up their produce were accused of being kulaks—dangerous speculators who were undermining the revolution.[138] Grain collection detachments were sent to the villages to seize any grain the peasants were unwilling to hand over, often leaving them without enough food to survive. As army performance was closely tied to central policy, such practices alienated many peasant soldiers in the ranks and sparked mutinies and desertions. However, peasant soldiers also rebelled over poor conditions and inadequate supplies, and in protest of being drafted into the Red Army in the first place. The Bolsheviks in general terms drew little support from the Russian peasantry. The number of peasant soldiers deserting to the Greens from the Red Army was extremely high and destabilizing. It has been recorded that as many peasant soldiers deserted from the Red Army as remained in the ranks throughout the civil war. Moreover, these were not just individual cases of desertion. At times, entire detachments joined the peasant rebels or refused to fight.[139] Cases of mutinous soldiers murdering communists were not uncommon.[140]

The Bolsheviks used merciless force to quell mutinies in the ranks. For instance, in the case of the rebellion led by a peasant rebel officer, Sapozhkov, in Samara in mid-1920, who had taken up arms after being dismissed from his position for his opposition to grain requisitions, Trotsky ordered that those responsible should be "mercilessly punished." Trotsky was concerned about the risk that the revolt might develop into a more widespread uprising. Sapozhkov had already managed to attract not insignificant numbers of followers.[141] Furthermore, in order to cope with the scale of the problem of peasant soldiers deserting to the Greens, the Cheka was given additional resources in order to keep a closer observation of the troops.[142] The problem was not just uprisings, however. The Bolsheviks believed that the Greens could easily infiltrate the ranks and establish intelligence networks to undermine the war effort.[143] In this sense, concerns that the Red Army could be internally subverted did not only stem from fears about foreign agents, military specialists, or former Whites, but applied as much to the ordinary soldiers in the rank and file. The lower ranks were judged to be porous and open to hostile enemies.

Although it was not too surprising that discontented peasant soldiers might rebel against the Bolsheviks, what was perhaps more alarming was that even the most effective fighting units were ill-disciplined. One of the prestigious Red Army units, the First Cavalry Army (Konarmiia), for instance, which was led by the famed commander and Stalin ally, Semen Budennyi, was notorious for its bouts of violence and looting. One political commissar, V. Chernov, described the Konarmiia as behaving like Budennyi's private army. In a letter to the Central Committee from December 1919, Chernov recalled that some of the cavalry men had shouted slogans such as, "Let's kill the Whites first, and then we can start killing the Communists!"[144] Later, in September 1920, approximately half of the Konarmiia rebelled for three weeks, murdered their commissar, and went on a looting spree before Budennyi brought them under control.[145] That the unit claiming to be one of the most elite in the Red Army could show such disobedience reveals the extent to which problems with stability affected all levels, not just unreliable peasant soldiers.

Of course, despite the high levels of internal turmoil experienced by the Red Army, it managed to win the civil war and could still wield its power effectively to crush rebellions.[146] One of the largest uprisings crushed by the Red Army was in Tambov in September 1920. This uprising was sparked by widespread discontent toward forced grain requisitions and was led by the Green rebel Aleksandr Antonov. Peasant bands had deployed effective guerrilla warfare tactics against Bolshevik forces. However, when Tukhachevskii arrived in May 1921, the Tambov rebellion was finally put down. Tukhachevskii showed both unwavering loyalty and brutality in his conduct of the operation. He described the peasant rebels as an "epidemic" and used poison gas and chemical weapons.[147] After suppressing the Tambov rebellion, similarly brutal methods were used to put down bandits on the Don in 1921.[148] Of similar notoriety was the regime's reaction to the mutiny at the Kronstadt naval fortress during February and March 1921, where soldiers and sailors joined with Petrograd workers in protest over widespread hunger, the lack of democracy within the Bolshevik regime, and the repressive measures taken against strikers. The Kronstadt mutiny was brutally suppressed by Red Army units, once again led by Tukhachevskii. Thousands of the rebels were executed.[149] The Kronstadt rebellion, however, had special significance. Even though the mutiny was overcome, it was undoubtedly alarming. One of the key support groups for the Bolsheviks during the revolution had been the very sailors who rebelled at Kronstadt. The mutiny was a clear warning that valuable supporters could turn against the Bolsheviks at times of social strain. As we will see in chapter 3, similar problems with the reliability and stability of the lower ranks appeared again at the end of the 1920s during a time of dramatic social upheaval and transformation, and on a much larger scale.

The civil war was a formative experience for the Red Army in that it was immediately identified as a target of counterrevolutionaries, foreign agents, and other subversives infiltrating the lower ranks. However, on a personal level, the civil war was also a formative experience for party members and officers, who served side by side in combat and who continued to work together after the conflict. As one historian has noted, between 1918 and 1921, 70 percent of Moscow's communists had served in the Red Army.[150] Stalin in particular spent large amounts of time at the front, and his early military experiences helped shape his future working relationship with the Red Army leadership. Indeed, in the literature on the military purge, a great deal is often made of an alleged dispute between Stalin and Tukhachevskii over the military defeat against Poland, a conflict that began in the closing years of the civil war. This dispute has commonly been depicted as almost a feud, and it is often emphasized as contributing to Stalin's later alleged hostility toward Tukhachevskii and part of the reason why he had him executed in 1937.[151] Yet how long-lasting this particular dispute was and its impact on Stalin's later relationship with Tukhachevskii are questionable. What was much more important for Tukhachevskii was how a visible power group comprising Stalin and his close military colleagues, Voroshilov and Budennyi, was cemented during the civil war. Tukhachevskii was excluded from this close circle despite being a far more capable military professional.

In December 1919, the Allied Supreme Council marked a line running through Brest-Litovsk that recognized claims to territory on the former eastern front between Russia and the newly resurrected Polish state.[152] Just a few months later, in April 1920, however, Polish forces attacked the southwestern front in an invasion of Ukraine.[153] The Red Army was mobilized to repulse the Polish offensive, but a hapless performance at the battle for Warsaw in August 1920 heavily undermined the Bolshevik offensive and resulted in the loss of the war. The chief reason for the defeat was the division of the Red Army forces, which weakened its overall power. In repelling the Polish forces, the Red Army had been divided into two fronts, western and southwestern. Tukhachevskii, who headed the western front, had advanced toward Warsaw, but he did not have sufficient forces to overcome Polish resistance. Indeed, the southwestern front had been supposed to have traveled northward in support. However, under Stalin, Voroshilov, and Aleksandr Egorov's direction, and after receiving permission from the commander in chief, Sergei Kamenev, the Konarmiia was ordered to attack Lwów, the Polish stronghold in Galicia. Adding to the confusion, the 12th Red Army was also delayed in marshy terrain.[154] It looked like Tukhachevskii would not receive his support. However, the strategy quickly changed, and on 11 August, Kamenev ordered that the forces of the southwestern front should travel northward to support Tukhachevskii. This time, Stalin refused.[155] Stalin wanted to concentrate instead on the defense of Russia from Wrangel's forces in the Crimea rather than dispatch troops to support Tukhachevskii's march to Warsaw.[156] Tukhachevskii's support thus never arrived. The Polish leader, Józef Piłsudski, then launched a counterattack on 16 August, the battle for Warsaw was lost, and the entire conflict with Poland became a stalemate. An armistice was signed in October 1920, and the Treaty of Riga was signed on 18 March 1921, which transferred parts of Ukraine and Belorussia to Poland.[157]

Who carries the most blame for the failure of the Polish campaign is more complex than it first seems. The obvious issue of Stalin and his allies' refusal to transfer their forces was only part of the problem. As Robert Ponichtera and David Stone point out, the entire war with Poland was confused from the very beginning. There was little clarity over whether the war was defensive or offensive, whether the Bolsheviks meant to capture Warsaw, or whether the war was really a means to spread European revolution.[158] Moreover, because the Red Army had been divided from the beginning, by the time the order came through in August to send Stalin's forces northward, it was difficult to disengage these from battle with Wrangel's forces in the Crimea. Furthermore, the distance these troops would have to cover to join with Tukhachevskii was considerable. Lenin also sent conflicting signals at crucial points in the conflict. On 11 August, the very day Kamenev ordered that the Konarmiia and the 12th Red Army should join Tukhachevskii's western front, Lenin urged Stalin to concentrate on defeating Wrangel instead. Lenin incorrectly believed that Tukhachevskii did not need any reinforcements and that victory had nearly been achieved.[159] When Lenin was better informed about the need for reinforcements on 12 August, he ordered Trotsky to create reinforcements from conscripted Belorussian peasants. As one historian notes, it was naive to think that this would be sufficient.[160] There were further complications when Tukhachevskii sent an order to Budennyi, the commander of the Konarmiia, to coordinate their troops, but this was queried by the latter as the order contained only Tukhachevskii's signature and had not been countersigned. By the time a new order arrived, Budennyi, Stalin, and Egorov were already heavily engaged in Lwów. Stalin no doubt used the problem with Tukhachevskii's order as an excuse to delay having to respond to Kamenev's order of 11 August. This probably suited Stalin's own purposes.[161] He made no effort to find out the truth between the conflicting orders sent by Lenin and Kamenev, and it appears that the confusion gave him the opportunity to concentrate on Lwów, which was his preferred choice.[162] In short, the war with Poland was badly planned, it had confused intended outcomes from the very start, and contradictory orders were made at crucial moments. What matters is not who individually was the most responsible for the defeat, but rather that in the aftermath, everyone blamed the failure on someone else.

As noted above, the alleged ill feeling between Stalin and Tukhachevskii stemming from the defeat against Poland has been a persistent theme in the literature on the military purge. It does have some level of substance, but the significance is often exaggerated. First, both Stalin and Tukhachevskii share some blame in losing the conflict. Stalin clearly disobeyed an order, probably for his own purposes. Lenin criticized Stalin at the Ninth Party Conference in September 1920 and accused him of being "biased" against the western front.[163] Yet Tukhachevskii also received criticism in the years after the war, mainly for advancing too hastily toward Warsaw to try and ignite a European revolution. Tukhachevskii took risks in how he conducted his drive to Warsaw, leaving his forces stretched.[164] At the Ninth Party Conference, Stalin pointed to poor organization as a factor in the loss of the war, and his ally, Sergei Minin, blamed the western front for hastily attacking Warsaw.[165] This was an obvious reference to Tukhachevskii. In addition, in 1920, the party's Politburo produced a resolution that criticized Tukhachevskii's actions during the campaign as undermining the party and government.[166] In this respect, Lenin believed that alongside Stalin, Tukhachevskii shared some of the blame for the loss of the war for acting too impulsively. It appears, however, that Tukhachevskii did not accept this verdict. In a lecture given later in February 1923, he argued that the main reason for the failure of the Polish campaign was strategy, and that there would have been a different outcome had the two fronts been better coordinated. Tukhachevskii did not name anyone specifically, but he likely had the actions of the leaders of the southwestern front in mind—namely Stalin, Egorov, Budennyi, and Voroshilov.[167]

Although there was blame on both sides, it is going too far to suggest that Stalin and Tukhachevskii were hostile to each other from this point on, or that Stalin had a burning desire to settle the score. The defeat against Poland would certainly not be forgotten, and it is likely that both men continued to blame each other for the outcome. However, this issue did not define Stalin's later relationship with Tukhachevskii. Before the war against Poland, Stalin showed confidence in Tukhachevskii's military skill and his ability to achieve results. In February 1920, for instance, Stalin sent a telegram to Voroshilov and Budennyi describing Tukhachevskii in laudatory terms as "the conqueror of Siberia and victor over Kolchak."[168] After the war with Poland, Stalin may have held Tukhachevskii responsible for the defeat, but this did not stop the two from working closely together. As we shall see, Stalin would again praise Tukhachevskii's talent and abilities.[169] Stalin and Tukhachevskii clashed during the conflict with Poland, but this did not destroy their working relationship. Stalin continued to respect the ability of the young officer and probably saw him as an important asset for the Red Army. This is not to say that Tukhachevskii was one of Stalin's close allies. Stalin had formed a close alliance with Voroshilov and Budennyi during the civil war. This was strengthened by their shared experience at Tsaritsyn and further cemented in the war against Poland. Tukhachevskii was never part of this close circle, which created tensions within the future military elite. Stalin recognized Tukhachevskii's military skill, which allowed him to rapidly progress up the army hierarchy in the 1920s, but he was never trusted to the same extent as Voroshilov and Budennyi. The latter two, in particular, were among the few senior officers to survive the military purge of 1937–1938. That Tukhachevskii was not one of Stalin's closest allies in the army, and that Voroshilov and Budennyi were likewise promoted in the years after the civil war, would have far greater consequences for Tukhachevskii's later career than any apparent feud with Stalin over the defeat against Poland. The army leadership quickly became an awkward mixture of professional talented officers like Tukhachevskii alongside inexperienced Stalin loyalists such as Voroshilov and Budennyi. These were the conditions for conflict.

Both the civil war and the Polish war were formative experiences for the Bolshevik Party, the political police, and officers who would soon become members of the Red Army elite. From the renewed German offensive in 1918 to the fierce combat against the White forces, Lenin and the party leadership were delivered a lesson in reality. For the revolution to survive, any ideological principles against standing armies had to be put aside and fears about betrayals by military specialists overcome. None of this was without resistance. The military opposition opposed the move to transform the early volunteer Red Army into a regular standing force, and the distrust of military specialists was widespread and entrenched. Indeed, when a military specialist betrayed the Bolsheviks, the impact was much larger than a mutiny by an ordinary rank-and-file soldier or Red commander. Military specialists were considered to be the enemies within, a notion reinforced by persistent class prejudices. Further, the pragmatic use of opposition to military specialists from party members like Stalin, alongside the Cheka's use of forced confessions in their search for enemies, helped inflate the perceived scale of the threat posed by military specialists and former White officers. Importantly, there was no single agreed-upon view of the threat posed by the military specialists to the Red Army. Different groups and institutions judged this differently, and perceptions of threat were informed by institutional interests and individual priorities. This created competing narratives about perceived threats to the Red Army that competed for dominance. The use of former imperial officers, however, was not the only problem for the new Red Army. The lower ranks experienced widespread discontent during the civil war, and peasant rebellions could seriously undermine the war effort. The lesson was clear: during periods of social strain, the rank and file proved to be unstable and unreliable. Finally, as this chapter has shown, the experience of battle in the civil war was formative in terms of army organization and for the party members who had a direct combat role. Importantly, what became a long-lasting alliance between Stalin, Voroshilov, and Budennyi had a profound effect on the dynamic within the later military elite. This was more influential than any alleged grudge between Stalin and Tukhachevskii about the failed war against Poland. Indeed, Tukhachevskii would rapidly rise through the army hierarchy after the civil war, but so would Voroshilov and Budennyi. In the 1920s, neither would hide their hostility to Tukhachevskii, but, as we shall see, this had nothing to do with military defeat against Poland. Yet for now, the conduct of the new Red Army in the civil war had proved disorganized, chaotic, rebellious, and not at all confident. The Red Army displayed a lack of professionalism, and all agreed that it was an attractive target for dangerous enemies. However, as the next chapter will show, even with victory in the civil war, fears about betrayal in the Red Army and recognized problems with its political reliability and stability refused to subside. The Red Army was only at the very beginning of a long process of reform and consolidation. The 1920s were equally fraught with accusations of army betrayal and new fears about a military coup. Most importantly, the gulf between the perception and the reality of threats began to grow wider.

2 | The Red Army in Consolidation

With its victory in the civil war, the Red Army had passed its first serious test. The conflict had been hard fought, and the Bolsheviks had at times been pushed to the point of collapse. However, a lack of unity among the White leaders, along with a failure to win the support of ordinary people, handed the Red Army opportunities to recover its strength and for the Bolsheviks to eventually consolidate control over Russia. Yet victory in the civil war was not entirely reassuring. Serious concerns had been raised about the reliability of the Red Army at all levels during the war, including the dominance of the upper ranks by supposedly untrustworthy military specialists and widespread instability in the rank and file. It had been impossible for the Bolshevik leaders to trust their military. The 1920s proved little different. Even though the Bolsheviks emerged from the civil war as victors, this was not the end of the struggle against the Whites. As this chapter will show, even though the White armies had been scattered and driven into exile, they were still seen as an active and dangerous force. In the years after the civil war, the White leaders altered their tactics to allow them to carry on the struggle for Russia from abroad. The infiltration of agents carrying out espionage and terrorist attacks, for instance, became more widely deployed in the 1920s, and the Red Army remained a primary target. As far as the Bolshevik leaders and political police were concerned, the Red Army remained no less exposed to subversion even in peacetime.

The security threats judged to be arrayed against the Red Army in the 1920s were not just a continuation of those seen in the civil war; entirely new external and internal perceived dangers soon emerged. In particular, the apex of the Red Army high command was subject to widespread rumors in the early 1920s that several senior officers were disloyal and ready to betray the regime. The most common rumor described a supposed Russian Bonaparte in the high command who would overthrow the Bolsheviks. This type of hearsay was particularly common outside of the newly established Soviet Union, and some officers, notably Tukhachevskii, were almost permanent subjects of speculation.

However, as we shall see, the political police was one of the primary sources of these rumors; it used them as part of counterintelligence operations targeted against genuine White conspirators. The end result, however, left the Red Army elite continually surrounded by persistent whispers of disloyalty. Moreover, further concerns about the reliability of the Red Army were sparked by the power struggle in the party after Lenin's death in 1924. Trotsky's platform found a level of support within the ranks in the early 1920s that led to exaggerated fears about military assistance in a possible Trotskyist coup. Finally, in the 1920s, the gulf between how threats were perceived and their reality began to grow wider. Since the end of the civil war, the real and immediate danger to the survival of the regime had subsided, but the Bolshevik leaders saw the world differently. From their perspective, the threats facing the Soviet Union and its military had not dissipated. Instead, they had only evolved and taken new forms.

Fears of Subversion and the Military Specialists

The civil war had a devastating impact on Russia and created an economic crisis. The grain harvest had collapsed, a famine had started to spread in 1921, and by 1922, inflation was running at 40 percent per month.[1] Under these conditions, it was impossible to maintain the Red Army at the size it had swelled to during the civil war, and an extensive demobilization was now unavoidable.[2] Consequently, from its peak strength of over five million soldiers in the civil war years, the Red Army was reduced to 562,000 by 1924. Many military specialists who had been reluctantly conscripted solely for the purpose of winning the war were among the first to be discharged as part of extensive demobilization. The early 1920s marked the beginning of their steady removal from the army and the promotion of a new generation of academy-trained communist Red commanders. However, the replacement of the military specialists proved to be a more drawn-out process than expected. The Soviet leaders could not afford to discharge them all as a result of a persistent skills shortage. At the end of 1922, just half of all Red Army officers had what was deemed to be a sufficient level of military training, and there were distinct shortages of experienced officers in the infantry and artillery.[3] Even in the late 1920s, after several years of demobilization, military specialists still occupied over 10 percent of command positions.[4] In this respect, throughout the decade, former tsarist officers remained a visible and influential cohort in the army. Certain military specialists who had won accolades as heroes of the civil war, notably Tukhachevskii, were not only secure in their positions but also rose quickly up the Red Army hierarchy.

Moreover, as military specialists were discharged from the army in the early 1920s, the number of communists was also gaining ground. From a low point of 10.5 percent in 1920, party membership reached 31.8 percent in 1924, but there was still a long way to go.[5] More direct measures were taken to increase the weight of communist officers in the army, such as the 1924 *chistka* (purge) of the personal staff, which gave a boost to their number in comparison to the supposedly unreliable military specialists.[6] However, while this sort of intervention helped alter the ratio of Red commanders to military specialists, there were limits. Military specialists were found clustered in the higher ranks and still tended to staff the most influential positions. The Red Army could not afford to discharge all of its military specialists and replace them with more reliable, if comparatively inexperienced, communist Red commanders. Too much valuable military knowledge would be lost. This meant that questions could still be raised about the overall reliability of the Red Army, and notably of the officer corps, which contained a sizable cohort of bourgeois officers. This did little to dampen concerns about treachery within the Red Army. That the class enemy was still seen to be working from within the army remained a flash point.

A central reason why the lingering presence of military specialists was worrying for many in the party and the Red Army was that the White armies may well have lost the civil war, but they had not ended their struggle against the Bolshevik regime. After being driven from Russia, the Whites had been exiled throughout Europe and congregated in cities such as Berlin, Paris, and Istanbul, as well as in the Far East. As Lenin noted in 1921, "Now, after we have repulsed the attack of international counter-revolution, there has been formed abroad an organization of these Russian bourgeoisie and of all the Russian counter-revolutionary parties. The number of Russian émigrés who are scattered through all foreign countries, might be counted at from one and a half to two million."[7] The threat from the Whites was certainly real, but Lenin overestimated their strength. More realistically, they numbered between 60,000 and 80,000.[8] Moreover, what Lenin did not adequately grasp was that the exiled White movement was even less unified than it had been during the civil war. Its forces were not only fragmented geographically but also divided between competing groups, such as monarchists and liberals, who had conflicting visions about the future of Russia.[9] The Whites also lacked the military power they had once had and were grouped together in small military associations and units. It was not until the White leader Piotr Wrangel founded the Russian General Military Union (ROVS) in 1924 that greater cohesiveness was brought to the dispersed forces. ROVS was to act as a new center in the ongoing struggle against the Bolshevik regime and as an instrument for maintaining White identity. It soon became the largest center of the White movement.[10] However, even with the greater coherence provided by ROVS, the Whites were still in a weak position. ROVS was hindered by organizational chaos, funding problems, and a lack of commitment from its membership.[11] It would certainly be a mistake to suggest that the Whites could have actually undertaken any sort of new military campaign against the Soviet Union so soon after their defeat in the civil war. Yet despite the problems, Wrangel still intended to fight the Bolsheviks and win control of Russia, though he knew that a change of tactics would be necessary.

Lacking the means to launch a new military campaign, from the early 1920s, the Whites began to place greater emphasis on covert methods, including intelligence operations and the infiltration of agents into key Soviet institutions. One major part of this new offensive was attempts to make contacts with Soviet officers and infiltrate the Red Army.[12] A successful overthrow of the Soviet regime was out of the question without parts of the Red Army turning against their leaders, and the Whites were optimistic that this was not an unrealistic prospect. Aside from a perceived common soldier bond, the Red Army still employed large numbers of military specialists in the 1920s whom the Whites believed could be potentially recruited. The counterintelligence department of ROVS consequently kept the Red Army officer corps under close observation.[13] In response to this threat, the Cheka carefully monitored military specialists and put many under close surveillance. Indeed, the end of the civil war had not reduced the importance of the political police. Furthermore, as the Whites had done, the Cheka also changed its tactics. Its methods were altered to suit the post–civil war period and became, according to one historian, far more conspiratorial.[14] Observation and careful monitoring of the reliability of the Red Army remained an important task at the same time as espionage and counterintelligence took on a far larger role.[15]

Details of covert operations supposedly hatched by the exiled Whites against the Red Army can be seen in Soviet political police intelligence materials. Of course, any intelligence can be inaccurate or even entirely false, and not all of the material collected by the political police was legitimate. Nonetheless, it does appear that they were genuinely concerned about the subversion of the Red Army by the Whites in the early 1920s. In September 1921, for instance, the Cheka's foreign department reported on a meeting of former imperial officers in Petrograd who had supposedly discussed how to infiltrate agents into the Soviet Union. Specifically, the Cheka recorded the group as having talked about "the organization of an 'expedition' to Moscow with the aim of the possible activation of old Wrangel cells and the creation of new ones for infiltration into the ranks of the Red army, the VChK [Cheka], and other Soviet institutions."[16] In March 1922, when the Cheka had been succeeded by the State Political Directorate (GPU), it reported that groups of monarchist and exiled Constitutional Democratic Party émigrés intended to unite their efforts to gain the allegiance of senior officers in the Red Army and Red Navy and how they planned to use military specialists to carry out espionage.[17] Moreover, it was not just the Cheka/GPU that was worried about White infiltration of the Red Army. Some Red Army officers showed as much concern about the reliability of their military specialist comrades. In a letter sent to the Central Committee in February 1924, fourteen officers, including Pavel Dybenko and Ivan Fedko, both of whom later became senior figures in the military establishment, alleged that some serving military specialists maintained links to counterrevolutionaries and leaders of the White movement. When he received this letter, Stalin requested it be sent to all members of the Central Committee, suggesting he believed its contents were noteworthy.[18] In this sense, the view that military specialists were potentially treacherous and could turn against the Bolsheviks was still potent after the civil war. This may well have become further ingrained by intelligence reports showing that the Whites were on a covert offensive and looking to use military specialists as a recruiting pool.

The Whites, however, had a more effective method of infiltrating agents into the Red Army than trying to recruit serving military specialists. They could use their own men. Former White officers were still allowed to serve in the Red Army after the civil war. In 1921 over 14,000 former Whites were still in the ranks. Ten years later, this number had seen a significant reduction to 1,537, with just 122 in command positions.[19] Yet continuing to permit former White officers to serve in the Red Army throughout the 1920s meant that the White leaders could send their agents to the Soviet Union under the guise of returning soldiers wanting to join the Bolsheviks. Indeed, a series of amnesties running from 1920 to 1923 allowed White officers to return from exile.[20] On the surface, it seems a strange decision for the Soviet leaders to allow those who had fought so vigorously against what they believed to be an illegitimate regime to serve in the Red Army. However, the amnesties did serve a purpose, even if they seemed to almost invite the subversion of the army.[21] First, in the immediate aftermath of the civil war, the Red Army still desperately needed qualified officers, and employing former Whites, if they were available, could not be refused entirely.[22] A secondary motivation can be seen in a letter from the deputy of the GPU, Josef Unshlikht, to one of Stalin's closest allies, Viacheslav Molotov, sent in June 1921. Unshlikht noted that the large number of Whites residing abroad represented a very real threat to the Soviet Union. This was an extensive power base for the defeated but still hostile White generals. Using amnesties was one way to disarm this foreign power base by draining the White support from abroad to the Soviet Union. Unshlikht did point out, however, that this was a potentially dangerous strategy because there would certainly be some hostile agents among the returning Whites: "I understand that to allow onto the territory of Soviet Russia so many soldiers, among whom undoubtedly will be a significant percentage of counterrevolutionaries and spies, is a dangerous thing."[23] Similarly, a GPU circular from 1923 on the filtration of repatriates also recognized the underlying problem with the amnesties: "Return to the homeland undoubtedly was used by Wrangel's counterintelligence for sending agents, organizers, and spies to Russia." The circular called for surveillance to be refocused toward exposing White agents among reemigrants and to monitor their associations with the local population, including servicemen in the Red Army.[24] Another GPU order from March 1923 emphasized that the threat from White subversives had grown larger in recent years: "The activity of Wrangel's intelligence and counterintelligence organs has increased on a large scale. A number of new intelligence institutions have opened, the main aim of which is the collection of information about the Red army's condition and armament, as well as breaking down the morale (*moral'noe razlozhenie*) of the latter through planting agents in commanding positions in units of the Red Army." The order noted that White agents were entering the Red Army under the cover of returning soldiers and called for a greater observation of the former Whites serving in the military.[25]

Clearly the policy of disarming the White movement through amnesties had attached difficulties and new obligations. Kliment Voroshilov, who became head of the Red Army as people's commissar of military and naval affairs in 1925, recognized that former White officers were more likely to betray the army than ordinary military specialists.[26] There was a difficult balancing act in using former Whites in order to boost levels of military knowledge and experience in the Red Army. Aside from GPU surveillance, strict controls were put in place mandating which regions former Whites could be stationed at, the number permitted in each region, and clearance from the GPU was needed before they could actually serve in the military.[27] The policy remained contentious throughout the 1920s and was a source of complaint from within the Red Army. In 1929, for instance, Budennyi complained to Voroshilov that too many White officers were serving together in the Siberian Military District, including those who had previously served under Kolchak. This was judged to be dangerous because officers who had fought alongside Kolchak in Siberia in the civil war were now serving in the Red Army in exactly the same place. As far as Budennyi was concerned, this was impermissible.[28] Despite such complaints, however, former White officers who proved loyal were undoubtedly an asset. The Soviet leadership began to reward former Whites who turned out not to be traitors. For example, in December 1924, the presidium of the Central Executive Committee ordered that former Whites serving in the military who had shown heroism and loyalty could have their names removed from special observation lists.[29] However, it remained the case that despite these official recognitions of reliability, for many (most notably the GPU), former Whites represented an additional subversive threat to the Red Army, and one that added further weight to the fear of the enemy within.

As well as trying to subvert the Red Army from the inside, the White leaders took a more direct approach in the 1920s and launched a terrorist campaign to try and undermine the Soviet state. Even though these terrorist attacks did not target the Red Army exclusively, they did lend greater credibility to the overall White threat. Examples of the terrorist threat in the early 1920s include the assassination of the Soviet representative to the Lausanne conference by a White émigré in 1923. Months later, in early 1924, Dzerzhinskii warned Trotsky about a possible attempt on his life from information he had received from Berlin.[30] The central figure in the organization of this White terrorism was General Aleksandr Kutepov, a senior member of ROVS who later headed the organization after Wrangel's death in 1928. Kutepov coordinated underground operations targeted at individuals and institutions in the Soviet Union from 1924, and from 1927 he launched a broader terrorist campaign.[31] However, despite controlling well-trained and experienced White officers, Kutepov lacked sufficient funding and numbers. Soviet counterintelligence also proved to be effective against his efforts.[32]

Yet Kutepov's group did land several successful terrorist attacks that had significant impact and undeniably alarmed the regime. In 1927, a bomb was successfully exploded at a party club in Leningrad, injuring twenty-six people. In the same year, the Soviet special envoy in Poland, Piotr Voikov, was assassinated by a White monarchist. Tellingly, and revealing of Stalin's worldview, his immediate reaction was to point the finger at the British government in arranging the assassination in order to spark a war. As he put it in private correspondence, the British wanted to "repeat Sarajevo."[33] Even though Stalin grossly misjudged who was behind the assassination, it was nonetheless a stark demonstration of the danger posed by White terrorism. The exiled Whites had shown that they could be a formidable threat. Notably, after the Voikov assassination, Nikolai Krylenko, the deputy commissar of justice, proposed reinstating extraordinary tribunals for individuals implicated in counterrevolutionary crime, espionage, and banditry. Those arrested under these extraordinary procedures would not be permitted defense in court, and any sentence would be applied immediately.[34] That Krylenko was urging restoring the type of extrajudicial sentencing used during emergency situations such as the civil war suggests that the regime had been rattled by the Voikov assassination. The Politburo soon awarded the political police the right to issue extrajudicial sentences, including executions, for arrested Whites.[35] Although these extrajudicial powers were quickly taken away again in 1928, Voikov's assassination clearly had a strong impact on Stalin, as this knee-jerk reaction shows. As we shall see, it was one of the events that contributed to the war scare that spread throughout the Soviet Union in 1927.[36] Moreover, when informed of Voikov's death, Stalin wrote to Molotov and proposed that a number of imprisoned monarchists should be shot in reprisal (twenty were eventually executed), and that more should be killed in the event of future assassinations. Stalin also wanted intense searches to uncover White terrorists in the Soviet Union and the "elimination of monarchist and White Guard cells."[37] In this respect, the White terrorist and subversive threat was perceived to be real and substantial in 1927. Soviet intelligence continued to report, accurately or not, that preparations for further attacks were being made in several European cities. Indeed, just a year later, in July 1928, two of Kutepov's men managed another successful strike when they bombed the political police's headquarters in Moscow, accomplishing a direct attack on their long-standing enemy.[38] A combination of high-impact terrorism, alongside the broader subversive threat already embodied by the movement, made the Whites a top priority for the Soviet political police throughout the 1920s.[39]

Even though the Whites managed to carry out several successful terrorist attacks in the 1920s that alarmed the Bolshevik leadership, and even though their intention to infiltrate the Red Army was well known to the political police, there is a great deal to suggest that the overall subversive threat posed to the military by the exiled White movement was actually judged to be more dangerous than it really was. The gulf between the perception and the reality of threats remained wide. One important reason why can be seen in the deeply entrenched class prejudices toward military specialists still potent after the civil war. Many members of the party and newly qualified Red commanders continued to distrust military specialists and were unhappy with the slow speed of their replacement. With the emergency of the civil war now over, some Red commanders thought that they should be awarded the prestigious posts occupied by the military specialists who were no longer necessary. That military specialists tended to cluster in the upper ranks provoked hostility, and they were frequently accused of having bourgeois values alien to the Soviet state. In this respect, the difficulty of disentangling the reality of the threat posed by military specialists to the Red Army from how they were perceived remains the same. As a cohort, the military specialists were disliked and distrusted; this only fed suspicions about the enemy within. This in turn made the White movement appear more formidable and dangerous than it was in reality, as the military specialists represented a recruiting pool inside the Red Army. This is no doubt one of the reasons why the disorganized White movement was judged by the political police to be one of the primary dangers in the 1920s. With so many supposedly unreliable military specialists still serving in the ranks, class prejudices were important in making the Red Army appear disproportionally exposed to subversion. In this way, how security threats to the Red Army were understood continued to be shaped by ideology, context, and, as we shall see, institutional and individual interests.

An example of persisting feelings of resentment and distrust toward military specialists can be seen in a report sent to the Central Committee from a military academy party cell on 19 February 1924. The authors made their negative opinions about the military specialists obvious:

> In the army commanding staff, there is no unity in political goals or tasks. The class point of view of the Red commanding staff runs up against the "a-politicalness" (*apolitichnost'*) of the military specialists. . . . Alongside this, there is a completely incomprehensible proliferation of specialists in all main sections of the army hierarchy. . . . The quantity of former officers in the general staff in comparison with their quantity in the army at the time of the civil war has significantly increased.[40]

Relations were particularly tense over the disparity of power between the military specialists and Red commanders. For instance, a thesis prepared by the head of the mobilization department, N. L. Shpektorov, in January 1924 highlighted the disadvantages that Red commanders faced compared to their military specialist colleagues. Qualifications and military knowledge were at unequal levels, and (probably not unrelated) a large number of former imperial officers had managed to find positions in the central army apparatus. Traditional approaches to military discipline and ordering the rank and file that had raised tensions during the civil war were still being employed by military specialists. According to Shpektorov, some military specialists were also trying to introduce one-man command and place curbs on the power of the political commissars.[41] This discontent from the Red commanders toward the military specialists could turn violent. The political police did record cases where Red commanders had apparently attempted to murder military specialists.[42]

Further complaints about the domination of the upper ranks by military specialists and the slow speed of their removal were also aired in party circles. At a plenum of the Central Committee in February 1924, for instance, Sergei Gusev, secretary of the Central Control Commission and virulent critic of military specialists, accused the Revolutionary Military Council of not doing a good enough job of replacing bourgeois officers with newly trained Red commanders, fresh from the academy of the general staff. According to Gusev, the majority of new graduates were being tossed aside and simply "demobilized from the Red Army." Moreover, Gusev quoted a letter from Ieronim Uborevich, the commander of the 5th Red Banner Army, to support these accusations. Uborevich had complained that the army center was saturated with the customs (*dukhe*) of the military specialists. Stalin's ally and the first secretary of the Transcaucasian Regional Committee, Sergo Ordzhonikidze, supported this view and remarked that Uborevich's opinion was not isolated. Apparently both Tukhachevskii and Aleksandr Egorov had raised similar concerns. Furthermore, speaking for the Political Administration of the Red Army (PUR), Gusev's civil war comrade, M. M. Lashevich, a senior political commissar, complained that not only was the officer corps dominated by military specialists but also that they did not understand the "psychology of the Red Army" and that the political commissars lacked support from the center.[43] In short, several influential party figures, not all attached to the Red Army, were frustrated with the current condition of the officer corps. They believed that it was out of touch with the ideals of a revolutionary workers' state and had become a center of bourgeois customs and habits. Admittedly, it is unsurprising that someone like Gusev would take a tough line against military specialists. Previously the head of PUR, he had believed that the political commissars were the main bulwark against Bonapartism in the military.[44] Yet the discontent against military specialists had evidently spread beyond the hard-liners like Gusev. Uborevich's unease toward prerevolutionary specialists can be seen again in a letter he sent to Voroshilov a few years later in 1929 when he was stationed in Germany. On the question of whether German specialists could be employed in Soviet industry, Uborevich tellingly remarked that he believed they would be no "politically worse or more dangerous than our Russian specialists."[45]

Countering the accusations leveled at military specialists at the 1924 plenum of the Central Committee was the deputy chairman of the Revolutionary Military Council and Trotsky's close ally, Efraim Sklianskii. Replying to Gusev's complaint that freshly trained Red commanders were being demobilized from the army, Sklianskii argued that the levels of pay were much better in industry, which was attracting the military graduates away. It was thus wrong to say that the Red commanders were being purposely demobilized. It appears that Sklianskii was right on this point. Gusev was later forced to acknowledge his errors and his use of anecdotal evidence.[46] What really mattered in this debate is not whether Gusev or Sklianskii was right, but that military specialists were being scapegoated. They continued to be perceived as outsiders in the Red Army and as objects of suspicion, particularly the older military specialists. Persisting class prejudices only made it easier to accept allegations of betrayal and treachery against them. Moreover, it is also almost certain that some of the accusations leveled at the plenum were politicized and partly aimed at weakening Trotsky's position. As we shall see in the next chapter, by 1924, in his final months as war commissar, Trotsky was increasingly embattled, and Gusev in particular had allied more closely with Stalin since the civil war. His attack on military specialists at the plenum no doubt served the dual purpose of venting his personal hostility and launching an attack on Trotsky.

Some of the strongest attacks on military specialists came from the fringes of the Communist Party. V. M. Smirnov, for instance, who had been the main spokesman for the military opposition at the Eighth Party Congress in 1919, unsurprisingly remained a stern critic of military specialists. Indeed, the pressure from the military opposition at this time was evidently enough to force Voroshilov, recently appointed head of the army, to mount a defense of military specialists, the speed with which they were being replaced by Red commanders, and the stability and reliability of the Red Army as a whole. Voroshilov delivered this defense in a speech to the *Krasnopresnensk raion* party conference on 2 November 1927, during which he raised one of the military opposition's most alarmist accusations: that the employment of military specialists increased the chance of a military coup. The military opposition had claimed that the continuing use of military specialists meant, in Voroshilov's words, that "the Red Army is threatened by becoming a loyal instrument in a Bonapartist coup . . . for currently the proletariat is deprived of the chance to influence the education, studies, preparation, organization, [and] all the life of the Red Army."[47] In the same speech, Voroshilov addressed a similar attack from political oppositionist Grigorii Zinoviev, who had argued earlier in the year that "there is no doubt that in the period of the NEP [New Economic Policy], in relation to the growth of the kulak and the new bourgeoisie in general, there has grown and is still growing people among the military specialists who are dreaming about the role of a Russian Chiang Kai-shek."[48] Voroshilov labeled this slander and lacking evidence. He used his speech as an opportunity to stress that the army and navy were both fully reliable, and he presented a range of supporting statistics.[49] For example, Voroshilov noted that in 1927, the percentage of workers in the Red Army had increased to 16 percent and the number of peasants had fallen to 59 percent. Fifty-four percent of the officer corps were now members of the party. Voroshilov did not deny that there were no unreliable servicemen or traitors in the army whatsoever, but the picture he presented was of a military that was becoming more cohesive, stable, and reliable.[50] Of course, it would be wrong to gauge Voroshilov's genuine level of concern about military specialists from his public speeches and selective Soviet statistics. Since taking on the position as head of the Red Army in 1925, it is understandable that Voroshilov would seek to downplay any problems with its stability or reliability, especially in a public speech. He had a vested interest in doing so to avoid the risk his authority might be undermined. In this respect, as soon as Voroshilov became the head of the Red Army, he moderated his stance on military specialists. Voroshilov had been happy to side with the military opposition and criticize suspicious military specialists during the civil war, but as the head of the Red Army, and now directly accountable for its reliability, these criticisms ended. Voroshilov would not have wanted to sow doubts about his leadership and the direction he was taking the army. He had only been head of the Red Army for two years at the time of this particular speech. Voroshilov emphasized the ideological strength and unity within the Red Army, and this became a fixed pattern. As we shall see, however, Voroshilov soon found himself out of his depth as the head of the Red Army.

In light of the concerns about the reliability of the Red Army shared by the party leadership, political police, and military elite—concerns that included the threat posed by White subversives, terrorists, and treacherous military specialists, as well as the more outlandish fears of a military coup—the important question is, how successful was the White movement at actually subverting the Red Army in the 1920s? Was the army overrun with military specialists who were working for Whites, or did class prejudice and unwarranted suspicion act to exaggerate these threats? These questions are difficult to answer definitively because access to important archival documents remains restricted, particularly those that would shed light on the activity of the political police during the 1920s. However, one historian with access to documents held in the Central Archive of the Federal Security Service of the Russian Federation has pointed out that the political police did not arrest large numbers of military specialists or former White officers in the Red Army until the late 1920s. Between 1924 and 1930, there were no mass arrests of military specialists. Some political police materials reported a total absence of suspicious activity by military specialists.[51] As we have seen, the political police certainly received intelligence sketching out the White subversive threat to the Red Army. This intelligence inevitably varied in accuracy, but there is little to suggest that it was not taken seriously. The danger from military specialists and former White officers in the Red Army had been made clear since the civil war. High-profile mutinies left a lasting impression. The political police did make preemptive arrests to counter subversive threats to the military in the 1920s. In 1924, for instance, operatives of the recently reformed GPU (now renamed the OGPU)[52] were convinced that a group of former imperial officers serving in the navy were active counterrevolutionaries after supposed links were revealed between sailors in Kronstadt and Leningrad and the White movement. Several arrests followed. Similarly, many Whites were arrested in 1926 after their return to the Soviet Union on suspicion of having joined subversive groups.[53] However, crucially, none of these arrests was on a large scale. There is a disparity between the level of attention the political police gave to the exiled White movement and how many arrests followed. The White movement was understood to be a primary threat facing the Soviet Union in the 1920s, and one that intelligence reports claimed placed the Red Army in danger. Still, any resulting arrests remained at a low level for the time being. In this respect, it is unlikely that there was a genuine and pressing domestic threat from military specialists or former White officers to the Red Army. There is, of course, little doubt that the exiled White leaders did all they could to undermine the Soviet regime. A certain number of military specialists serving in the Red Army will have held negative, and sometimes openly hostile, opinions about the Soviet system. Similarly, there will have been military specialists with secret connections to the White movement. Some were undoubtedly working as agents. However, at the same time, the great majority of military specialists, even if they disliked the new Bolshevik regime, posed little threat to the Red Army. That there were relatively few arrests of military specialists or former Whites in the 1920s makes clear that White leaders' attempts to subvert the Red Army failed. The White movement was disorganized, lacked adequate funding, and probably had difficulty finding willing volunteers to risk dangerous missions to the Soviet Union. Beyond the infrequent, if dramatic, attacks carried out by a small network of terrorists, neither the Soviet state nor the Red Army was destabilized.

In this sense, what can be said is that fears about the subversion of the Red Army were heightened by strong class prejudices and inaccurate or exaggerated intelligence describing various active White plots, some of which, it is worth noting, warned of a full-scale military intervention into Soviet territory led by the Whites and backed by foreign powers.[54] Moreover, even though they were rarely successful, terrorist attacks carried out by the Whites lent them a certain credibility. This made their disparate movement seem more formidable than it really was. In this way, the perceived threat from the White movement to the Soviet state and toward the Red Army could be exaggerated. The difference between how threats were perceived and their reality is important to recognize, particularly in the case of the military specialists, who, despite posing little real threat to the Red Army, nonetheless often attracted the label of the enemy working within. In the coming years, the perception of threats facing the Red Army became increasingly disconnected from reality.

Divergent judgments of the reliability of the Red Army also continued to run against each other during the 1920s and were still shaped by institutional interests. As much as Voroshilov tried to publicly downplay the subversive threat to the military from his position as the head of the Red Army, the political police tended to do the opposite. In the 1920s, the primary goal of the OGPU remained the unmasking of dangerous enemies even though the Soviet state was no longer facing total destruction in a civil war. This was partly due to potent anxieties about the capitalist encirclement of the Soviet Union, but in terms of lobbying for funding and continuing to prove their value, regularly exposing dangers was important. The political police had again come under pressure at the close of the civil war from party moderates, notably Grigorii Sokol'nikov and Nikolai Bukharin, who wanted cuts to its budget now that the immediate threat to the revolution had passed.[55] The Cheka did see significant curbs on its power when it lost the right to investigate and try political cases independently as part of the transformation into the GPU in 1921. Stronger judicial oversight was also introduced into the investigation process as part of this reform.[56] Concerning the Red Army, the special departments lost much of their power after the civil war.[57]

The political police naturally resisted efforts to reduce its power and freedom of action.[58] However, the limits placed on its authority provided a strong impetus to inflate the threat to the Soviet state from a host of dangerous enemies, including the still widely employed military specialists. In doing so, Dzerzhinskii could make a stronger case that the political police remained an indispensible institution to a still-vulnerable Soviet regime and that state security was under threat. The political police thus had an incentive to continue an active search for supposed counterrevolutionaries across the Soviet state and in the Red Army. While Stalin tended to agree with Dzerzhinskii that the revolution remained in danger in the 1920s, and he tried to protect the political police from too-stringent budget cuts, resources and manpower allotted for the defense of the Red Army were nonetheless reduced. Stalin did not always manage to impose his will successfully before his consolidation of power at the end of the decade, and budgets were tight during the 1920s.[59] Until its numbers began to recover in 1930, OGPU manpower in general declined precipitously during the 1920s, and the special departments were particularly hard hit.[60] This does not suggest that there was a consensus within the regime that the political police required additional resources to prevent the army from being swamped by an array of dangerous subversives. Yet although the GPU/OGPU did not manage to arrest large numbers of military specialists in the 1920s or expose any major subversive organizations in the Red Army, in later years, they had much more success.

The Myth of the Russian Bonaparte

The exiled White leaders wanted to infiltrate the Red Army not only because it was an essential support for the Soviet regime but also because some Whites were optimistic that senior officers from the high command could be recruited to their side; they thought that a successful coup was not entirely unrealistic. A military coup was the only feasible way that the Whites might hope to wrestle control of Russia from the Soviet leadership. In reality, however, there was no chance of this happening. The Whites did not have a foothold in the Soviet high command. Nonetheless, they continued to hold out hope for a military coup. To understand this misplaced optimism, it is important to stress that White subversion and corresponding Soviet countermeasures operated within an atmosphere of unrelenting rumors about betrayal in the Red Army. At the same time that the Soviet political police were receiving intelligence about White espionage and subversion, they were gathering information and reports about a Russian Bonaparte who would supposedly emerge from the Red Army high command, unleashing a Soviet Thermidor. Comparisons between the Russian and French revolutions were common inside and outside of the Soviet Union from 1917, and that rumors of a Russian Bonaparte began to spread is unsurprising. These rumors fed into fears (but also hopes) that the Soviet regime would likewise collapse.[61] For the Whites, this gave them greater confidence that their subversive efforts might eventually pay off and help usher in a military dictatorship. By contrast, the Soviets typically rejected the rumors as disinformation, although they would never be entirely forgotten. It is likely that reports of these rumors were recorded and stored in secret police files, leaving a mass of damning information that could be interpreted more literally in the future. Although the regime took no action against the senior officers named in the incriminating rumors in the 1920s, there were nonetheless probably some lingering nagging doubts about whether the high command could be fully trusted. When the Red Army later faced a much larger wave of discharges and arrests during the Great Terror, the rumors that had sprung up in the 1920s added fuel to the fire.

Certain senior officers in the Red Army high command received more attention than others as the rumors about a Russian Bonaparte began to spread in the early 1920s. Tukhachevskii in particular attracted a great deal of hearsay and became most closely associated with the idea of a Soviet Thermidor. Tukhachevskii was a hero of the civil war, an intelligent and ambitious young officer, and the Whites rightfully regarded him as a powerful figure in the Red Army hierarchy.[62] After proving his capability in the civil war, Tukhachevskii was awarded with more responsibility in the 1920s. He became deputy chief of staff in July 1924 and was promoted to chief of staff in November 1925. Tukhachevskii's career was quickly advancing, and he established himself as a leading figure in the military elite. He had evidently lost none of the ambition he had shown during the civil war, and it would be difficult to find a better candidate for the role of a prospective Russian Bonaparte. Some White publications began to portray him as a careerist obsessed with power.[63] It did not take long for the rumor mills to set to work.[64]

Historian Sergei Minakov has explored the different channels through which rumors about betrayal in the Red Army gained a wider audience during these years. For instance, White publications such as *Voina i mir* produced stories about Bonapartism in the Red Army from 1922.[65] Moreover, the notion of a Russian Bonaparte was entertained at the apex of the White movement. The White general Aleksandr von Lampe, a prominent Wrangel aide in ROVS, made regular references to Bonapartism as well as comparisons between Tukhachevskii and Napoleon in his diary.[66] The rumors also appeared in White intelligence reports and were presumably given some credibility. One report from 15 February 1922, for instance, detailed that "a person, closely acquainted with Tukhachevskii, has indicated that he is a person of outstanding ability and great administrative and military talents. But he is not without ambition, and having recognized his own strength and authority, [he] imagines himself as a Russian Napoleon."[67] Similarly, the Soviet political police received their own intelligence describing Bonapartism in the Red Army. Some of this material suggested that plans were already in preparation for an attempted military coup. For instance, a report from the OGPU's foreign department from March 1924 detailed that a White officer, a certain Samoilov, an aide to General Kutepov, intended to make contact with Tukhachevskii to offer him a role in a military coup and in the establishment of a military dictatorship.[68] Seemingly, Tukhachevskii's ambition and the rumors about his supposed Bonapartism had encouraged opportunist White officers to try and make contact. It is unlikely that Samoilov would have wanted to get Tukhachevskii on board if his public reputation was one of a dedicated Bolshevik loyalist. Similar material was reported by the political police in December 1925, when a Soviet agent drew attention to two strains of thought apparently visible among the Red Army officers, one monarchist and the other Bonapartist, both of which apparently concentrated around Tukhachevskii.[69] It is important to stress that such reports were undoubtedly stored in political police files, but they were also doubtless sent directly to the leadership.

However, there is nothing to suggest that the Soviet leadership or the political police truly believed that certain members of the Red Army elite were plotting a coup or imagined themselves as a Russian Bonaparte. The political police did keep Tukhachevskii under observation in the 1920s. They opened a file on him that presumably grew thicker with every new piece of hearsay or rumor, including those concerning Bonapartism. Despite this, it appears that the political police did not believe that Tukhachevskii styled himself a future dictator. As Aleksandr Zdanovich has pointed out, the GPU special department was keeping Tukhachevskii under surveillance in 1922, but this was because they suspected that he was misusing state funds. Yet at the same time, they compiled a telling character assessment (*kharakteristika*) of Tukhachevskii. This described him as a highly capable military figure, but someone less capable in party life. Tukhachevskii was also deemed to be arrogant and prone to acting impulsively.[70] As such, according to this early profile of Tukhachevskii, he may have been seen as arrogant, incautious, and impulsive, but there was nothing to suggest he was a potential Russian Bonaparte.[71] In this respect, there was probably a level of overlap between the White and Soviet character assessments of Tukhachevskii; however, their conclusions diverged. Whereas the Whites were more likely to interpret Tukhachevskii's impulsiveness as suggesting an independence from the Bolsheviks and perhaps showing a desire for more personal power (only fueling rumors about his Bonapartism), the political police interpreted these traits simply as a man prone to taking risks. So although there is nothing to suggest that they genuinely believed Tukhachevskii was planning a coup, from an early stage, the GPU kept him under observation and marked him out as a potential problem. New pieces of potentially compromising information would subsequently be placed in his secret file. Even if at this point Tukhachevskii was not considered a threat to the regime, such files only got thicker, to become dangerous ammunition for the future.

However, the most important indication that neither the Soviet leadership nor the political police were taken in by the story of the Russian Bonaparte is the simple fact that they used these rumors for their own ends. The political police launched a number of counterintelligence entrapment operations against the Whites in the 1920s that played on the very same rumors of treachery that were circling the Red Army elite. Although this demonstrated the potency of the idea of betrayal in the Red Army high command, it almost certainly proves that the political police knew they were false. They knowingly kindled hopes of a Russian Bonaparte to use as disinformation. In short, the operations worked through publicizing well-known names in the Soviet high command as members of fictitious counterrevolutionary organizations. The chief objectives were to obtain information about genuine White organizations, to spread disinformation, and to flush out any active conspiracies. That the political police were turning to this type of more sophisticated counterintelligence operation is a further indication of the tactical change forced on them after the civil war. Espionage and counterintelligence were becoming increasingly important during the unresolved struggle against the Whites in the 1920s. The most notable entrapment operations launched during the decade were Operation Sindikat-4, which began in November 1924 and created a fictional White organization, the Internal Russian National Organization; and Operation D-7, which created the bogus Military Organization.[72] The most successful by far, however, was code-named Operation Trust (*Trest*).

Operation Trust was launched in November 1921 and ran for nearly six years until it was finally exposed in April 1927. A key to its success was the creation of the fictional counterrevolutionary organization, the Monarchist Union of Central Russia (MOTsR), which was advertised to the Whites as including a large part of the Red Army officer corps among its membership. It was claimed that the organization was in a position to overthrow the Soviet regime.[73] The individuals acting in the role of the organization's leaders were the former prerevolutionary general A. Zaionchkovskii and A. Iakushev, a Soviet official. Both were secretly working for the political police.[74] Among the first targets of Operation Trust were the leaders of the Berlin-based Supreme Monarchist Council. In this case, in December 1922, Iakushev, playing the role of a member of MOTsR, met with the head of the Supreme Monarchist Council, N. E. Markov. Using the fictitious organization's impressive credentials, he soon managed to gain Markov's trust. What appears to have been decisive was that MOTsR was presented as having supporters within the Red Army high command, including Tukhachevskii, so a military coup might seem entirely possible.[75] Indeed, they quickly began creating a plan for a new campaign against the Bolsheviks. With Markov willing to open up to Iakushev and work with MOTsR to formulate plans to subvert the Soviet Union, the political police now had a direct line into the Supreme Monarchist Council.

From 1922, the scope of Operation Trust began to widen. Its operatives made more fixed contact with the leaders of the White movement, including Grand Duke Nikolai Romanov (second cousin of Nicholas II) and White generals Wrangel, Kutepov, and Evgenii Miller.[76] The operation also began to target foreign intelligence services.[77] In 1923, for instance, the Polish and Estonian intelligence agencies made inquiries to MOTsR about senior officers in the Red Army, seemingly believing it was a genuine White organization.[78] When ROVS was founded in 1924, Operation Trust was deployed to establish contact and to neutralize the organization. This was particularly important in light of the White's nascent terrorist campaign launched against the Soviet state. Once again, in order to gather intelligence on ROVS, Operation Trust spread false information that Tukhachevskii and other senior officers, including Boris Shaposhnikov, Aleksandr Svechin, Pavel Lebedev, and Sergei Kamenev, were members of MOTsR and hostile to the Soviet regime. Kutepov, who, as we have seen, was the central figure orchestrating White terrorism, was completely taken in by Operation Trust, and the Bolsheviks gained important intelligence about his activity.[79] In order to make MOTsR even more convincing, fabricated documents were passed to White groups and foreign intelligence agencies that included real information and intelligence about the Red Army and its military elite, with genuine signatures from the named officers.[80] These entrapment operations were undoubtedly some of the political police's greatest successes in the 1920s. They gained valuable information about the activity of the White movement, their plans to undermine the Soviet state, and where they found their supporters. This is no doubt one major reason why the White leaders' subversive efforts failed to have much impact on the Soviet state. Foreign governments were duped as successfully. In the final year of Operation Trust, its leader, Artur Artuzov, was confident that the information held on the Red Army by Poland, France, Germany, Estonia, and Japan was almost exclusively disinformation.[81] Moreover, Operation Trust's exposure in April 1927 still managed to have a negative impact on the Whites. When they learned of the reality of the Soviet deception, their suspicions that they were surrounded by enemies and provocateurs were only reinforced. Mutual trust was undermined, and Kutepov in particular came under pressure to resign after being so willfully taken in.[82]

The extensive use of disinformation about the military elite by the Soviet political police in the 1920s guaranteed that there would be no respite from stories of treachery and betrayal in the Red Army high command. The rumors were purposely spread to ensure that the fictitious White organizations appeared more credible in order to gain valuable intelligence on real anti-Soviet activity. Consequently, the hopes that some Whites placed on a Russian Bonaparte emerging from the Red Army elite and overthrowing the Bolsheviks were ideas reinforced by the Soviet political police. Even though the influence of this disinformation was clearly more potent outside of the Soviet Union, it probably had some internal impact. The disinformation campaigns carried out by the political police were highly secretive, and few inside the Communist Party would be aware of their existence. In this sense, it is perhaps easier to understand why, against a backdrop of such widespread disinformation, people such as party outsiders Grigorii Zinoviev and V. M. Smirnov produced alarmist claims that the Red Army was at risk of being used for counterrevolutionary purposes. Like the Whites, some members of the party were surely taken in by rumors of military betrayal. Because the atmosphere of the 1920s was heavy with disinformation about the high command, this may have helped those not privy to the mechanics behind the operations to accept some of the stories they were hearing. Military coups elsewhere in Europe—in Bulgaria in 1923 (which led to the crushing of the Bulgarian Communist Party), General Józef Piłsudski's military coup in Poland in May 1926, and the military coup in Lithuania in December 1926—must have only further heightened concerns about Bonapartism in the Red Army inside the Soviet Union.

The end of Operation Trust in 1927 did not bring an end to the rumors of betrayal that encircled the Red Army. One year later, the foreign press reported on a supposed insurrection in the Red Army apparently led by Tukhachevskii.[83] It seems that the sheer success of the Soviet disinformation campaigns, while helping gain valuable intelligence, had reinforced a wider tendency toward questioning the reliability of the Red Army high command that was difficult to shift. Even though rumors about a military coup and a Russian Bonaparte were not taken seriously by the political police in the 1920s, they did provide constant suggestions both inside and outside the Soviet Union that the military elite's loyalty was not guaranteed. As we shall see, entirely new rumors appeared in the mid-1930s, meaning that the high command never escaped the speculation that its senior officers were untrustworthy. These later rumors built on the foundations of those publicized in the 1920s. Indeed, it is likely that any rumors about treachery in the Red Army (however skeptically they were seen) were still added to political police files on prominent senior officers. They would never be entirely forgotten. A mass of potentially compromising information was steadily building up against members of the high command. This would contribute to their later repression during the Great Terror.

The Threat from Foreign Governments

While neither the Soviet leadership nor political police believed that senior Red Army officers were actually plotting a coup in the 1920s, they were certainly concerned that a coalition of capitalist powers was planning a military intervention to crush the revolution. This was the impression gleaned from the intelligence gained from the disinformation campaigns against the Whites. These reports were valuable precisely because they gave insight into the hopes among White groups of one day overthrowing the Soviet regime and their optimism that European states would lend assistance. European political elites had hoped for a White victory in the civil war and now had to adjust to life with the Soviet Union. In reality, there was no chance of a full-blown military assault on the Soviet Union led by an alliance of European states. Yet as far as the Soviet leadership was concerned, any intelligence connecting the Whites to capitalist powers was worth taking seriously. The Soviet leaders were convinced that the Soviet Union was surrounded by foreign governments hostile to the revolution. They may have won the civil war, but the Soviet Union remained a pariah state in the world, and another major conflict was believed to be only a matter of time. Moreover, with some European governments continuing to provide financial support for the exiled White movement and hosting their scattered forces, it is easy to see why the Soviet leaders were alert to a possible future invasion. The perception of the foreign threat is central to understanding the behavior of the Soviet regime throughout the interwar period.[84]

In addition to intelligence gathered from the Soviet disinformation operations against the Whites, a regular stream of supposed espionage cases seemed to provide further evidence that capitalist states had nothing but hostile intentions toward the Soviet Union. Espionage in general terms was widespread in the interwar years. All governments aimed to find out as much as they could about the military power of their potential enemies; this became a more pressing concern as an arms race began in the years before the outbreak of World War II. The Soviet Union created the largest intelligence network in Europe in the 1920s, and European governments likewise wanted to gather information on the military power of the Red Army. All this meant that spy networks and foreign intelligence agents were frequently exposed in the Soviet Union—though, as we shall see, not all were genuine.[85] Moreover, as had been the case during the civil war, the Red Army was still understood as being a prime target for foreign spies wanting to get hold of valuable military information. Trotsky had taken action against this particular threat early on. In 1922, he prohibited soldiers from having contact with foreigners without first notifying a political commissar.[86] However, alleged foreign agents were discovered in the Red Army throughout the 1920s at a low but frequent level. In June 1924, for instance, the counterintelligence department of the Kiev OGPU arrested a group on charges of Polish espionage. The majority were military specialists who had served in the Red Army, and one was still in service.[87] In March 1925, the army newspaper *Krasnaia zvezda* reported on the exposure of another Polish spy network in the army. The organization had apparently included a number of former imperial officers who were allegedly working for Poland. All had previously served in the Red Army. Details of a similar case were published in April.[88] Agents supposedly working for the British, Finnish, and Latvian governments were also discovered in the military in the mid-1920s.[89] In October 1926, the head of the inspectorate of the Moscow Military District staff, Pavel Filin, was arrested for espionage, along with his wife, Nona Filina. Filin was accused of having British connections.[90] In a revealing move, after this particular case, Voroshilov ordered that even the families of soldiers were forbidden to have any contact with foreigners.[91] The espionage threat to the Red Army was seemingly in need of greater attention. Foreign intelligence agencies were also believed to be closely collaborating with the White movement to subvert Soviet institutions. The Soviet leadership saw the outlines of a worldwide conspiracy against them. The so-called Center of Action, for instance, a White organization controlled from Paris, was believed to be financed by Poland and France. Among many of its tasks was the recruitment of agents from the Red Army in order to gain valuable intelligence.[92] In terms of which country was identified as the most dangerous threat to the Soviet Union in the 1920s, Poland topped the list. Relations had continued to be tense in the years after the Russo-Polish war, and when the staunch anticommunist Józef Piłsudski came to power in 1926 in a military coup, they only got worse. From this point on, the political police reported an increase in Polish espionage activity and attempts to recruit from within the Red Army.[93]

What many of these espionage cases had in common was how traitorous military specialists were singled out as being the tools of hostile
foreign governments. A report from the Military Procuracy on counterrevolutionary organizations inside the Red Army covering the period October 1926 to October 1927 raised this issue. According to the
Military Procuracy, to carry out espionage, "foreign intelligence agents
use social aliens and those with harmful moods toward Sov[iet] power,
elements/former noblemen (*dvoriane*) . . . [and] in the main, individuals from the command."[94] It was believed that foreign powers, like the
White leaders, were taking advantage of disaffected outsider elements
in the Red Army; this meant military specialists.[95] The Military Procuracy, however, also pointed out that this espionage activity was on a small
scale and less common than other types of criminal activity in the military. In 1927, the Military Procuracy reported, "The infiltration of foreign intelligence agents into the RKKA is on an insignificant scale."[96] In
this respect, at least during the 1920s, foreign agents were understood
to have the ability to infiltrate the Red Army, and there was an identified
pool of potential recruits among the military specialists, although the
problem was not yet widespread.[97]

However, it would be a mistake to evaluate the wider significance
of the espionage threat to the Red Army from the Military Procuracy
alone. This was the mainstream judicial arm responsible for crime in
the Red Army. It valued evidence-based investigation far more than the
political police, who, in contrast, tended to rely on their revolutionary
instincts. Nor did the Military Procuracy have the same vested interest
in arresting enemies to justify its value. It is certain that the political
police judged the relatively small number of espionage cases in the Red
Army as more sinister and dangerous than the Military Procuracy. The
political police was not alone in exaggerating the significance of foreign
espionage. The Soviet leadership in general (and Stalin in particular)
tended to see the espionage threat to the Soviet Union in graver terms
than was justified. What matters is not the physical number of so-called
spies discovered across the Soviet state but how the regime interpreted
these cases in accordance with a worldview shaped by the idea of capitalist encirclement. The Soviet leaders believed that they were surrounded
by a coalition of capitalist powers who were actively making preparations for war to capture new territory and resources. This can be seen
early on, when Stalin tellingly claimed in 1920 that Britain, France, and
America had instigated the Russo-Polish war.[98] From the regime's per-

spective, the Soviet Union was under siege, and a new war was not just a possibility but was unavoidable. The communist and capitalist worlds were incompatible, and a major clash was only a matter of time.[99] This deeply held belief in capitalist encirclement created a heightened sensitivity toward future conflict, meaning that even low levels of foreign espionage (but especially targeted at the Red Army) only confirmed this much larger looming danger.

The civil war experience seemed to confirm this prophecy of inevitable war. The fate of the revolution had hung in the balance, and the Soviet leaders would never forget the assistance given to their enemies by European governments or the landing of foreign troops on Soviet territory. This was ample evidence of their hostile intentions. Over the course of the 1920s, a profound sense of anxiety about a new war shaped the regime's responses to international affairs. Indeed, so-called evidence that foreign powers were still working hard to bring down the revolution was not difficult to find. Several European governments, for example, maintained links with the exiled White movement in the 1920s and continued to subsidize their intelligence operations.[100] White agents were sometimes directly used as part of foreign intelligence operations.[101] There is, of course, a considerable gulf between subsidizing the White movement and actively participating in a coalition of powers bent on destroying the Soviet Union. European political elites were certainly hostile to the Soviet Union. They were worried about communist subversion and the spread of communist revolution across Europe. Anticommunism was a potent force after the stabilization of Soviet power after the civil war. However, this anticommunism never translated into any concerted attempt to overthrow the Soviet regime. There was no appetite for another major conflict among the European powers so soon after World War I, and the status of Germany in the postwar world was seen as a bigger problem than the Soviet Union. Indeed, the Soviet Union was not long in its diplomatic isolation. Over the course of the 1920s, it was recognized by all major European powers. However, the Soviet leadership saw things differently and could never be complacent. Any hostile rhetoric from abroad or new alliances and treaties ratified between foreign powers could easily be interpreted as evidence that plans were being devised to crush the Soviet state.

Judging by the instability in Europe in the early 1920s, it is easy to see why the Soviet leaders believed that a new war was on the horizon. In 1923, for instance, French troops occupied the Ruhr region in January after the German government failed to honor its reparations payments. This was not just a major international crisis but also sparked fears within the Soviet regime that an invasion was imminent. When the Weimar government ordered workers in the Ruhr to go on strike in response to the French occupation (which only added to Germany's economic woes), an insurrection led by the German Communist Party further destabilized the government. The Soviet leaders were now convinced that the country was at the point of revolution. Preparations were made for the mobilization of the Red Army to intervene on Germany's behalf.[102] Indeed, although the prospect of a new communist government being established in the heart of Europe was an exciting one, the Soviet leaders were also worried that it risked provoking a military intervention by Poland, whose government was concerned that the Ruhr crisis would leave Germany aligned more closely with the Soviet Union. Moreover, the Soviet leaders feared that Poland might crush the German revolution and then turn attention once again toward the Soviet Union. The Soviet political police also worried that the impulsive Tukhachevskii might needlessly use the unrest in Germany as a pretext to make a drive into Poland to revenge the lost war.[103] However, despite ambitious plans to send the Red Army to Germany and the belief that another revolution was vital for Soviet security, in reality, the Soviet Union was in too weakened a position to adequately defend itself in a new European conflict. Although there was much optimism surrounding a revolution in Germany, there were also many uncertainties surrounding the Ruhr crisis, including the possibility of a war that the Soviet Union could not win. In any case, the communist insurrection in Germany, having received no support from the German Social Democratic Party, soon failed, bringing the crisis to an end. The German revolution was left to succumb to its own weaknesses. The uprising collapsed before it gathered momentum.[104]

The failure of the German revolution did not mean that the Soviet leadership gave up on their attempts to spread communism around the world. This was still perceived as a critical task of the Russian revolution. However, in general, they were cautious and wanted to avoid overly antagonizing other European powers. They believed that the capitalist world had managed to stabilize itself after the upheaval of World War I and that it constituted a serious threat to Soviet power that should not be needlessly provoked. Soviet leaders were suspicious in particular of the intentions of the British government as the preeminent imperialist power; they incorrectly believed, for instance, that it was attempting to form an anti-Soviet bloc with Poland, Romania, and the Baltic states.[105] Low points in Anglo-Soviet relations, such as the Curzon ultimatum of May 1923, did little to dampen suspicions of British hostility. France was similarly judged to be making plans for war. For example, the OGPU reported in 1923 that a French attack would be launched in the following year, supported by Poland, Romania, and the exiled Whites.[106] The concern that the Entente powers would make use of proxies to attack the Soviet Union can be seen in directives sent in February 1923 to the Western Red Army stationed in Ukraine from Sergei Kamenev, the commander in chief of the Red Army. These stated that in the near future, the Red Army may be required to defend the borders and that the most probable aggressors would be the White movement with Polish and Entente assistance. Moreover, according to Kamenev, it was possible that other countries bordering the Soviet Union would join the attack, including Finland, Estonia, Latvia, Lithuania, and Romania.[107] The Soviet leaders, in short, were watching the international situation carefully in the 1920s, but their perspective was skewed, and they misread the outside world. Diplomatic ties and trade links between foreign powers were misinterpreted as evidence of hostile intentions and conspiracy.[108] This misreading created an expectation of looming conflict. The Soviet leaders believed that the capitalist world was actively making plans for war, that it would never reconcile to the existence of the Soviet state, and that the only question was when the attack would come.

In this respect, the discovery of supposed foreign intelligence agents in the Red Army had special significance, even if this was at a relatively low level in the 1920s. When seen in the context of perceived capitalist encirclement, the continuing assistance given to the White movement by foreign governments, and the Soviet leaders' own misplaced views about inevitable war, espionage against the Red Army appeared as one part of a much larger conspiracy to crush the Soviet Union. This confirmed the regime's sense of isolation and the ever-present threat from the capitalist world. Stalin clearly made these connections. After the assassination of Soviet special envoy Piotr Voikov in Poland in 1927, which Stalin interpreted as a British attempt to spark a war between Poland and the Soviet Union, Stalin, in a letter to the new OGPU chief, Viacheslav Menzhinskii (who had taken over after Dzerzhinskii's death in July 1926), called for stronger countermeasures against British intelligence. Stalin believed that its agents were more deeply infiltrated in the Soviet state than anyone had previously thought, and he suggested staging several show trials of supposed British spies for propaganda purposes, along with widespread searches for any agents, to be carried out by the OGPU. Notably, Stalin specifically ordered Menzhinskii to pay "special attention to espionage in the military, aviation, and navy."[109]

In contrast to other European countries, Germany was given extensive access to the Red Army during the 1920s. Germany was seen as an important ally for the Soviet Union and a means to bring it out of diplomatic isolation, as both countries were pariah states in the years after World War I. The two countries had begun to collaborate in May 1921 with the signing of a commercial agreement that also established military–industrial contacts.[110] Formal diplomatic relations came a year later, in April 1922, with the signing of the Treaty of Rapallo. The growing cooperation between the two countries suited both their interests. The Soviet Union lacked the technical ability essential for strengthening its industrial base, while Germany needed locations it could use to secretly rearm and work around the restrictions imposed by the Treaty of Versailles. Germany also gave assistance to building Soviet military power, helping the Red Army's chemical weapons program and its tank and aircraft production.[111]

However, any hopes that this collaboration would satisfy the Soviet leaders' needs were short-lived. By late 1925, it was clear that the Soviet Union needed to industrialize independently and build up its own armaments industry rather than rely on others. The rejection of several Soviet proposals by the Germans and their desire to collaborate only at a low level also became sticking points in the relationship.[112] Nonetheless, despite these problems, a military collaboration did continue and was one of the longest-lasting features of the partnership. This primarily involved an exchange of officers between the two countries. One of the first Red Army officers to spend a significant period of time in Germany was Uborevich, who was there for thirteen months beginning in November 1927. Uborevich studied with German officers and was given open access to large amounts of military technology. (There are indications that Uborevich was favored by the Germans and given freer access than other Soviet officers.[113]) Following in his footsteps, a further 192 Red Army officers trained in Germany between 1925 and 1932, and twelve visited twice. Uborevich, Iakir, and Ivan Belov spent at least a year in Germany; however, most spent one to three months in the country.[114]

It is clear that this partnership, though it had obvious benefits, would put the Red Army at risk of infiltration by German intelligence agents. Voroshilov warned Uborevich against striking up too friendly of relations with the Germans during his stay in the country, and the Soviet political police were suspicious of this from the very beginning. Dzerzhinskii believed that the Germans were planning to overthrow the Soviet regime and suspected that they were working with White organizations.[115] An OGPU circular from 1924 highlighted an espionage threat from Germans in the Soviet Union.[116] Moreover, with the establishment of the Junkers aircraft company on Soviet territory, the political police began to make a range of accusations, including that the company was attempting to forge links with the Red Army officer corps for intelligence purposes and that it was a counterrevolutionary organization working with the British government.[117]

Dzerzhinskii was not wrong in suspecting that German representatives in the Soviet Union were after intelligence. However, it seems in many cases what they were engaged in cannot be justly described as serious espionage. Some German representatives did gather material during their visits to the Soviet Union. They sent home information from the Soviet military press, as well as their personal observations of military maneuvers and conversations with Red Army officers.[118] This type of information gathering is documented in interrogation transcripts of German diplomats and military attachés who were arrested in the 1940s.[119] This activity, if it can be classified as espionage, was certainly on a low level and appears to have been tolerated. On 24 December 1928, for instance, the head of military intelligence, Ian Berzin, sent a letter to Voroshilov in which he raised the issue but showed little alarm:

> There is no doubt that all the German enterprises, apart from their direct task[s], also have the task of economic, political, and military information/ espionage. . . . But this espionage, according to all information, is not directed along the lines of the extraction and collection of secret documents but is conducted through personal observations, conversations, and verbal information (*ustnikh informatsii*). This espionage is less dangerous.[120]

This hardly suggests that Berzin believed the Germans were trying to undermine or sabotage the Red Army. This was not the theft of highly secret material that might cause harm to the Soviet Union's military power. Moreover, in his letter to Voroshilov, Berzin expressed his wish that the collaboration continue, and he suggested an exchange of intelligence on Poland with Germany.[121] The threat from Poland was evidently rated more highly than German espionage. Even though Voroshilov had had some doubts during the collaboration and believed that the Germans were holding back information and exploiting the Soviet side, he also took advantage of the closer contact. Voroshilov instructed officers visiting Germany to find out specific information about the organization of the Reichswehr and its military technology.[122] Before Uborevich's long stay in Germany in 1927, Voroshilov asked him to find out information about the organization and armaments of the German military. Soviet military intelligence likewise instructed those visiting Germany to bring back information.[123] In this way, both the Soviet and German governments profited from the collaboration. It offered mutual benefits and some intelligence at a low risk. Even though a closer partnership with Germany would leave the Red Army open to infiltration, in the early 1920s at least, the collaboration was seen as important in helping the Soviet Union develop its military power and prepare for the inevitable war. This was the overriding consideration. The military collaboration, however, took place before Hitler's ascendance to power. As Germany took an increasingly hostile stance toward the Soviet Union in the early 1930s, it was quickly brought to an end. However, that such a partnership had been maintained in the 1920s—with personal connections established between Soviet and German officers—had unintended consequences in later years.[124] When the espionage threat from Nazi Germany started to be judged as a major problem in the 1930s, it helped cast suspicion on the Red Army officers who had spent time in the country.

Trotskyism in the Red Army

The perceived security threats to the Red Army from the White movement and foreign intelligence agencies were regarded as serious enough problems, but it faced one final threat to its stability in the 1920s. This came from what the Soviet leadership labeled the Trotskyist Left Opposition, which found a small level of support in the Red Army. The subversive threat embodied by Trotskyists differed from the external threats posed by the Whites and foreign agents in one important respect. The opposition did not depend on infiltrated agents. It could potentially easily spread from one army party organization to another. More than any other problem faced by the military, Trotskyism was seen as an issue of the enemy within. Yet in the literature on the Red Army and the military purge, the scale of the support Trotsky found in the ranks is usually only briefly commented upon. There has been little examination of how the danger from Trotskyists was understood, and on what terms. The small number of military supporters who rallied to Trotsky's platform in the 1920s is another demonstration of how conflicting judgments about the vulnerability of the Red Army existed in competition and how these were predominately shaped by institutional interests.

In the early 1920s, the Communist Party was divided over what to do about the devastating economic crisis created by the civil war. The regime was facing a wave of strike actions, and in the countryside, the peasants were in rebellion because of widespread shortages and an intensifying food crisis. A change of direction was essential if the regime was going to avoid collapse. Consequently, the highly unpopular and authoritarian policy of war communism, which had sanctioned forced grain requisitions and kept the Bolsheviks afloat during the civil war, was abandoned. However, its replacement proved to be divisive. At the Tenth Party Congress in March 1921, the foundations were laid for what became known as the New Economic Policy (NEP). This program of reform aimed at producing economic recovery by introducing a limited private sector and allowing peasants some freedom to engage in their own economic activity. Among a raft of measures, grain requisitions were to be replaced by a lower level of taxation, and peasants would be permitted to keep their surpluses. Heavy industry would remain under the control of the state, but it was now required to function according to market rules.[125] In essence, the NEP was a radical change in direction, especially for revolutionary-minded Bolsheviks. This was precisely the problem. Many party members saw the reestablishment of central features of a capitalist economy as a step backward from how they had imagined the state at the time of the revolution. Trotsky in particular did not agree with the changes ushered in by the NEP. He believed that in allowing limited private enterprise, the NEP gave too much freedom to the rich peasants, the reviled kulaks. He also began to argue for a much faster-paced industrialization of the state, going against the consensus in the party at this time.[126]

The NEP, however, was not the only cause of Trotsky's growing opposition to the party line. Underlying tensions within the Communist Party were exacerbated by Lenin's worsening health. After suffering a number of strokes in the early 1920s, he was forced to withdraw from public and party life. With Lenin unable to carry out his duties as party leader, everyday leadership was transferred to a ruling triumvirate of Stalin, Grigorii Zinoviev, and Lev Kamenev in 1922.[127] However, Trotsky now began to openly criticize Stalin, accusing him of centralizing power. He called for stronger democratic practices and denounced what he saw as a creeping bureaucratization in party life. Yet Trotsky's own position was not as strong as it had once been. His popularity within the party had been in sharp decline since the civil war, and in the early 1920s, a new dispute erupted over the role of the trade unions that drew further dividing lines. Trotsky's weakened support was evident at the Tenth Party Congress in March 1921, where he only managed to come in tenth in the vote for the new Central Committee, and the number of his supporters was reduced.[128]

Trotsky came under further pressure when his record as war commissar was put under increasing scrutiny. The employment of military specialists had continued to cause Trotsky damage, but he was also facing pressure as a result of the poor condition of the Red Army.[129] In 1923, a military commission found a series of alarming problems with the army, chiefly related to manpower and supply, for which, as war commissar, Trotsky was held accountable.[130] Another commission in 1924, which included a number of Stalin's allies and both future heads of the army, Mikhail Frunze and Voroshilov, delivered another blow to Trotsky's authority, again condemning the condition of the military.[131] Even though both military commissions were undoubtedly politicized and used to weaken Trotsky's position, this does not mean that the defects in the Red Army were concocted. The Red Army needed to undergo a long period of reform before it resembled anything like a professional standing army, especially after the destructive civil war. Shortages in adequately trained officers were acute, and the military as a whole suffered from poor organization. Trotsky then lost some of his key allies in the Red Army. In 1924, his deputy, Sklianskii, was replaced by Stalin's ally, Mikhail Frunze, and Voroshilov took command of the Moscow Military District, ousting another Trotsky ally, Nikolai Muralov.[132]

Even though Trotsky was in a weakened position in the early 1920s, he continued to find supporters. In October 1923, forty-six party members sent a letter to the Central Committee repeating Trotsky's criticisms of economic policy and bureaucratism in the party. The letter, known as the platform of the forty-six, was denounced by the Central Committee, and before long, Trotsky was accused of factionalism by the ruling triumvirate. Trotsky also still had allies in the Red Army. The most important were Vladimir Antonov-Ovseenko, who was head of PUR until his removal in 1923, and other senior officers, such as Muralov, who commanded the Moscow Military District until his replacement with Voroshilov, and the commander of the Volga Military District, Sergei Mrachkovskii. Other notable Trotskyist officers included Vitalii Primakov and Vitovt Putna. Trotsky also found support from among the military specialists, within the military academies, in the navy, in PUR, and among the youth.[133] In terms of scale, the support for Trotsky could in places reach quite high levels. In 1923, for instance, he had the support of approximately a third of Moscow's military party cells.[134]

Ruling circles in the party regarded this support for Trotsky as dangerous and destabilizing for the Red Army. One incident causing particular scorn was Antonov-Ovseenko's unsanctioned distribution of a PUR circular on 24 December 1923 that called for the reestablishment of democratic practices in the military with the election of party cell secretaries. The circular prompted a counterresolution from the party's disciplinary body, the Central Control Commission, in January 1924, which accused Antonov-Ovseenko of having created a "harmful mood" among military party members. The Central Control Commission presented his actions as a challenge to the party leadership and as an attempt "to raise the military workers against the leading organs of the party and all the party as a whole."[135] Subsequently, during the Thirteenth Party Conference in January 1924, Antonov-Ovseenko was again criticized for sending the circular and was removed from his position as the head of PUR. He was soon sent overseas on diplomatic work.[136] Moreover, Antonov-Ovseenko's replacement (and Stalin ally), Andrei Bubnov, immediately set out to find out why Trotsky was finding supporters in the ranks. He was ordered to quash the democratic movement in the Red Army.[137] The situation only worsened for Trotsky in 1924. When Lenin finally died on 21 January, the infighting inside the party intensified. The ruling triumvirate of Stalin, Zinoviev, and Kamenev was now even more determined to stop Trotsky from becoming the next party leader. The pressure on Trotsky and his allies began to build throughout the year.[138] Trotsky had already been criticized in two military commissions, and now an assembly of senior political workers organized by Bubnov called for his resignation in November 1924. This was followed by a call from the Revolutionary Military Council demanding the same thing. Without Lenin to lean on for support, and suffering from malaria, Trotsky caved in to the pressure. In January 1925, he resigned as the head of the Red Army.[139] His replacement, Mikhail Frunze, was one of Stalin's allies in the military who, as we shall see in the next chapter, unleashed a raft of reforms in the military. Frunze would serve less than a year; he died in October 1925 while undergoing surgery. Frunze's replacement with Voroshilov cemented Stalin's control over the Red Army.

The party may have come down hard on Trotsky in the mid-1920s, but in general, reactions to the Trotskyists in the Red Army varied widely and were shaped by institutional interests. PUR, for instance, typically downplayed the Trotskyist impact in the military. In a range of reports throughout the 1920s, PUR consistently noted that Trotsky had only a minor level of support in the armed forces. For example, in a PUR survey from February 1925, compiled in reference to the previous year's publication of Trotsky's critical essay, "The Lessons of October," it was noted that support for Trotsky was only at a low level in the army and navy.[140] In September 1926, another PUR report stressed the unity of army party organizations in face of Trotskyist agitation. The report noted that despite oppositionist speeches at a recent plenum of the Central Committee, "the resolutions, accepted in the party meetings, meetings of the *aktiv* etc., utterly and completely endorse the decisions of the plenum, sharply condemning the opposition and welcome the firm Lenin line (*leninskuiu liniiu*) of the TsK [Central Committee]."[141] One month later, Anton Bulin, a senior political commissar, sent Voroshilov a report on the scale of the Trotskyist presence in a number of military districts. According to Bulin, Trotsky's platform was only having limited impact in the ranks. He reported that in the Volga Military District, for instance, "the oppositionists have shown their political wretchedness, poverty, and full unscrupulousness. It absolutely has no trust and influence in the wider party masses."[142] Bulin recorded a similar reaction from the troops in the Central Asian Military District.[143] Notably, a PUR report from 1927 placed Trotskyists at only 0.25 percent of all army party organizations.[144] In this way, PUR was reporting that Trotsky had failed to gain any real traction in the ranks. This was certainly justified in terms of numbers. Trotsky never gained a mass following in the Red Army despite his pockets of support. However, PUR was the organization directly responsible for the political reliability of the Red Army, and it had a vested interest in downplaying problems with its stability. It is only natural that it would look to emphasize the stability and reliability of the Red Army and not admit too easily to any weaknesses.

To do so would draw attention to how PUR was failing to instill a proper political education into the soldiers. As the newly installed head of PUR, Bubnov would not want to be seen as having failed to get control over the Trotskyist influence in the military.

In contrast, there are glimpses of how some members of PUR estimated the oppositionist threat, painting a different picture than that of the above reports. For instance, on receiving information about oppositionist activity within the Leningrad Military District, the deputy head of PUR in the region, Mikhail Landa, reacted with alarm and contacted the Central Control Commission on 18 September 1926. The Leningrad PUR had received a letter from a political worker, a certain Khvatskii, who had until recently been a member of the opposition. In his letter, Khvatskii had detailed the activities of his former oppositionist group and its military wing, the so-called Military Bureau. According to Khvatskii, the Military Bureau had members working in positions in a range of units; he described his former political position as "practically against the party."[145] In his letter to the Central Control Commission, it is evident that Landa was deeply troubled by these revelations:

> This letter paints a scandalous picture of the opposition's underground work in the army. From this letter, it is apparent that in parts of the Leningrad Military District, the opposition has organized underground troikas, which are organizing underground meetings. . . . Such dissenting and disruptive work is dangerous for the party organization of the army. I consider it necessary to bring a decisive end to such unprecedented irresponsible and hugely harmful disorder. Therefore I request that the TsKK [Central Control Commission] bring all mentioned in the letter to account.[146]

Beyond the PUR reports that attached little significance to the Trotskyist influence in the army, the reality is that some political commissars—people like Landa—saw a greater danger. In this sense, it is likely that PUR did see a genuine danger posed by Trotskyists to the Red Army but perhaps saw danger in admitting this too openly.

Like PUR, Voroshilov tended to downplay the oppositionist threat to the army in public. As the head of the Red Army, he was ultimately accountable for its political reliability, and he had a similar vested interest in not admitting too easily to any serious problems. Indeed, at the time of Voroshilov's promotion to people's commissar of military and naval affairs in 1925, Trotsky had managed to hold onto a small number of military supporters, and Voroshilov did his best to downplay their significance. For instance, in a speech on the achievements of the party organizations delivered on 10 January 1927, Voroshilov congratulated the army for having stood firm in the face of the Trotskyist threat: "The interparty events that happened in the past year were in my opinion a serious examination for our party organizations, and we should note with satisfaction that our party organization brilliantly passed this examination in political Leninist maturity." With a comment that he would repeat in later years, Voroshilov added: "The Red Army is the most delicate organization in all of the Soviet system, and therefore party work here should be arranged the most correctly."[147] Voroshilov's tendency to downplay or outright ignore problems with the internal stability of the Red Army soon became routine.

The political police, however, held a very different view of the army Trotskyists. They were far more concerned about the harmful effects of political agitation in the ranks, even though the number of Trotsky's military supporters was still relatively small. The political police took counteraction after receiving reports of underground and illegal oppositionist propaganda and agitation within the army.[148] From December 1925 to November 1927, eighty oppositionists were discharged from the ranks and expelled from the party.[149] Moreover, the political police were not just concerned about propaganda and agitation; they were also alert to any attempt to use military Trotskyists as part of a coup. An early investigation into this potential threat concerned the case of Iakov Dvorzhets, a subordinate of Antonov-Ovseenko.[150] In this particular case, Antonov-Ovseenko had persuaded Dvorzhets to speak out against Zinoviev (at the time one of the members of the ruling triumvirate) during a discussion meeting in 1923. Zinoviev responded by claiming that Dvorzhets's speech was counterrevolutionary. This attracted the attention of the OGPU.[151] When Antonov-Ovseenko heard about the case against his subordinate, he sent an ultimatum to the Central Committee that threateningly noted that there were members of the party, and in particular within the Red Army, who "will at some point call to order those leaders who have overstepped the mark."[152] Antonov-Ovseenko was clearly bluffing. He had nowhere near enough supporters in the army to call anyone in the leadership to order. The threat made little difference, however, and Dvorzhets was formally arrested on 11 January 1924.[153] Nonetheless, Antonov-Ovseenko's ultimatum is another reminder of the fact that on a certain level, loyalties were being contested in the Red Army in the 1920s. The army could not help but be drawn into the sharpening political struggle inside the Communist Party, and the OGPU took this seriously. Notably, when they interrogated Dvorzhets, they tried to find out specific information about a possible military coup led by Trotsky, although they failed to uncover any proof.[154] However, the lack of evidence did not end the OGPU's search to uncover plans for a Trotskyist coup.

In 1926, Trotsky's defiance of the ruling party was reinforced after Zinoviev and Kamenev had broken with Stalin a year earlier, left the triumvirate, and went into opposition. Indeed, it was not long after Trotsky's resignation as war commissar in early 1925 that Zinoviev and Kamenev began to criticize what they saw as the overly pro-peasant orientation in the NEP as well as Stalin's growing personal power. Both men were subjected to stern criticism as a result and were punished with demotion: Kamenev lost full membership in the Politburo and was downgraded to candidate status, and Zinoviev lost his position as chairman of the Leningrad Soviet. Despite this, both Old Bolsheviks continued to denounce Stalin and the economic policies of the party. They soon became members of a reformed opposition group, the United Opposition, which included both Trotsky and Lenin's widow, Nadezhda Krupskaia. The year 1927 was the peak of the group's activity: its campaign was broadened beyond party circles, thus representing a firmer challenge to party authority and necessitating a tougher response. Trotsky and Zinoviev were subsequently expelled from the Central Committee in October alongside Kamenev, who had already been sent overseas. All three were later expelled from the party. This clampdown on the opposition had consequences for the Trotskyists serving in the Red Army. In particular, in 1927, Trotskyist officers Primakov and Putna lost their commands and were sent overseas on diplomatic assignments. Primakov became the military attaché in Afghanistan and Putna took the same position in Japan, though both managed to retain their party memberships.

Events finally came to a head in November 1927, when the opposition planned demonstrations for the tenth anniversary of the revolution. The OGPU believed these were not simply demonstrations but that the opposition's supposed combat organization was planning a coup. Menzhinskii, as the recently appointed head of the OGPU, duly informed the Central Committee of his concerns. According to Menzhinskii, the conspirators planned to take over the Kremlin and the OGPU headquarters, with similar operations in the works in Leningrad and Kharkov. However, no evidence exists to support Menzhinskii's version of the conspiracy. It may well have been based on inaccurate or entirely fabricated information.[155] The OGPU may have exaggerated the threat. They had already raised concerns that the opposition had formed a subversive military group in September and had notified the Central Committee. This smaller case involved the arrest of a group of men apparently working in a supposed illegal Trotskyist printing press, some of whom were serving in the Red Army. However, under interrogation, one of the arrested men supplied evidence (likely coerced) that he was part of a military group that was planning a coup, with inspiration taken from Józef Piłsudski. The case was discussed at a joint plenum of the Central Committee in late October. However, at this point, Menzhinskii was ordered not to further interrogate members of the arrested group. It seems that merely the accusation of a possible oppositionist military coup suited Stalin's purposes for slurring Trotsky.[156] As such, Menzhinskii may have claimed that there was further evidence of a coup in November as a pretext to push for stronger action to be taken against the opposition, which included its supporters in the Red Army, who were apparently central to the so-called conspiracy. (According to Menzhinskii, the preparations for the coup had coincided with sustained and vigorous agitation within the Red Army.) Although Menzhinskii would have been well aware of Voroshilov's and PUR's repeated assurances that the army had remained reliable and stable in the face of the opposition's attempts to find supporters in the ranks, it is unlikely that he agreed. Moreover, if the OGPU did manage to prevent a coup while demonstrating that the Red Army had been internally compromised, Menzhinskii could use this to undermine Voroshilov and convince Stalin that his own concerns about the vulnerability of the Red Army were worth listening to.

If this was Menzhinskii's reasoning, events nearly went to plan. The coup, of course, never materialized, but the OGPU was commended anyway for forestalling a dangerous plot. Stalin praised the decisive action taken by Menzhinskii and Voroshilov in stopping the oppositionists, reiterating the threat they posed to the regime.[157] Ultimately, however, Menzhinskii failed to convince Stalin that his concerns about the vulnerability of the Red Army were justified. In his initial letter about the opposition's supposed combat organization, Menzhinskii wrote:

> In this secret report of the combat organization it is further stated that propaganda among the workers and in the Workers' and Peasants' Army should continue by all possible means until further orders. Especially in the

army. The destructive effect of this propaganda in the army, I have already pointed out many times—though, unfortunately, not always with the desired results. . . . We must therefore expect, in the time immediately ahead, that opposition propaganda will be at least as vigorous as it has been until now. It will be directed first of all, judging from the present state of affairs, at subverting the army. Comrade Voroshilov has acknowledged to me without question the pernicious effect of the opposition slogans. . . . It makes me very sad to have to assert here, in this place, that the army today, unlike before, has already been partly contaminated and that the commanders now are often not reliable in the full sense of the word. Comrade Voroshilov is thoroughly aware of the seriousness of the situation and fully shares my pessimistic mood.[158]

Menzhinskii evidently did not hold much faith in the Red Army's ability to withstand agitation and propaganda. Yet his opinion was not universally accepted. Unsurprisingly, PUR held a different view and continued to display little concern about the influence of the opposition in the ranks.[159] Even though PUR had an incentive to downplay problems with political reliability, they were supported by military intelligence, which reported to Voroshilov in October 1927 that the opposition's agitation had been firmly rejected by the army party members.[160] Most importantly, however, Stalin did not share Menzhinskii's view of the threat to the Red Army from the opposition. In a separate letter to the Central Committee, Stalin distanced himself from Menzhinskii, noting that he could not "fully share the very pessimistic viewpoint of the GPU Collegium." Stalin added that because of the countermeasures already taken, it was more difficult for the opposition to agitate in the army; he regarded industry and the Central Committee as targets more open to subversive propaganda.[161]

It is difficult to know for sure to what extent Stalin believed that the Trotskyists posed a credible threat to the Red Army when he received Menzhinskii's warning about the coup. It is possible that he accepted the OGPU's evidence of the oppositionist threat simply as another means of disgracing Trotsky. Stalin undoubtedly wanted to destroy Trotsky's influence, although there were some limits to how far he would go. He did not accept that the Red Army needed to be subject to an OGPU crackdown, which is clearly what Menzhinskii was angling for. Notably, Menzhinskii complained in his letter to the Central Committee that he had raised the issue of oppositionist propaganda in the army before but that this had not met with the desired results—by which Menzhinskii probably meant permission for a serious crackdown on the military. The OGPU's complaints about the oppositionist threat to the Red Army were still failing to find resonance with Stalin, even with the warnings about a coup. In this sense, it seems that Stalin had hesitated. It is likely that from his point of view, the Trotskyists were a dangerous force that had to be crushed, but the military was not yet at a crisis point and did not represent a serious threat to the state. There was no need to unleash the OGPU and sanction a destabilizing crackdown. In contrast to Menzhinskii, Stalin favored restraint, which meant, at least for now, the OGPU would not get their desired results.

There is also more that can be read into Voroshilov's response to the supposed oppositionist coup attempt than appears on the surface. At least in public, Voroshilov continued to stress that the Red Army was loyal, and he defended its reliability throughout 1927. For instance, just one month before Menzhinskii's letter to the Central Committee about the supposed oppositionist plot, Voroshilov publicly chided Trotsky and Zinoviev for only having a weak level of support in the military:

> Comrades Zinoviev and Trotsky, in regard to all their spiteful hatred toward everyone who is not with them, who are against them, are not able to dispute the fact that in a Red Army of 600,000 people, we have 95,000 party and candidate members, and 120,000 members of the Komsomol (*komsomol'tsev*). The opposition also knows well that regardless of all its efforts, and having sent a factional infection into the party ranks, it has not seen success.[162]

Moreover, in his speech delivered to the *Krasnopresnensk raion* party conference on 2 November 1927, Voroshilov did note that an oppositionist plot had been exposed by the OGPU. However, he argued that the majority of those arrested had nothing to do with the Red Army.[163] Yet despite these public defenses of army loyalty, it is unlikely that Voroshilov held such positive views in private. Menzhinskii's letter to the Central Committee reveals a discrepancy between Voroshilov's private and public views, and suggests that the strength and influence of the opposition in the ranks was hushed up as a result of the Red Army's importance to the regime.[164] In his letter to the Central Committee, Menzhinskii specifically noted that Voroshilov shared his pessimism about army reliability. Although it is doubtful that Voroshilov fully agreed with Menzhinskii, he surely saw the oppositionist threat to the military as a more serious problem than he let on in public. He must have recognized that oppositionist agitation undermined the stability of the Red Army at a time when the Communist Party was divided; but he equally would not have wanted to draw criticism of his own leadership. The Trotskyists had managed to retain their foothold in the ranks under his watch, and it is hardly likely that Voroshilov wanted to bring this to wider attention. This might lead to criticism of his leadership of the Red Army. Indeed, the year before, in 1926, Zinoviev had suggested, not unjustly, that Voroshilov had little authority in the Red Army.[165] Voroshilov's public defenses of the Red Army were thus probably partly designed to cover his own back. Although he was not as alarmist as Menzhinskii (and it is doubtful he would have willingly endorsed a serious crackdown on the military), Voroshilov surely understood that the Trotskyists still in the Red Army were a potential problem.

Moreover, it is possible that there was some tension between Voroshilov and Menzhinskii on the issue of the reliability of the Red Army and that each struggled to convince Stalin of his own view. Different power groups within the political police often intrigued against one another during the 1920s and 1930s. They competed for influence over policy and for greater control over the apparatus of repression.[166] It would be surprising if the Red Army was not drawn into these intrigues or that Menzhinskii might purposely try to undermine Voroshilov in order to gain more influence over military security. Luckily for Voroshilov, however, Stalin did not agree with Menzhinskii this time, and for now, the Red Army escaped a round of repression in 1927. This did not mean that the army was entirely free of OGPU attention. It remained under close OGPU scrutiny nonetheless, and arrests and discharges for Trotskyism continued in the late 1920s. Between the end of 1927 and February 1928, there were another 131 cases of Trotskyism in the ranks, and during 1928, the OGPU arrested more than ten alleged Trotskyist military groups. Some of these cases were high profile. Trotsky's ally, Mrachkovskii, who had commanded the Volga and West Siberian military districts, was arrested in early 1928 for Trotskyist activity and supposedly belonging to a military group.[167]

However, in the late 1920s, the OGPU was facing criticism from the Military Procuracy for its cavalier approach to arrests in the Red Army. In a report examining crime in the army during 1927, the Military Procuracy noted that the OGPU special departments had investigated 578 cases during the year and that half of these investigations had been initiated without sufficient evidence. The report also criticized the heavy reliance of the OGPU on extrajudicial methods and their inter-rogation practices, noting, "Too long periods of investigation and inter-rogation and long periods of custody for those arrested are used by the special departments even for petty, insignificant matters. The procura-tor considers all of this abnormal."[168] The OGPU's tendency to inflate the scale of threats based on circumstantial evidence had not gone un-noticed. Indeed, there are some indications that Voroshilov himself was skeptical of the credibility of some OGPU investigations. In a letter sent to Mikhail Tomskii, head of the All-Union Central Council of Trade Unions, on 2 February 1928, Voroshilov questioned whether the OGPU was fabricating a case against a group of bourgeois specialists that culmi-nated in the notorious Shakhty trial.[169] That the OGPU had the ability to likewise fabricate cases inside the Red Army must have been at the back of Voroshilov's mind.

The opposition was effectively crushed between 1927 and 1928, and its leaders were expelled from the party and sent into exile. Trotsky was deported to Alma Ata in Kazakhstan in 1928; he would be deported from the Soviet Union in the following year. Stalin had thus taken a further step in consolidating his power over the Communist Party in the late 1920s. Yet crushing the opposition did not mean that its sup-porters were forbidden from ever returning to the party fold. As long as they were willing to recant their so-called political errors, oppositionists were allowed to rejoin the party from the end of the 1920s. This of-fer applied equally to the Red Army Trotskyists. In this respect, officers Vitalii Primakov and Vitovt Putna, who had been sent into diplomatic exile as military attachés as punishment for supporting Trotsky, pre-sent particularly interesting cases. Not only were both given significant responsibility abroad despite their recent opposition to the party line, but Voroshilov appears to have placed a great deal of trust in the pair. He became a vocal advocate of Putna in particular and did what he could to improve his circumstances. This is hardly suggestive of a lin-gering distrust toward the Trotskyist officers or that Voroshilov saw the Trotskyist threat in as alarmist terms as the OGPU. Indeed, even though the opposition had been defeated, the nature of the threat it posed to the Red Army continued to create divides. Notably, both Primakov and Putna would later stand alongside Tukhachevskii during the trial of the ringleaders of the military-fascist plot in June 1937.

The OGPU had established that Putna, a midranking officer, had been working on Trotsky's orders in the mid-1920s. He was sent to Japan in 1927 to take up the role of military attaché as punishment, but Putna soon wanted a new position. To this end, he secured the help of Aleksandr Troianovskii, the Soviet ambassador in Japan. Troianovskii wrote to Stalin in April 1928, forwarding a letter he had received from Putna, which contained an appeal to find a new position in the army, perhaps as a corps commander: "I must express a wish that the CC [Central Committee] of the party create the possibility and accept active measures for the return to the party ranks of excluded comrades who have declared their intentions, joy, and unity with the party, and to fully submit to the decisions of the party congress."[170] In his covering letter, Troianovskii praised Putna, writing that there were just a few like him in the Red Army and that he was "very businesslike and very dedicated to military work."[171]

Voroshilov also came to Putna's assistance; his character assessment was even more glowing. In May 1929, Voroshilov wrote to Nikolai Krestinskii, the Soviet ambassador in Berlin, where Putna was soon to be a military attaché, having moved on from Japan (Putna had not yet received his coveted position as a corps commander, but at least he had gotten out of Japan). In his letter, Voroshilov gave Putna high praise and asked Krestinskii to give him "comradely support" on his arrival in Berlin.[172] Later in September, Voroshilov interceded once more on Putna's behalf and made a complaint to Krestinskii about the poor relations between the Soviet embassy and Putna, which were apparently hindering his work and making his life difficult. Voroshilov went on to write:

> I very much request of you to take into consideration that in the person of com[rade] Putna, we have one of the best of our commander-party men (*komandirov-partiitsev*). I, the RVS of the USSR, and the party fully trust him, and I have entrusted to him extraordinarily serious and responsible tasks, which he will be able to fulfill only in conditions of full support from . . . you and your embassy apparatus. . . . Over the last few years, com.[rade] Putna, as you well know, had a hard experience of a party and personal character, [and] our responsibility is to help him to now finally eliminate these remaining difficult traces, creating real comradely circumstances for him.[173]

Voroshilov even requested that Putna be allowed access to top-secret documents, which he had not had previously.[174] Voroshilov's letters to Krestinskii are striking because it seems that in less than two years after the concerns about Trotskyism in the military, and despite the OGPU's fears of a military coup, he had become an advocate of a prominent ex-Trotskyist. We can only speculate about the "extremely serious" work that Voroshilov had entrusted to Putna, but information collected by British intelligence agents indicated that Putna was heavily involved in espionage while working as a military attaché, particularly while stationed in Berlin. Putna had apparently also controlled Soviet agents in Finland, where he played a coordinating role. According to British intelligence, Putna was responsible for the collection of information about British defense and the placement of agents within the British war department.[175] Furthermore, the Soviet ambassador in Britain, Ivan Maiskii, later described Putna's post as military attaché in Germany as "extraordinarily important."[176]

Trotskyist officer Primakov was also given important duties abroad during his exile. Like Putna, Primakov was also sent overseas as a military attaché in the late 1920s, first to Afghanistan and then to Japan from mid-1929. However, Primakov's experience abroad was less smooth than Putna's. In April 1930, for instance, Ian Berzin, the head of Soviet military intelligence, wrote to Voroshilov complaining about Primakov's conduct in Japan. Berzin was mainly concerned with Primakov's careless and uneconomical attitude toward state funding, but more importantly, he also mentioned the following:

> The promotion of c.[omrade] Primakov as military attaché and leader of secret service work (*agenturnoi raboti*) in Japan has not brought a substantial improvement to the leadership of our military apparatus in Japan, not in relation to the obtaining of intelligence (*agenturnikh*) materials. . . . On the contrary, for the past six months a weakening in the flow of the necessary materials from Japan has been noted.[177]

Berzin requested that Primakov be transferred elsewhere.[178] That Berzin was not happy with Primakov's performance in Japan is not the key point here, although perhaps his performance was indeed substandard. What is interesting is that, like Putna, Primakov had been given an espionage role while stationed in Japan. Again, for an individual whose political convictions were of such concern not long before his posting abroad, it is certainly worth noting that he was given this responsibility at a time when Soviet relations with the Far East were increasingly strained. Voroshilov must have backed Primakov for his intelligence role in Japan.

The experiences of Primakov and Putna strongly suggest that Voroshilov believed that certain former military Trotskyists could be trusted enough to be given intelligence assignments. His letters about Putna in particular reveal what seems to be a genuine faith that Putna could be relied upon. It is hard to say for certain why Voroshilov vouched for these two officers. It is possible that his confidence was isolated to these two men alone and did not stretch to other ex-Trotskyists. Primakov and Putna might well have been previous acquaintances (Voroshilov and Primakov had commanded partisan units in Ukraine in 1918).[179] However, it was not only Voroshilov who placed trust in the two men. Stalin similarly had no problem with helping Putna. Replying a few weeks later to the letter he had received from Troianovskii in April 1928 about Putna, Stalin remarked, "We will do everything possible for Putna. Voroshilov is thinking of keeping him for military work."[180] Moreover, it is unlikely that Primakov would have been given an intelligence role in Japan without Stalin's sanction. There is a broader point here: although Primakov and Putna had compromised political pasts, so did many people in the Red Army and in other Soviet institutions. Having a stained record in the late 1920s and early 1930s did not automatically preclude a person from ever working again. Prominent former Trotskyist, Georgii Piatakov, for instance, rose to become the deputy people's commissar of heavy industry in the 1920s. Similarly, Ivar Smilga, a Trotsky supporter and former military officer, later became the vice chairman of the State Planning Committee (Gosplan). Smilga was given significant defense responsibilities in 1930 when he was put in charge of the Mobilization-Planning Directorate.[181] The regime made compromises regularly, and Voroshilov evidently believed that Primakov and Putna could be trusted enough for intelligence work. He certainly pushed for Putna to be given more freedom of action and access to classified materials. Yet it seems that neither Primakov nor Putna ever fully turned their backs on their Trotskyist pasts. This put Voroshilov in an awkward position when the two were arrested in 1936.

In this respect, although Voroshilov most likely appreciated the danger from the opposition to the Red Army—more than his public speeches suggest—and although he may well have shared some of Menzhinskii's pessimism about its reliability in 1927, these concerns were short-lived. In addition, by not indulging Menzhinskii in 1927, Stalin also signaled that he believed that the Trotskyist danger to the Red Army was not urgent. A serious crackdown at this point was not necessary. However, this does not mean that Stalin would forget that the opposition had managed to gain a foothold in the ranks or its alleged role in the attempted coup of November 1927. This surely left some nagging doubts about the political reliability of the Red Army. Although Stalin was willing to reinstate former Trotskyists who recanted their political views in the late 1920s, including Primakov and Putna, their opposition to the party would never be forgotten. Indeed, nothing was ever forgotten in the Stalinist system. As we shall see in chapter 4, even if Voroshilov had faith in Primakov and Putna, the OGPU was far less certain. The OGPU remained uneasy about former oppositionists serving once again in the Red Army and maintained close surveillance.

For the Soviet leaders, victory in the civil war did not bring a sense of security. Facing what was still a tense international situation and what the regime saw as hostile capitalist encirclement, the Red Army remained of paramount importance. Neither Lenin nor Stalin believed that the capitalist world would peacefully reconcile to the existence of the Soviet Union; indeed, they believed that it would actively seek its destruction. Both leaders were certain that as the Soviet state slowly consolidated its strength, class enemies would only struggle more fiercely against it.[182] Yet the institution most critical for defense, the Red Army, was still judged as displaying vulnerabilities to a range of perceived external threats, particularly from foreign agents and White counterrevolutionaries. Because the policy of employing military specialists and former White officers could not yet be abandoned, this only served to heighten these security concerns. For many, the use of military specialists and former Whites acted to sabotage the stability of the Red Army at the very point that an aggressive capitalist coalition was being assembled. The political police were accordingly forced to maintain a close watch over the Red Army into the 1920s to guard against any damaging infiltration. Although one of the most important tools in the struggle against the White movement were entrapment operations such as Operation Trust, the frequent use of disinformation by the political police meant that there was no respite from the rumors of betrayal surrounding the high command. The constant drip of hearsay and speculation about the loyalty of certain senior officers never fully dissipated. In later years, and in a very different political context, these rumors had more serious consequences.

Despite fears that the Red Army was vulnerable to subversion from a range of enemies, any related arrests were on a relatively small scale in the 1920s. How security threats to the military were typically perceived was an exaggeration of their reality. Furthermore, the gulf between perception and reality only increased in the aftermath of the civil war. The 1920s was a decade when the Red Army did not face any immediate crises but when several major perceived threats persisted nonetheless. Although the regime did not face the same pressing challenges to its survival, as had been the case in the civil war, Soviet leaders still regarded their position as under threat from the Whites and an alliance of capitalist powers. A new war was only a matter of time. Although everyone recognized this broader existential danger, opinions, shaped by institutional interests, differed about the specific nature of the threat facing the Red Army. Voroshilov and PUR tended to downplay subversive dangers, whereas the political police tended to overplay their significance. In the 1920s, different and competing narratives about the nature of the threats arrayed against the Red Army began to emerge more visibly. The political police's perspective was clearly the most pessimistic; however, because no serious crises hit the Red Army in the 1920s, it was unable to become dominant. Menzhinskii failed to convince Stalin of the danger posed by the Trotskyists to the army in 1927, and the OGPU never arrested enough military specialists, former Whites, or foreign agents to bring the army to a crisis point. Stalin had no cause to order any kind of serious crackdown on the Red Army. He could have unleashed Menzhinskii on the military, but he hesitated. The resulting crackdown would inevitably destabilize the army, and a credible threat first needed to be presented. It is possible that Stalin took such a pragmatic approach because Trotsky had already been politically crushed by 1927, and he believed that it was now easier to control the Red Army. Whatever his reasoning, it remains likely that Stalin nonetheless harbored some doubts and lingering suspicions about the Red Army after the supposed coup attempt of November 1927. Despite his disagreement with Menzhinskii, he would not easily forget how the Trotskyists had gained a foothold in the ranks or that the army remained a target for the Whites and foreign spies.

The 1920s, however, were only the beginning of a long period of flux in the Red Army as the regime grappled with what it saw as a range of difficult external and internal challenges. The struggle against internal Trotskyist counterrevolutionaries, Whites, and foreign agents would continue into the 1930s and became ever further removed from reality as the international situation deteriorated in the years before the outbreak of the Great Terror. However, as the next chapter will show, an entirely different set of internal pressures, divisions, and infighting existed inside the army establishment during these years. Concerns about the subversion of the Red Army played out alongside bitter disputes within the military elite and a major upheaval in the rank and file sparked by the regime's efforts to industrialize the Soviet Union. Almost immediately after the civil war, the Soviet leaders had realized that along with safeguarding the political reliability of the Red Army, it needed to be reformed and modernized. This soon became a source of further conflict.

3 | Reorganization and Crisis in the Red Army

In the early 1920s, the Red Army was not adequately prepared for the anticipated war with the capitalist world. In the years after a damaging civil war, it could not hope to compete with the military power of the other major European states. The Red Army lacked sufficient equipment and arms to sustain a period of war beyond a couple of months.[1] There were no easy solutions to this problem. Facing the stark economic realities of the 1920s, the Red Army leadership struggled for investment against civilian needs within a sluggish economy. Giving large boosts to military spending was, in short, impossible. The military elite fiercely lobbied for investment, but they were far from united about the best way to carry out reform.[2] The arguments put forward regarding the direction, speed, and scale of rearmament revealed bitter disputes between senior members of the high command, and it is possible to see the formation of power groups within the army establishment at this time. Moreover, even with the launch of rapid industrialization and the start of the first five-year plan at the end of the decade, the army leadership still did not receive the funds they believed were necessary to build Soviet military power. Although it was evident that a worldwide communist revolution had failed to take hold and Stalin understood that the Soviet Union now, more than ever, needed to be self-reliant and strengthen its own defenses, he also believed there was some breathing room to do this. Despite the tense international situation in the 1920s, as well as the Soviet leaders' personal convictions that a final clash with capitalism was inevitable, a new war was not seen as imminent. War would certainly arrive in the future, but not anytime soon. In this respect, radically increasing spending on the Red Army was not an urgent priority. The ambitions of the military elite were frustrated on the outset of the industrialization drive, but this did not mean that the discussion about rearmament was shelved. It remained hotly debated, but questions about levels of authority in the army establishment also became points of tension. Efforts to overcome military weaknesses had thrown into sharp relief the divides that existed under the surface of the high command. These fissures, however, were not solely about rearmament; they contained a subtext of institutional interest, power politics, and pure ambition.

On Trotsky's resignation as war commissar in January 1925, his deputy, Mikhail Frunze, was promoted as people's commissar of military and naval affairs. Frunze did not have a particularly strong military background; like Trotsky, he had little military experience before the civil war. He had led a Red brigade during the October revolution, but the bulk of his experience was acquired during the civil war itself, where he had gained a solid reputation as a successful commander, scoring several critical victories against the White armies.[3] Frunze was also a leading party member with a long history of revolutionary activity before 1917. Yet above all, the central factor in his promotion was the fact he was one of Stalin's allies in the Red Army. Frunze's elevation to the leadership of the Red Army in 1925 not only represented a consolidation of the power of the Red commanders in the military elite but also strengthened Stalin's personal influence.[4] With Trotsky out of the way, Stalin could now exert greater control over the military. In terms of what changes Frunze introduced to the Red Army, he launched a series of reforms intended to improve military organization. The Frunze reforms represented the first serious attempt toward creating a modern and efficient Red Army, but the results were mixed. Frunze's program created more problems than it remedied, particularly in terms of organizational confusion and the interarmy tensions that resulted. In any case, his time as the head of the army was prematurely cut short. Frunze died while undergoing stomach surgery in October 1925, paving the way for his deputy, Voroshilov, to take over the army leadership.[5]

Because Voroshilov was Stalin's old comrade from Tsaritsyn, his promotion further increased Stalin's influence in the Red Army. Not everyone, however, welcomed the appointment. Following what had become a familiar pattern for heads of the army, Voroshilov did not have enough military experience for the role, and what little experience he did have was confined to the civil war years. In comparison to Tukhachevskii, the newly promoted chief of staff—the second most powerful position in the army—this disparity in knowledge and experience created a rift between the two. The tensions between Tukhachevskii and Voroshilov have been well documented. For example, Georgii Zhukov remarked in his memoirs that Voroshilov hated Tukhachevskii and that Tukhachevskii considered Voroshilov incompetent. Zhukov described Voroshilov's military knowledge as poor.[6] As one historian has noted, in a stark contrast to Tukhachevskii, a skilled military thinker, Voroshilov never wrote anything worth remembering.[7] Tukhachevskii was forthright and ambitious, and he had grand plans for Red Army development. He must have resented having to work under someone he regarded as militarily inferior. Notably, even Voroshilov's ally, Budennyi, considered him underqualified for the role. In 1926, Budennyi's secretary recorded that he had remarked that the Red Army had been entrusted to an idiot.[8] Undoubtedly, Voroshilov had risen to the army leadership purely because of Stalin's patronage, and other senior officers surely believed that they were better suited for the position. Tukhachevskii was certainly a stronger candidate. Although both men had a shared interest in working together for the benefit of the Red Army, particularly in terms of trying to increase its budget, they often had very different views about the direction of army reform. Tukhachevskii was more capable of driving forward army modernization, but he was not one of Stalin's close allies. As a result, he could be easily sidelined and ignored. The tension between the two top figures in the Red Army elite remained a permanent feature of army life until Tukhachevskii's execution in June 1937.

Upon his death in 1925, Frunze left a legacy of reform, much of which was positive. He improved discipline, pay, regulations, housing, and food provisions. However, some of his reforms proved more controversial. The introduction of single command, for instance, which transferred power from the political commissars to the officers, provoked a negative reaction from PUR.[9] Moreover, the weakening of the authority of the general staff, set in motion under Frunze, provoked the first major rift between Tukhachevskii and Voroshilov. Before the Frunze reforms, the staff had been a dominant force in the military hierarchy and had wielded great influence. Although the staff was a powerful body, it was also seen as too large and cumbersome and in need of reorganization. In a bid to increase its efficiency, Frunze split the staff into three bodies, creating an administrative staff, an inspectorate, and a smaller staff for mobilization planning. As newly appointed chief of staff, Tukhachevskii was unhappy with the changes, and not just because of the confusion stemming from overlapping lines of authority.[10] Tukhachevskii thought that the reform meant there was no single dominant institution now responsible for defense, and he fully intended to reassert the power taken from the staff. Consequently, throughout 1926–1927, he continually pressed the notion that the staff needed to assume greater authority and take charge of directing rearmament for the entire Red Army.[11] Notably, Tukhachevskii believed in the staff's place in directing army reform, but in practice, this meant his own place in directing this reform. Tukhachevskii went even further in arguing that the staff should have even greater power in forging a closer relationship with the main economic institutions of the state.[12] Tukhachevskii wanted to extend his influence beyond the confines of the Red Army. In addition, upon his promotion to chief of staff, the organization lost control over military intelligence. As a result, in January 1926, Tukhachevskii appealed to Voroshilov, complaining that without access to military intelligence, the staff would be unable to adequately study foreign countries and draw up mobilization plans.[13] He interpreted the loss of military intelligence as a lack of trust in his department, even though, as he put it, the staff was now "almost 100 percent communist."[14]

Tukhachevskii probably had some grounds for his complaints, but it is clear that not everybody wanted his personal authority increased. Almost immediately, interdepartment rivalry put a brake on Tukhachevskii's ambitions. Tukhachevskii clashed with Sergei Kamenev, the head of the main administration of the Red Army, after he blocked his attempts to gain more power for the staff and its control over the central directorates in the People's Commissariat for Military and Naval Affairs.[15] Tukhachevskii saw this as a deliberate attempt to weaken the staff. In a letter sent to Voroshilov in February 1927, he accused Kamenev of leading a campaign against the staff from the very beginning of the Frunze reforms.[16] It seems that Kamenev, reluctant to allow Tukhachevskii so much influence in the Red Army, was putting up resistance. But Tukhachevskii did not stop there. In February 1928, he also accused Voroshilov of weakening and discrediting the staff, and that by not supporting its authority, he was working against it.[17] It is clearly an understatement to say that Tukhachevskii had difficulty coming to terms with his reduced influence. His demands were increasingly pushing against the fixed power relations inside the army hierarchy. Indeed, in challenging Voroshilov, Tukhachevskii was also challenging one of Stalin's closest allies.

Why Voroshilov did not give in to Tukhachevskii can be seen in a letter (which was never sent) that addressed his complaints and ambitions: "You insisted on concentrating this enormous power in the Staff of the Red Army. I was categorically against this, because I considered that this task must also be accomplished by the civilian authorities and be directed by a government organ."[18] The mention of "enormous power" is instructive of how Tukhachevskii's ambitions were being perceived by his colleagues. Tensions about the position of the staff then reached breaking point in mid-1928. In April, a group of senior officers, Egorov, Budennyi, and Pavel Dybenko (all Voroshilov's allies), sent a letter to the Revolutionary Military Council addressing the overlapping lines of authority between military departments. However, this letter also included a criticism of the attempt by the staff "to take into its hands a leading role in all questions of construction and operational leadership of the RKKA."[19] Tukhachevskii's ambitions were becoming divisive. Those allied with Voroshilov were closing ranks, unhappy with Tukhachevskii's attempts to gain enhanced power. Egorov, Dybenko, and Budennyi called for Tukhachevskii to be transferred from the staff.[20] Tukhachevskii, however, struck back with an even more radical proposal that envisioned a highly centralized staff taking over many of the duties of the army administration and inspectorate, not only controlling mobilization and rearmament but also taking a leading role in guiding industrial policy at large.[21] Unsurprisingly, these new proposals went too far and were rejected. After this defeat, Tukhachevskii resigned from the staff and took a position as commander of the Leningrad Military District. His vacated space as chief of staff was taken by the more moderate Boris Shaposhnikov—someone who could be trusted not to challenge the status quo.

The exact reason why Tukhachevskii resigned as chief of staff is still a matter of speculation, but there is nothing to suggest that he was pushed out. When Tukhachevskii's proposals for increasing staff authority were rejected, rather than acquiesce, he probably saw resignation as the only option. He would rather resign than go along with a policy he did not agree with. His replacement with Shaposhnikov is telling in this sense. Shaposhnikov was an experienced military specialist, and one of the few people from the army elite who managed to survive the Great Terror. This was a testament to both his moderation and his reluctance to push boundaries. Yet as David Stone has noted, after Shaposhnikov's promotion to the staff, many of the more radical changes that Tukhachevskii had proposed were actually put into practice. Shaposhnikov had managed to achieve what Tukhachevskii could not. Eighteen months after Tukhachevskii's resignation, for instance, overall responsibility for army mobilization was given to the staff.[22] Either Tukhachevskii's proposals had become more palatable eighteen months after his resignation, or, more likely, because Shaposhnikov did not show Tukhachevskii's level of ambition, he was entrusted with increased staff power. Shaposhnikov was not seen to be craving authority and influence. He did not represent the same type of threat to established interests in the Red Army. In this respect, Tukhachevskii's defeat probably stemmed more from how his motives were interpreted by his colleagues than the substance of his proposed reforms. Moreover, it cannot be ruled out that the rumors spread about Tukhachevskii by the political police as part of the disinformation operations against the Whites did have an impact inside the high command. Out of all the military elite, it was Tukhachevskii who most actively challenged power structures and tried to increase his personal authority, and he was widely rumored to be disloyal. However, there is nothing to suggest that Tukhachevskii would have made any attempt to actually seize control of the Red Army leadership from Voroshilov—or attempt a military coup, for that matter. Tukhachevskii may well have been dissatisfied with his situation, but this does not mean that he was a prospective Russian Bonaparte. Yet the forceful way that Tukhachevskii tried to increase his influence and his tendency to push boundaries, when seen alongside rumors about his lust for power, may have helped turn his colleagues against him.

Despite his defeat and resignation, however, Tukhachevskii continued to conduct research into army organization in Leningrad in the late 1920s; this thus should not be seen as too much of a demotion. Leningrad was a strategically important military district, and its command was prestigious. Leningrad was an important industrial center and a vital defensive outpost against any attack from the north or the Baltic states. Tukhachevskii, despite his self-removal from the center, thus remained very much a key individual in the army leadership. Nor did his resignation from the staff bring an end to the divides and tensions among the military elite or Tukhachevskii's own tendency to provoke his comrades.

Tukhachevskii was a military professional committed to a vision of the Soviet Union possessing a mechanized Red Army that could compete with the armies of the capitalist states. Mechanization quickly became another divide between Tukhachevskii and other officers in the high command, following on the heels of the arguments about staff power. Even though no one denied that the Red Army had to undergo reform and become a modern military force, there were a number of influential officers, most notably Budennyi, who remained nostalgic for tradition, and particularly about the role of the cavalry in modern war. The cavalry had undeniably played an important role during the civil war, and as leader of the First Cavalry Army, Budennyi had won accolades for his battle successes. However, as part of the demobilization of the Red Army in the years after the civil war, the cavalry army was largely disbanded. Only a few divisions remained in active service in the 1920s, and Budennyi became their most vocal advocate.[23] Yet Budennyi's influential connections to Stalin and Voroshilov did not stop the cavalry from coming under further pressure. Although the Red Army would not see a serious expansion in its tank forces until the early 1930s, in the late 1920s, Tukhachevskii was pushing his military theory of deep operations, which left little room for the cavalry in its current form. Deep operations called for a powerful strike behind enemy lines to destroy the enemy's rear and required a large mechanized force, including large numbers of tanks.[24] On this basis, a clash between Tukhachevskii and Budennyi was inevitable.

The cavalry supporters were put on the defensive after coming under pressure at meetings of the Revolutionary Military Council in the late 1920s. At a meeting in 1928, for instance, the cavalry leaders were accused of not utilizing modern communications technology and criticized for the poor performance of the cavalry during the recent Belorussian maneuvers.[25] One year later, it became clear that a divide had formed within the military elite over the role of the cavalry. During a meeting of the Revolutionary Military Council in 1929, the main proponents of army modernization, Tukhachevskii and Uborevich, argued for increasing the development of technical troops, triggering a reaction from Budennyi, who was certain that this would result in the cavalry's being sidelined. He accused Tukhachevskii of wanting to convert the cavalry into infantry; he leveled the same accusation at Iakir, another advocate of army modernization.[26] According to Budennyi, Iakir had been "with the Germans, they indoctrinated him (*emu mozgi svernuli*), he wants to turf the cavalry out on foot." Luckily for Budennyi, he was not alone in fearing the loss of the cavalry. Voroshilov was on his side and registered his support, adding, "I am against those who believe that the cavalry has had its day."[27] Having Voroshilov's backing was obviously important to Budennyi's cause. Voroshilov recognized the need to expand tank forces, but like Budennyi, he did not want the cavalry entirely discarded. Voroshilov's support of Budennyi in this instance, however, did not bring an end to the dispute about the position of the cavalry in the Red Army.[28]

Over the course of the late 1920s and early 1930s, Budennyi made a number of written complaints to Voroshilov about the cavalry question; his contempt for the supporters of extensive mechanization, particularly Tukhachevskii and Vladimir Triandafillov, was clear. Triandafillov was chief of the operations directorate before he died in a plane accident in 1931. Sharing Tukhachevskii's view about deep operations, having written a key text on the subject, Triandafillov was committed to increasing the pace of mechanization in the Red Army. In November 1929 Triandafillov came under fire from Budennyi after he had written a report on the cavalry that criticized its performance during the Belorussian maneuvers and its poor application of technology. Triandafillov also alluded to Voroshilov's support of Budennyi, describing him as "a wingmate to the cavalry."[29] In response, in a letter to Voroshilov sent in November 1929, Budennyi accused Triandafillov of defaming both the head of the army and the Revolutionary Military Council; he interpreted the report as a planned attack on the cavalry. Budennyi was nothing short of indignant. He remarked, "These scoundrels are leading a systematic campaign for the liquidation of the cavalry," adding that he believed the cavalry question had acquired a "political character."[30] In this respect, at least from Budennyi's point of view, this was not just a dispute about the future role of the cavalry in the Red Army. Rather, it was also a question of power politics in the high command. Budennyi had been part of the group of officers who had criticized Tukhachevskii's ambitions for the staff in 1928. It is entirely possible that he interpreted the criticisms of the cavalry as another means by which Tukhachevskii was attempting to expand his personal influence. Budennyi certainly felt that underhand tactics were being used in the debate. Moreover, in March 1930, he leveled another accusation against Tukhachevskii and Triandafillov, this time arguing that they were trying to "indoctrinate" their ideas into the army under the guise of "progressivism." Budennyi again accused Tukhachevskii and Triandafillov of discrediting the cavalry and its command, arguing, "Demagogic methods are used in all of these speeches—to attribute to the cavalry staff what they in fact never defended, namely, that the cavalrymen, supposedly, in every way possible deny technology, that the cavalrymen recognize the exclusive mode of action in all cases only as attack on horse."[31] In short, Budennyi felt that his arguments were being misrepresented, that Tukhachevskii and Triandafillov were being dishonest, and that the subtext to this entire debate was one of power.

In this respect, alongside the grouping of Egorov, Budennyi, and Dybenko, who had positioned themselves against Tukhachevskii's grandstanding over staff authority in 1928, a loose alliance of Iakir, Uborevich, Triandafillov, and Tukhachevskii, connected by a shared commitment to mechanization, clashed with Budennyi during the next year.[32] Facing this kind of opposition, it is possible that Budennyi felt under siege. Indeed, he complained that Tukhachevskii and Uborevich expressed total solidarity with Triandafillov.[33] Debates—often heated ones—over modernization are of course common to all militaries. In this case, however, Budennyi interpreted the dispute as having a subtext of a power struggle, which may be immediately paralleled with the recent conflict about staff power. From the criticisms leveled at Tukhachevskii's ambitions for the staff (specifically the accusation that he was trying to gain enormous power) to what Budennyi regarded as the politicization of the cavalry question, Tukhachevskii's critics implied an ulterior motive. The ambitious Tukhachevskii and his allies wanted to strengthen their position in the army leadership and take control over the direction of army reform. It cannot be discounted that there may have been some suspicions that Tukhachevskii wanted to seize control of the entire army. Budennyi believed that Tukhachevskii was criticizing the cavalry in order to jockey for influence, and Voroshilov may have had similar suspicions—especially as he had so recently chastised Tukhachevskii for desiring more power. Importantly, Stalin could not have been ignorant of these disputes in the high command. He no doubt carefully watched the debates unfold and clearly grasped the military elite's competing alliances. The biggest controversy, however, was still to come. Tukhachevskii created further waves shortly after the cavalry dispute. This time, he would finally raise Stalin's ire. The wider context to the debate about the role of the cavalry was how much funding could be allocated to the Red Army and the speed of rearmament. Tukhachevskii was already the most vocal member of the military elite for increasing the Red Army's technological development and achieving parity with the West.[34] However, in the late 1920s, he began to argue for much higher levels of military spending than previously. This proved highly controversial.

From the point of view of the Soviet leaders, the international situation worsened during 1926–1927. In May 1926, Józef Piłsudski returned to power in Poland through a military coup, reviving the danger from the Soviet Union's old enemy. Indeed, just weeks after the coup, Dzerzhinskii was already writing to Stalin with supposed evidence that he believed confirmed that Poland was ready to attack and seize Belorussia and Ukraine.[35] Then a few months later, in December, the secret collaboration between the Red Army and the Reichswehr was finally exposed by Frederick Voigt, a journalist at the *Manchester Guardian*, sparking a diplomatic crisis. Tensions reached a peak in 1927, when a wave of panic about an impending war gripped the Soviet Union. People began buying essential foodstuffs in bulk and hoarding whatever they could, fearing that the country was sliding to the brink of war.[36] In reality, the Soviet Union was not on the edge of a new conflict; rather, the war scare was sparked by deteriorating Soviet diplomatic relations with Britain and China throughout April and May 1927. In April, the Soviet embassy in Beijing was raided, with documents seized and personnel arrested. Shortly afterward, large numbers of Chinese communists were massacred by the Chinese nationalists as part of a crackdown. In May, the All-Russian Cooperative Society (ARCOS), a Soviet trading company based in London, was raided by the British authorities. The raid supposedly uncovered compromising documents showing Soviet intelligence activity. After receiving a belligerent response to the action from the Soviet Union, diplomatic relations between the two countries were severed. Finally, as we have already seen, the Soviet ambassador to Poland was assassinated by a White monarchist in June 1927—an event Stalin misinterpreted as further evidence of an aggressive British government.

Yet within this threatening international climate, the Red Army remained underfunded and technologically backward.[37] Despite the assessment from the defense sector of the State Planning Committee (Gosplan) in early 1927 that the army was not ready for war, military spending was still not substantially increased.[38] The Soviet economy remained too financially restricted to allow any serious boosts in military spending, even though the international situation had noticeably degraded.[39] Budgets were tight, and defense was no exception. Moreover, spending priorities were informed by the regime's particular expectation of the timing of any future war. The international situation was certainly judged as more threatening in 1927, reinforcing fears that the capitalist powers were bent on destroying the Soviet Union, but the probability of war breaking out in the imminent future was estimated as low.[40] There is little to suggest that the Soviet leaders were concerned about the immediate outbreak of war. They were not gripped by the same level of fear that spread through the Soviet population during 1927. The British raid on ARCOS, for instance, did not spark panic in the leadership and was interpreted more calmly as evidence of a more assertive British stance against the Soviet Union.[41] Nor did Stalin think that Poland would launch a conflict immediately. Even though Poland was still believed to be the most pressing military threat facing the Soviet Union (and one that was assumed to be allied with the hostile British government), Soviet leaders also assumed that Piłsudski would avoid war because of the resulting domestic political consequences.[42] Soviet military intelligence also estimated the likelihood of war against European powers to be low in 1927.[43] All of this meant that despite the pleas for more money for the Red Army, military spending was not noticeably increased. Voroshilov failed to secure his preferred budget of 807 million rubles for 1927–1928, receiving 742.4 million rubles instead. The worsening diplomatic relations between the Soviet Union and its European neighbors did not lead to a substantial increase in defense spending on the scale that the military leadership had been lobbying for.[44]

The Red Army leadership was given some cause to hope for higher levels of investment with the move toward rapid industrialization and the announcement of the forthcoming first five-year plan in October 1928. The onset of industrialization saw rapidly rising production targets and massive investments in heavy industry, pushing the Soviet Union toward breakneck economic growth. The limited private sphere permitted under the NEP was finally abolished, and centralized planning soon came to direct all economic activity. New construction projects, such as the Volga–Don canal and the enormous metallurgical plant at Magnitogorsk, symbolized the plan's soaring ambitions.[45] Even though the first five-year plan never fulfilled its unrealistic production goals, creating huge upheaval, waste, and inefficiency along the way, it did achieve an impressive level of industrial expansion.[46] Accompanying this radical transformation of industry, Stalin ordered the collectivization of agriculture to fund industrialization. This was to come under total state control, which created uproar in the lower ranks of the army.

Both industrialization and collectivization had their roots in 1926–1927, when several factors produced a shift in party opinion toward endorsing rapid state-driven economic growth. These included the recovery of industry to almost pre–World War I levels and the war scare of 1927.[47] Most importantly, Stalin had become an advocate of rapid industrialization by 1927. He abandoned his earlier support of economic growth within NEP limits and argued that the Soviet Union needed to quickly expand its industrial base. The country needed to become economically independent and less reliant on foreign imports. This new program of industrial expansion was in tune with the arguments of the now-defeated political opposition, but it is a mistake to see Stalin's adoption of these policies as purely cynical politics. That the opposition had been smashed certainly made it easier for Stalin to become a public advocate of faster-paced economic growth, but his actions were guided by far more than political calculation. The most important factor behind Stalin's abandonment of the NEP was his belief that a mixed-market economy would never allow the Soviet Union to overcome its backwardness and catch up—and eventually overtake—the capitalist states in terms of economic power. Moreover, increasing the Soviet Union's ability to defend itself and bolster its military power was another central motivation. War was not understood to be imminent, but Stalin believed that it was inevitable that the capitalist world would one day attack the Soviet Union. The country needed to be prepared for when war finally came. In this way, Stalin would lead the Soviet Union headlong into a period of radical transformation. The Soviet Union's industrial base was to be rapidly expanded with little consideration of the economic and human costs.

Because one of its main goals was increasing military power, the Red Army was a beneficiary of the industrialization drive, and it did receive an increase in funds. However, the high command was still left dissatisfied by the amount of spending allocated to the military.[48] During 1928, total state spending continued to be subject to financial constraints, and military spending in particular was at risk of cutbacks. One reason for this was that even though the Soviet Union's industrial base was now expanding, it was at the expense of light industry. This in turn meant that fewer commercial goods were being delivered to market, meaning that peasants had less incentive to sell their grain in return. This caused a contraction in the grain supply to the cities, which in turn threatened the pace of industrialization. Reducing the military budget and using any spare funds to maintain the pace of industrialization, rather than further decreasing investment in light industry, was one way to avoid further aggravating the regime's relationship with the peasant farmers.[49] What this meant was that the high command was still required to strenuously lobby for higher levels of investment during the late 1920s and into the early 1930s. Yet Tukhachevskii once again began to push too far. From his position in Leningrad, he sent several proposals to the center calling for dramatically increased levels of military spending.[50] Tukhachevskii's calculations highlighted the potential resources to be released over the course of industrialization and collectivization, and he based his armament proposals on these assumptions. The resulting figures were hypothetical and highly ambitious.[51] Tukhachevskii believed that crash industrialization had provided an opportunity for the rapid expansion of the Red Army, and he was going to take it. However, what he was proposing far exceeded the capacity of the Soviet economy. It is possible that Tukhachevskii actually believed that the economy could deliver his plans for Red Army development, or he may have been simply caught up in the frenzy of rising targets that characterized the first five-year plan and did not want the army to be left behind. Tukhachevskii was not alone in producing outlandish figures. Rather than set targets in accordance with economic realities, at the outset of industrialization, planners were seized by revolutionary optimism that incredible tempos of growth could actually be achieved. Targets rose higher and higher, becoming ever removed from reality. Anything resembling Tukhachevskii's suggestions for radical increases in defense spending would not materialize until 1931, and not before he had clashed with Stalin.[52]

In 1930, Tukhachevskii drew up a far-reaching and ambitious rearmament plan that was unrealistic in view of the Soviet Union's current industrial capacity and spending restrictions. He projected massive increases in tanks, cavalry, and rifle divisions, increased communication lines, and improvements to chemical industry.[53] His memorandum of January 1930 predicted that industry could produce over 100,000 tanks and aircraft for the first year of war and deploy at the very least 240 infantry divisions.[54] Tukhachevskii sent these optimistic projections to Voroshilov, Shaposhnikov, and Uborevich, who rejected them immediately. According to Shaposhnikov's calculations, in order to fulfil Tukhachevskii's plan, boys aged just fourteen would need to be called up for military service. Further, the required budget exceeded the combined state budgets for the previous three years.[55] This was the picture that was presented to Stalin, along with the following note from Voroshilov, who took (and no doubt relished) the opportunity to undermine his ambitious rival: "Tukhachevskii wants to be original and . . . 'radical.' It is bad that in the R[ed] A[rmy] there are these sort of people, who take this 'radicalism' at face value."[56] Moreover, as Lennart Samuelson had shown, in another unsent letter intended for Tukhachevskii, Voroshilov accused him of neglecting his duties in Leningrad in order to draw up his unrealistic proposals and characterized Tukhachevskii's views as "incorrect" and "politically harmful."[57] While Stalin understood that increasing military spending was an essential part of the industrialization drive, Tukhachevskii's proposals far exceeded anything he had in mind. He replied to Voroshilov in March, writing that though he respected Tukhachevskii and considered him an "unusually capable comrade," his proposals for military spending were "fantastic," lacked realism, and would squander and waste equipment. Stalin went so far as to say that to put the Tukhachevskii plan into operation would be "worse than any counterrevolution."[58]

Tukhachevskii had suffered another defeat. This time, however, he had not only angered Voroshilov but had also—and more seriously—managed to annoy Stalin. Indeed, after the rejection of his armaments proposals, Tukhachevskii was banned from raising the subject again.[59] However, circumstances quickly changed. In December 1930, Tukhachevskii appealed to Stalin about the rejection of his memorandum, complaining that his figures had been distorted by Shaposhnikov and asking for them to be looked at again.[60] Despite not immediately winning Stalin over, in June 1931, Tukhachevskii returned to the center from Leningrad and was appointed the Red Army's director of armaments, replacing Uborevich, who, at his own admission, had been having difficulty in the role.[61] In this new position, Tukhachevskii had much greater power in directing army reform.

That Tukhachevskii could be brought back into the heart of the military establishment so soon after his armament proposals had provoked such a negative reaction from Stalin in 1930 requires explanation. On the one hand, as David Stone has noted, Tukhachevskii was fortunate in that there was growing momentum behind radical rearmament in the late 1920s and early 1930s. The Politburo was making moves in this direction in July 1929 when it awarded priority to defense leading to increases in the military budget. The Politburo also approved the reorganization of war industries, mobilization capability, and production methods.[62] From 1930, Stalin assumed a more direct role in military affairs, and in June, he agreed to look at Tukhachevskii's armament proposals again.[63]

Perhaps more importantly, in March 1931, Stalin received a report from Soviet military intelligence concerning a possible military strike by Japan. In an intercepted telegram, the Japanese military attaché in Moscow had made the case for carrying out a quick war against the Soviet Union before the first five-year plan was completed.[64] The relationship between the Soviet Union and Japan had become increasingly strained since the Japanese seizure of the jointly owned Chinese Eastern Railway in 1929, but this new intelligence represented a further deterioration. It is likely that Stalin decided to look again at Tukhachevskii's armaments proposals now that the Soviet Union faced the possibility of imminent war in the east. Just two months after Tukhachevskii's return to the center from Leningrad, the Council of Labor and Defense approved a massive expansion in tank production known as the big tank program.[65]

When the Japanese military invaded Manchuria in September 1931 after an explosion on the South Manchurian Railway (which had been orchestrated by the Japanese Kwantung army and used as a pretext for the invasion), there was now a pressing impetus to increase military spending along the lines Tukhachevskii had been urging. The Soviet Union faced a hostile enemy very close to a sparsely defended border, and defense became a priority. The production of armaments, for instance, increased 75 percent during October and December 1931, and the military budget increased markedly over the course of 1932. The tank program in particular saw one of the largest expansions.[66] In this respect, even though the Soviet leadership was beginning to pay greater attention to defense from the late 1920s, the crisis sparked by the Japanese invasion of Manchuria finally pushed the regime toward rapid and extensive rearmament. From this point on, the Soviet economy was put practically on a war footing.[67] Tukhachevskii was eventually fully rehabilitated in May 1932, when Stalin sent him a rare letter of apology for what he admitted was his misunderstanding of Tukhachevskii's 1930 armament proposals.[68] Tukhachevskii had thus been the beneficiary of a shift in the regime's approach toward rapid rearmament in the late 1920s, which had been accelerated by a new threatening international crisis.

The conflicts and disputes within the Red Army elite about rearmament and reform are important for several reasons. First, the army leadership was divided over most questions aside from the need for a larger share of the state budget. The Red Army was still a fledgling force, and attempts at reform had only just begun. These efforts would have been difficult enough without the awkward mixture of professional and party officers that occupied key positions in the high command. Individual ambitions and strong personalities only made these efforts harder. Clashes and conflicts were almost inevitable. The disputes about the reorganization of the army took the form of power politics as senior officers tried to assert their vision for a modernized Red Army. Tukhachevskii in particular was subject to stern criticism and suspicion over what were seen as personal ambitions to increase his own power and politicize military disputes. The need to reform and reorganize the Red Army to overcome its military weaknesses thus revealed deep weaknesses in the unity of the high command. None of this would escape Stalin's attention. However, most surprisingly of all, even after all the controversy he caused, Tukhachevskii's vision for army development was victorious, and he managed to win Stalin's support. It is doubtful that this pleased some of his colleagues, particularly Voroshilov and Budennyi. Tukhachevskii's return to the center of the military establishment and the power he gained as director of armaments would only fuel resentment against him. Yet beyond the quarrels created at the top of the military establishment, the need to industrialize and build economic and military power generated far greater problems for the stability of the lower ranks. The regime's agricultural policies accompanying the industrialization drive produced a widespread crisis in the rank and file.

Collectivization and the Peasant Mood

Crash industrialization was impossible without the collectivization of agriculture. If enough resources were to be funneled to industry to maintain the pace of the first five-year plan, it was up to the peasants to bear the burden. From the late 1920s, the peasants saw a squeeze on their living standards, and peasant farmers were soon forcibly organized into large collective and state-run farms. No longer able to sell grain surpluses privately on the open market, as permitted under the NEP, they now had to surrender their produce directly to the state. In doing so, the regime aimed to secure enough grain to feed the expanding industrial sector. This radical and ambitious agricultural experiment, however, was a disaster. The collectivization years resulted in declining agricultural production and sparked a huge outpouring of resentment toward the regime.[69] Facing rising levels of dissent in the countryside, the regime responded with a campaign of repression in order to secure a steady supply of raw materials and grain. Hundreds of thousands of resisting peasants were deported from their villages and sent to the rapidly expanding labor camp system, the gulag. Millions of peasants were to suffer from the collectivization drive, either through direct state repression or from the resulting famine that struck between 1932 and 1933.

The decision to collectivize agriculture to fuel industrialization was driven by several factors, including the backwardness of peasant farming methods and the lower amount of grain that was being delivered to market under the NEP than before World War I.[70] A more immediate cause was an agricultural crisis that erupted in 1927; this more than anything finally broke the compromise the regime had maintained with the peasantry during the NEP years. The 1927 harvest was lower than the year before, meaning that there was less grain to take to market in the first place. However, the situation was made worse by the grain prices offered by the state. These were set at a lower level than for other produce, and in response, peasants turned to trying to sell meat, dairy, and industrial crops rather than their grain. In addition, a general shortage of consumer goods provided little incentive for peasants to bring their grain to market. With a lack of incentive to sell, and urged on by the 1927 war scare, peasants began to hoard their produce. An agricultural crisis quickly developed.[71] This affected internal grain supply and exports, leading to a shortfall of several million tons compared to the previous year's harvest. Grain supplies to urban areas were adversely affected, threatening the industrialization drive. The regime decided on a draconian response. They turned to forced grain requisitions, which had not been used since the civil war. During 1928, party opinion increasingly turned toward squeezing the peasantry in order to fuel the rapid industrialization of heavy industry. Stalin believed that by withholding their grain, the peasants were engaging in speculative practices that were causing the state to lose out. This would only slow the pace of industrialization and weaken the Soviet Union in the long run. A crackdown against speculation was launched, and 1928 saw rising levels of repression against the peasantry and widespread use of grain requisitions.[72] This was the start of a growing wave of violence in the countryside that would give way to the wholesale collectivization of agriculture under state control and an attempt to "liquidate" the kulaks as a class, an expropriation of their assets known as dekulakization.

Opposition to the regime's increasingly repressive agricultural policies came from the upper echelons of the Communist Party. Party theorist Nikolai Bukharin, head of Soviet government Alexei Rykov, and trade union organization head Mikhail Tomskii formed a loose alliance that Stalin labeled the Right Deviation. The group opposed the use of grain requisitions and argued that peasants should not be forced to shoulder the burdens of industrialization. Instead, they endorsed a continuation of the NEP settlement with the peasantry, believing that this model could produce stable economic growth—enough to fund industrialization. However, by the late 1920s, Stalin had enough support within the Politburo to overcome this challenge easily. As had been the case with Trotsky and his supporters, the Right Deviation was accused of factionalism, and all three members were eventually removed from their positions. However, a much stronger challenge to the regime came from within the countryside itself. The mass resistance from the peasantry to collectivization has been well documented. Peasants rebelled against the regime in huge numbers, and the countryside saw a spike of violence that nearly brought the country to the edge of another civil war.[73] Part of this upsurge in protests was the resistance of large numbers of rank-and-file soldiers to collectivization. This discontent in the military has been less well examined by historians, with some notable exceptions.[74] Indeed, according to Soviet statistics, at the height of the collectivization drive in 1930, peasants constituted 57.9 percent of the Red Army.[75] With so many peasants in the lower ranks, some kind of negative reaction to collectivization was unavoidable.

The regime's turn toward forced grain requisitions placed the Red Army under serious strain. Many peasant soldiers retained close ties to their home communities in the countryside and were soon made aware of the repressive measures being imposed. Army reliability quickly began to waver. The crux of the problem lay in the Red Army's territorial structure. In an effort to cut costs, a process to transform the army into a territorial force had been launched in 1923. This reform was completed under Frunze and left the Red Army composed of a standing cadre and a number of territorial militia divisions.[76] The greater reliance on territorial divisions increased the number of peasants in the ranks as a whole. By 1926, territorial divisions constituted 65.8 percent of the Red Army.[77] In some places, such as the Volga Military District, there were only territorial divisions. The Moscow Military District was not far behind, at 90 percent.[78] There had been dissenting voices against this reorganization scheme for precisely this reason. Aside from the fact that territorial forces tended to suffer from poor discipline, the OGPU was unhappy with the changes; it saw a danger in giving peasants too much influence in army life, which might potentially undermine the army's reliability.[79] Iagoda, the deputy head of the OGPU, had expressed concern that territorial divisions were more vulnerable to peasant agitators and counterrevolutionaries.[80] In September 1925, a law was promulgated barring disenfranchised rich peasants (the kulaks) and other supposedly unreliable elements from serving in the army proper. The law was used in the territorial divisions to stop them having access to weapons.[81] However, this focus on subversives did little to stop the wave of discontent that spread through the ranks at the end of the 1920s. The main problem was not with so-called unreliable elements but rather with ordinary peasant soldiers.

The upheaval in the rank and file during the collectivization drive was nothing new; rather, it was only the scale of the problem that was unforeseen. The OGPU had dealt with similar problems in the ranks before the collectivization drive. As early as 1923, Iagoda had been notified about the hostile reaction among groups of soldiers toward agricultural taxes. In a series of letters from a subordinate in the Far East, Iagoda was briefed about the appearance of a sharp "demobilization mood" within the ranks and how some soldiers had formed agitation groups— an activity deemed to be "counterrevolutionary."[82] In this respect, it was already clear that tensions in the countryside could quite easily manifest in the Red Army and affect its reliability. Similar concerns were also raised by Dzerzhinskii in early 1925, when he acknowledged that if the Red Army was to be a powerful force, the mood of the peasants had to be carefully watched.[83] Moreover, presaging the forms of peasant agitation seen under collectivization, the OGPU recorded the circulation of anti-Soviet letters from peasants to their relatives serving in the Red Army that contained complaints about poverty and abuses of power carried out by the party.[84] These formed an important link between the rank and file and the villages. Dzerzhinskii kept track of the ratio of positive to negative letters in the mid-1920s, suggesting that he understood their potential influence on the soldiers.[85] Such letters would become crucial in spreading the word about the harsh economic policies that the regime forced on the peasantry just years later.[86] Yet in the years before the launch of the collectivization drive, despite receiving thousands of complaints from soldiers about taxes and witnessing a steady flow of letters between the villages and Red Army, there was no pressing crisis. The so-called peasant mood (*krest'ianskoe nastroenie*) had not yet gripped the ranks to the extent that it later would during collectivization.[87] Before 1928, it was understood that peasant dissatisfaction in the ranks was nothing that PUR could not handle.[88]

In this respect, it was already clear that there would be some negative and destabilizing consequences for the Red Army when forced grain requisitions were again used in the countryside. Whether there was opposition from the army leadership to collectivization for this very reason is difficult to establish. Those pushing for rapid rearmament, such as Tukhachevskii, appear to have had no concerns about the negative consequences of collectivization in the rank and file. Tukhachevskii's calculations for his ambitious armament proposals were based on the potential resources released by both collectivization and industrialization. He saw state control of agriculture as a necessary step toward creating a powerful military. In a book published in 1931, he gave his full backing to collectivization.[89] There is some circumstantial evidence that Voroshilov was against launching collectivization. Documents from the British Foreign Office suggest that Voroshilov warned Stalin that he could not be responsible for the reliability of the Red Army if he continued to force collectivization on the countryside.[90] These sources are too removed from the decision-making processes within the Politburo to permit any firm judgment. Voroshilov had given Bukharin, a member of the Right Deviation, support on a different issue in 1929, when the former petitioned not to be transferred to the Commissariat for Education as punishment for his opposition to the regime's economic and agricultural policies (as Oleg Khlevniuk notes, this transfer would have meant political exile). Bukharin instead wanted to become the head of the Scientific Technical Administration.[91] Voroshilov went against Stalin on this issue and supported Bukharin. It is doubtful, however, that Voroshilov's support for Bukharin in this instance would have translated into support for his stance against collectivization. As David Stone convincingly argues, there was considerable animosity between Voroshilov and Rykov, member of the Right Deviation and head of the Soviet government, over the latter's efforts to block the army's attempts to get more funding. The bad relations between the two men made any wider alliance between Voroshilov and the Right Deviation unlikely.[92] However, it would be surprising if Voroshilov had not foreseen that collectivization would generate strong hostility in the rank and file. He probably expected a bad reaction on some level. Yet aside from his show of support for Bukharin in 1929, Voroshilov was loyal to Stalin. He may have had private doubts about the impact of collectivization on the Red Army, but it was not in his character to openly dissent from the general line in any significant way.[93]

As soon as forced grain requisitions were enforced in the countryside, problems with army morale became evident. In the autumn of 1927, many rank-and-file soldiers were showing increasing dissatisfaction with the regime's new agricultural policies.[94] This trend continued into 1928, and it was at this point that the peasant mood became a serious subject of study.[95] In early 1928, PUR compiled a series of reports on the peasant mood that went some way in reaching an understanding of how the military was being affected by peasant discontent. Among its conclusions, the reports noted that, unsurprisingly, dissatisfaction with forced grain requisitions was largely confined to the lower ranks. Responses were more diverse from within the officer corps and depended on how closely officers were connected to the villages.[96] Moreover, some soldiers were not just acting in solidarity with the peasants but were also apparently engaged in direct action and agitation—something typically blamed on subversive kulak influences. For example, an order from the Revolutionary Military Council in 1928 noted that growing rank-and-file hostility toward grain requisitions was a reflection of the class struggle and attempts by kulaks to agitate within the barracks.[97] The discontent in the rank and file was thus perceived through the well-established lens of the army's vulnerability to subversion. On 10 July 1928, the Central Committee ordered that additional efforts were needed to combat the discontent in the ranks, and it criticized the inability of PUR to stop the negative influence that class aliens were having on the soldiers.[98] In terms of the scale of the rank-and-file hostility toward grain requisitions, the reports compiled in 1928 did not note this precisely, but they described a "large wave" that might get stronger as more information fed into the barracks.[99] Indeed, PUR noted that even after a brief lull in levels of hostility in February 1928, questions about grain requisitions remained the center of attention for many soldiers.[100]

PUR also highlighted that discontent was spreading throughout the ranks by letters and envoys sent from the villages in which peasants asked their serving relatives to assist in direct action against grain collections.[101] The volume of letters was impressive, with one garrison in the North Caucasus Military District receiving 6,000 letters in one day.[102] From excerpts from these letters, it is possible to see the picture of hardship in the countryside being presented to the rank-and-file soldiers. For example, in the first two months of 1928, a Caucasus infantry battalion received letters with the following complaints: "In the village and at the shop they're not giving out goods for money, they're only giving them out for wheat." Another letter noted, "One village (*stanitsa*) was saddled with a mandatory assignment of 100,000 poods of grain, and we can't sell the surplus without permission from the village soviet."[103] A report from 1928 recorded a letter sent to a soldier from the Kuban Oblast' typical of visible incitements to violence. The sender complained that the peasants were being "fleeced" and called for direct action from the Red Army: "You are silent in the army. Put pressure on your commanders, bring about a revolt (*bunt*), we have to go to war."[104] Appeals for soldiers to revolt were common in intercepted letters and sometimes were successful in turning army opinion against the regime.[105] A letter sent by a political commissar to Alexei Rykov noted that "extraordinarily abnormal and dangerous moods" were fomenting in the ranks. He added that "many students" declared that the "workers live at the expense of the peasantry" and that "they fleece the peasants now more than under the tsars."[106] In the Volga Military District, the following comment was recorded from a member of a machine gun regiment: "When there was a campaign to collect taxes, we supported Soviet power, but now Soviet power has neglected us—it does not give us bread. We must liberate the poor from collection and the kulaks must be made to serve." From the same group of soldiers, and in response to the question of whether they were loyal to the government, there was the outcry, "We all hate Soviet power!"[107]

Both Voroshilov and the OGPU called for better monitoring of the growing discontent in the rank and file. In February 1928, for instance, the OGPU called for the seizure of all letters addressed to soldiers from the villages so that they could be checked for any counterrevolutionary content.[108] More drastic measures were also needed. Consequently, in July 1928, an army purge was launched. This targeted individuals regarded as "socially alien" (*sotsial'no chuzhdye*), including the sons of priests, judicial bureaucrats, and other nonworker professionals. A second category concerned servicemen classified as "class harmful elements" (*klassovye vrazhdebnye elementy*), including kulaks and the sons of kulaks, as well as those deprived of voting rights. By January 1929, 4,029 discharges from the army had already been approved.[109] This was not a purge carried out without excess. Soldiers were sometimes discharged from the ranks not because they fit into either subversive social category, but simply because they did not want to join a collective farm.[110] Before the launch of this purge, the discharge of socially alien elements from the Red Army had been done on a case-by-case basis. This purge, which brought discharges on a mass scale, was inevitably a blunt instrument.[111]

The resort to mass discharges shows how concerning the peasant mood spreading throughout the Red Army was estimated to be.[112] However, as was the case with the alleged Trotskyist attempted coup of November 1927, there was a divergence in opinion between PUR and the OGPU about the nature and scale of the threat in the lower ranks. Vested interests continued to shape what were conflicting depictions of the dangers facing the Red Army. Unsurprisingly, the OGPU were most concerned about the peasant mood. Notably, in 1929, they believed that this wave of discontent was the primary cause of trouble in the ranks. The OGPU was also more likely to connect manifestations of the peasant mood to what they saw as increasing anti-Soviet activity.[113] In this way, the peasant mood was interpreted as further evidence of how the Red Army remained open to subversion and infiltration. It cannot be entirely discounted that in depicting the turmoil in the ranks through the lens of subversion, the OGPU was trying to show how it remained indispensable to the security of the army compared to PUR, which had seemingly been unable to adequately secure the military against dangerous enemies. PUR was certainly more sanguine about the peasant mood, particularly toward the end of 1929. At this point, it argued that the trouble in the lower ranks had largely been overcome and that the army was stable once again. In materials prepared for the May 1929 Fifth Congress of Soviets, for instance, the verdict from PUR was, "It is possible with full foundation to characterize the general political condition of the Red Army as fully stable, healthy."[114] Of course, PUR continued to have a strong incentive to downplay anything that might weaken army political reliability. The growth of the peasant mood would surely be seen by some as a powerful indictment of the organization's ability to carry out political education in the ranks. In this sense, it is not surprising that PUR seized on the lull in the peasant mood (which did dip in intensity in mid-1929) to declare the army stable and reliable.

The lull in the peasant mood in 1929, however, did not last. As forced grain requisitions gave way to the wholesale collectivization of agriculture in late 1929, another wave of the peasant mood was recorded.[115] Moreover, dekulakization served to increase the scale of repression in the countryside. Correspondingly, the peasant mood in the Red Army now became known as the kulak mood, showing once more how discontent in the ranks tended to be framed as instigated by subversives rather than the expression of legitimate concerns of peasant soldiers. By mid-1930, PUR was recording growing levels of "kulak agitation" inside the Red Army, and the OGPU reported on "counterrevolutionary" groups within the ranks.[116] The turbulence created by collectivization and dekulakization was reaching a breaking point. Roger Reese argues that during the winter of 1929–1930, the entire Red Army should be seen as unreliable because of its high levels of internal turmoil.[117] The purge of the army thus needed to be continued, but at a faster pace. During the first six months of 1930 alone, a further 5,703 soldiers were discharged from the army.[118] Indeed, an army resolution of January 1930 called for greater class vigilance and stronger repression of the enemy.[119] At approximately the same time, the new head of PUR, Ian Gamarnik, spelled out the danger facing the army:

> The kulak will send provocative letters to the barracks. The attempts by the kulak "to knock at" (*stuchat'sia*) the barracks, to influence it, undoubtedly will increase in the near future. This should force the political organs, party organizations, and members of the Komsomol to strengthen class vigilance, to improve political work, mass work, [to] mobilize all the Red Army masses around the slogans of the party—to liquidate the kulak as a class. . . . More than it has even been, the political organs are required to watch the mood of the Red Army men, to study them and react to them in good time.[120]

As the new head of PUR, Gamarnik was surely coming under pressure. His organization had already been criticized by the Central Committee for its failure to safeguard the reliability of the soldiers in the face of perceived kulak agitation, and the discontent in the ranks was only getting worse. Gamarnik's solutions were hardly radical. He called for more observation, better political work, and more vigilance against enemies. However, this would do little to restore army stability. Discharging soldiers en masse was the only realistic way that order might be returned without giving into demands from below. Gamarnik no doubt realized this, but at the same time, he had to be seen to be doing something to ensure that the discontent did not get any worse and to make an effort to improve the performance of PUR, especially because the OGPU continued to present an image of an army open to infiltration by an array of dangerous enemies. An OGPU report from October 1930 noted that there had apparently been an intensification of counterrevolutionary activity in the ranks, with some groups connected to subversive organizations outside of the Red Army. The participation of junior, middle, and even senior ranking officers in this supposed counterrevolutionary activity had also "significantly grown."[121] Gamarnik was no doubt conscious that all of this was happening under his watch and that he needed to be offering credible solutions to reinforce army reliability. Yet merely calling for greater vigilance suggests that he had few ideas about how to solve the crisis in the rank and file.

It was not until the end of 1932 that the situation in the Red Army improved and was, in the opinion of PUR at least, stable again.[122] On a certain level, a change in policy toward the protesting soldiers had helped accomplish this, suggesting that the regime had realized that the instability in the ranks could not be solely attributed to subversive enemies. The families of soldiers, for instance, were eventually exempted from the dekulakization campaign.[123] Between late 1929 and early 1930, a propaganda campaign was launched that involved soldiers writing to the villages promoting the benefits of collectivization.[124] However, the crude method of mass discharges alongside the winding down of dekulakization and collectivization in the early 1930s were the most important factors in regaining control over the rank and file. This came at a heavy cost to the army: almost 37,000 soldiers had been discharged by the end of 1933.[125] Moreover, there would be different lessons taken about the specific causes of this huge turmoil in the lower ranks. The OGPU would see further weaknesses in army reliability and more evidence of how it remained susceptible to infiltration. As far as the OGPU was concerned, PUR had failed to control the peasant mood.[126] Because the peasant and kulak moods had overwhelmingly been interpreted as fomented by kulaks and suspected counterrevolutionaries rather than stemming from legitimate grievances, this played directly into the OGPU's hands. It is likely that they came out of these crisis years in a stronger position than PUR.

Despite the widespread discontent in the ranks, Voroshilov publicly denied that the Red Army had been affected by collectivization. He hushed up the problem. At the Sixteenth Party Congress in July 1930, at the height of collectivization, Voroshilov remarked,

> The difficulty with collectivization and the sortie of kulak elements, the intrigues of the Right Deviation—these are all factors, comrades, that gave us

the full opportunity to fundamentally verify the political stability and loyalty of the Red Army masses to the matter of the proletarian revolution. After these checks, we are able to declare with pride that, regardless of the difficulties, despite the sharpening of the class struggle during these two and a half years, the Red Army never once wavered.[127]

As we have seen, it was manifestly false to declare that the army had "never once wavered" in the face of collectivization. Voroshilov was once again masking the problems with army reliability. In reality, the regime had been given a clear lesson that, when under certain social strains, the Red Army could not be fully relied upon. Another clear lesson—at least from the regime's point of view—was that enemies and subversives could easily infiltrate the ranks and create havoc. However, Voroshilov would hardly want to admit this in public. To do so would damage his authority. Stalin would no doubt listen to both Voroshilov and the OGPU about what lessons should be taken from the hostile reaction from the Red Army to collectivization, but ultimately, he would see a military that had cracked under pressure and was wide open to being subverted. This is something he would not forget. Yet the crisis in the Red Army in the early 1930s did not stop at the rank and file. At the same time that mass discharges were spreading throughout the lower ranks, a supposed large military specialist conspiracy was unfolding in the upper ranks.

Operation Vesna

During 1930–1931, the OGPU carried out Operation Vesna (springtime), which led to the discharge and arrest of thousands of military specialists serving in the Red Army and its military academies. The operation was focused in Moscow, Leningrad, and Ukraine, and the arrested military specialists were accused of being members of monarchist and White counterrevolutionary groups allegedly involved in a range of anti-Soviet activities, including espionage, sabotage, and so-called wrecking. The overall aim of these traitors was supposedly to assist in bringing down the Soviet state in a time of war.[128] Although this was undoubtedly the largest counterrevolutionary plot yet discovered in the military, it had no basis in reality. The plot stemmed from long-standing security anxieties about the perceived risk to the Red Army from traitorous military specialists financed by hostile foreign powers. However,

Stalin seems to have fully accepted the notion that the military specialist plot was genuine, even though forced confessions provided the necessary evidence. As far as the regime was concerned, Operation Vesna made clear how the Red Army could be deeply infiltrated by enemy agents. In addition, the exposure of this apparently extensive conspiracy among the military specialists would do little to support PUR and Voroshilov's repeated assurances that the Red Army was reliable and would only strengthen the more pessimistic view held by the OGPU. Finally, because this large conspiracy was unmasked at the very same time that the regime was being forced into discharging soldiers en masse from the rank and file in attempt to control the fallout from the collectivization drive, it is not unjustified to see the late 1920s to early 1930s as a period of severe crisis for the entire Red Army.

Operation Vesna did not come out of nowhere. As we saw in chapter 2, ever since the end of the civil war, military specialists had still attracted the suspicions of the political police. They were judged to be potential agents of hostile capitalist powers, the exiled White movement, or both. Military specialists were arrested throughout the 1920s on charges of counterrevolutionary activity and espionage, but these arrests never reached a large scale. During 1927, there had been a slight increase in the number of military specialists charged for counterrevolutionary activity in Leningrad and Moscow, but this still did not represent mass arrests.[129] The increase in 1927 is best explained by the Soviet Union's worsening relationship with the outside world. The OGPU had already initiated closer observation over military specialists in 1926 because of the Soviet Union's worsening diplomatic relations. As we have seen, the Soviet leaders believed that the capitalist powers and their proxy states represented a credible military threat; these security fears were pronounced during the war scare of 1927. Notably, the OGPU believed that military specialists would welcome a new war because this would hasten the fall of Soviet power.[130]

There is, however, an important domestic context to the greater scrutiny of military specialists in the mid- to late 1920s. During these years, specialists in all Soviet institutions were increasingly persecuted as the regime forced through rapid industrialization and the first five-year plan. These were years of utopian optimism and unrealistic industrial targets. Moreover, the regime mobilized younger and more idealistic party members, and encouraged them to challenge their prerevolutionary superiors.[131] There was little room for either the realism or expert guidance that experienced specialists could bring to the planning process. Rather, resistance to the impossible targets of the plan was often interpreted as revealing insufficient revolutionary optimism and a desire to purposely hold back, perhaps even sabotage, production tempos. Relationships between bourgeois specialists and their party counterparts in industry became increasingly strained during the first five-year plan. Specialists often found themselves used as scapegoats for any failure to meet the spiraling economic targets. This officially sanctioned campaign against specialists culminated in several high-profile trials, the most notorious of which was the Shakhty trial in May to June 1928. Fifty-three specialist coal engineers from the North Caucasus were convicted of sabotage and of working with foreign powers. The entire case was a sham, but the trial was meant as a public demonstration of how specialists were believed to be holding back the tempos of industrial development. As industrial shortages increased toward the end of the 1920s, campaigns against wrecking and sabotage flourished.

Alongside the Shakhty case were several other trials and high-profile specialist arrests. Former general Vadim Mikhailov, head of the main industrial directorate, for instance, was arrested in May 1928 for apparently coordinating a wrecking group in military industry. He was later executed in 1929, along with several other specialists. In general terms, 1929 saw a spate of arrests of specialists working in military industry, inside the weapons arsenal trust in March, and in the artillery administrations and ammunition trusts in summer and autumn.[132] A second highly publicized specialist trial began in late 1929, this time of the so-called Industrial Party. The charges were in the same vein as the Shakhty trial. The specialist defendants were accused of carrying out sabotage to prepare the ground for a foreign invention. Moreover, many lecturers classified as prerevolutionary "former people" (*byvshie liudi*) were also arrested in Leningrad at this time. They were forced to acknowledge their supposed monarchist sympathies and were accused of holding counterrevolutionary views.[133] The Red Army could not avoid being pulled into the persecution of specialists that accompanied the first five-year plan. The large numbers of military specialists still serving in the army made this impossible. Indeed, in a report from September 1930, Ia. K. Ol'skii, head of the OGPU special department, raised concerns that wreckers and saboteurs financed from abroad were hidden in the armed forces.[134] A number of supposed wrecking groups were discovered across the artillery, navy, topographic department, and sanitary department. The arrested wreckers were once again outsiders in the Red Army, including former White officers, former socialist revolutionaries, sons of kulaks, and military specialists. The OGPU unearthed what they believed were connections between these saboteurs and foreign governments. In the military topographic department, for example, military specialist wreckers were apparently also carrying out espionage for Poland.[135] As long as industrial tempos remained impossibly high, and as hysteria was whipped up about sabotage, there would be no shortage of similar cases exposed in the future.[136] As one historian has argued, the atmosphere was such that almost all former Whites in military service were seen as potential wreckers and as members of counterrevolutionary organizations during the late 1920s and early 1930s.[137]

In this respect, the increase in the number of arrested military specialists in the Red Army in the mid- to late 1920s should be seen as one part of the wider state-sponsored campaign against sabotage and wrecking in industry. That the Red Army was receptive to fluctuating currents in Soviet party politics and the mobilization campaigns launched by the regime is unsurprising. As the party promoted specialist baiting, the military specialists also felt pressure. Moreover, it seems that the antiwrecking trials of the late 1920s helped sketch out the broader outlines of the military specialist "conspiracy" that would later be exposed through Operation Vesna in 1930. The arrested specialists working in industry were accused of sabotage and being connected to foreign powers, as well as planning to hasten the fall of Soviet power. In this sense, the background was already primed for a military specialist plot to be unmasked inside the Red Army. Yet while the atmosphere of specialist baiting certainly contributed to the exposure of a supposed large military specialist conspiracy over the course of 1930–1931, undoubtedly giving it a certain credibility, the specific trigger was the perceived foreign threat.

We have already seen that the OGPU decided to keep military specialists under closer observation in the mid-1920s as a result of the worsening international situation. In the late 1920s, the OGPU believed that there was a significant danger from abroad and that preparations for an attack on the Soviet Union were underway. For example, they had received information in December 1927 that Ukrainian nationalist leaders had supposedly met with British prime minister Stanley Baldwin and chancellor of the exchequer Winston Churchill, who had apparently agreed to some kind of joint attack against the Soviet Union involving several foreign powers and Ukrainian nationalists. Several counterrevolutionary groups were subsequently rounded up by the OGPU in Odessa, Umani, Kremenchug, Lugansk, Krivoi Rog, and Dnepopetrovsk.[138] Similar wild fears were running high in mid-1928, when the OGPU suspected that the British government was planning to take advantage of the tense relationship that still existed between the Soviet Union and Poland in order to spark a war. According to intelligence received by the OGPU's foreign department, the British had supposedly paid Piłsudski £100,000 in 1927 to organize an anti-Bolshevik uprising in Ukraine. This revolt was to be headed up by nationalists of the then-obsolete Ukrainian People's Republic (UNR). The plan purported to make use of both UNR forces and Red Army troops that had been successfully turned against the regime. This British-inspired uprising was exactly the type of foreign-sponsored conspiracy that the OGPU feared was being concocted by the capitalist states. Yet for now, the operation had apparently been placed on hold. Intelligence later obtained by the OGPU suggested that the plan had been delayed until spring 1929 because Piłsudski had fallen ill.[139]

It is difficult to authenticate this type of intelligence. Instead of representing real British efforts to undermine the Soviet Union, it is much more likely that this was disinformation or simply plainly inaccurate. Nonetheless, the OGPU appears to have accepted the information as credible. As such, when further intelligence was obtained with information about a supposed collaboration between Poland and members of the UNR, indicating that the recently aborted plans for the Ukrainian uprising were once again active, a decision was made to make arrests.[140] In Ukraine, the OGPU searched for Polish intelligence agents; the majority of people arrested were former imperial officers. Although most of these officers no longer served in the military, some did have connections to officers still serving, primarily military specialists. The OGPU's focus now swung toward the Red Army, and surveillance was set up of serving officers connected to the first round of arrests in Ukraine. This all took place under the operational name Vesna.[141] Menzhinskii soon contacted Stalin to inform him that several counterrevolutionary organizations had been discovered that were trying to infiltrate the Red Army. Menzhinskii then gave the order to shift the focus of the operation toward exposing counterrevolutionary activity inside the Red Army, something he believed was being overlooked.[142] From early 1930, the OGPU began to arrest growing numbers of military specialists.

Within months, the arrests had spread throughout the military academies, numbering into the thousands.[143] Notably, the arrested military specialists were accused of being members of monarchist and White counterrevolutionary groups that were engaged in widespread espionage and sabotage. Operation Vesna was first concentrated in Moscow, but the arrests soon spread to Kiev and Leningrad in early 1931.[144]

The discovery of this supposed counterrevolutionary military plot had significant impact. Two senior OGPU operatives, Efim Evdokimov and Ia. K. Ol'skii, remarked that the unmasking of the plot represented a powerful strike on the Whites and had exposed the main base of White counterrevolutionary agents in the Soviet Union.[145] Although the sheer numbers arrested in the military plot perhaps justified this reaction, many of the associated arrests were confined to military academies.[146] At the end of the 1920s, military specialists still represented a sizable cohort in the Red Army, but they were increasingly concentrated in teaching roles as a steady influx of newly trained Red commanders took positions as officers. In this respect, the victims of Operation Vesna were in the main army outsiders and not those directly in the chain of command. This is a key difference to the later and much larger military purge of 1937–1938, which struck at the heart of the military elite. However, the high command was not completely insulated from Operation Vesna, and some of the most senior officers found themselves drawn in.

In August 1930, several senior officers were implicated in Operation Vesna for their supposed membership of counterrevolutionary organizations. This included Mikhail Tukhachevskii, which in many respects is unsurprising. As we have seen, Tukhachevskii's reliability was the subject of persistent rumors throughout the 1920s, and in the early 1930s, the OGPU was still collecting rumor and hearsay about him.[147] Tukhachevskii's incrimination in the military specialist plot came when two military specialists employed at the Frunze Military Academy, N. Kakurin and I. Troitskii, were arrested during Operation Vesna. Under interrogation, they gave evidence in August 1930 that claimed that Tukhachevskii was sympathetic to the Right Deviation and that portrayed him as the head of a conspiracy planning to stage a military coup.[148] That Kakurin had served with Tukhachevskii during the civil war may have lent some weight to these accusations, even though they were entirely baseless.[149] Indeed, it seems that the evidence given by Kakurin and Troitskii was extracted by torture. Kakurin claimed as much in 1939 in a statement given to the military collegium of the supreme court, stating that his evidence in 1930 had been false.[150] Moreover, the OGPU's regular use of torture was evidently prevalent enough in the early 1930s that even Iagoda was forced to complain about it in 1931.[151] In this respect, it is likely that some OGPU leaders were already looking to find incriminating information about Tukhachevskii before Kakurin's arrest and used torture to get the necessary evidence, perhaps in view of discovering a conspiracy deep inside the high command. The OGPU already had a large file of rumors and hearsay purporting to show Tukhachevskii's disloyalty and alleged ambitions for power. Although it seems that these rumors were treated with suitable skepticism in the 1920s (primarily because the political police spread similar disinformation about Tukhachevskii for their own ends), the military specialist plot uncovered during Operation Vesna may have prompted the OGPU to partly rethink the hearsay about Tukhachevskii. They may have wanted to dig a little deeper. Noticeably, the testimony given by Troitskii and Kakurin that incriminated Tukhachevskii had similarities to the rumors about a Russian Bonaparte so common in the 1920s. Among other charges, Tukhachevskii apparently planned to seize power and establish a military dictatorship.[152]

Menzhinskii, for one, now believed that Tukhachevskii represented a threat to the state and that there was a military conspiracy in the high command. On 10 September 1930, he sent the details of Kakurin's and Troitskii's interrogations, along with the following note about Tukhachevskii and officers incriminated alongside him, to Stalin:

> To arrest the participants of the group one at a time—is risky. There are two possible conclusions: either immediately arrest the most active participants of the group, or wait for your arrival, having applied covert observational measures in order not to be caught off guard. I consider it necessary to add that now the whole insurgent group is maturing very quickly and the later solution presents a certain risk.[153]

Stalin, however, did not follow Menzhinskii's advice and decided to write first to his close ally, Ordzhonikidze, on 24 September:[154]

> Please read as soon as possible the testimony of Kakurin—Troitskii and think about measures to liquidate this unpleasant business. This material, as you see, is strictly secret: only Molotov, I, and now you know about it. I do not know if Klim [Voroshilov] is informed about it. This would mean that

Tukhachevskii has been captured by anti-Soviet elements from the ranks of the right. That is what the materials indicate. Is it possible? Of course it is possible, it cannot be excluded. Evidently the Rights are preparing to install a military dictatorship just to get rid of the Central Committee, the kolkhozes and sovkhozes, the Bolshevik tempos of development of industry. . . . It is impossible to finish with this matter in the usual way (immediate arrest and so on). It's necessary to think about this carefully. It would be better to postpone a decision on this question, raised in Menzhinskii's memorandum, until mid-October, when we will all be gathered again.[155]

Stalin's note to Ordzhonikidze is important for several reasons. First, it suggests that Voroshilov had not even been informed of Tukhachevskii's incrimination, showing that the OGPU went directly to Stalin and not through army channels, despite this being a military matter. In doing so, it is entirely possible that Menzhinskii was trying to undermine Voroshilov by leaving him in the dark about Tukhachevskii. Even though (judging by his past form) Voroshilov probably would have welcomed the arrest of his troublesome subordinate, the whole case would reflect badly on his leadership. If someone as senior as Tukhachevskii turned out to be a counterrevolutionary or working for a foreign power, this would be a clear demonstration for Stalin that enemies were operating at the highest levels of the Red Army and that Voroshilov had seemingly not noticed. However, as had been the case at the time of the alleged Trotskyist coup attempt in November 1927, Stalin hesitated. He had doubts about the next step. He waited two weeks before acting on Menzhinskii's letter of 10 September and confided in Ordzhonikidze for advice. Stalin was not entirely certain about the case against Tukhachevskii, writing in his letter that whether he was in fact a counterrevolutionary was "possible" and "cannot be excluded." Stalin wanted to tread carefully and avoid knee-jerk responses. In the end, he put off the issue until the end of October for discussion in the Politburo. In the meantime, Kakurin provided further material on 5 October. No doubt once again under OGPU pressure, he claimed that Tukhachevskii had spoken about an attempt on Stalin's life by a "fanatic." He also cryptically hinted that Tukhachevskii would be the candidate for military dictator in a struggle with "anarchy and aggression." These were serious insinuations, and corroborating material was received from the interrogation of Troitskii. In October, Stalin met with Ordzhonikidze and Voroshilov, and they conducted a face-to-face confrontation with Tukhachevskii,

Kakurin, and Troitskii. Also present at the meeting were Gamarnik and senior officers Iakir and Ivan Dubovoi, all of whom were interviewed about Tukhachevskii. At this point, the accusations were dropped. After this confrontation, Tukhachevskii was released from suspicion.[156] Stalin later wrote to Molotov on 23 October, remarking, "With regard to the case of Tukhachevskii, he turned out to be 100 percent clean. This is very good."[157]

Tukhachevskii had escaped arrest despite the damaging testimony from both Kakurin and Troitskii. Evidently Stalin's doubts about the case against him carried the day. These had been visible from the very start in his delay in acting on Menzhinskii's September letter, and the face-to-face confrontation in October finally convinced Stalin of Tukhachevskii's innocence. That Tukhachevskii's incrimination came so soon after Stalin's harsh rejection of his radical armament memorandum is worth highlighting. Despite previously describing Tukhachevskii's proposals as Red militarism and "worse than any counterrevolution," Stalin did not take the opportunity to have Tukhachevskii removed from the army elite when the chance presented itself. He could easily have had the troublesome Tukhachevskii arrested. Stalin's decision to exonerate Tukhachevskii does not appear connected to any doubts about the wider military specialist plot unmasked by Operation Vesna. He did not show the same level of skepticism toward the thousands of other arrested military specialists as he did toward Tukhachevskii. Moreover, Stalin's personal correspondence from this time suggests that he accepted the premise of the supposed military plot. At the height of Operation Vesna in September 1930, for instance, Stalin wrote to Molotov with his concerns that Poland was joining forces with the Baltic states and that they were planning to wage war against the Soviet Union.[158] Operation Vesna similarly stemmed from concerns about a Polish intervention into Ukraine. Furthermore, a few months earlier, in January, the Politburo had called for a strengthening of the OGPU's foreign department to help it find out whether England, France, Germany, Japan, Poland, Romania, Finland, and the Baltic states were planning aggressive actions against the Soviet Union.[159] That the threat from abroad was heightened in 1930 no doubt made the "military plot" discovered by the OGPU seem entirely credible to the Soviet leadership. In this sense, we can speculate that in the absence of doubt about Operation Vesna itself, Stalin did not act on Tukhachevskii's incrimination because he felt a level of respect for his military skill and abilities, despite his tendency to push boundaries. Indeed, as noted above, in his letter criticizing Tukhachevskii's rearmament plan of 1930 as "worse than any counter-revolution," Stalin also remarked that he respected Tukhachevskii as an "unusually capable" comrade. Because the face-to-face confrontation after Tukhachevskii's incrimination in summer 1930 had convinced Stalin that he was innocent, it served no purpose to have him arrested on the basis of evidence that did not stand up. The Red Army needed people of Tukhachevskii's talent for any modernization plan to be successful, even if he was a recognized troublemaker.

Voroshilov, however, was much less forgiving than Stalin. Even after Tukhachevskii had been judged clean of any participation in a military conspiracy, Voroshilov continued to send Stalin compromising information about his rival.[160] In doing so, Voroshilov may have sensed an opportunity to play on Tukhachevskii's incrimination to try and ignite fresh doubts in Stalin's mind, perhaps in attempt to have Tukhachevskii demoted. If this was Voroshilov's intention, it was not an entirely unrealistic gambit. Even though Stalin leaned toward restraint in 1930 and supported Tukhachevskii, he would not forget Operation Vesna or the serious accusations leveled against certain members of the high command. Suspicions about the reliability of the Red Army would linger, and Stalin may have decided to keep a closer eye on Tukhachevskii. He was not part of Stalin's close circle; nor was he a close ally, like Voroshilov. Stalin could not be as certain of Tukhachevskii's loyalty. Consequently, while he was safe for now, Tukhachevskii's incrimination in 1930 may have left him the object of greater scrutiny. Certainly it would be surprising if the OGPU left Tukhachevskii alone from this point on, having got so close to having him arrested.

In early 1931, Operation Vesna reached its apogee. The different strands of the investigation in Ukraine, Moscow, and Leningrad were finally tied together on 16 February 1931, when the head of the OGPU in Ukraine, Vsevolod Balitskii, sent a telegram to Menzhinskii and Iagoda with evidence apparently proving the existence of an "all-Union military-officer counterrevolutionary organization."[161] In making this claim, Balitskii was in fact doing little more than following Menzhinskii and Iagoda's direction. Both had urged him to apply harsher repressive measures in Ukraine to find evidence of a much broader plot.[162] Menzhinskii no doubt fully believed that the true scale of the military plot was yet to be fully uncovered, but he probably had an ulterior motive in pushing his subordinates to find fitting evidence of a unionwide conspiracy. If a much larger plot was unmasked, it would strengthen the position of the OGPU in general terms, but it would also highlight the failures of PUR and the army leadership in safeguarding the ranks from subversion. As Stalin accepted Menzhinskii's claims about an extensive military plot, it is possible that he drew this lesson.[163] Operation Vesna had supposedly uncovered, for the first time, an extensive conspiracy inside the Red Army with connections to foreign powers, and whose members apparently planned to assist in overthrowing Soviet power during war. The OGPU discovered this plot, not the Red Army, which would have only strengthened its position.

Operation Vesna was finally wound down in May 1931, but it is safe to say that it contributed to what was already a period of acute crisis in the Red Army.[164] The regime believed that a major military specialist conspiracy had been uncovered at the very same time as mass discharges were hitting the lower ranks. In this respect, the early 1930s represent a tipping point for the Red Army in terms of repression. From Stalin's point of view, it would appear that his military was open to infiltration at all levels. As the international situation worsened over the coming years, it is possible that Stalin remained concerned about whether his armed forces could be relied on when the capitalist states finally launched their long-awaited attack on the Soviet Union and whether the military would prove resistant to subversion. The foreign threat had loomed large throughout Operation Vesna. Not only had a perceived threat from Poland provided the initial spark, but also information about a possible foreign invasion was gleaned from the subsequent investigation. Some arrested military specialists, for instance, claimed under interrogation that the peasant hostility toward collectivization would develop into uprisings in the countryside and weaken the strength of the Soviet regime. This, apparently, would provide foreign powers with the opportunity to attack.[165] Because forced confessions were liberally used by OGPU interrogators, such concerns about a foreign invasion reveal more about the private fears of the OGPU and what type of conspiracy its agents were seeking to uncover than any genuine threat. Even before Operation Vesna was launched, the OGPU had already expressed concern that capitalist powers might take advantage of social strain in the Red Army and look to stir discontent in the ranks.[166] The wider discontent in the rank and file against collectivization and the military specialist plot unmasked by Operation Vesna were not understood to be discrete security problems.

In this way, Operation Vesna had confirmed the OGPU's long-standing fears about the Red Army's vulnerability to subversion, and it is likely that the organization came out of the crisis of 1930–1931 in a stronger position. The OGPU had played a leading role both in tackling the discontent in the rank and file and in uncovering the military specialist plot. In contrast, PUR had been criticized by the Central Committee for carrying out poor political work among the rank-and-file soldiers, and Menzhinskii seemingly did not even bother to inform Voroshilov about Tukhachevskii's incrimination in Operation Vesna. This is hardly an indication that Menzhinskii held Voroshilov in high regard or believed he was capable of preserving the security of the Red Army. Leaving Voroshilov out of the loop was probably intended as a means to undermine him. This type of behavior, as we have seen, was nothing new for the OGPU. Senior OGPU leaders intrigued against each other in a struggle for influence inside the political police. The Red Army was sometimes drawn into these power struggles.[167] However, from Stalin's point of view, whatever the intrigue coming from the OGPU, it was Menzhinskii who had delivered results, whereas Voroshilov had failed to avert a major crisis in the Red Army.

A final point on Operation Vesna concerns its longer-term impact. Even though recent research on the Red Army often mentions Operation Vesna, more often than not, this is without a comment upon its significance. Even in more detailed examinations of the operation, a possible connection to the later military purge of 1937–1938 is not fully explored.[168] Indeed, it is easy to see Operation Vesna and the military purge of the Great Terror as separate episodes. On the surface, their targets were very different. Operation Vesna was directed at military specialists who were already objects of suspicion and increasingly outsiders in the Red Army. In contrast, during the Great Terror, it was the Red Army elite and officer corps who bore the brunt of the military purge. Those who had contributed so much to the reform and reorganization of the army—people like Tukhachevskii—were executed. Although the targets of Operation Vesna and the military purge differed, the triggers were almost identical. Operation Vesna was sparked by the perceived foreign threat, and the arrested military specialists were accused of plotting the downfall of the Soviet state with the assistance of foreign powers. Sabotage and wrecking featured heavily in the charges. These were the exact accusations later used against members of the high command and officer corps in 1937–1938. In this respect, the regime's concerns that foreign governments were ordering their agents to infiltrate the Red Army and undermine Soviet power never went away. However, before large numbers of senior officers could be accused of treachery and arrested en masse in 1937, they—like the military specialists in the early 1930s—needed to be perceived with just as much suspicion. Tukhachevskii's incrimination during Operation Vesna was an early signal that the OGPU was beginning to develop more concrete suspicions about the loyalty of some of the Red Army's most senior officers.

In chapter 2, we saw how the Red Army was still understood to be vulnerable to internal and external subversives even though the Bolsheviks had won the civil war. This chapter has shown how throughout the same period, the Red Army was also militarily weak and in no condition to fight a major conflict. It still lacked sufficient military expertise and desperately needed modernization. However, attempts to push through vital military reforms to strengthen the Red Army and bring it in line with the armies of other major foreign powers only exposed new problems. First, the high command proved to be sharply divided about the direction and speed of military reform. Resulting disputes were often highly acrimonious, especially among Tukhachevskii, Budennyi, and Voroshilov. By petitioning Stalin with their personal grievances, Voroshilov and Tukhachevskii reinforced the impression of disunity in the army leadership. The poor relationship between both men persisted into the 1930s and would not escape Stalin's attention. Second, the collectivization drive, indispensable to the success of the first five-year plan and in increasing Soviet economic and military power, sparked widespread hostility from peasant soldiers. A wave of discontent undermined the Red Army's ability to wage war and led to a major crisis in the rank and file. The actual cause of this crisis was not correctly identified (or openly admitted). Rather than see peasant soldiers with legitimate grievances, unhappy with how their relatives were being squeezed by grain requisitions, any hostility from below was explained as the consequence of kulak agitation or counterrevolutionary groups operating in the lower ranks. This reinforced an image of the Red Army as vulnerable to infiltration and subversion, and raised questions about its reliability under pressure. In this sense, collectivization and industrialization increased the power of the Soviet Union but at the same time exposed weaknesses in the institution most vital for defense. Finally,

Operation Vesna demonstrates how the perceived foreign threat to the Red Army loomed continually. Even though the operation unrolled in an atmosphere of officially sponsored specialist baiting and dramatic staged trials of prerevolutionary industrial experts, it was the specific perceived threat from Poland toward Ukraine, supposedly backed by Britain, that provided the initial trigger. Moreover, that Stalin believed that Operation Vesna had exposed a large foreign-backed conspiracy among the military specialists for the first time no doubt only further reinforced fears that the Red Army was under assault from an array of hostile capitalist powers. This supposed military specialist plot would never be forgotten, and not only because it incriminated some of the most senior officers in the high command. More than anything, from the Soviet leadership's point of view, it showed how easily a large foreign-sponsored conspiracy could take root inside the Red Army.

By 1932, more stability was brought to the military. The collectivization campaign had eased, and Operation Vesna had already been brought to an end. A period of crisis had passed. Of course, for the Red Army, the end of the 1920s and early 1930s was not a time entirely defined by crisis. It continued to modernize, defense spending was finally seeing substantial increases, new tank and aircraft programs were underway, and military doctrine was being revised. The Red Army was reaping the rewards of industrialization and becoming more advanced and modernized in anticipation of the inevitable future war. However, what were understood to be problems with the reliability of the Red Army did not disappear so easily. As the next chapter will show, even though overt manifestations of discontent in the lower ranks never again occurred after collectivization, and even though it was not until mid-1937 that the political police managed to expose another supposed major military conspiracy, the image of the Red Army as open to subversion stubbornly persisted. As pressure inside the Communist Party in particular began to rise throughout the 1930s, the perceived vulnerability of the Red Army manifested in new forms.

4 | The Red Army and the Communist Party, 1930–1936

With the end of Operation Vesna and the scaling down of the collectivization drive, tens of thousands of military specialists and rank-and-file soldiers had been discharged from the Red Army and thousands arrested.[1] The crisis period of 1928–1932 may well have passed, but this by no means brought an end to the security problems that plagued the Red Army. The mass discharges sanctioned by the regime over the late 1920s and early 1930s were an emergency response to regain control. They were not designed to purge the military of all potential enemies. Consequently, the threat posed by perceived subversives of different stripes remained potent in the years before the Great Terror. Large numbers of socially harmful and socially alien Red Army men continued to be unmasked, alongside more dangerous foreign agents and counterrevolutionaries. Although the regime did not turn to any sort of mass purge to deal with these supposed subversives (which would only be sanctioned later, during the Great Terror), serious efforts were made to improve the internal composition of the Red Army, particularly because espionage was understood to be a growing problem in the 1930s and the army was judged to be a primary target. These efforts, however, were doomed from the very beginning. Both the officer corps and PUR proved incapable of independently rooting out enemies in the ranks to a satisfactory level. Alleged counterrevolutionaries and foreign agents continued to go undiscovered even as the wider espionage threat to the Soviet Union was believed to be increasing. There are many indications that fundamental weaknesses existed in military self-policing, as well as evidence that a number of officers were consciously avoiding scrutinizing their own commands. Yet Voroshilov proved utterly incapable of coming to grips with these problems. He ignored the root causes of the Red Army's failure to adequately police itself; instead, he called vaguely for increased vigilance. This did little to improve the number of hidden enemies found by the military; indeed, it only ceded further ground to the political police, who were far more adept at finding apparently dangerous subversives in the ranks. All of this put Voroshilov in an increasingly difficult position. Over the course of the 1930s, the political atmosphere in the party steadily began to tighten as Stalin assumed more direct control, and the Red Army could not avoid being drawn in. The former political opposition was now increasingly persecuted, making it impossible to ignore the former oppositionists still serving in the Red Army. Because Voroshilov was unable to resolve the stubborn problems in army self-policing, it was the political police who scored major victories in unmasking supposed Trotskyist groups in the Red Army. A key moment in the run-up to the military purge came in the summer of 1936, when the political police discovered the so-called Trotskyist Military Center, which, as far as the Soviet leaders were concerned, provided evidence that the Red Army had been internally compromised by dangerous counterrevolutionary Trotskyists. It was the political police, rather than any military body, who uncovered this supposed conspiratorial group, and it provided the basis for a deeper investigation of the army that would lead directly to the military purge in 1937. In this respect, a year before the launch of the military purge, the political police had become the driving force behind the growing repression in the Red Army, and Voroshilov's leadership was looking more weak and ineffectual.

From the point of view of the Soviet leadership, imminent war was a genuine prospect for the first time in the early 1930s. The earlier certainty that some breathing room existed before the next major conflict had been shattered by the Japanese invasion of Manchuria in September 1931, and a war along the Soviet Union's sparsely defended eastern border now seemed like a real possibility. Indeed, the Japanese made rapid gains after the invasion of Manchuria, quickly consolidating their position and occupying the region by February 1932. By September, they announced the creation of a new puppet state, Manchukuo. The number of Japanese troops in Manchuria also steadily increased, reaching nearly 65,000 in 1931. Frequent low-level fighting along the border against Soviet troops became commonplace.[2] What made matters worse, however, were the reports prepared by Soviet intelligence indicating that the Japanese planned a quick and decisive war against the Soviet Union.[3] Looking for a way to prevent this looming conflict, a diplomatic offensive was immediately launched. The Soviet foreign commissar, Maxim Litvinov, offered a nonaggression pact in December 1931, but it was rebuffed by the Japanese leadership. Alongside these failing diplomatic efforts, a central strategy for protecting the Soviet Union in an increasingly hostile international environment was to rapidly increase its military power. As the new director of armaments from 1931, Tukhachevskii had been entrusted by Stalin to make this a reality. Although bottlenecks, shortages, and unfilled orders were stubborn problems for military industry as it struggled to fulfill growing demand, the Soviet Union was finally getting onto a war footing in the early 1930s.[4] Yet rearmament on the scale now desired by the regime would still take time, and from the regime's point of view, Japan was not the only hostile threat arrayed against the Soviet Union.

The main reason why a war with Japan was so alarming was that it raised the possibility that the Soviet Union would be forced to fight a war on two fronts. From the perspective of the Soviet leaders, the Japanese threat was just one part of what they saw as an increasingly unstable world. Notably, they also continued to see what they believed was a hostile coalition of capitalist powers in the west. Even though the Great Depression was deepening in Europe in the early 1930s, which made any major European conflict extremely unlikely, Stalin saw things differently. In accordance with Lenin's theory of imperialism, it was precisely when capitalism was going through a crisis that war became more likely. Economic crises would spur capitalist states onward to seek out new markets through conflict.[5] In this respect, war in the west was judged as a real possibility, and there was little movement in which countries were believed to be the most aggressive. Poland, Britain, Latvia, Lithuania, Romania, and Finland remained high on the list of potential belligerents. Stalin received intelligence along these lines at the end of 1931 and early 1932. In an intercepted letter from the Japanese military attaché in Moscow to the Japanese general staff from February 1932, for instance, it was claimed that Poland, Romania, and the Baltic states would join a war against the Soviet Union, with France playing a supporting role.[6] The hopes that the Japanese military attaché placed on a war against the Soviet Union were certainly misplaced or fabricated (and there are questions about how much weight Stalin attached to the opinion of a military attaché[7]), but this type of intelligence conformed precisely to Stalin's view of the world and the perceived threat of capitalist encirclement. Moreover, additional intelligence Stalin received from other sources throughout the year appeared to confirm the imminent threat of war.[8] A war on two fronts, however, was a prospect both the Red Army and Soviet military industry were woefully unprepared for, even though momentum had now swung behind rapid rearmament.

Now, however, Germany represented an additional threat to Soviet security. Since the Geneva peace conference in July 1932, where the German government had declared it would no longer be bound by the Treaty of Versailles, Soviet–German relations had quickly deteriorated. When Hitler came to power in January 1933, a formal end was brought to the collaboration between Germany and the Soviet Union that had held over the past decade.[9] From this point on, the new threat posed by Nazism gradually became the main focus of Soviet foreign policy. The possibility of a new war in Europe soon came to eclipse any other danger. This did not mean that old foes were entirely forgotten. The exiled White movement, for instance, was still in operation and as intent as ever on overthrowing Soviet power. Admittedly, as a result of its aging membership, ROVS had lost much of its dynamism. Its leader, General Kutepov, had been kidnapped by the OGPU in Paris in January 1930 and never made it to the Soviet Union alive.[10] His replacement, General Evgenii Miller, was less forthright and moved the organization away from terrorism, but he still represented a serious threat to Soviet interests. Miller favored infiltrating agents into Soviet territory, who, at a point of internal crisis or foreign intervention, would aid the overthrow of the regime. Subversive groups like the White youth intelligence organization, Belaia ideia (White idea), operated inside the Soviet Union in the early 1930s.[11] This continual subversive activity from the Whites was a further complication to what the Soviet leadership regarded as an already tense international situation. Indeed, the political police believed that White groups were actively working together with hostile foreign governments. In December 1934, for instance, they alerted the military leadership to the presence of Japanese–White guard groups that were apparently attempting to agitate among Red Army troops stationed on the eastern border to try to persuade them to turn against the regime.[12] It is difficult to know how accurate such reports were, but that its enemies were collaborating remained a potent concern for the regime.

One way that Stalin tried to avoid the slide into war in the 1930s was to normalize diplomatic relations with other major powers. Although Litvinov's offer of a nonaggression pact to Japan in 1931 after the invasion of Manchuria had been unsuccessful, relations with other countries showed marked improvement in these years. Prompted by a desire to lower international tensions, in 1933, for instance, Soviet leaders responded positively to President Franklin Roosevelt's efforts to reestablish contacts that had been severed after the Russian revolution. In November 1933, the United States officially recognized the Soviet Union for the first time. In September 1934, the Soviet Union joined the League of Nations and was soon trying to forge security pacts with other European countries. This attempt to establish a system of collective security—a policy normally associated with Litvinov—sought to use international alliances to counter the growing threat of fascism. This more open diplomacy did not necessarily mean that the Soviet leaders now fully trusted the motives of the capitalist states. It remained an article of faith that the Soviet Union was encircled by hostile powers. In this respect, the use of covert methods to gain advantage over a potential adversary could not be abandoned. At a time of approaching war, espionage was widespread among all countries.[13]

In a climate of looming war and escalating military power, enhancing knowledge about a potential enemy has obvious importance. Espionage can be an indispensible tool for gaining vital military secrets, despite its vulnerability to disinformation and falsehoods. Since the early years of the revolution, Soviet leaders had understood the value of espionage and had established a large intelligence network in Europe in the interwar period. Although their agents infiltrated foreign embassies and institutions, Soviet leaders were also acutely aware that the Soviet Union's own porous borders left it alarmingly open to foreign espionage. Stalin was kept closely informed about supposed foreign agents and spy rings, which were frequently discovered inside the Soviet Union in the 1930s.[14] Unsurprisingly, at a time when international tensions were rising, the Red Army was judged to be a prime target of foreign intelligence agents. Throughout the 1930s, alleged spies were frequently found in the military, some of whom held positions of responsibility.[15] Notably, heightened concerns about the security of military secrets can also be seen in the more severe punishments meted out to deserters, especially those charged with stealing classified documents. The late 1920s had already seen a steep rise in reported cases of soldiers deserting across the borders; this increased further in the early 1930s.[16] The severity of punishment was ratcheted up in 1934. Now the families of servicemen who fled abroad were at risk of receiving ten years' imprisonment. Even if they had no knowledge of the desertion, they were still liable for five years' imprisonment.[17]

Most of the spies exposed in the Red Army at this time were unlikely to have been genuine. The OGPU continued to use brutal interrogation methods and had a vested interest in obtaining confessions of counter-revolution and espionage. Moreover, responding to the pressure of an increasingly hostile international environment, they no doubt searched even more attentively for any hidden foreign agents. This almost guaranteed that a larger number would be found in the Red Army as the OGPU looked for anyone who fit the profile. Indeed, having non-Russian nationality or a connection abroad put a person in greater danger. An exaggerated espionage threat would remain firmly separated from reality; it only reinforced the impression among the Soviet leadership that a host of foreign governments were intent on subverting the Red Army, further fueling concerns about capitalist encirclement. In December 1931, for instance, Gamarnik wrote to Stalin about a group of Latvian spies who had managed to enter Soviet territory, apparently having gained access to positions in the Red Army through a member of Soviet military intelligence.[18] In September 1932, spies allegedly working for the Japanese and Chinese intelligence services were supposedly discovered in the Special Red Banner Far Eastern Army. Indeed, after the invasion of Manchuria, Soviet intelligence services increasingly reported on the activity of Japanese spies, targeted in particular at Red Army units in the Far East region.[19] In March 1933, Finnish spies were found in the Leningrad Military District, also apparently within Soviet military intelligence.[20] Foreign agents supposedly working for Turkey were also discovered in the army.[21] Yet out of all the foreign intelligence services, the Polish threat was regarded as particularly grave.[22] Even though the Soviet Union signed a nonaggression treaty with Poland in July 1932, significant mistrust lingered. Just months later, in November 1932, an OGPU circular reported an increase in Polish espionage activity and noted that some agents had established connections with the Red Army.[23]

The overall espionage threat to the Red Army was analyzed in a report compiled by the OGPU in 1933. Its findings must have been concerning for the Soviet leadership. The authors of the report argued that the more frequent discovery of foreign agents in the military in the early 1930s was a sign that war was approaching. The ground was being prepared for an invasion, and according to the report, the Red Army was now, more than it had been at any other time, the target of counterrevolution.[24] The authors detailed that during 1932, 112 Red Army men had been arrested by the OGPU for espionage out of a total of 8,599 spy cases. In 1933, the number of military cases had doubled to 224 from an increased grand total of 23,190 spy cases.[25] Thus, aside from the doubling in military cases, the total number of arrests for espionage had risen dramatically from 1932 to 1933. Arrests for Polish espionage alone had seen a threefold increase. Moreover, the authors of the report gave the impression that the Soviet Union was under a sustained assault from foreign agents on all sides, with Japanese agents collaborating with White groups in the Far East and German spies coming from in the west, targeting both the Red Army and the defense industry.[26]

The OGPU's 1933 analysis also noted that the majority of foreign agents in the military had been discovered in units stationed in the border regions of the Ukrainian, Belorussian, and Leningrad military districts, as well as the Far East region.[27] These regions were on the periphery, and their borders were porous. Here the OGPU would not struggle to find foreign agents. Back in the 1920s, Dzerzhinskii had concentrated OGPU attention in these areas.[28] Several very large spy rings were exposed in the border regions in the early 1930s. In 1933, for instance, an extensive spy ring of 1,640 people was discovered by the OGPU on the border strip between Leningrad and Karelia, apparently organized by Finnish and Estonian intelligence.[29] The great majority of those arrested for espionage by the OGPU were, in all likelihood, not genuine spies. A larger number of foreign nationals lived in the border regions compared to the interior, which provided a pool of innocent people who could be labeled foreign agents and swept up for arrest. However, all of this meant that Red Army troops stationed in the border regions were perceived to be at greater risk of infiltration, and the OGPU wanted more robust defenses. In the Belorussian Military District, for example, they called for more attention to be paid to security weaknesses and stronger countermeasures applied, having calculated that three quarters of the troops were stationed close to the border, leaving them open to infiltration by foreign agents.[30]

The most likely explanation behind the sharp spike in espionage cases reported in 1933 was the worsening international situation. Hitler's rise to power in early 1933, along with Japanese aggression after the invasion of Manchuria and existing suspicions about the true intentions of old enemies such as Poland, certainly heightened the perceived subversive threat. Throughout 1933, the OGPU began to search more attentively for infiltrated agents and regularly reported to Stalin with their findings. For example, Iagoda sent Stalin a long report in March detailing the number of foreign agents, spies, and diversionaries who had been discovered in the western regions, which included a network of Finnish agents in the Leningrad Military District.[31] The OGPU also carried out large-scale sweep operations, often in the western border regions, against supposedly suspicious national groups. By the mid-1930s, German nationals in particular were seen with much more suspicion as potential agents of fascism.[32] This had an immediate effect in the Red Army, and soldiers of German nationality were now kept under closer observation.[33] Indeed, with a stronger threat emanating from Europe, western military districts could not escape increased OGPU scrutiny. In an OGPU operation carried out in March 1933, for instance, eight diversionary groups were apparently discovered in the Leningrad Military District.[34] The OGPU was now paying more attention to "unreliable" national groups in the early 1930s, which best explains why reported espionage cases increased by such a degree over the course of 1932 to 1933.

Yet even though larger numbers of espionage cases were being reported by the OGPU, the number of arrests in the Red Army was not yet significant in comparison to the grand total. The OGPU reported just 224 spy cases in the military, from a grand total of more than 23,000 cases in 1933. The number of military cases had doubled in one year but still remained at a relatively low level. Yet the actual scale of the espionage problem in the Red Army may not have been the main cause for alarm for the military leadership. That both PUR and the officer corps proved to be incapable of independently rooting out enemies posed a more difficult challenge.

Problems of Vigilance

Voroshilov was clearly troubled with how easily foreign agents were managing to infiltrate the Red Army and to occupy positions of responsibility. On 2 January 1932, he published an order through the Revolutionary Military Council on this very question. This concerned the case of a former tank commander in the Belorussian Military District, Mikhail Bozhenko, who had recently been awarded a promotion. However, according to Voroshilov, as it turned out, Bozhenko had actually been a Polish agent all along and had later fled to Poland. Voroshilov was clearly agitated that Bozhenko was able to slip through the net, and he blamed the district staff for not running adequate background checks, even though Bozhenko had accumulated an impressive list of "antimoral" offenses before his promotion. He had already been charged with having "demobilization" and "counterrevolutionary Trotskyist" moods and had actually been slated for discharge from the army the year before; this had even been ordered by the Revolutionary Military Council.[35] It is hardly surprising that all of this was highly displeasing for Voroshilov, who accused the district staff of ignoring the calls from the previous year for greater scrutiny of officers serving in important units. He also criticized what he saw as negligent attitudes toward the promotion of officers. Voroshilov went on to stress the need for unremitting Bolshevik vigilance and closer scrutiny of officers by the officer corps, PUR, and the Communist Youth League, the Komsomol. In particular, he stressed the importance of officer selection in the border regions, especially within the air force, artillery units, and motorized and mechanized units, which were judged to be more sensitive in terms of internal security.[36]

Despite Voroshilov's complaints about insufficient background checks and the promotion of unreliable officers, standards were not improved. On 2 April 1933, his order from 1932 was republished.[37] This was clearly a reminder. Then, a year later, in August 1934, a Politburo commission issued an order concerning the promotion of officers and referenced the Bozhenko case. This Politburo commission called for several improvements in the promotion of officers, including running more detailed background checks, focusing in particular on nationality and family connections; it also called attention to what it saw as inattentiveness in the study of the officer corps in general. Moreover, the commission reaffirmed a recent order from the Revolutionary Military Council mandating that officers serving in the border districts be checked within a three-month period and that less politically reliable officers be transferred to interior districts—another clear indication of the wider perceived espionage threat.[38] The Politburo evidently felt the need to intervene to try and raise the standard of self-policing in the Red Army. In recognition of concerns that unreliable officers were potentially serving in sensitive positions, the Politburo commission ordered that commanders in air, tank, and artillery divisions should be drawn from members of the party or from the Komsomol only.[39] Thus, in short, the Bozhenko case was used as an example three times between 1932 and 1934 to highlight the poor background checks of commanders in the Red Army. The original case was not a stand-alone issue, and the problems it raised were deemed serious enough to attract Stalin's attention.

Of course, that more attention was being focused on the reliability of some individuals in the officer corps does not mean that it was overrun with enemies and foreign intelligence agents. Even if Bozhenko had been a genuine Polish agent (he may have been yet another deserter to Poland), the majority of spies, counterrevolutionaries, or anti-Soviet elements discovered in commanding positions would have been entirely innocent of any crime. Moreover, not only did the OGPU have a vested interest in finding "enemies" in the Red Army, but it also had clear advantages over any military body when it actually came to doing so. The OGPU used forced confessions and blackmail to their advantage; the army's own efforts to keep its house in order could only pale in comparison.

However, there was probably more at work here than the OGPU simply making baseless arrests in the officer corps, which Voroshilov would struggle to do something about. Notably, regardless of whether or not he was a spy, Bozhenko had faced little serious scrutiny from his superiors or colleagues. He had black marks on his record before his promotion, and he had actually been up for discharge. Why, then, was he given a promotion? What will be argued below is that there was a wider culture of avoidance and looking the other way in the Red Army when it came to unmasking enemies identified as particularly dangerous. There is evidence that some officers were reluctant to do too much digging into another person's background, which only hindered the regime's periodic calls for enemies to be rooted out. Indeed, in the early 1930s, in the aftermath of Operation Vesna—which involved mass arrests often made on the basis of incrimination by association—it is understandable that there may have been a level of wariness (and even active resistance) toward being overly vigilant. If officers were constantly on the lookout for any potential foreign agents and counterrevolutionaries serving beside them, they may well be rewarded, but such vigilance also risked drawing unwanted attention. Questions might be asked about why such dangerous people had not been noticed before, especially when it had long been abundantly clear that the Red Army was a target of dangerous subversives. Officers thus may have thought it easier to avoid digging too deeply into each other's backgrounds in the search for dangerous enemies. Because the danger of incrimination by association was real, calling attention to a colleague's or subordinate's suspicious background could carry risks equal to or greater than simply looking the other way. In the years leading up to the Great Terror, before intense pressure was placed on Soviet citizens to denounce each other to find hidden "enemies of the people," ignoring Voroshilov's orders about increasing vigilance may have been seen by some officers as the safer option for the time being.[40]

Whatever the reason behind the poor internal scrutiny of officers, it is without question that Voroshilov's calls for more vigilance would change very little. By demanding greater vigilance, he was not addressing the root cause of why it was so poor and why adequate background checks were not being performed. Simply calling for more vigilance did not engage with the problem seriously and would ultimately prove ineffective. Rather, what it does suggest is that Voroshilov had little idea about how to improve the verification of officers and military self-policing. He must have realized that it was better to be seen doing something rather than nothing. Publicly calling for more vigilance served this purpose even if it had little real impact. The problems with army self-policing had been identified at the same time that the perceived threat from foreign intelligence services was on the rise. In 1934 the Politburo commission cited above specifically highlighted that nationality and the family connections of officers needed to be looked at more closely. In this sense, it is entirely possible that Voroshilov was starting to feel some pressure from above. He would certainly be expected to make sure that the military was insulated from what was understood to be a growing espionage threat. The reference to the Bozhenko affair by the Politburo commission suggested that Stalin wanted more done to improve the security of the officer corps. Yet Voroshilov would never be able to deliver. The continued failures in military self-policing would only strengthen the more pessimistic views about the reliability of the Red Army, most importantly held by the OGPU. Voroshilov's calls for greater vigilance, although temporarily covering his own back, would do nothing to alter this.

Seemingly without a means to resolve the failures in its self-policing, as well as call for more vigilance, Voroshilov continued to publicly downplay any weaknesses in the political reliability of the Red Army. At a joint plenum of the Central Committee and the Central Control Commission in January 1933, he took the opportunity to praise the apparent increasing reliability of the Red Army as a whole. According to Voroshilov, the number of officers with worker backgrounds had now reached 40 percent, and 61 percent of officers were party members.[41] Voroshilov made similar comments during another speech in March, proclaiming that the number of peasants in the army had now dropped to 47 percent during 1933. He pointed out that all the main commanders of the military districts were now party members. Voroshilov's tendency to inflate the achievements of the Red Army in public was made particularly clear when he remarked, "Without any kind of exaggeration, it is possible to say that in the business of the preparation of Bolshevik military cadres, we have achieved enormous, decisive results."[42] Voroshilov made a great deal of the military's good performance in the membership purge (*chistka*) in the Communist Party carried out in 1933. Membership purges were regularly undertaken in the party and were used to weed out anyone not living up to the proper standards of party life, be it for reasons of careerism or criminality, or simply being passive and disengaged.[43] Officers and soldiers were expelled from the party during the 1933 *chistka* for a variety of reasons, including hiding a past as a social alien (or keeping secret a connection to one); having an anti-Soviet mood; or for being passive or performing inadequate party political work.[44] The 1933 *chistka* expelled 4.3 percent of the army party organizations, which was much lower than the 17 percent excluded from ten other civilian party organizations.[45] In his speech to the Seventeenth Party Congress on 10 January 1934, Voroshilov called attention to this achievement, describing a "significant" divergence in the *chistka* results between the army and the civilian party organizations.[46] Moreover, the 1933 *chistka* had also excluded slightly fewer army party members than the previous *chistka* in 1929, which had seen just over 5 percent of people excluded from army party organizations.[47] Soviet statistics are of course notoriously unreliable, but what matters in this case is not the validity of the figures but rather Voroshilov's possible motive in deploying them in public. The results from the 1933 *chistka* were undoubtedly welcome news for Voroshilov, and he may have been using them as tangible proof (which presumably he hoped could not be ignored) that the Red Army was more reliable than other civilian organizations. Voroshilov was using these statistics to present an image of the Red Army as growing in internal cohesion and political reliability. However, while on paper these statistics painted a positive picture of the

Red Army, they also masked a range of other underlying problems with its political reliability that existed in addition to those already identified in the poor verification of officers.

Even after thousands of soldiers had been discharged from the lower ranks during the collectivization crisis of 1928–1932, the composition of the Red Army remained far from ideal. Large numbers of soldiers labeled as socially alien and socially harmful continued to be discharged from the ranks from 1933. In that year alone, 22,308 servicemen, including kulaks, former Whites, and other anti-Soviet elements, were discharged from the Red Army. Similarly, 1933 saw a recorded increase in the number of kulak groups apparently operating in the army alongside other counterrevolutionaries discovered by the OGPU (some of whom were charged with highly serious crimes, including arranging terrorist acts and supposedly planning to murder Stalin).[48] Aviation in particular was singled out as a vulnerable target. The OGPU believed that sabotage explained a recent increase in aircraft accidents.[49] Straightforward problems with inefficiency and poorly trained pilots were thus being framed as evidence of wrecking. In addition, alongside the continuing activity of various enemies inside the Red Army, the OGPU recorded a growth in negative behaviors among ordinary soldiers in the last quarter of 1932 and into early 1933, including alcoholism and what was labeled as general dissatisfaction.[50]

In all, it seems that there was still much to do to improve the internal composition of the Red Army. That so many discharges were being sanctioned into 1933, after collectivization had eased, suggests that the regime understood this and saw the presence of so many supposedly unreliable elements in the ranks as posing an internal security threat. The OGPU argued precisely this point in 1933, noting that the large numbers of unreliable peasant soldiers still serving in the army gave foreign agents greater opportunity to organize espionage networks.[51] It is possible that the Soviet leaders were also concerned about another flare-up of mass discontent in the rank and file and a potential repeat of the hostile reaction to collectivization. This reaction had made it clear that the lower ranks could not be relied upon when placed under social strain, and a new surge in discontent risked undermining military stability at the very time that the international situation was further deteriorating. The OGPU had continued to detect anticommunist sentiments and pro-peasant attitudes in the Red Army into the mid-1930s.[52] Moreover, a severe famine in Ukraine during 1932–1933, the most serious consequence of the rush to collectivize agriculture, had already sparked a new outpouring of discontent in the rank and file in the region.[53] The regime surely wanted to avoid risking any further revolts. Consequently, it is likely that the perceived subversive threat to the Red Army from foreign agents coincided with ongoing concerns about the reliability of the rank and file in general terms. There was a pressing need to improve the internal reliability of the Red Army; large numbers of discharges and arrests would thus soon follow.

Further evidence that the Soviet leaders were increasingly concerned about the reliability of the Red Army in the first half of the 1930s can also be seen in the strengthening of the OGPU special departments. From an all-time low in 1930, their numbers soon tripled, reaching 3,769 operatives by January 1935.[54] This additional manpower not only suggests that Stalin was paying more attention to unreliable servicemen in the Red Army, but also indicates that he had less confidence in the army leadership's ability to do anything about this independently. Despite Voroshilov's public assurances that the Red Army was more reliable than it had ever been, his protests were almost certainly undermined by the OGPU's recent success in uncovering the supposed military specialist plot from Operation Vesna. From Stalin's point of view, the OGPU had delivered results. Because PUR also had seemingly failed to ensure the reliability of the soldiers during the collectivization drive, from now on, Stalin may well have started to side more closely with the OGPU when it came to questions of army security. More resources were thus given to the special departments, and Voroshilov no doubt found himself on the back foot. Even though the Politburo ordered in July 1931 that no specialists, including military specialists, could be arrested without the permission of the corresponding people's commissar—recognition of the fact that the state antiwrecking campaign had become counterproductive—Voroshilov would still feel the pressure.[55] With additional resources, a greater number of criminal military cases brought by the OGPU would only further solidify the perception that the Red Army was open to subversion and incapable of dealing with this by itself.[56] It is hardly likely that the OGPU leaders had accepted Voroshilov's public defenses of the reliability of the Red Army, and their recent achievement in Operation Vesna may have emboldened them toward trying to undermine the military leadership. Indeed, although Voroshilov continued to push an image of a united and loyal Red Army, this view became increasingly untenable over the next few years.

In the face of growing OGPU attention on the Red Army, its leadership made efforts to deal with officers and soldiers deemed unreliable in the first half of the 1930s. Purge commissions, chaired at military district and Revolutionary Military Council level, were regularly convened to approve discharges or transfers.[57] The reasons for discharge were wide-ranging. Many people fell under the category of being a social alien, including secret former Whites and the sons of kulaks or priests. Consistent with the perceived espionage threat, many soldiers were discharged for having undeclared relations abroad. Servicemen were also discharged for more serious crimes, including membership in supposed counterrevolutionary groups or the more common crime of possessing an anti-Soviet mood. A great many discharges, however, were approved for more mundane reasons, such as alcoholism, poor discipline, weak political work, or simply being in poor health.

Yet in a similar way that problems were evident in the verification of officers (as in the Bozhenko case), the process of discharging officers and soldiers from the Red Army was not without errors. On 4 July 1933, for instance, Voroshilov sent a circular to all military districts concerning the numerous complaints that he and the main administration of the Red Army had received from officers who had been incorrectly discharged. Voroshilov argued that there was a lack of sufficient attention being paid to the important task of discharging officers. Using similar language to the Bozhenko case, he argued that a "formalistic" approach to discharges was not a minor problem and that he could provide many examples.[58] In another order from April 1934, Voroshilov again raised the issue of incorrect discharges, describing the mistaken demobilization of a Red Army man and publicizing the reprimand given to the officer responsible.[59]

The problem of incorrect discharges was evidently widespread enough to warrant Voroshilov's personal intervention, and when seen alongside the problems surrounding the promotion of reliable officers, there are signs that the whole system of verification of army personnel was breaking down. However, Voroshilov would face an uphill struggle in trying to fix these problems. For example, even though he had demanded action on incorrect discharges, a report from the main administration of the Red Army from April 1934 noted that in the Leningrad Military District, the necessary materials required to discharge army men were not being studied correctly; it suggested that no one was even bothering to read the relevant paperwork.[60] Again, there is probably more at work here than some officers simply being negligent in properly checking the grounds for discharge. It is possible that some were making conspicuous demonstrations of their vigilance in sanctioning discharges for minor crimes. As we have seen, the danger of incrimination by association was very real in the 1930s. If a dangerous enemy (such as a spy or counterrevolutionary) was discovered in a unit, the commanding officer was likely to attract scrutiny in turn. Therefore, another strategy officers could use to avoid properly responding to Voroshilov's call to raise vigilance to combat hidden enemies was in sanctioning discharges for minor crimes on tenuous grounds in an attempt to cultivate a reputation for vigilance. This avoided the unforeseen and potentially dangerous consequences attached to drawing attention to supposed counterrevolutionaries or spies while appearing attentive to the internal security of a unit. Indeed, the justification given for the incorrect discharge highlighted by Voroshilov in his order of April 1934 was for being the son of a kulak that turned out to be baseless. In this respect, as in the Bozhenko case, there are further suggestions that some officers were knowingly avoiding carrying out the search for dangerous enemies in their commands as intended by Voroshilov. Cultivating a reputation for vigilance through making unnecessary discharges was little more than looking the other way. It was also a way to deflect attention and scrutiny. The next two years saw further criticism from the army leadership along similar lines; specifically, some officers were sanctioning large numbers of discharges for minor crimes and giving out reprimands en masse while more dangerous enemies were going undetected.

It is likely that Voroshilov appreciated the deeper reality behind what he described as formalism in military self-policing. He must have realized that he was not just dealing with negligent discharges and poor standards of verification of officers, and that these were only the symptoms of a more serious underlying disease in the Red Army. The attitude and approach of certain officers in searching out internal enemies needed to be confronted, especially in the years of growing international crisis. By simply calling for more vigilance and attacking formalism, Voroshilov was not tackling this problem head-on. It is entirely possible that this was not his real intention. His criticisms may have been primarily designed as his own demonstration of vigilance. As head of the Red Army, Voroshilov needed to be seen as addressing any security weaknesses. Even if calling for vigilance would actually do very little, it at least provided him with some cover by indicating that he had been trying to make improvements to the Red Army's security and that he understood the seriousness of the situation.

The consequences of poor vigilance in the Red Army were soon revealed again on 5 August 1934, when A. S. Nakhaev, the chief of staff of the artillery battalion of Osoaviakhim (Society to Assist Defense, Aviation, and Chemical Development), attempted to lead a revolt from the Moscow barracks after convincing 200 infantrymen to join him. Angry at living under an undemocratic regime, Nakhaev complained to the assembled soldiers that it was wrong that the party elite controlled industry and agriculture rather than the workers and peasants. He called on them to bring down the government. Unfortunately for Nakhaev, however, few soldiers were inspired enough by his speech to run the risk of being arrested. The attempted revolt was easily overcome, and Nakhaev was taken in by the political police.

After Nakhaev had been arrested and questioned, Stalin's deputy, Lazar Kaganovich, wrote to Stalin about the incident and informed him that the initial investigation had given the impression that Nakhaev had psychological problems. Kaganovich added that Voroshilov agreed with this assessment and had described Nakhaev as a psychopath. Moreover, Kaganovich placed blame on Osoaviakhim in particular for having "messed up here."[61] In this respect, in the first instance, there was nothing particularly unusual about the case. Nakhaev had been identified as unstable, and Osoaviakhim should have better vetted its personnel. However, in his reply, Stalin presented a very different view of events. On 8 August, he wrote back to Kaganovich:

> The Nakhaev affair is about a piece of scum. He is, of course (of course!), not alone. He must be put up against the wall and forced to talk—to tell the whole truth and then severely punished. He must be a Polish–German (or Japanese) agent . . . He called on armed people to act against the government—so he must be destroyed.[62]

The difference between Kaganovich's and Stalin's explanations is striking. Stalin saw the influence of a foreign hand even though he was far removed from the case (he was in Sochi at the time). Stalin was acting entirely on his assumptions—on his revolutionary instincts—and he was certain that Nakhaev was a foreign agent. It is possible that Stalin's conviction that Nakhaev was working for a foreign power was connected to the recent rise in espionage cases seen the year before. Stalin may well have been using the case as a signal that he believed espionage was a problem in need of stronger counteractions. The regime had already started paying more attention to national minorities whose loyalty it believed was not guaranteed. The Politburo instructed Soviet intelligence agents, for instance, to pay as much attention to nationality as to social class in 1934. Between 1935 and 1936, Stalin sanctioned the deportation to the peripheries of the Soviet Union of hundreds of thousands of people from national minority groups deemed unreliable, including Poles, Finns, Koreans, Germans, and Ukrainians.[63] The Nakhaev case was in this sense an early indication of things to come. Of course, Kaganovich had little choice but to agree with Stalin's assessment of Nakhaev. He quickly fell into line, remarking in another letter that Stalin's view was "absolutely right."[64] Stalin's line was subsequently reflected in the investigation. Nakhaev was eventually connected to a former tsarist general Bykov, who worked at the institute of physical fitness and who was later arrested as a supposed Estonian intelligence agent. Under interrogation, Nakhaev claimed that Bykov had put him up to the revolt. These new revelations were sent to Stalin.[65]

Even though the Nakhaev case was primarily an Osoaviakhim matter, it had consequences for the Red Army. Because a revolt had been attempted at the Moscow barracks, Stalin ordered that Avgust Kork, the commander of the Moscow Military District, be called in and given a "tongue-lashing for the heedless and sloppy conduct in the barracks."[66] Kork was later transferred, and Stalin instructed Voroshilov to address the security problems at the Moscow barracks. Stalin evidently did not believe that Kork was up to the job of securing the troops in the Moscow Military District against dangerous subversives like Nakhaev. The political police also might have made note of Kork's Estonian nationality. It is possible there was an imagined connection between Kork and the supposed counterrevolutionary plot. However, the matter did not end with Kork alone. In a telegram to Kaganovich from the end of the month, Stalin wrote that Kork was not the only problem, that a sense of "complacency and gullibility" could be seen in all districts, and that PUR and the OGPU special departments needed to do more.[67] Stalin was already aware of the problems in military self-policing, and the Nakhaev case was another demonstration that insufficient standards of vigilance were being maintained by the officer corps. It also added to the stream of reports Stalin had received over the course of 1934 that detailed the activity of supposed enemies on Soviet soil with foreign connections. Some reports noted that spies were still managing to gain senior military positions.[68] For instance, a few months before the Nakhaev case, in February 1934, Iagoda sent Stalin an intercepted telegram from the Japanese military attaché in Moscow, detailing that the latter had been meeting with the head of foreign relations for the Red Army, B. B. Smagin. Iagoda interpreted this as possible espionage and requested that Smagin be removed from his position for passing secrets to the Japanese.[69] This was precisely the type of security risk that Stalin would expect Voroshilov to take measures to insulate the Red Army against; however, he was failing to do so. Nakhaev's attempted revolt at the Moscow barracks in August 1934 was another demonstration that not all was well in the Red Army.

The OGPU, importantly, also took a lesson from the Nakhaev case. One month later, they produced a report that noted that with war approaching, the special departments needed to work especially hard to combat enemies inside the Red Army. The report highlighted a range of counterrevolutionary cases that had been recently discovered in the ranks, which included Nakhaev's failed revolt.[70] In this respect, the OGPU fully intended to step up the pressure on the army in 1934, having seen a serious risk to its security. A final point on the Nakhaev case is that he had been a supporter of Trotsky's political platform in the late 1920s, which at that time had resulted in his expulsion from the party and discharge from the army.[71] Nakhaev's past political affiliations were not prominent in the charges against him in 1934, and Stalin's gut reaction that he was a foreign agent overrode anything else. However, just months later, in December 1934, after the assassination of Leningrad party boss Sergei Kirov, the former opposition quickly reemerged as a recognized subversive threat.

Growing Political Pressures

In the early 1930s, the atmosphere inside the Communist Party became much tenser as Stalin assumed greater power and control. By the late 1920s, Stalin had managed to consolidate his position as leader of the party after the defeats of the opposition and Right Deviation. Now he began to clamp down on any expression of resistance to the radical policies of collectivization and industrialization. There were still some dissenting voices in upper party circles to both policies, even though the opposition platforms of the 1920s had been thoroughly destroyed and the majority of their members had recanted. In mid-1932, for instance, the so-called Riutin platform (named after Moscow district secretary Martemyan Riutin) circulated a 194-page document among the party that was damning of Stalin's leadership and policies. Labeling Stalin an "unscrupulous political intriguer," it called for the destruction of the dictatorship. Stalin took this challenge very seriously. Even though the Riutin platform lacked the organization of previous oppositionist groups, it still posed a risk of attracting supporters from among the party rank and file. Soon enough, the Riutin group was rounded up and imprisoned.[72]

The Riutin platform was not the only challenge to Stalin's dominance in the early 1930s, and, notably, in other cases there were some reverberations for the Red Army. Indeed, the continuing resistance in some party circles toward industrialization and collectivization could at times converge with the rumors about a Russian Bonaparte that had long surrounded the high command. In December 1930, for instance, two senior party figures, Sergei Syrtsov, chairman of the Soviet government, and Vissarion Lominadze, first secretary of the Trans-Caucasian Regional Committee, came under fire for criticizing collectivization. Syrtsov was a supporter of Alexei Rykov, a leading member of the now-defeated Right Deviation, and he likewise believed that Stalin's economic policies were damaging to the state. Syrtsov and his supporters were accused of conspiring with a group of party members around Lominadze and were said to have planned to remove Stalin from the party leadership. All were subsequently expelled from the Central Committee after being accused of working against the party.[73] As part of the investigation into the group carried out by the OGPU, Uborevich's name was mentioned. Specifically, one piece of evidence used against Syrtsov was a denunciation given by a secretary of a party cell at the Institute of Red Professors, B. G. Reznikov. Among other damning statements, this denunciation detailed that Syrtsov had claimed that Voroshilov had been moved from the Red Army and might take Rykov's position as the head of the Soviet government. Uborevich apparently had taken over the leadership of the Red Army. However, according to Reznikov, Syrtsov was against this decision and described Uborevich in unflattering terms as "unprincipled," "devilishly proud," and a "clear Thermidorian."[74]

Stalin undoubtedly wanted Rykov ousted from the head of the Soviet government. He had been a member of the Right Deviation and was a potential troublemaker. In May 1931, Rykov was demoted anyway. It is also entirely possible that Stalin considered placing his old comrade, Voroshilov, at the head of the government. Voroshilov was clearly unsuited to a military career, and perhaps Stalin had thought about moving him. However, Voroshilov remained in place at the head of the Red Army. The idea was immediately abandoned or Syrtsov had been mistaken; it is unlikely he was privy to all important decision making behind the scenes in the Politburo.[75] Reznikov's denunciation also may well have been inaccurate. Nonetheless, any political intrigues aside, Syrtsov's negative description of Uborevich as told by Reznikov is reminiscent of the rumors about a Russian Bonaparte so common to the 1920s. In addition, a similar declaration was given by another party member, I. S. Nusinov, as part of the investigation that described a small gathering that had supposedly included Syrtsov, and during which the mood of the Red Army was said to have been discussed. According to Nusinov, Syrtsov mentioned Uborevich and described him as being talented but narcissistic. Nusinov acknowledged that he did not know Uborevich particularly well, but he did describe a separate incident where Uborevich had been proposed for candidacy to the Central Committee. Apparently his suitability had been heatedly discussed, with some members very opposed to his election.[76] Nusinov claimed that during the deliberations, he was passed a note describing Uborevich as a capable person but with little experience in party affairs, and as someone who regarded himself as a Napoleon.[77]

The accuracy of Reznikov's or Nusinov's accounts is difficult to know for certain; the whole affair is full of intrigue. It seems to have been manufactured by Stalin to punish his party critics. However, even if both Reznikov's and Nusinov's accounts were manifestly false, it is still noteworthy that Uborevich's name appeared during the investigation into the Syrtsov and Lominadze case, which on the surface had nothing to do with the Red Army. Uborevich's name seems to have had associations with disloyalty that he was unable to shake off. Some party members may well have worried into the early 1930s that he had hidden ambitions to become a military dictator. In this sense, the disinformation campaigns carried out by the OGPU against the Whites that painted the high command as full of traitors had seemingly left their mark on its image. Moreover, as Oleg Khlevniuk notes, in November 1930, in the immediate aftermath of the Syrtsov–Lominadze Affair, the Politburo had the Telegraph Agency of the Soviet Union respond to speculation in the foreign press that there had been an associated "military plot" and that this was entirely false.[78]

The year 1932 saw a similar case to the Syrtsov–Lominadze Affair, and this time Tukhachevskii's name surfaced in the investigation. During November and December, N. B. Eismont, the people's commissar of supply for the Russian Republic; V. N. Tolmachev, a department head in transport; E. P. Ashukina, chief of the personal planning department in the Commissariat for Agriculture; and another party member, V. F. Poponin, were arrested for allegedly having counterrevolutionary conversations. The group was said to have gathered at Eismont's apartment, drunk heavily, and spoken critically of Stalin. There had apparently been some talk of his possible removal.[79] The group was portrayed as a nascent faction, but what raised the seriousness of the case was the involvement of A. P. Smirnov, a senior party figure and chairman of the public housing commission of the Central Executive Committee. Smirnov was subsequently questioned about the antiparty discussions.[80] During the investigation into the group, Tukhachevskii's name surfaced in a similar manner as Uborevich's had two years earlier. In Poponin's account of the group's discussion, for instance, he remarked that Eismont had asked about Tukhachevskii's mood. Apparently this had been during a conversation between Poponin and Eismont concerning where the regime could find support if war and peasant rebellion were to break out.[81] Asking about Tukhachevskii's mood in this way suggested that Eismont believed his loyalty was not guaranteed.

As in the Syrtsov–Lominadze case, it is difficult to authenticate these remarks. Even if Poponin's testimony was entirely false, it remains interesting why Tukhachevskii's name appeared during the investigation. It would seem that, like Uborevich, Tukhachevskii's name was loaded with associations of potential disloyalty, which might surface when accusations were flying regarding counterrevolution activity. There is also the possibility that the OGPU had purposely steered both investigations toward the military elite. We saw above how Tukhachevskii had been incriminated in Operation Vesna, and even though Stalin declared him to be innocent, it is unlikely that the OGPU completely abandoned their suspicions about him. That Tukhachevskii's name appeared in the Eismont–Tolmachev case in 1932 may have stemmed from the doubts that the OGPU investigators continued to have about him. Notably, Tukhachevskii was still attracting rumors about his disloyalty in the 1930s. At the same time that the Eismont–Tolmachev investigation was underway in late 1932, the OGPU received further incriminating rumors about Tukhachevskii from abroad. Reports from Berlin, for instance, suggested that he was the leader of a counterrevolutionary plot.[82] Even though Iagoda, the deputy head of the OGPU, brushed these off as disinformation, this was another reminder that Tukhachevskii was subject to not insignificant speculation about his loyalty. Further reports from Berlin about alleged disloyalty in the high command and preparations for a military coup were received by the OGPU in December 1932, in June 1933, and in March, April, and December 1934.[83] These reports may well have produced some nagging doubts about the loyalty of the military elite among some OGPU investigators, who may have decided to take a closer look, even if Iagoda appears unconvinced at this point. What remains likely at the very least is that any new rumors about plots and conspiracies in the high command were added to the files on senior officers held by the political police.

Despite being named in the Syrtsov–Lominadze and Eismont–Tolmachev cases, neither Tukhachevskii nor Uborevich suffered any obvious consequences. It is possible that they fell under the OGPU's gaze to a greater extent, but both kept their positions, and Tukhachevskii's career in particular maintained an impressive upward trajectory. In February 1933 he received the Order of Lenin, and in 1934 he became a candidate member of the Central Committee.[84] Tukhachevskii and Uborevich had only been indirectly mentioned in the cases of party factionalism in the early 1930s, and this was evidently not enough to cause either any real trouble. Moreover, both were talented and experienced military leaders, and the Red Army would be worse off without them. Stalin no doubt understood this. He would have been kept closely informed about the course of the investigations into the Syrtsov–Lominadze and Eismont–Tolmachev cases, and he would have known that Tukhachevskii's and Uborevich's names had surfaced. However, Stalin would gain nothing from having either detained on the basis of indirect evidence about their characters. Both were important figures in the Red Army's efforts to modernize, and it made little sense to have them arrested or to put obstacles in their way for no good reason. Yet Stalin would not forget that Tukhachevskii's and Uborevich's names had surfaced in the investigations. The Soviet leadership judged the party factionalism of the early 1930s as posing a serious threat. Like the political police, Stalin may have chosen to keep a closer eye on Tukhachevskii and Uborevich in the future.

Besides the two cases of factionalism in the party that raised questions about loyalties in the high command, Trotskyism remained a simmering issue in the Red Army. Even though Stalin had successfully crushed the opposition a few years earlier and any Trotskyists serving in the military had been forced to recant their incorrect political views, crimes such as Trotskyist agitation and membership of Trotskyist groups remained reasons for arrest and discharge from the ranks.[85] The OGPU, however, did not just target open manifestations of Trotskyism; they also initiated surveillance over several former Trotskyist officers who had recanted their political errors and returned to the fold, but whom the OGPU believed had been insincere. In August 1933, for instance, they created a file on former Trotskyist Vitalii Primakov, who had been sent abroad as a military attaché in 1927 as punishment for his support of Trotsky but who recanted his opposition the following year. Primakov's military career does not appear to have suffered after this admission of his political errors. We have already seen that he was given an intelligence assignment in Japan in the late 1920s, and he became the deputy commander of the North Caucasus Military District in 1933 and trained in Germany between December 1932 to June 1933, presumably having been trusted enough to spend time in an increasingly hostile country.[86] However, an OGPU report on Primakov from 1933 registered serious doubts about his reliability. The report stated that "in June 1928 he [Primakov] gave a declaration about breaking with the opposition of a double-dealing (*dvurushnicheskogo*) character, having actually maintained his Trotskyist positions."[87] The OGPU called for closer observation of Primakov in view of exposing his hidden Trotskyist activity.[88] The OGPU did not have only Primakov in their sights. Former Trotskyist brigade commander M. O. Ziuk had already informed them that another former Trotskyist, Efim Dreitser, had contacted him and proposed resuming their underground activity.[89]

The truth in Ziuk's claim about Dreitser or whether Primakov was in fact a so-called double-dealer is difficult to gauge. The OGPU had shown undue alarmism about the Trotskyist threat in the 1920s, and it is unsurprising that they maintained a level of suspicion about Trotskyists who recanted their past political views. On the other hand, it is likely that a certain number of former Trotskyists did not sincerely admit their political errors when required to do this in the late 1920s, instead accepting the need to recant only for the sake of keeping their positions and party memberships. Privately, some would not have shed any of their dissatisfaction with the Stalinist regime. Some continued to meet together in secret, perhaps to talk politics, vent their criticisms of the leadership, or even conspire against the state. A secret Trotskyist network did continue to operate in the Soviet Union after Trotsky's exile in the late 1920s, largely coordinated by his son, Lev Sedov. A new secret underground opposition movement was even in the early stages of formation in the early 1930s, but it lost much of its momentum when several key members were arrested by the OGPU.[90] It seems that Primakov was involved in secret meetings with other former Trotskyists on some level around this time. When he was later placed under arrest in 1936, he sent a letter to Stalin denying being a Trotskyist or a counterrevolutionary, but he admitted to having met with other former Trotskyists in the early 1930s despite having publicly broken with Trotsky.[91] In this respect, the OGPU would have known something about the ongoing underground activity of former Trotskyists in the early 1930s. Primakov was not alone in being watched in 1933, and any secret gathering would be regarded with suspicion and perhaps even evidence of conspiracy.

However, the OGPU's observation of Primakov, interestingly, did not hinder his advancement in the Red Army. In January 1935, he was made a member of the Military Soviet and was promoted to deputy commander of the Leningrad Military District. This was an important position in a strategic area.[92] Being a former Trotskyist in the Red Army under OGPU observation evidently did not always stifle a military career. Voroshilov, of course, might have been unaware that Primakov was under surveillance. He had been kept out of the loop when Tukhachevskii was first incriminated during Operation Vesna, and Menzhinskii might have done the same thing again. The OGPU leaders were under no obligation to inform Voroshilov of their suspicions, and they perhaps saw another opportunity to undermine him in front of Stalin. If Primakov was up to anything suspicious, this would reflect badly on Voroshilov, who had promoted him. Alternatively, Voroshilov may have known about the OGPU's suspicions but did not take them too seriously at this point. It was only from the end of 1934, after the assassination of Sergei Kirov, that members of the former opposition were seen as posing a far more serious internal security threat. Indeed, Voroshilov appears to have lost none of the trust he placed in Primakov's fellow ex-Trotskyist, Vitovt Putna, whom he posted to the Far East after the Japanese invasion of Manchuria to help the military restructuring in the region.[93] Sending Putna to an unstable area is indicative of the support he still had from Voroshilov. Whatever the exact reason behind this tolerance of former Trotskyists, Voroshilov soon had to deal with a revived danger of Trotskyism in the Red Army.

The Kirov Murder

On 1 December 1934, the Leningrad first party secretary, Sergei Kirov, was shot dead in the city's party headquarters. The assassin, a disgruntled party member, Leonid Nikolaev, had acted alone. Walking into the Smolny Building, he happened to encounter Kirov outside his office and shot him in the back of the head.[94] Nikolaev had only personal motivations for the shooting. He was angry with the regime and blamed it for his unemployment and poor standard of living. The murder created nothing short of a sensation in the Soviet Union. A senior party boss had been gunned down with apparent ease in the daytime, and Soviet citizens soon began to speculate about why Nikolaev had turned assassin. More importantly, the Soviet leaders were immediately thrown into a panic. If Kirov could be killed so easily, which one of them might be next?

The repercussions of the Kirov murder were profound, and it is a central event in the years preceding the Great Terror. Immediately after the assassination, the apparatus of repression was scaled upward and an emergency degree rushed through the Politburo: the law of 1 December 1934. This shortened the process of arrest and trial for individuals accused of terrorism. Anyone arrested under the law now had no right to appeal; if found guilty, he or she would be immediately executed.[95] However, because such draconian legislation was so quickly promulgated after Kirov's death, historians speculated for decades that Stalin was the true mastermind behind the murder. Perhaps Stalin had Kirov murdered as a pretext to increase the apparatus of repression, which he could then deploy against any real or imagined opposition to his power. Moreover, in books on the Great Terror published during the Cold War and before the Russian archives opened, Kirov was typically presented as a popular and moderate figure in the party, as well as a potential rival for the leadership. In this way, Stalin needed Kirov out of the way, and his death was pointed to as the first act of a carefully orchestrated wave of terror lasting until 1938.[96] Yet since the opening of the Russian archives in the early 1990s, no convincing evidence has been found that Stalin had any hand in the murder itself. All available evidence points to

Nikolaev having acted alone. That he came across Kirov in the Smolny Building was nothing but pure chance. Furthermore, rather than being a moderate in the party, Kirov has been shown to have been a hard-liner. He sided with Stalin on nearly every issue and was an unlikely candidate to challenge his authority. Stalin had no prior knowledge of Nikolaev's intentions, although that he saw an opportunity to make use of Kirov's death is beyond question.[97]

Stalin immediately pointed the finger at the former opposition as being responsible for Kirov's death. Subsequently, in addition to Nikolaev, several supporters of the former opposition were arrested in Leningrad and accused of being part of a conspiracy to kill Kirov. During a trial in January 1935, the group was found guilty of having formed a terrorist cell, the so-called Leningrad center, and all were executed. The political police expended efforts to try and find any evidence that might link the leaders of the former opposition, Grigorii Zinoviev and Lev Kamenev, to the crime. Even though this came to nothing, Zinoviev and Kamenev were arrested anyway, alongside a further group of former oppositionists. Another trial was held in January. The second group was accused of having formed a Moscow center that supposedly had coordinated various counterrevolutionary groups from the capital. However, with no credible evidence linking Zinoviev and Kamenev to the Kirov murder, the two were charged only with having created the conditions necessary for the assassination to occur. It was Zinoviev and Kamenev's past opposition to the party line that was said to have given Nikolaev encouragement to commit such a grave crime. Subsequently, both men were found guilty of "moral complicity" and sent to the labor camps.[98]

A central figure in steering the investigation into Kirov's death toward the former opposition was Nikolai Ezhov, who at the time was deputy chairman of the Party Control Commission. In less than two years, however, he would take control of the political police and assume a leading role in pushing forward the Great Terror. Despite not yet having a formal role within the political police in December 1934, Ezhov was closely involved in the investigation into Kirov's death. He was someone whom Stalin felt he could trust. Stalin had given Ezhov permission to muscle in on the investigation and act as his eyes and ears on the ground. Ezhov searched to uncover an oppositionist conspiracy that he was convinced lay behind the murder; this led to a growing persecution of the former opposition during 1935–1936. What is perhaps most important about Ezhov's expanding influence in the mid-1930s is that he was far more accepting of conspiracy theories than Iagoda, the head of the political police at the time of Kirov's death. When Ezhov came to lead the political police in 1936, he was finally in a position to act on his conspiratorial view of the world and use this to justify increasing repression across the Soviet state and within the Red Army.

Ezhov, of course, was not solely responsible for pinning the Kirov murder on the former opposition. Even if he was certain that they were guilty, he was also responding to Stalin's cues, who immediately suspected opposition involvement. There are several possible reasons why Stalin jumped to this conclusion. First, Kirov had been party boss in Leningrad, a city that had formerly been Zinoviev's power base. Many of Zinoviev's supporters remained in the city, which helped ignite suspicions after Kirov's death. Second, Stalin had been keeping a close eye on the former opposition for any indication of renewed resistance ever since he had crushed them in the late 1920s.[99] It is admittedly impossible to know for certain on what level Stalin really suspected Zinoviev and Kamenev to be involved in the murder, or whether he was using Kirov's death simply as a means to have them arrested. We cannot know for sure what Stalin was thinking. There was certainly some political calculation behind Stalin's actions after the murder, but at the same time it does seem that he was genuinely shocked and even fearful at his colleague's death. In the months after Kirov's murder, Stalin voiced concern about further assassination attempts against himself or others in the party leadership. He began to claim that the party had been infiltrated by dangerous enemies and that there were other active terrorist plots.[100] This sense of shock was reflected in the investigation into Kirov's murder. This did not solely target the former opposition, and the general reaction is best seen as a knee-jerk one. It was not just former oppositionists who were rounded up: many White prisoners— people with no obvious connection to the murder—were executed in cities around the Soviet Union.[101] The regime was thrashing about in the wake of the murder of the Leningrad party boss.

All Soviet institutions felt the impact of the Kirov murder as the pressure inside the party increased dramatically over the next two years. On 18 January 1935, for instance, the Central Committee sent a secret letter to all party organizations setting out the charges against Zinoviev and Kamenev and detailing the discovery of a supposed Zinovievite counterrevolutionary group. Before long, hundreds of former oppositionists were arrested, and thousands were exiled from Leningrad.[102] The

Kirov murder, in this sense, was a key moment in escalating political tensions in the years before the Great Terror and firmly reestablishing a perceived threat from the former opposition. Yet there has been little examination of how the Red Army was affected by these rising political tensions. Although there was no strong connection to the Red Army, in the long term, the military purge would have been impossible without the Kirov murder.

The Kirov murder did have some immediate impact in the army in December 1934 and January 1935. During the subsequent investigation, sixty-three Red Army men, including twenty officers, were arrested for having connections to Zinoviev.[103] Other charges relating to the murder began to be leveled against other Red Army men. From 1 December 1934 to 20 January 1935, for instance, forty-three soldiers were arrested in the Moscow Military District for apparently having counter-revolutionary moods linked to the murder of Kirov.[104] Similar examples can be seen in other military districts.[105] These arrests, however, do not represent a targeted scrutiny of the Red Army specifically. The military leadership gave few indications that they were concerned about the Red Army after the murder. Nine days after the shooting, the Red Army held the inaugural meeting of the Military Soviet, a new advisory body attached to the Commissariat for Defense, and Kirov was hardly mentioned at all. His name came up just twice throughout the three-day meeting, and only once in terms of how the murder was a reflection of a growing class struggle.[106] There were no calls to launch an investigation in the army or to purge the ranks of any suspicious individuals. When Kirov was mentioned, his death was used as an example of how the army needed to be vigilant, which was hardly a new complaint. Yet despite the few references made to Kirov at this first meeting of the Military Soviet, it is doubtful that the military leadership had become any less uneasy about enemies in the ranks. Indeed, the tense political climate after the Kirov murder only made this a more pressing problem.

At the Military Soviet of December 1934, many speakers delivered formulaic speeches claiming that Red Army men were conducting better political work and that the troops were becoming ever more closely aligned around the party and Stalin's leadership. Meetings such as the Military Soviet were naturally used as forums to make these types of boasts, but there are hints of the deeper reality under the surface. Beyond the meaningless claims about Red Army successes, more worrying trends were noted by some participants that give a clearer impression of the type of security problems still persisting in the army. The deputy head of PUR, Anton Bulin, for instance, called attention to continuing weaknesses in the reliability of the army. He noted that in a recent check of the political reliability of forty-five military formations, thirteen were appraised as good, twenty-seven as satisfactory, and five as unsatisfactory. There was clearly room for improvement. Related to this, Bulin criticized what he saw as "forms of bureaucratic cabinet leadership," suggesting that some officers and political workers did not know their rank-and-file soldiers well enough.[107] According to Bulin, it was this kind of detachment that allowed enemies to go undetected. More worryingly, Bulin delivered criticisms relating to self-policing in the Red Army, which was continuing to malfunction and which represented a problem running deeper than weak vigilance. Notably, he argued that even when a satisfactory appraisal was awarded for political reliability, this could still mask the enemies working within a unit.[108] Good appraisals provided little incentive to root out enemies and encouraged complacency. Bulin, unsurprisingly, attributed this to a lack of sufficient Bolshevik vigilance, but again, there was probably more at work.[109] Although some officers surely did suffer from complacency on receiving a good appraisal, others may have used this as a good excuse to avoid digging any deeper to find enemies. A good appraisal provided effective cover. In this way, Bulin's complaints are another possible indication of a lack of drive among some officers toward the task of rooting out dangerous enemies in their commands. That Bulin felt the need to air these criticisms at the Military Soviet suggests that this was a widespread problem.

Gamarnik spoke in similar terms to Bulin at the Military Soviet. He criticized, for instance, what he called the formalistic manner by which reprimands were being given to soldiers that, according to Gamarnik, left some divisions with 60 to 70 percent of the soldiers having received some kind of reprimand, often for trivial matters. He argued that reprimands were being given out as an easy alternative to proper political education.[110] This type of reprimand would be used as punishment for a minor crime, and certainly not a political crime that would result in arrest and discharge. As such, reprimands for minor crimes were being given out en masse. As we have seen, these criticisms were similar to Voroshilov's earlier condemnation of incorrect discharges and may suggest another route by which some officers were trying to cultivate a reputation for vigilance. Giving out large numbers of reprimands could allow an officer to avoid tackling the thorny problem of having to uncover counterrevolutionaries and foreign agents in their units while still giving the impression of being duly alert against criminality. The discovery of a soldier who could potentially be portrayed as a dangerous enemy, and whose arrest would almost certainly draw some attention back to the commanding officer, was thus avoided. Moreover, and more damningly, Gamarnik noted that officers who gave inspections of their own troops often exaggerated these in a positive light. The defects and problems in the army were being smoothed over. Gamarnik cautioned against embellishing successes and criticized what he called "harmful boasting." It was this, he argued, that handed enemies the opportunity to get inside the army. Gamarnik remarked, "Under our very nose the enemy is huddled near us."[111] In this way, both Bulin's and Gamarnik's speeches to the Military Soviet provide further indications that some officers were using different tactics to avoid turning too much attention on themselves, including ignoring outright the calls to improve vigilance, exaggerating the reliability of their commands, or discharging soldiers and applying reprimands needlessly as a deflection. It is likely that this was the type of behavior that lay behind the army leadership's frequent and vague criticisms of inadequate vigilance and that was partly to blame for the breakdown in military self-policing. Neither Bulin nor Gamarnik offered any real solutions. The familiar calls for even more vigilance and better self-criticism heard at the Military Soviet would do nothing to get to the heart of the problem.

The political police had a presence at the Military Soviet in the person of M. I. Gai, the head of the Main Administration of State Security (GUGB) of the All-Union People's Commissariat for Internal Affairs (NKVD) for the Red Army. The OGPU had been abolished in early 1934 and its responsibilities subsumed into a reformed NKVD, which retained a close involvement with the military. At the Military Soviet, Gai struck a more alarmist tone than did the other speakers, presenting a picture of the Red Army as vulnerable to infiltration in what remained a hostile international environment. He pointed to a growing espionage threat and the increasing activity of foreign intelligence agents on Soviet soil. Indeed, Gai argued that foreign agents were not simply collecting intelligence but were preparing the ground for an invasion. They were apparently engaged in "the organization of diversionary acts." Supplies were being stockpiled and spy residencies organized that would activate at a time of war. From Gai's point of view, the Red Army was not sufficiently alert to this danger. He argued that he could give several examples of poor vigilance and made a note of the recent Nakhaev case.[112] Gai also complained that "socially harmful elements" were littered throughout the ranks and officer corps, remarking, "It is no secret that enough attention is still not given to the issue of the study of the personnel of the Red Army."[113] Allegedly, in some cases "direct agents of the enemy" were using false documentation to acquire responsible positions in the military. Gai provided examples where former White officers linked to émigré groups had managed to gain command positions.[114] In short, as far as Gai was concerned, the Red Army was still at high risk of infiltration, and this was no time to be complacent. However, he clearly had little confidence in the Red Army's ability to police itself adequately. The NKVD would keep up the pressure.

In the final speech to the Military Soviet, Voroshilov devoted some time to describing the deteriorating international situation facing the Soviet Union. Soviet relations with Germany, Poland, and Japan in particular remained poor. Moreover, Voroshilov believed that Germany and Poland were reaching out to Japan and considering a joint action against the Soviet Union.[115] It was not all bad news, however. Voroshilov declared that the Red Army was now recognized as a powerful force in the world. He stressed its apparent strengthening political stability and praised the hard work that had been done to achieve this. There were still persisting problems. Alongside not insignificant criminality, drunkenness, and detachment between officers and soldiers, Voroshilov recognized that enemies were still finding their way into the ranks: "It is nothing short of a disgrace, we cannot not consider it a terrible disgrace and shame that in 1934 in the ranks of our army . . . there are traitors, traitors who disgrace, who stain the entire Workers' and Peasants' Red Army." Despite this damning verdict, Voroshilov's remedy was, once again, more vigilance.[116] This would do nothing to get to the root of why some officers were lacking this in the first place. It was not a serious approach in trying to understand failures in army self-policing and why some officers may have been using deliberate tactics to avoid scrutinizing their commands. Voroshilov seemingly lacked credible solutions to the deeper failures undermining army security and was merely addressing the symptoms.

In this respect, there was a growing inconsistency between Voroshilov's rhetoric and action in the 1930s. Voroshilov frequently delivered stern criticism of how enemies were going undiscovered in the Red Army, but the solutions he proposed were consistently measured and focused vaguely on raising vigilance. The most likely explanation for this disconnect is that Voroshilov understood that he was in an increasingly difficult position, especially in the tense political climate after the Kirov murder. Importantly, it was far easier for the NKVD to unmask supposedly dangerous enemies in the Red Army than the officer corps or PUR. They did not have the same approach, brutal methods, or low standards of evidence. Voroshilov surely understood that the NKVD had the upper hand while also knowing that Stalin wanted any enemies in the Red Army found, particularly after the embarrassing Nakhaev case. Considering the difficulties Voroshilov was facing in getting his officers to correctly scrutinize their own soldiers (to which he had no credible solution), the army could never attempt to compete with the NKVD. Gai's speech to the 1934 Military Soviet made it clear that the NKVD was unhappy with the army's current efforts and would keep up the pressure. In this sense, calling for more vigilance may have been a way out for Voroshilov. It allowed him (and also Gamarnik) to at least be seen doing something about the problems with the security of the Red Army. It was a way to signal that they recognized the threat posed by undiscovered enemies in the ranks and to show that they were taking corresponding action. It would be surprising if both men did not realize that vaguely calling for more vigilance would not actually change a great deal, but this was better than doing nothing. In calling for more vigilance, Voroshilov and Gamarnik were probably as interested in protecting the Red Army as they were in covering their own backs.

In early 1935, German rearmament was progressing at such a rate that it was no longer possible to keep secret, and Hitler began to reveal his aggressive intentions for war.[117] On 10 March, during an interview with the British newspaper the *Daily Mail*, Hermann Göring declared that Germany had an air force, the Luftwaffe, and on 16 March, the German government reinstated universal conscription. Both announcements sparked international uproar. In the Soviet Union, Tukhachevskii was one of the most vocal figures in highlighting the renewed threat from Germany. He sounded the alarm in a *Pravda* article, edited by Stalin and published in March 1935, entitled "The War Plans of Contemporary Germany," which attacked German rearmament and expansionism. On the day this article was published, Stalin met with British conservative Anthony Eden and warned him that the danger of war was now greater than it had been in 1914.[118] Imminent war now seemed a certainty, and the Soviet leaders were fearful of a possible attack, seeing Germany, Japan, Poland, and Finland as their most probable enemies in a new conflict.[119] Consequently, in May 1935, the strength of the Red Army was bolstered. The territorial system was phased out, and cadre units increased by 600,000.[120] German–Soviet relations were particularly tense from this point on, and the Soviet leaders sought a range of diplomatic alliances as a counterweight to German aggression, signing mutual assistance pacts with France and Czechoslovakia in May 1935.

It was within this worsening international environment that former political oppositionists in the Soviet Union came under increasing pressure after the Kirov murder. During 1935, arrests for supposed oppositionist activity increased dramatically; this trend continued into 1936.[121] Accompanying this rise in political arrests, general cases of "counterrevolutionary crime" and "counterrevolutionary agitation" also saw an increase.[122] Despite not being subject to any specific scrutiny after the Kirov murder, the Red Army too felt the effects of this rising wave of repression. The chief military procurator, Naum Rozovskii, reported that counterrevolutionary crime totaled 27 percent of all criminal cases processed through military tribunals in 1935, constituting the most common crime. Anti-Soviet agitation had seen a ninefold increase since 1934, when there had been just 151 successful convictions, rising to 1,374 in 1935.[123] The Military Procuracy explained the rise in convictions for counterrevolutionary crime in 1935 as a result of Red Army men responding to Voroshilov's calls for more vigilance and the impact of the Kirov assassination.[124] However, it is more likely that the increase in counterrevolutionary crime seen in 1935 was the product of more focused NKVD attention on finding hidden counterrevolutionaries in the wake of the Kirov assassination rather than any real improvements in self-policing in the army. The officer corps continued to be criticized for displaying poor vigilance and being unable to independently expose dangerous enemies in the ranks over the next two years, suggesting that few real improvements had been made. Furthermore, while counterrevolutionary crime was on the increase in the army, this was at the same time as general criminality was in decline. According to Rozovskii, 5,062 cadre Red Army men were convicted of various crimes during 1935, a decline from 5,298 in 1934 and 7,091 in 1933. This decline continued into 1936.[125] In this respect, it was political arrests and counterrevolutionary crime specifically that were becoming the focus of attention in

1935—the territory of the NKVD. However, this was not without controversy. The NKVD was coming under criticism from the Military Procuracy for arresting large numbers of servicemen on weak grounds and
carrying out inadequate investigations, meaning that many cases were
being overturned—at times at a rate of over 30 percent in some military
districts. In any case, the NKVD was clearly applying more pressure on
the Red Army during 1935, even if this was resulting in larger numbers
of unfounded cases.[126]

Why general criminality was falling in the Red Army at the same
time as more officers and soldiers were being arrested for political and
counterrevolutionary crimes requires further explanation. The chief
reason behind this trend was most likely Voroshilov's gaining control
over sanctioning arrests in the Red Army. This meant that the political
police were now required to secure his permission before any arrest was
made. Specifically, greater authority in sanctioning the arrests of officers had been gained in April 1933, when the Central Military Procuracy mandated that agreement for such arrests was required from either
the Central Military Procuracy or the district military procuracies. Then
on 26 May 1934, the Politburo issued a further order forbidding the
political police from arresting soldiers and officers without the prior
agreement of a political commissar. By February 1935, only Voroshilov,
or in his absence Gamarnik, could sanction sending someone of the
rank of platoon commander or above to trial. Arrests at this level or
higher required Voroshilov's approval. This enhanced control over military arrests had an immediate impact. In a speech given later to a group
of Red Army party members in March 1937, Boris Fel'dman specifically
noted that awarding the army the right to approve its own arrests led to
a decline in arrest levels.[127]

Awarding the Red Army leadership more authority in sanctioning
arrests was in line with wider policing reforms initiated from mid-1933.
We have already seen how these reforms created a more powerful and
centralized all-union policing body, the NKVD, which absorbed the responsibilities of the OGPU in July 1934. At the same time, they also
produced a shift in Soviet policing and judicial policy toward having a
stronger grounding in legality. Greater power was awarded to the courts
and the extrajudicial powers of the political police were curtailed, particularly after the creation of a procurator of the USSR. Ultimately, the
purpose of these reforms was to ensure better supervision and centralization of the political police from the center. The new NKVD also did

not have the same level of extrajudicial power as the former OGPU. Indeed, in mid-1934, Stalin had criticized the illegal investigative methods used by the political police.[128] He wanted more oversight from the center, not an end to political repression. However, these policing reforms did have limits. They did not result in a full turn toward legality and complete abandonment of extrajudicial sentencing. The NKVD did retain some of its extrajudicial power in the form of the Special Boards, used for sensitive political cases. Accusations that the NKVD continued to abuse extrajudicial powers did not disappear.[129]

Despite their limits, the policing reforms of the mid-1930s were surely welcome news for Voroshilov. They granted him much greater control over arrests within the army and undoubtedly strengthened his position. The decline in arrests for general crime from 1934 would help support his case that the Red Army was in fact growing in reliability and stability. However, the policing reforms of the mid-1930s evidently had limited impact on the number of arrests for counterrevolutionary and political crimes in the military, both of which had surged in the immediate aftermath of the Kirov murder. The NKVD was applying pressure nonetheless. The Kirov murder remained a tipping point for the political repression inside the party, and it had a significant longer term impact for the Red Army. The murder shocked the ruling elite, and Stalin wanted a crackdown on the former opposition. In this respect, even if Voroshilov had wanted to use his enhanced powers to stem the flow of counterrevolutionary and political crimes, this would have been difficult. From early 1935, there was increasing pressure on institutional heads from above to clamp down on supporters of the former opposition, and Voroshilov needed to show that he was taking this seriously in the Red Army. It also cannot be excluded that Voroshilov sincerely believed that the Kirov murder proved that the party had been infiltrated by enemies, and he perhaps questioned his own safety. Whether or not Voroshilov was convinced that the former opposition now represented a dangerous internal cohort, in the aftermath of the Kirov murder, there was little room to do anything but follow Stalin and the NKVD's lead in the search for dangerous political enemies.

Consequently, arrests levels may well have been in decline in the Red Army from 1934 in general terms (thus showing that the military purge of 1937–1938 was not the culmination of a building wave of repression), but cases of counterrevolutionary and political crime saw a spike after the Kirov murder. Moreover, Stalin had clearly signaled that former oppositionists were dangerous political enemies, and if the Red Army was not seen as capable of guaranteeing its own security, the NKVD would gain the upper hand. They had the will and the brutal methods to find supposed political enemies in the army; they had much greater success than the officer corps and PUR in the years before the military purge. Indeed, there were few improvements in self-policing in the Red Army from this point on. People labeled as political enemies continued to be missed at the very moment it was imperative to find them. The various behaviors indicating a deliberate avoidance of scrutinizing subordinates and colleagues stubbornly persisted. In this respect, Voroshilov was placed in an increasingly difficult position after the Kirov murder. Even though he had greater control over arrests in the Red Army, he would still find it difficult to mount a credible defense of its reliability in such a tense political climate.

It is necessary to point to one particular case within the surge in counterrevolutionary crime in the Red Army in 1935. Tukhachevskii's name surfaced again during an investigation into a counterrevolutionary group. In this particular case, Gaia Gai, a former Trotskyist working as a professor of war history and military art (and unrelated to the NKVD's M. I. Gai), was arrested in June and accused of belonging to a counterrevolutionary group. The charges against Gai were serious. He was accused of spreading Trotskyist "slander" and having designs to "remove" (*ubrat'*) Stalin.[130] Despite denying any wrongdoing (Gai was said to have made the comments when he was drunk), he received five years in a labor camp and was eventually shot in December 1937.[131] Tukhachevskii's name appeared in the investigation when another arrested member of the group, a certain Avanesian, claimed that Gai had complained that he felt his career had been held back and that he blamed Voroshilov and Budennyi for this. Gai had supposedly remarked, "If Tukhachevskii was people's commissar then my chances would be much better."[132] Gai had met Tukhachevskii while serving in the 1st Revolutionary Army in 1918, and there are some indications that they were close acquaintances.[133] What is important here is not only the fact that Tukhachevskii's name had once again appeared during an investigation into a counterrevolutionary group, but also that Gai's supposed remarks cast Tukhachevskii in a positive light, as opposed to Voroshilov and Budennyi. Indeed, it is likely that the division in the high command between Tukhachevskii and Voroshilov had filtered down the ranks and was known to the wider army. The hostility between the two men was no doubt common knowledge. There were almost certainly other officers like Gai who would have preferred Tukhachevskii at the head of the Red Army rather than Voroshilov.

Tukhachevskii suffered no obvious consequences after being named by Gai. Admittedly, this case was not as serious as the previous Eismont–Tolmachev investigation in 1932, when Tukhachevskii's loyalty to the state had supposedly been discussed by the arrested party members. Tukhachevskii's career continued on an upward trajectory in 1935. He was one of the five officers to be given the rank of marshal of the Soviet Union when military ranks were restored in the Red Army during that year, and he had greater influence than ever before. Tukhachevskii became a stronger voice in foreign policy in 1935, demonstrated by his *Pravda* article attacking German aggression, and he took on further diplomatic responsibilities over the next two years. In short, there is little to suggest that Tukhachevskii was being sidelined as a result of questions about his character, judgment, or political reliability in 1935. Yet this new association with counterrevolution from the investigation into Gaia Gai, like any past cases, would almost certainly be kept on file by the NKVD. It was another event that may have sparked a few nagging doubts about Tukhachevskii's loyalty—and sufficient enough for the NKVD to continue to keep a close eye on him.

Gaia Gai's arrest is also a good example of how renewed pressure on the former opposition from the Kirov murder had an impact on former Trotskyists serving in the Red Army. Gai was a reasonably senior military figure imprisoned on spurious grounds because of his past support for Trotsky. The imperative from above to search out political enemies was shaping the course of repression in the Red Army as much as it did in other Soviet institutions. Indeed, the Military Procuracy highlighted a number of so-called Trotskyist double-dealers who had been found in the army in 1935.[134] According to one set of statistics, 268 officers were discharged for Trotskyism in 1935, slightly surpassing the 239 for counterrevolutionary agitation.[135] In this politically charged atmosphere, Voroshilov undoubtedly knew that the military needed to renew its efforts to find any hidden enemies, although there was no change in how he instructed his subordinates to do this. All he could seemingly come up with was to call for vigilance to be raised to even higher levels. In April 1935, Voroshilov published two orders on the question of enemies in the ranks that demonstrate that he was still not getting to the root cause of why self-policing in the army was breaking down. The first order detailed a case of a "scoundrel and swindler" who, having impersonated a party member, had managed to gain a position in an aviation brigade. The imposter had been so convincing that he had even been allowed to fly airplanes. Voroshilov noted that the reason the man was able to do this was because of his close acquaintance with several officers. This, then, was a question of nepotism. Voroshilov must have felt that there were enough comparable cases to warrant highlighting this case in the first place. However, aside from stating that the officers in question should be punished harshly, Voroshilov's evaluation of the case simply focused on a lack of vigilance toward the class enemy.[136] The second order in April was along similar lines. This time, Voroshilov criticized the low levels of vigilance in a particular regiment. Apparently, its chief of staff had engaged in counterrevolutionary conversations for an extended period of time, but no one had seen fit to report this. Voroshilov ordered the guilty to be reprimanded and removed from their positions.[137] Voroshilov's criticisms, however, were once again primarily framed in terms of weak vigilance, and this was unlikely to bring about any substantial improvements in army self-policing. The underlying reasons behind why there was insufficient vigilance in the officer corps were not being addressed. Voroshilov was again merely responding to the symptoms. Why were counterrevolutionary conversations going unreported? What specific circumstances allowed nepotistic behaviors to flourish? It is unlikely that Voroshilov had answers to these more complex questions. The easy (and perhaps only) option he had was to simply proclaim the need for more vigilance as a catchall solution to the army's security problems. It was better to be seen doing something rather than nothing. Indeed, the need for better vigilance in the Red Army was pushed publicly in 1935 and was the subject of several front pages of *Krasnaia zvezda* during the year.[138]

Voroshilov was soon given the opportunity to find out whether his frequent calls for more vigilance were paying off when, in May 1935, the party conducted another *chistka*: the verification of party documents (*proverka partdokumentov*). The *proverka* aimed to improve the chaotic state of party record keeping and simultaneously flush out any corrupt and criminal members. It uncovered a variety of people who should not have had party membership, including social aliens, kulaks, and Whites, but also more dangerous Trotskyists, Zinovievites, and alleged spies. This party purge is generally passed over in research on the Red Army, but its results are revealing. During the *proverka*, the army party organizations expelled 5,311 full party members and 2,472 candidate members, representing 3.6 percent and 5.3 percent of their total numbers, respectively.[139] The combined total of full and candidate members expelled from the army party organizations was consistent with the 9 percent expelled from the party nationally.[140] The most common reason for expulsion from the army party organizations was hiding one's social origins; having a connection to a suspected socially harmful element; or not having admitted to previous service in the White armies during the civil war. These reasons alone led to 3,350 exclusions. For Trotskyism and Zinovievism, 261 people were expelled. There were a mere 114 expulsions for espionage—just 1.5 percent of total expulsions in the *proverka*. In this respect, while demonstrating the ever-present perceived danger from more threatening enemies in the army (such as spies and former oppositionists), these were by no means prominent in the *proverka*. Cases of espionage in particular were at a low level in the purge, and on the surface, they should not have represented a pressing danger.[141]

However, on 26 June 1935, Gamarnik gave a speech to the heads of the political organizations in the Belorussian Military District in which he spoke candidly about the results of the *proverka*. It is clear that he did not view the results positively. Gamarnik remarked that the *proverka* showed that people in the Red Army were still being studied "very badly" and that political workers "did not know people well."[142] Moreover, despite Trotskyists and spies coming in on the lower end of the expulsions, Gamarnik chose to highlight them specifically:

> The fact of the matter is 555 people were excluded in total in the Belorussian district. This figure is not so large, it is four or something percent. Among those now exposed and excluded from the party are clear enemies—spies, White guards, Trotskyists—whom we had not revealed before the *proverka* of party documents although the people were studied. The *proverka* of party documents helped us to identify the enormous quantity of people whom we did not know earlier or knew poorly.[143]

Gamarnik acknowledged that the total number of expulsions from the *proverka* in the Belorussian Military District was in fact quite small: just 4 percent. Even though socially harmful elements comprised the bulk of these expulsions, he seemed more concerned that the more dangerous enemies—foreign agents and Trotskyists—had not been discovered before the *proverka* had taken place. This would be understood as evidence that standards of vigilance had not been improved despite Voroshilov's frequent complaints. Indeed, it had taken an independent party purge to actually reveal hidden enemies still in the ranks. At precisely the time that Soviet leaders were showing growing concerns about foreign agents infiltrating the Soviet Union, and alongside the perceived threat embodied by the former opposition after the Kirov murder, this failure in army self-policing should have been concerning for Gamarnik as head of PUR. The Red Army was missing the enemies working within, and it is unlikely that this was going unnoticed by the ruling elite or the NKVD.

That Gamarnik pointed to a danger from foreign agents specifically in his speech in the Belorussian Military District corresponds with how they were beginning to be perceived as a much more serious threat to the state in broader terms. For example, Ezhov, the organizer of the *proverka* who later became head of the NKVD, reported to Stalin in the summer of 1935 that foreign agents had infiltrated the party. He later repeated this claim at a conference of regional party secretaries in September. Alongside this infiltration of foreign agents, Ezhov remarked, "Trotskyists undoubtedly have a center somewhere in the USSR."[144] As William Chase has noted, Ezhov spoke of Trotskyists and foreign spies in much the same terms. He saw little difference between them in either aims or methods.[145] Ezhov would soon start joining the dots, making supposed connections between members of the former opposition and fascist states that would feature heavily in the charges against the many Soviet citizens arrested and executed during the Great Terror.

There were other clear signs in 1935 that the perceived spy threat and questions about the loyalty of non-Russians were moving up the regime's agenda beyond Ezhov's pronouncements. The regime began to strengthen the Soviet Union's borders, and large numbers of national minority groups were deported from the border regions for fear they would turn against the regime in a future war. In early 1935, approximately 50,000 Poles, Germans, and Ukrainians were deported from the western Ukraine border.[146] Hitler's consolidation of power in early 1933 had also seen an increase in the number of German communists fleeing to the Soviet Union, bringing with them another potential security threat. Questions were raised about whether the communists arriving from Nazi Germany could be trusted, and a plenum of the Central Committee in December 1935 called for all political émigrés to be carefully checked.[147] Notably, some of these new security measures were aimed directly at the Red Army. In 1935, the special departments began to register foreigners and political emigrants serving in the Red Army.

There had been some reports of some German Red Army soldiers in the western border districts apparently displaying positive attitudes toward Hitler.[148] It was in this climate of growing spy mania that the Red Army was failing to adequately police its own ranks.

When the Military Soviet assembled again in December 1935, many speakers delivered the usual formulaic statements and boastful claims describing apparently significant gains in both military and political preparation in the Red Army. These self-serving comments remained standard practice, but among the superficial rhetoric, it is clear that many of the problems aired during the previous year's Military Soviet remained unresolved. For instance, in his speech, Gamarnik outlined the persisting problems with vigilance highlighted anew by the recent *proverka:*

> The *proverka* of party documents, great in its organizational and political significance, carried out according to the initiative of c[omrade] Stalin, again showed that we still badly, often only formally, know people, that often we miss enemies—spies, Trotskyists, Zinovievites, swindlers—and very often we do not notice, promote, cultivate, [those] truly loyal to the party, able and valuable people.[149]

This was the same complaint that Gamarnik had made in the Belorussian Military District in June: it had taken the independent *proverka* to actually reveal the dangerous enemies still hidden in the Red Army. This should not have been the case if the officer corps and PUR had been sufficiently alert to possible threats. Although Gamarnik did see a small silver lining, arguing that the *proverka* had led to some improvement in the study of people in the Red Army, there was obviously much room for improvement. Gamarnik's displeasure with the current state of army self-policing remained unchanged.[150]

There were, however, further indications at the 1935 Military Soviet that some officers were deliberately avoiding behaving as Gamarnik wanted and avoiding turning too much attention on their own commands. Specifically, the commander of the Siberian Military District, Ia. P. Gailit, highlighted what he described as an extraordinary number of court cases and discharges from the Red Army, arguing that soldiers were being dismissed far too easily. This criticism was similar to Gamarnik's complaint at the previous year's Military Soviet concerning the large numbers of reprimands being sanctioned by officers, as well as Voroshilov's earlier criticisms of incorrect discharges. Indeed, according to Gailit, dismissal was still taking precedence over political re-education. Investigations into criminal cases were also not being carried out properly, and the officers and political workers were to blame. Gailit noted that in many cases, no one from the command had adequately examined a discharge case, or even spoken to the individual in question.

Gailit explained this behavior as a result of officers responding incorrectly to Voroshilov's calls to raise vigilance.[151] Gailit was probably not wrong here on a certain level, but it is possible that some officers knew exactly what they were doing. In sanctioning large numbers of discharges on weak grounds, some officers may have been trying to make conspicuous demonstrations that they were responding to the call to raise vigilance. This provided cover for accusations of their not being sufficiently vigilant while at the same time putting off the delicate task of digging deeper for potentially dangerous political enemies and foreign agents—something that could rebound against a commanding officer. Even though there was growing pressure to locate anyone who could be regarded as a dangerous political enemy or foreign subversive in 1935, this remained a hazardous task. Not all officers would be willing to run the risk of turning the NKVD's attentions on their own commands or on themselves personally.[152] In this respect, Gailit's comments build on the criticisms aired at the previous year's Military Soviet—that some officers were giving overly positive appraisals of their own units' political reliability. Moreover, this adds further evidence that some officers may not have been fully engaging with the task of rooting out enemies despite the increasingly tense political and international climate. It is possible that, for some, this was deliberate behavior. The calls to locate enemies in the ranks could be ignored or deflected. Either way, Voroshilov and Gamarnik were no doubt increasingly concerned about the Red Army's failure to produce results.

In 1936, the Soviet leaders decided to conduct a further internal party membership purge similar to the *proverka*: the exchange of party documents (*obmen partdokumentov*). There had been several problems with the *proverka*, primarily the cursory attention given to the task by local party leaders, who were anxious about turning too much official attention on their own centers of power.[153] The *proverka* consequently did not finish on time, and the *obmen* was a second attempt to sort out the chaos of the party record system and be rid of any member deemed unsuitable or criminal. During the course of the *obmen*, more members of the army party organizations were expelled for various reasons. Passivity, being deemed a social alien (or being linked to one), and "moral degeneracy," constituted the majority of the military expulsions.[154] However, once again, supposed political enemies were also discovered during the course of the purge. Speaking in early 1937, Voroshilov noted that the *obmen* expelled 244 Trotskyists and Zinovievites from the army party organizations, which was just short of the 261 expelled during the *proverka*.[155] In this respect, the *obmen* reaffirmed the lesson delivered by the *proverka*. It was another demonstration that despite the mounting calls for the army to increase its levels of vigilance, dangerous enemies were still going unnoticed in the ranks. It had taken a second independent party purge to actually root these out. It is likely that the results of the *obmen* added to concerns that the Red Army was failing to manage its own internal security effectively.

Rising international tensions throughout 1936 only made the task of safeguarding the internal security of the Red Army more urgent. A succession of crises in the first half of 1936 made European war seem even more of a certainty. On 7 March, Germany took possession of the Rhineland; Italy annexed Abyssinia in May; and in July, the Spanish civil war began. For the Soviet leaders, who had attentively watched the international situation for years and who had long expected a final showdown with capitalism, it seemed that world war had at last begun. As Oleg Khlevniuk notes, the war in Spain convinced Stalin that Britain and France were unable to put up resistance to Germany. Soviet defense spending now rose sharply.[156] As the international situation worsened, concerns about espionage only increased.[157] In February 1936, the Central Committee accepted Ezhov's draft report, "On Measures to Protect the USSR against the Penetration of Spy, Terrorist, and Sabotage Elements," which pointed to a supposedly growing spy threat among political émigré circles inside the Soviet Union. The perceived Polish espionage threat in particular was also now attracting more of the NKVD's attention.[158]

These growing concerns about espionage manifested inside the Red Army during 1936. Indeed, one of the main themes in Gamarnik's complaints about poor self-policing in the Red Army and the results of the *proverka* was that spies had managed to get inside the army. In a speech given in February 1936, for example, he remarked:

By way of verification of party documents in the personnel of the RKKA, we found real enemies who deceived us, who got into the army using false documents. We revealed spies in the army, who were not only expelled from the army and party but sent to prison. . . . Much to our shame, we are still allowing such scum into the army. . . . And at the same time there are often people whom we are not allowing into the army but who ought to be permitted, who ought to be in the army.[159]

Gamarnik's remark that many people "who ought to be permitted" in the Red Army were barred from doing so suggests that there were ongoing problems with discharges in 1936. Gamarnik seems to have been grappling with this issue at some level. This can be seen in comments he made on a list of discharges prepared by officers N. A. Efrimov and A. M. Vol'pe during the same month, which Gamarnik thought had been incorrectly assembled. He noted that many of the people selected for discharge had not in fact committed any serious crimes, remarking, "This list is formally and mechanistically compiled. It is possible there are enemies here, but there are quite a few good men whom it is necessary to educate."[160] Again, it is possible that these two officers were purposely trying to give an impression of vigilance by sanctioning discharges on spurious grounds, or their mistakes may have stemmed from a lack of attention or basic misunderstanding about the nature of the task. In his February 1936 speech, Gamarnik instructed his listeners to take sufficient time to study people and their lives carefully rather than simply extract information about a person from official files.[161]

In another speech delivered to the Moscow Garrison on 1 April 1936, Gamarnik once again raised the danger posed by spies in the ranks, but this time in clearer terms than in the past. On the subject of expulsions resulting from the *proverka,* he remarked, "There are many crooks among them, having infiltrated the party with false documents. There is a group—not large—of spies."[162] Although Gamarnik felt the need to highlight this group of dangerous spies specifically, his solution was a familiar one:

We have to close all gaps for the enemy, and it must still be admitted that not only gaps but all the doors and windows were wide open, and any clever person, any clever crook, was able to infiltrate anywhere. . . . Linked with insufficient vigilance of the individual army party organizations, in our organizations we revealed spies, White guards, crooks; we revealed a group of Trotskyists and Zinovievites who led subversive work.[163]

In this respect, Gamarnik, like Voroshilov, was still failing to offer any credible solutions to the failures in military self-policing aside from continuing to blame low levels of vigilance. It is possible to speculate about his motivations. Gamarnik would have understood the need to draw attention to spies and Trotskyists in the Red Army within what was a worsening international climate. Gamarnik had no choice but to show that he was aware of the danger facing the Red Army, even if he had no credible solutions. As head of PUR, he was chiefly responsible for the political reliability of the Red Army and had to be seen to be taking action. Such signaling, however, appears to be the full extent of Gamarnik's efforts. Unfortunately, calling for more vigilance would do nothing to close the "gaps" identified in his speech that had supposedly allowed enemies to infiltrate the military. Over the course of 1936 and 1937, the perceived threat from foreign subversives only grew stronger.

It must be stressed, however, that despite rising political tensions, the worsening international situation, and the clear problems in military self-policing, there is no indication that anything as extreme as an all-army purge was looming in the first half of 1936. We have already seen how general crime levels were in decline in the army during the first half of the 1930s, and this trend continued. According to a report compiled by Fel'dman, the head of the main administration of the Red Army, approximately 7,500 people from the officer corps and other leading army bodies had been discharged in 1935, and 6,000 were discharged in 1936.[164] Moreover, a report compiled by Vasilii Ulrikh, chairman of the military collegium of the supreme court, noted that within the cadre element of the Red Army during the first half of 1936, there had been 1,692 convictions, whereas during the same months in 1935, the number was 2,839. This downward trend was for both officers and ordinary soldiers.[165] A decline in cases of counterrevolutionary agitation within commanding bodies was also recorded for 1936; however, discharges for Trotskyism, notably, continued to climb.[166] This is consistent with the pressure placed on supporters of the former opposition after the Kirov murder, which only saw greater intensity in 1936.[167]

Consequently, in the first half of 1936, there was no indication that the level of repression was increasing in general terms in the Red Army or that a mass military purge was on the horizon. If anything, only former Trotskyists were being increasingly targeted, yet they had only ever been a minority in the Red Army in the 1920s and remained so in the mid-1930s. In this respect, the military purge beginning in early June 1937 was in no sense a culmination of a rising tide of repression. In reality, general arrest levels were in decline before a sudden explosion of violence in the summer of 1937. But that political arrests continued to increase in 1936 is important. Stalin wanted a crackdown on the former opposition. The NKVD duly obliged, but as we have seen, Gamarnik and Voroshilov were failing to make any real improvement to self-policing in the Red Army. They vaguely appealed for raised vigilance, but clearly neither really knew how to improve the unmasking of enemies by the officers or PUR. This was already a difficult enough task as the enemies that the officers and PUR were expected to search out were more often than not imagined enemies—supposed spies and treacherous former oppositionists. Even without the defects in its self-policing, the Red Army would struggle to compete with the NKVD on this basis. Indeed, the army leadership's failure to come to grips with the problem of poor vigilance would give the conspiratorially minded NKVD the space it needed to more intensely scrutinize the Red Army in just a few months' time.

At the same time as foreign agents and Trotskyists were judged to be pressing security threats for the Red Army in the mid-1930s, the rumors that certain senior officers in the high command were disloyal continued to filter into the Soviet Union. Although there was still no serious response to these rumors (and certainly no arrests), it remains likely that the NKVD continued to log each piece of material suggesting that the loyalty of the high command was not guaranteed. One report of disloyalty in the high command, for instance, surfaced in Czechoslovakia in December 1935 and was published in the Russian journal *Znamia Rossii*, which reported that an underground organization was supposedly operating in the Soviet Union under the name of Kraskomov. According to *Znamia Rossii*, the members of the organization were from the Red Army high command and planned the overthrow of Soviet power.[168] As had been the case in the 1920s, some officers still received more attention than others. Tukhachevskii was as much an object of speculation as ever. For example, while on his way to England in January 1936 to attend the funeral of King George V, Tukhachevskii gave an interview to the Polish newspaper, *Ekspress Poranni*, which contained the following passage: "Tukhachevskii has always gone 'with the wind' (*po vetru*). In the past, when it had a purpose, he was considered to be a very staunch supporter of Trotsky. But he first turned his back on his patron as soon as he felt Trotsky was losing and firmly took Stalin's side."[169] At a time of increasing pressure on the former opposition, being associated with Trotsky and depicted as politically capricious was potentially damaging.

The most prominent reports and rumors in the mid-1930s, however, concerned connections that supposedly existed between the Red Army and German military elites. In December 1935, a supposed secret connection between German officers and the Red Army high command was reported by the head of Soviet military intelligence.[170] Then in April 1936, an intelligence report forwarded to Stalin with intercepted communication from the German embassy suggested that Tukhachevskii was close to the German high command. The report's account of his behavior noted, "Tukhachevskii's conduct was significant. . . . They say that he is a Francophile. Now in an extremely courteous tone he asked about the acquaintances of the German officers with interest. This is completely different behavior than before."[171] Further suggestions that Tukhachevskii was sympathetic to the Germans were received by Voroshilov from another military intelligence report in May 1936 that contained comments allegedly made by Hermann Göring during a meeting with the Polish minister of foreign affairs. According to this report, Göring said he had met with Tukhachevskii when the latter stopped in Berlin on his way back from George V's funeral. Tukhachevskii had apparently raised the possibility of resuming the military collaboration between Germany and the Soviet Union.[172] Göring's supposed remarks may have been misinformation or incorrectly relayed by Soviet intelligence. Stalin publicly rejected the idea that Tukhachevskii met Göring when he spoke with Anthony Eden in March 1935 (though Stalin no doubt wanted to put some distance between the Soviet Union and Germany at a time when he was also seeking to establish a system of collective security with other European states).[173] The idea of resuming collaboration with Germany appears to have been popular, at least in the early 1930s, among several senior Red Army officers, including Voroshilov, who was recorded by German representatives expressing his disappointment at the end of the military collaboration in 1933.[174] Yet to speak favorably of the Germans during 1933 was very different than doing so just a few years later. By 1936, Germany was the most likely enemy for the Soviet Union in the coming war. It was now possible to be arrested for merely expressing views about Germany or Hitler that could be construed as positive or flattering. In May 1936, a teacher at the Frunze Academy was arrested for supposedly saying that Hitler reflected national sentiment in Germany.[175]

In March 1935, it seems that the NKVD's foreign department did start to take more of an interest in a possible connection between the Red Army high command and Germany. A Soviet agent operating in Germany was instructed to investigate the connection.[176] Nonetheless, it remains difficult to judge how credible and threatening these rumors were estimated by the NKVD or Soviet leadership. It is likely that any new incriminating materials obtained by the NKVD would be added to files already held on certain senior officers. It is also likely that observation of the high command was stepped up as a result. There were no obvious consequences for the high command, and Tukhachevskii's career continued uninterrupted, reaching a high point in 1936. In April, he was awarded with promotion as Voroshilov's first deputy, reaching the same seniority as Gamarnik.[177] Because relations between Voroshilov and Tukhachevskii remained poor, it is possible that Stalin engineered this promotion. Voroshilov's star was perhaps beginning to fade, and he risked being eclipsed by his ambitious rival. Certainly as far as outside observers like the Japanese military attaché in Moscow were concerned, Tukhachevskii was recognized as one of the most important figures in the army establishment in the years before the military purge.[178] Tukhachevskii was also given other new responsibilities at this time, namely the authority to supervise the combat training department.[179] In this sense, if Tukhachevskii was a marked man, and if there were serious questions about his loyalty, it would have been strange to award him with a promotion and give him additional responsibilities. It would, however, be surprising if the NKVD had not maintained closer observation of Tukhachevskii because of the new rumors about his supposed German sympathies. Stalin may also have had his own nagging doubts. Although at this point, these were probably neither strong nor credible enough for any serious action to be taken.

Tukhachevskii's promotion as his first deputy was unlikely to have pleased Voroshilov. Indeed, the tensions between the two men were still simmering in the mid-1930s. At the Seventeenth Party Congress in 1934, for example, Voroshilov took the opportunity to dig up the dispute about the role of the cavalry in the Red Army. Mentioning no names, but using loaded language, Voroshilov argued that it was necessary to bring "wrecking theories" (*vreditel'skimi teoriiami*) about the cavalry to an end. He clearly had Tukhachevskii in mind.[180] However, a much more serious clash came two years later, on 1 May 1936, when several senior military figures, as well as Stalin, gathered in Voroshilov's apartment after a military parade. The tension between Voroshilov and Tukhachevskii now came to a head. In Stalin's presence, Tukhachevskii accused Voroshilov and Budennyi of being part of an exclusive clique that was dominating military politics. This was a serious charge. Stalin called an end to the argument and offered to examine the issue in the Politburo. Tukhachevskii, probably sensing that he had no choice but to back down, withdrew his accusations at this session.[181] He was then publicly criticized in *Pravda* on 24 May when an anonymous writer accused Tukhachevskii of pushing harmful theories that undermined the cavalry.[182] In this respect, Voroshilov probably would have welcomed the removal or demotion of Tukhachevskii from the army leadership, but there was little chance of this happening. Even though Stalin knew that his military leadership was divided, rising international tensions meant that the Red Army needed someone of Tukhachevskii's caliber in a senior position. Neither the persisting rumors about his disloyalty, the supposed connection to Germany, nor the long-running personal animosity with Voroshilov would lead to Tukhachevskii's losing any of his influence.

Where these ongoing internal conflicts in the high command fit into the military purge was in giving the military-fascist plot some surface credibility once it had been exposed by the NKVD in 1937. Tukhachevskii was known to be ambitious, and his poor relationship with Voroshilov was no doubt common knowledge (at the very least in the Red Army). It might have seemed plausible to some, including within the party elite, that Tukhachevskii had in fact conspired to seize control of the military from Voroshilov and perhaps wanted to bring down the regime, as the NKVD's supposed evidence of the 1937 military plot suggested. However, there is little to say that the divides in the high command provided any urgency for Stalin to purge the Red Army in the first place. While Voroshilov and Tukhachevskii were at loggerheads, the other senior officers executed as leaders of a military conspiracy in 1937 were not causing any trouble. Notably, in June 1936, Voroshilov wrote to Stalin requesting that a number of military reprimands be removed from several senior officers because four years had passed since their application. This included reprimands against Kork, Uborevich, Iakov Alksnis, and L. N. Aronshtam.[183] In August 1936, Kork had another reprimand removed, which he had received as part of the fallout from the Nakhaev case at the Moscow barracks.[184] Kork, Uborevich, Alksnis, and Aronshtam would all be executed during the military purge. Kork and Uborevich in particular would be publicly presented as two of the ringleaders of the conspiracy. For now, however, their positions were secure. It seems that whatever problems Voroshilov had with Tukhachevskii, these did not extend to all of the members of the future military-fascist plot.

Rather, the first major step toward the military purge can be seen during the summer of 1936, and it came from outside the Red Army. As we shall see, over the first six months of 1936, the NKVD's pressure on the former political opposition finally paid off, and they were able to announce the discovery of the so-called Zinoviev–Kamenev Counterrevolutionary Bloc. Importantly, the investigation into this supposed former oppositionist group quickly established connections to a number of middle-ranking former Trotskyist officers, which in turn led to a concerted NKVD investigation into the Red Army resulting in the discovery of an alleged Trotskyist military organization. It was this discovery that represented the first major step toward the military purge. The early momentum behind what would soon become an explosion of repression in the Red Army in 1937 came from a deeper level of NKVD scrutiny of the middle ranks in 1936 rather than any concerns about the reliability of the high command.

The First Moscow Show Trial and the Trotskyist Military Center

In January 1936, the NKVD arrested Valentin Ol'berg, a member of the German Communist Party, after his arrival in the Soviet Union from Germany on suspicion of being an emissary from Trotsky. There were loose grounds for suspicion. Ol'berg had once been an associate of Trotsky's, but the NKVD's subsequent line of questioning soon became divorced from reality. Under interrogation, Ol'berg was forced to admit to counterrevolutionary activity and eventually confessed to working on Trotsky's orders and planning to assassinate Stalin. Ol'berg was forced to name his fellow conspirators. This became the starting point of a growing series of arrests among the former opposition as the NKVD (no doubt making liberal use of forced confessions) obtained further admissions of criminality. By April, over 500 former Trotskyists had been arrested, and the NKVD announced the discovery of a major counter-revolutionary group.[185] As had been the case at the time of the Kirov murder, it was Ezhov who was once again the driving force behind this investigation, even though he was still not yet the head of the NKVD. As Arch Getty and Oleg Naumov note, Ezhov had been working to undermine Iagoda and was slowly positioning himself to take his place, which was not a difficult task. Under Iagoda's leadership of the NKVD, not only had Kirov been murdered, but six months later, Ezhov discovered a serious security breach in the Kremlin staff.[186] It seems that Stalin, increasingly frustrated with Iagoda's failures, gave Ezhov the freedom to muscle in on the NKVD's investigation into the former opposition in early 1936.

Ezhov, importantly, was far more conspiratorially minded than Iagoda. He was prone to seeing the outlines of complex imagined conspiracies that he believed were a pressing threat to the regime's survival. Ezhov had already been collating an increasingly large file on supposed Trotskyist subversive activity, and his conspiratorial worldview is best seen in a manuscript he had been working on since 1935, "From Factionalism to Open Counterrevolution." This set out details of a conspiracy theory linking the political opposition of Zinoviev and Kamenev to acts of terrorism and counterrevolution.[187] The manuscript laid many of the foundations for how Ezhov would frame the imagined oppositionist conspiracy the NKVD gradually exposed from 1936, which became integral to the overarching narrative of the Great Terror. The string of arrests targeting the former opposition after the arrest of Valentin Ol'berg in January 1936 represented the culmination of Ezhov's push to confirm his suspicions. The whole investigation, of course, was based on nothing more than a conspiracy theory, but Ezhov was convinced that he had discovered a major counterrevolutionary center.

Crucially, in late spring 1936, Ezhov began to push a theory that Zinoviev and Kamenev had a direct hand in the Kirov murder and had acted on Trotsky's orders. As far as Ezhov was concerned, their crime was no longer the "moral culpability" for which they had originally been charged in 1935.[188] With mounting numbers of former oppositionists now being arrested by the NKVD in the early months of 1936, Stalin decided to reopen the investigation into the Kirov murder. Zinoviev and Kamenev were taken from prison, interrogated again, and forced to confess to terrorist activity and their role in killing Kirov.[189] On 29 July, the Central Committee published a secret letter entitled "Concerning the Terroristic Activity of the Trotskyist–Zinovievist Counterrevolutionary Bloc." Sent to all party organizations, the letter detailed Zinoviev and Kamenev's purported role in the Kirov murder and Trotsky's overall direction of the unmasked counterrevolutionary center's plans to murder other Soviet leaders, including Stalin, Voroshilov, Kaganovich, and Ordzhonikidze.[190] In August, Zinoviev, Kamenev, and another fourteen defendants were forced to admit their guilt in a heavily publicized show trial, the proceedings of which had been carefully scripted. All were executed on 24 August. The first Moscow show trial was the starting point of the Great Terror. It was a public demonstration of how a dangerous conspiracy had been exposed by the NKVD that threatened the state. The trial was meant as a lesson to Soviet citizens that former oppositionists could not be trusted and that all party members needed to be alert to the danger.[191]

This attack on the former opposition in the first half of 1936 had an immediate impact on the Red Army. Importantly, the series of arrests from January stemming from the Ol'berg case had revealed several connections to former Trotskyists still serving in the military who were soon arrested because of associations with the Zinoviev–Kamenev Counterrevolutionary Bloc or for membership in a separate Trotskyist military organization. On 4 July, for instance, R. V. Pickel, who at one time had been in charge of Zinoviev's secretariat and who was put on trial in August, claimed under interrogation that former Trotskyists Dmitri Shmidt, Efim Dreitser, and Vitovt Putna were members of a counterrevolutionary military organization.[192] With the exception of Dreitser, who was the deputy director of the Cheliabinsk factory Magnezit, the other two were serving officers. Shmidt was a battalion commander in the Kiev Military District, and Putna was the Soviet military attaché in Britain. Dreitser had already been arrested at the end of June, and Shmidt was picked up on 6 July.[193] Moreover, Shmidt served with another corps commander, S. A. Turovskii, who was arrested in September and accused of belonging to the same military organization. When Shmidt was interrogated by the NKVD, he was coerced into giving evidence that a Trotskyist underground organization existed in Moscow. This was apparently the center for other Trotskyist organizations, and Shmidt claimed that there was an associated military organization.[194] Another former military Trotskyist arrested in the summer was Sergei Mrachkovskii, one of Trotsky's most senior allies in the Red Army in the 1920s.

It was perhaps for this reason that he was selected to be one of the defendants at the Moscow show trial in August 1936. In this way, there was a direct connection between the August show trial and the Red Army. Finally, Vitalii Primakov, who had been under NKVD observation from 1933, was also arrested in August alongside another former Trotskyist, B. I. Kuz'michev, the chief of staff of an aviation brigade and one-time secretary to Primakov.

This series of arrests must have been vindication for the NKVD. They had kept some of these very same former Trotskyists under observation since the early 1930s, refusing to believe that they had abandoned their support for Trotsky. This included Dreitser, who was now understood to be a key conspirator and who was named in the secret letter from the Central Committee in July that described the exposed oppositionist organization. Trotsky had apparently ordered Dreitser to assassinate Stalin and Voroshilov.[195] However, it seems that some of these now-arrested former Trotskyists, including those from the Red Army, had continued to meet with each other in the 1930s even after recanting their incorrect political views. Some of these meetings continued right up to their arrests. Dreitser, for instance, was a close acquaintance of Putna, and the two met in Britain, where Putna was the Soviet military attaché. According to a letter sent to Voroshilov in early September 1936 from the deputy head of military intelligence, Artur Artuzov, Putna had been in regular contact with Dreitser. Artuzov relayed a conversation he had had with Putna's wife, who, aside from arguing that her husband was innocent of any crime, remarked that Putna and Dreitser often saw each other in London. Apparently, upon hearing the news about the exposure of the Zinoviev–Kamenev Counterrevolutionary Bloc, Putna's wife recalled that her husband worried that because of his contact with Dreitser he would now come under suspicion.[196] Although former military Trotskyists like Putna and Dreitser did meet in secret from time to time, it is unlikely that they were actually planning the overthrow of the regime. Whatever oppositionist network existed in the Soviet Union in the mid-1930s was weak and ineffectual, and it is questionable whether Putna and Dreitser were in fact conspiring. Yet from the NKVD's point of view, any meeting between two ex-Trotskyists could be nothing but conspiratorial. What other business would they need to discuss in secret and outside of the Soviet Union apart from how to undermine the Soviet state? As Arch Getty has noted, as far as the party elite were concerned, merely to share critical thoughts about the regime was akin to treason.[197] Putna had not been oblivious to the danger of meeting with other members of the former opposition. Five days after his arrest on 20 August, Voroshilov received a letter from A. Orlov, the Soviet military attaché in Germany, who was writing after reading about Putna's alleged involvement with the Zinoviev–Kamenev Counterrevolutionary Bloc in the German newspapers. In his letter, Orlov recalled meeting Putna in Paris in January 1935 and how their conversation had turned to the recent Kirov murder. According to Orlov, Putna had remarked, "I ran into Kamenev. He invited me to come and visit him as an old friend. For some reason I did not go. What would you think about me now if I had gone to see him, in connection with my past?"[198] If Orlov's account is accurate, it shows that Putna clearly understood that his background as a former Trotskyist remained potentially compromising, despite his recantation and demonstration of loyalty to the party. Putna knew how the Stalinist system worked. Past black marks were never forgotten, and Putna had to tread carefully to make sure they were not used against him. Moreover, if Putna did consider himself an old friend of Lev Kamenev, it is possible that the NKVD watched him with particular interest in the years after the Kirov murder.

For Putna, being a former Trotskyist was not his only problem. We saw evidence in chapter 2 to suggest that Voroshilov gave Putna an intelligence role after he had publicly turned away from Trotskyism in the late 1920s. Putna may well have carried out espionage in London, as the British authorities suspected. The British security service materials on Putna, however, also suggest that he had been in regular contact with a German intelligence agent named Erich von Salzman.[199] If this is true, a close association with a German intelligence agent, alongside the secret meetings with Dreitser, would have been damning for Putna. The NKVD surely seized the opportunity to arrest him in August 1936. This is a critical point. It was only when the Zinoviev–Kamenev Counterrevolutionary Bloc was arrested in summer 1936 that the NKVD could act on whatever prior suspicions they had about Putna and finally have him arrested. This applies equally to the other former military Trotskyists arrested during the summer of 1936. Primakov, now deputy commander of the Leningrad Military District, was arrested in August 1936 despite having been under surveillance in 1933.[200] A day later, former Trotskyist and commander of the 25th Rifle Division M. O. Ziuk was also arrested. Ziuk had likewise been on the NKVD's radar as a potentially unreformed Trotskyist in the early 1930s. It was the Zinoviev–Kamenev

Counterrevolutionary Bloc that gave the NKVD the opportunity to at last capitalize on their suspicions.

Unsurprisingly, and no doubt sensing trouble ahead, Voroshilov immediately tried to put some distance between himself and the arrested former Trotskyists in the Red Army. On 7 June 1936, around the time the incriminating evidence was beginning to surface against the group of former Trotskyist officers, Voroshilov sent a letter to Stalin that was damning of the arrested former oppositionists. In reference to the testimony emerging from the interrogations of Dreitser and Pickel, he remarked, "What an abomination, how low people can sink. But the worst of this scum, nevertheless, is Mrachkovskii. . . . This should serve as a lesson: it is impossible to have any kind of business with these people."[201] As we saw in chapter 2, however, Voroshilov had had dealings with precisely "these people" in the past. He had been a strong advocate of Putna in the early 1930s, describing him as "one of our best commander-party men,"[202] and had even petitioned for him to have access to secret documents while he was a military attaché in Germany. That Putna was now implicated in a major counterrevolutionary group should have alarmed Voroshilov. It raised serious questions about his judgment. His letter to Stalin was no doubt intended as an exercise in damage control after he realized the difficult position he was now in.

In this respect, the pressure on former Trotskyists, which increased markedly over the course of 1936 and culminated in the NKVD's discovery of the Zinoviev–Kamenev Counterrevolutionary Bloc, had dragged in the Red Army. In truth, this was all nothing more than an imagined conspiracy. It was revealing of the conspiratorial worldview of the ruling Soviet elite and of their willingness to accept that the former opposition were dangerous terrorists. Evidence to fit the narrative was extracted by the NKVD by forced confessions. Notably, the arrested former Trotskyist officers connected to this oppositionist conspiracy were not from the military elite. These officers were not on the level of Tukhachevskii, but their arrests were still significant. Primakov, for instance, had been deputy commander of the Leningrad Military District, a member of the Military Soviet, and a member of the Central Executive Committee.[203] These arrests were more serious than any previous cases of Trotskyism in the Red Army. The NKVD claimed to have discovered the counterrevolutionary center responsible for the Kirov murder with ties to the military. Moreover, the exposure of these connections provided the opportunity for arrests to spread further within the Red Army. After the arrest of Dmitri Shmidt, for instance, in early August, Voroshilov received a denunciation from the head of a military political academy leveled against another army man, a certain Rubinov. According to the denunciation, Rubinov had been close to Shmidt. They had served together, and Rubinov was said to have defended him. The denunciation added, "I would not be very surprised if an attentive investigation would establish that Rubinov was close to this entire band, and in any case, knew about Shmidt's mood."[204] It is unclear what happened to Rubinov as a result of this letter, but such denunciations would feature much more heavily in 1937–1938.

The Red Army, then, may well have regained some stability after Operation Vesna and the scaling back of collectivization, but the army leadership could not be confident that all enemies had been expunged from the ranks or that the military was now fully reliable. Large numbers of soldiers continued to be discharged throughout the early 1930s and beyond. The Red Army was still judged to be the target of various subversives, particularly foreign agents. This perceived vulnerability to subversion became a more pressing issue as the international situation deteriorated throughout the 1930s, meaning that having a powerful (and reliable) military was even more of a priority. For the Soviet leaders, the surge of Japanese aggression in the east and the rise of Hitler in the west meant that a war on two fronts seemed a likely prospect. However, what was particularly concerning for the army leadership was the persistent lack of vigilance shown by the officer corps toward self-policing in the ranks. Enemies, including foreign subversives, were believed to be going undiscovered at the same time that international tensions were rising. However, Voroshilov had no credible solution to this problem. His criticisms of weak vigilance merely masked deeper problems in self-policing in the Red Army. We have already seen many indications that poor vigilance may have in fact stemmed from some officers' desire not to attract too much official scrutiny, to protect their own interests, or to deflect attention by making conspicuous demonstrations of being alert. Voroshilov was as guilty of this as anyone else. It is almost certain that he was feeling pressure from Stalin about undiscovered enemies in the army, especially in the aftermath of the Kirov murder, but his only solution was to call for even more vigilance. This was not a serious engagement with the problems existing in the Red Army and was probably intended more for show than substance. As the next chapter shows,

Voroshilov's failure to properly come to grips with the security of the Red Army meant that it was difficult for Stalin to feel confident that Voroshilov had matters in hand and that the army was sufficiently insulated from what was understood to be a growing threat from subversives. Indeed, rather than discover enemies independently, it had taken separate party purges, the *proverka* and *obmen*, to expose the supposed spies, Trotskyists, and Zinovievites who had seemingly been missed by the army. Former Trotskyist officers connected to the Zinoviev–Kamenev Counterrevolutionary Bloc had of course been arrested by the NKVD.

In this respect, the perceived threat from Trotskyist counterrevolutionaries in 1936 began to solidify concerns that the Red Army had been infiltrated by a conspiratorial organization. As Stalin and the NKVD actively targeted supporters of the former opposition, and as connections were unearthed between the group of former Trotskyist officers and the imagined Zinoviev–Kamenev Counterrevolutionary Bloc, it was impossible to ignore the potential threat posed by the former Trotskyists still serving in the Red Army. Over the next six months and running into 1937, the NKVD would arrest a growing number of former Trotskyists in the military. Yet for the time being, the most senior officers in the high command were not at risk of arrest. Despite persistent rumors about members of the high command working against the regime or being sympathetic to Germany, and even with tensions peaking between Tukhachevskii and Voroshilov, there is no indication that the Red Army elite was being primed for a purge. Reprimands were removed from the files of several officers who would be executed just a year later. Importantly, no one from the military elite had ever supported the opposition. In the summer of 1936, there was little indication that the arrests spreading throughout the Red Army would move beyond an exclusively Trotskyist purge. General arrest levels and criminality in the army continued to decline. A mass purge was not being prepared.

As we shall see in the next chapter, the primary importance of the arrests of the former Trotskyist officers in 1936 was that it focused attention on the Red Army. This was a decisive moment in the lead-up to the military purge in 1937. Even if it was not apparent at the time, the exposure of a Trotskyist military organization prepared the ground for Ezhov and the NKVD to conceptualize a much broader imagined conspiracy in the Red Army over the coming months. Indeed, the direction of the investigation soon changed in early 1937 as the NKVD began to make more supposed connections between arrested former oppositionists and fascist states. The convergence of these two threats—the domestic and the external—greatly widened the circle of officers who could now be arrested, going far beyond the former opposition. Once the NKVD turned greater attention to the threat posed by foreign agents, even those at the heart of the upper military establishment were put at risk.

5 | The Military Purge

The arrest of the small group of former Trotskyist officers during the summer and autumn of 1936 was different in many respects from earlier cases of counterrevolutionary Trotskyism in the Red Army. The connections between members of the Zinoviev–Kamenev Counterrevolutionary Bloc and still-serving officers in the Red Army were far more serious. Since the summer of 1936, a group of middle-ranking officers was now understood to be complicit in a conspiracy to assassinate leading party members. The existence of a supposed Trotskyist military organization gave form to what had previously been a disparate, if not growing, string of arrests for Trotskyism in the army over the past few years. These earlier arrests had typically been on a case-by-case basis and showed few signs of organized conspiracy.[1] Now the situation was very different, with the unmasking of a secret military group, supposedly masterminded from abroad by Trotsky, that had subversive designs against the party elite. Moreover, it is not surprising that after the arrests of Primakov, Putna, and the other former Trotskyist officers, the Red Army would face more intense scrutiny. As we have seen, the previous years had seen repeated calls from the army leadership about raising Bolshevik vigilance, criticism of incorrect discharges and promotions, and the discovery of dangerous "enemies" in the ranks who had seemingly gone unnoticed by the officer corps and PUR. The exposure of a new Trotskyist military group in 1936 would be taken as further evidence that army self-policing remained entirely inadequate. The Red Army was missing the dangerous conspirators working from within. Furthermore, it had not been any improvement in vigilance in the army that had produced these recent arrests but rather a separate NKVD investigation. It is doubtful that this provided much assurance to the Soviet leadership that the Red Army was able to manage its own security. Ezhov and the NKVD's influence in military affairs only grew from this point on.

As the Primakov–Putna group was being arrested by the NKVD, there were immediate calls for the Red Army to be more closely scrutinized. One such call came from Voroshilov's old comrade and ally, Budennyi, who sent him a letter on 22 August containing his thoughts on the first Moscow show trial:

> The trial of the counterrevolutionary band going on now in Moscow as never before clearly shows the world's humanity to what point these degenerates and their mangy ringleader—Trotsky—have sunk. But this, in my view, should not be the end. I think that it is necessary to raise all the working people, both in the Soviet Union and in all countries of the world, to demand the extradition of Trotsky and his foreign company, to put him on trial in our country. . . . It is clear that the network of this organization has penetrated into the army, into the railways, industry, agriculture, into the organism of our state in general. . . . It seems to me that it is necessary to check especially carefully people in the army, since in the ranks we see people from the command, the officers and political workers, who on the one hand have careerist tendencies and on the other a tendency to consider serious questions not from the point of view of the state but from a narrowly personal point of view—a local "oligarchy" (*bat'kovshchina*) and also people who easily give in to any kind of influence, in particular counterrevolutionary.[2]

Because of his close relationship with Voroshilov, Budennyi surely believed his letter would carry weight; he may well have been trying to influence Stalin. That Budennyi specifically chose to commit his views to writing suggests that he wanted them shared; if this was the case, he got what he wanted. Voroshilov, presumably seeing the importance of the letter, forwarded it to Stalin, Ezhov, and A. A. Andreev, a secretary of the Central Committee, on 1 September.[3]

The significance of Budennyi's letter is not only in his call for a careful scrutiny of the Red Army but also in that he specifically singled out the officer corps. Aside from the fact that the officers would bear much of the weight of the later military purge, by accusing them of choosing their own narrow self-interest over that of the state, Budennyi touched on the type of complaints about the officer corps that had been raised in previous years and that had typically been captured under the umbrella of poor vigilance. Using the term *bat'kovshchina* (oligarchy) implied that some officers were principally concerned with maintaining their own networks of power and influence rather than working for the good of the Red Army as a whole. It suggested that systems of patronage and nepotism existed in the military and that these were having a detrimental effect on its security. For Budennyi, these local networks gave dangerous enemies the opportunity to operate freely. If officers were looking after their own self-interest, what motivation would they have to locate any possible Trotskyists, Zinovievites, or foreign agents working within their own commands? The discovery of such enemies could bring down the entire local network under NKVD pressure. In this sense, Budennyi's comments add further weight to the accumulating evidence suggesting that some officers may have been reluctant to search for enemies in their own commands and were more concerned in maintaining their own positions and spheres of influence. Finally, it is possible that in writing the letter, Budennyi was attempting to disassociate himself from Voroshilov despite their long alliance. He was making efforts to point out in written form that there were serious problems with the behavior of the officer corps—problems that had consequences for the security of the Red Army. Budennyi perhaps sensed that further arrests were around the corner after the unmasking of the Trotskyist military organization, and he may have thought that Voroshilov was in a precarious position. Budennyi may have wanted to make sure that he had given suitable signals about the threat to the army in good time.

The NKVD matched Budennyi's call, declaring that the Red Army should be investigated more thoroughly. However, a change in leadership proved decisive. On 25 September, Iagoda was finally replaced by Ezhov as the head of the NKVD. Since the investigation into the Kirov murder, Ezhov had been encroaching into Iagoda's territory. When the Zinoviev–Kamenev Counterrevolutionary Bloc was exposed in 1936, it spelled the end of his time as the head of the NKVD. Stalin criticized Iagoda for having been four years behind in the group's discovery. (The interrogations of the arrested former oppositionists revealed that the group had supposedly formed as early as 1932.) There was, of course, no truth to this, but as far as Stalin was concerned, Iagoda had allowed dangerous conspirators to operate freely for several years. Iagoda was then further undermined by serious gas explosions at the Kemerovo coal mines in Western Siberia in September, which was presented as further evidence of Trotskyist sabotage.[4] With the head of the NKVD seemingly allowing dangerous enemies to slip by, Stalin finally brought in someone he believed would deliver results: Ezhov.

Ezhov's appointment as the head of the NKVD was a key moment for both the wider Great Terror and the military purge. Ezhov was far more conspiratorially minded than his predecessor, and he had a lower standard of what constituted reliable evidence. Iagoda had justifiably expressed some skepticism about the idea that Trotsky was masterminding an oppositionist terrorist network inside the Soviet Union from his exile abroad.[5] Ezhov had no such doubts. His appointment as head of the NKVD meant that the Zinoviev–Kamenev Counterrevolutionary Bloc would inevitably achieve much greater proportions and that the conspiracy would move in new directions. Indeed, in the months after the August show trial, Ezhov turned his attention toward former oppositionists working within the Soviet state apparatus. Industry was hit particularly hard.[6] Managers and engineers working under the severe pressures of the five-year plan were vulnerable targets. In the tense climate after the arrest of the Zinoviev–Kamenev Counterrevolutionary Bloc, unavoidable shortfalls in output or industrial accidents were even more likely to be explained as evidence of sabotage rather than as the consequence of pushing the factories too far and too fast. From August 1936, the NKVD arrested increasing numbers of people working in industry connected to the former opposition or with other black marks on their party records as responsible for industrial sabotage. The most significant arrest was that of Georgii Piatakov, deputy people's commissar of heavy industry, on 11 September 1936. Piatakov had been a leading Trotskyist in the 1920s but had risen to a powerful position as Ordzhonikidze's deputy in the People's Commissariat for Heavy Industry. Under arrest, he was forced to confess to having carried out acts of industrial sabotage that located the conspiracy of former oppositionists further up the party hierarchy. The parameters of the imagined conspiracy were gradually shifting as the NKVD widened the scope of the investigation. Moreover, in November, a number of senior industry officials were put on trial and found guilty of carrying out the explosions at the Kemerovo mines in September, which, as Arch Getty notes, provided a clear signal that there were senior officials in the economic establishment actively engaged in industrial sabotage. It was no longer just former oppositionists living on the fringes of Soviet society who represented a threat. Now individuals with real power and influence—those directly responsible for the Soviet economy—were being unmasked as supposedly working against the regime.[7]

It would be a mistake, however, to see Ezhov as the sole driving force behind this expanding wave of repression. Ezhov was undeniably a conspiracy theorist who, as head of the NKVD, had been given one of the most powerful positions in the Soviet state. This was a dangerous combination. He now had the opportunity to capitalize on his suspicions and bring his conspiracy theories to life. But at the same time, Stalin always had the last word. Ezhov could certainly present Stalin with his evidence of underground conspiracies and terrorist groups, but there was no guarantee that these would be accepted, or in what form. Stalin had in fact shown some skepticism toward Ezhov's theory that Zinoviev and Kamenev were involved in the Kirov murder when he raised this supposition in 1935.[8] Stalin eventually came around to this view a year later when he ordered that the investigation into the Kirov murder be reopened, but Ezhov failed to convince him before this point. Stalin exercised ultimate control over the path of repression—an important point. However, it does seem that Stalin came to trust Ezhov more than he had Iagoda.[9] Ezhov had succeeded where Iagoda had failed. After the arrest of the Zinoviev–Kamenev Counterrevolutionary Bloc in summer 1936, it appears that Stalin gave Ezhov the green light to widen his investigation. Despite having shown some skepticism toward Ezhov's ideas in the past, for the time being, Stalin was probably willing to see what else he might come up with. This gave Ezhov more freedom to take his conspiracy theories in new directions.

The Red Army could not avoid being drawn into his widening net. The military had long been recognized as an attractive target for potential saboteurs and enemies. In terms of investigating the Red Army specifically, Ezhov signaled his intentions early on. Just before his appointment as head of the NKVD, in a letter to Stalin on 9 September 1936 concerning the arrested former oppositionists, Ezhov remarked that he believed that there must still be Trotskyist officers undiscovered in the Red Army.[10] This letter was sent to Stalin just days after Ezhov received Budennyi's letter calling for more scrutiny of the officer corps, and it may have had some influence. However, with Ezhov now at the helm of the NKVD, and with Budennyi calling for careful scrutiny of the officer corps, two powerful influences coincided to push the investigation of the Trotskyist military organization deeper into the Red Army.

Guilt by association was the most direct way that repression in the army gathered pace in the second half of 1936. In the first instance, anyone connected to the former oppositionists arrested over the summer was vulnerable. For example, on 26 September, M. I. Gai, the head of the special department of the NKVD, sent Voroshilov a request to demobilize four army men who were supposedly linked with arrested former Trotskyist, Dreitser.[11] However, the active participation of Red Army men themselves also accelerated the pace of repression. Because a Trotskyist military group had been supposedly found in the Red Army—and one connected to the Zinoviev–Kamenev Counterrevolutionary Bloc—the ground was set for a spike in denunciations. This participation from below was not unique to the Red Army. A central reason why the Great Terror achieved such a vast scale between 1937 and 1938 was because ordinary people helped perpetuate the wave of violence. There were powerful impulses toward denouncing another person to the authorities during these years. Once someone had been arrested, all of his or her social connections, friends, and family were in danger of guilt by association. In response, and as a means of self-preservation, some people chose to denounce another person in order to put some distance between themselves and their arrested associate. A denunciation in this sense could be intended to prove that the denouncer was sufficiently vigilant against enemies. Moreover, a number of ordinary people certainly wrote denunciations out of a sense of duty, having fully accepted the regime's warnings about enemies of the people. Others had far baser motives, perhaps sensing an opportunity to get rid of a rival by using a well-timed denunciation. Ultimately, however, even for those who did not believe the regime's rhetoric about the enemy within, it was almost impossible to avoid complicity in spreading the gathering repression.[12] To do nothing at all in an increasingly tense political climate was potentially risky and might raise suspicions about one's own background or personal loyalties. These pressures and tough choices played out in the Red Army as much as they did in other Soviet institutions. Consequently, denunciation letters soon flowed in after the August show trial, with some Red Army men choosing to write directly to Stalin. On 10 October 1936, for example, Stalin received a denunciation from a political commissar in the Black Sea fleet with a list of ten people whom he claimed were dangerous former oppositionists. On 15 November, Gamarnik was sent a long list of army men who were apparently former Trotskyists. Ninety-two people were named.[13] It also appears that Stalin was kept well informed about the number of former Trotskyists discovered in the Red Army at this time. Georgii Malenkov, director of the department of leading party organs of the Central Committee, for instance, sent Stalin the details of Trotskyists working in the central army apparatus and the military academies in November 1936.[14]

During the investigation into the Zinoviev–Kamenev Counterrevolutionary Bloc, it seems that the NKVD already had suspicions about the specific role that might be played by a Trotskyist military group. In the interrogation transcripts of some of the arrested former oppositionists, a possible military plot (*voennyi zagovor*) was recorded on several occasions. For example, during the interrogation of Isaak Reingol'd, a former Trotskyist and chairman of the cotton syndicate, Reingol'd mentioned two ways that power could be seized by the counterrevolutionaries: either through "double-dealing" or a "military plot."[15] Senior party figure and journalist Karl Radek, who had been implicated during the August show trial and arrested soon after, also claimed under interrogation in December that there was a military plot that included several of the arrested former Trotskyist officers. Around the same time, former oppositionist Grigorii Sokol'nikov, the first deputy people's commissar of light industry, also spoke under interrogation about preparations for sabotage and treachery by Trotskyist officers at a time of war.[16] These examples are a reminder that the NKVD had the power to shape interrogation evidence and push it in a particular direction. Sleep deprivation, violence, intimidation, and blackmail helped interrogators get the confessions they were looking for. That a military plot was mentioned several times by senior former oppositionists in the latter half of 1936 indicates at the very least that this threat was on the NKVD's radar. Some people within the NKVD (probably Ezhov) may have believed that a nascent military conspiracy already existed in the Red Army in mid-1936 and intended to see how high up the ranks it extended.

The Military Soviet met again in October 1936, not long after the Primakov–Putna group had been arrested over the summer. What is surprising about this meeting, however, is that there was almost no discussion of the arrested former Trotskyist officers. Their arrests were not specifically addressed; only the wider trend of former oppositionists being arrested was mentioned, as well as their responsibility for the Kirov murder.[17] It is possible that the army leadership saw the arrests of Primakov, Putna, and the other former Trotskyist officers as primarily an NKVD matter; this explains the lack of discussion at the Military Soviet. However, it is also entirely likely that they were not too alarmed over what were, at this stage, only a small number of arrests of officers connected to the Zinoviev–Kamenev case. Whatever the reason for the silence about the Trotskyist military organization, the Military Soviet undertook its customary discussion of political reliability in the Red Army. Alongside the usual formulaic statements about apparent advances in the military's political consciousness, several negative trends were still causing problems—trends that raise further questions about the effectiveness of self-policing in the Red Army.

In his speech to the Military Soviet, the deputy head of PUR, G. A.

Osepian, noted several ongoing problems with the reliability of the Red Army. Although he claimed that general reliability had actually seen some improvement over the past year, stubborn unresolved issues included poor discipline levels and young officers not receiving adequate political education. In addition, many political workers were apparently themselves poorly trained. Drunkenness was also a serious problem and was identified as the primary cause of accidents. However, more seriously, Osepian warned that the threat from subversives remained high. He remarked that even though the previous two party purges, the *proverka* and *obmen,* had expelled class enemies and harmful people from the army party organizations, this was not the time to be complacent. Not all enemies had been found, and the army needed to be alert to the danger within. At the same time, Osepian made further suggestions that self-policing in the army continued to function poorly. According to Osepian, some officers had been classifying harmless conversations between servicemen as something more dangerous (presumably counter-revolutionary), and this was leading to unnecessary expulsions from the party and discharges from the army.[18] It is undoubtedly true that some officers reacted with excessive zeal to the widely publicized—and sensational—revelations of the first show trial, but it is possible that within an increasingly tense political climate, like so many other ordinary Soviet citizens, a greater number of officers felt the need to make conspicuous demonstrations of vigilance out of a sense of self-preservation. Denouncing the supposedly counterrevolutionary conduct of others was a way of proving one's vigilance. So while the army leadership gave little impression of being panicked by the Red Army's connection to the Zinoviev–Kamenev group at the October Military Soviet, some officers lower down the chain of command may have had more cause for concern. The possibility of guilt by association, as we have seen, was very real in the months after the first Moscow show trial, and baseless denunciations must have been happening on a large enough scale for Osepian to raise the issue at the Military Soviet. The sense of panic in the Red Army only grew stronger throughout 1937.

Pavel Smirnov, the head of PUR in the Leningrad Military District, also called attention to the presence of subversives in the ranks at the Military Soviet. Making a similar point to Osepian, he argued that the *proverka* and *obmen* had revealed that class aliens, harmful elements, and foreign elements had managed to infiltrate the army and its commanding structures. He gave examples of the Belorussian and Leningrad military districts, where apparently a number of Polish and Finnish nationals had infiltrated the army. Notably, these agents, according to Smirnov, had been sent by "fascist elements."[19] Moreover, Ian Berzin, the deputy commander of the Special Red Banner Far Eastern Army and former head of military intelligence, also raised the security threat posed by foreign agents. He noted that because of the location of his forces on the eastern border, there was a high risk of treachery from non-Russian soldiers and that some were actively working against the Red Army.[20] The perceived threat posed by foreign agents in the border regions was nothing new. The OGPU had wanted closer observation of the troops serving in border regions since the early 1930s. Because world war looked more likely from the Soviet point of view, the threat from foreign agents was being taken more seriously, and it would become the defining issue for the Red Army in 1937. Voroshilov used the Military Soviet to comment on the deteriorating international situation. Germany and Japan were the most likely opponents in any war, and Italy was moving closer to Germany. As far as Voroshilov was concerned, war was approaching with speed, and the Red Army still had a lot of work to do to maximize its military strength.[21] However, as the discussion at the Military Soviet revealed, there was still some way to go before the Red Army leadership could feel satisfied that the military was adequately securing itself from enemies. Importantly, there were hints that the nature of this threat was changing. Fascist agents would soon become the main security threat for the Red Army rather than members of the former opposition.

However, in the second half of 1936, the perceived internal threats posed by former Trotskyists and other supporters of the former opposition were still the main causes of concern for the Soviet leadership. This explains why, as of yet, there was no large wave of repression in the Red Army. According to a report summarizing arrests within the command and other leading army institutions, between 1 August and 31 December 1936, there were 212 arrests for counterrevolutionary Trotskyism, of which thirty-two were from the officer corps. The number of such arrests over the previous six months (from January to 1 August 1936) was 125, with six from the officer corps. As such, from August 1936, the number of arrests had certainly increased in these commanding bodies, though by less than 100 cases. From 1 January 1937 to 1 March 1937, the pace of arrests seen in the latter half of 1936 was maintained, with 125 further arrests, forty-three from the officer corps.[22] These are not large numbers compared with the thousands arrested during the military purge between 1937 and 1938. Furthermore, between July 1936 and February 1937, those arrested belonging to the rank of major and higher included only the officers connected to the Zinoviev–Kamenev Counterrevolutionary Bloc, namely Putna, Primakov, Turovskii, Shmidt, Ziuk, and Kuz'michev. Another two former Trotskyists officers joined this group. I. L. Karpel', the head of staff of the 66th Rifle Division, was arrested in December 1936, and Iu. V. Sablin, a battalion commander, had been incriminated as part of the case against the Trotskyist military organization.[23] However, members of the military elite were as yet unaffected by the gathering arrests. Senior officers such as Tukhachevskii, who in less than a year would be put on trial as a leader of the military-fascist plot, were not in danger of arrest at this point because they had never had any involvement with the former political opposition. For the time being, the NKVD was focusing most of its attention on Stalin's former political opponents. This focus widened in the early months of 1937.

Another indication that the Red Army leadership was not thrown into a panic over the discovery of the alleged Trotskyist military organization can be seen from the Military Procuracy. In late January 1937, the chief military procurator, Naum Rozovskii, wrote to Fel'dman, head of the main administration of the Red Army, about the possibility of releasing N. Kakurin from prison. Kakurin, as we saw in chapter 3, was arrested during Operation Vesna in 1930, and his interrogation evidence incriminated Tukhachevskii as the leader of a supposed counterrevolutionary group—an accusation that Stalin eventually dismissed. In 1937, Rozovskii was contacting Fel'dman about the possibility of releasing Kakurin after he had received an appeal from his wife. He wanted Fel'dman's opinion about whether Kakurin could now be reinstated in the army as a specialist.[24] Unfortunately, Fel'dman's judgment is unknown, but that the chief military procurator was considering releasing a convicted conspirator and giving him a new military role suggests a certain level of complacency about enemies within the Red Army. Admittedly, the original charges against Kakurin might have been viewed more skeptically seven years later, but nonetheless, if there was genuine growing panic about the danger from subversives in the military, it is unlikely that the idea of releasing Kakurin would be entertained. Yet this does not mean that the army leadership was entirely complacent. The continuing threat to the Red Army from enemies had been made clear at the Military Soviet in October 1936, and the Primakov–Putna group, despite its small size, was recognized as comprising dangerous conspirators. A cautious approach was being taken in the Red Army. For instance, at the same time that Rozovskii was writing to Fel'dman about Kakurin, Gamarnik ordered that officers discharged from the ranks for political or moral reasons would not be able to rejoin the army even in the early phase of a war.[25] This was an attempt to improve the political reliability of the officer corps, but there was no indication that a major purge was planned.

There is also evidence of a level of pushback from within the army leadership against unfounded cases brought by the NKVD in the military at this time. This can be seen most clearly from Fel'dman, who took a stand against the NKVD on several occasions throughout 1936 and early 1937. Fel'dman frequently defended officers and soldiers charged as counterrevolutionaries or for espionage, and he lobbied Voroshilov and Gamarnik for more lenient punishments. At times, he argued outright that the charges were baseless. Fel'dman typically made a case that the accused was in fact a good officer or soldier who denied the accusations against them, and that a transfer would be a better solution than a discharge.[26] One example concerns a wrecking group that had supposedly been uncovered in the chemical industry by M. I. Gai, who notified Voroshilov about it on 26 August 1936. Two workers from the chemical administration, a certain Nikitin and Ostovskii, also sent Voroshilov a denunciation naming almost thirty alleged Trotskyists working alongside them.[27] Voroshilov then ordered Fel'dman and G. A. Osepian, deputy head of PUR, to investigate the case, alongside N. I. Dobroditskii, a deputy at the NKVD special department. When Fel'dman and Osepian reported back to Voroshilov on 19 September, they challenged the NKVD's story. They argued that without carefully scrutiny of the work and activity of the accused men, they could not advise arrest with full confidence.[28] Moreover, they stated that there was no concrete evidence against the group, and in fact their individual appraisals had shown them to be loyal and disciplined.[29] Fel'dman and Osepian also challenged the denunciation sent in by Nikitin and Ostovskii that named the other Trotskyists.[30] The outcome of this case is unknown, but Fel'dman and Osepian were challenging the NKVD on the need for better evidence. It is hard to imagine that it would be possible to consistently intervene in this way if the army leadership was making preparations for a major purge of the military. The risks of defending those accused of sabotage or counterrevolution would be too great.

Fel'dman's attempts to uphold legality would, however, do little to forestall the military purge when it was finally sanctioned in June 1937. Fel'dman was certainly an influential military voice, but he had nothing like Ezhov's power. In the months after the first Moscow show trial, the Red Army was not thrown into crisis, but Ezhov seemed intent on seeing how far the Trotskyist presence extended in the ranks. At an NKVD conference in December 1936, he remarked, "I think we have still not fully investigated the military Trotskyist line. I think there are not only Trotskyists in the army, but every other scum since the army is not isolated from the population. . . . We opened a diversionary-wrecking organization in industry. What grounds are there to believe that it is impossible to carry out diversionary acts in the army? There are more opportunities here anyway than in industry, not fewer."[31]

A final indication that senior officers in the high command were safe from arrest for the time being is that Voroshilov pushed for the promotion of some of those who would later be accused of leading the military-fascist plot. On 10 November 1936, he wrote to Stalin about the possibility of moving Uborevich from the head of the Belorussian Military District and promoting him as his deputy and as the head of the air force.[32] Voroshilov similarly requested that Eideman be promoted from his position as the head of Osoaviakhim to the head of the antiaircraft administration, as, in his words, it needed someone of "major authority."[33] Voroshilov had previously tried to have Uborevich transferred to the head of the air force, in 1935, but at that time, Uborevich had written to Stalin and asked not to be moved, arguing that he was in poor health and not up to the demands of working in the central apparatus.[34] When Voroshilov raised this again with Stalin in November 1936, Uborevich resisted once again. That Voroshilov proposed splitting the Belorussian Military District into two alongside sending Uborevich to the center may have been the source of his resistance.[35] It is possible to interpret Voroshilov's plan to split the Belorussian Military District as an attempt to dilute Uborevich's regional influence.[36] We have already seen Budennyi's complaint about the existence of oligarchies in the Red Army, and Voroshilov may have wanted to break up Uborevich's own center of power. Then again, he might simply have believed Uborevich would be better employed in the center as his deputy and head of the air force, and that his district should be split for efficiency's sake. It is impossible to know for certain. However, it is less likely that Voroshilov wanted Uborevich moved because he saw him as a potential military conspirator. When Uborevich was eventually incriminated in the military-fascist plot in mid-1937, rather than being brought to the center, the opposite happened: he was transferred even further away from Moscow to a backwater military district before his arrest.

In the end, Stalin had no problem with Uborevich staying where he was and did not sanction the transfer.[37] Nor was Eideman moved from Osoaviakhim. Eideman's transfer might not have been approved as a result of doubts about his suitability. Stalin will have not forgotten Nakhaev's revolt at the Moscow barracks just two years before, and as head of Osoaviakhim, Eideman had been Nakhaev's superior. Stalin may have questioned his competence. Whatever motivations lay behind Voroshilov's wanting the two officers transferred and Stalin's refusal to do so, in 1936, there was nothing to suggest that either would be arrested anytime soon. There might have been questions about Eideman's competence or the level of Uborevich's regional influence, but there was no evidence tying either to a conspiracy against the state. Stalin possibly had his own private concerns about the loyalty of the high command. He would know that Ezhov suspected that more enemies in the Red Army were yet to be found and that some of the arrested former oppositionists had referred to a military plot during their interrogations. Even if Stalin had nagging doubts, including doubts about those who would in the future be named the ringleaders of the military-fascist plot, it does not seem that he had communicated these to Voroshilov. It is hard to imagine that he would have proposed promoting Eideman or asking for Uborevich to be made his deputy if this had been the case. Stalin either did not believe that the newly exposed Trotskyist military organization reached up into the military elite, or he was waiting to see, if anything, what the NKVD discovered.

In this respect, as political repression focused on the former opposition gathered pace within the Communist Party over the course of 1936, it was impossible to ignore the former Trotskyists still serving in the Red Army. By mid-1936, the army had fallen under Ezhov's gaze, and he was pushing for a more intense investigation. However, there was nothing to suggest a large purge of the military was imminent or even planned at this point. Trotskyists had only ever been a minority in the Red Army, and they were absent from the military elite. The officers arrested during the investigation into the Trotskyist military organization were undoubtedly judged to be dangerous counterrevolutionaries. In a letter to Stalin from mid-November 1936, Ordzhonikidze had commented that "a cunning enemy [in the army] can carry out an irreparable strike." However, at the same time, he remarked that "to begin to slander people will sow distrust in the army," and he urged a cautious approach.[38] This appears to have been the case during the last six months of 1936 and early 1937. Arrests were steadily increasing in the ranks, denunciations were gathering pace, but this was not enough to spark a panic. For a much larger military purge to be considered by Stalin, the NKVD would need to expose a much more serious threat to Red Army security—enough to convince him that drastic action was necessary. For this to happen, the imagined conspiracy uncovered by the NKVD in mid-1936 would need to move on from the perceived threat of Trotskyist counterrevolution to something that could encompass a far larger circle of officers. If the investigation remained at the level of targeting former oppositionists, the upper ranks and those who had never supported Trotsky would remain untouched. The last few months of 1936 and in early 1937, however, saw a shift in the parameters of the investigation. The charge of counterrevolutionary Trotskyism began to align with the charge of foreign espionage and sabotage. This convergence of threats allowed the NKVD's investigation of the Red Army to move beyond Trotskyism and, at the very last moment, provided the momentum needed to affect a much wider circle of officers.

Foreign Espionage and the Military-Fascist Plot

Connections between the former oppositionists convicted at the first Moscow show trial in August 1936 and the German government had supposedly been unearthed as part of the NKVD's investigation into the Zinoviev–Kamenev Counterrevolutionary Bloc. Zinoviev, Kamenev, and their codefendents were said to have worked with the Gestapo in the preparation of terrorist acts. Moreover, a gradual alignment of the perceived foreign threat with the internal Trotskyist threat can be seen even before the August trial. The case of Valentin Ol'berg, the member of the German Communist Party whose arrest in January 1936 touched off a chain of arrests among supporters of the former opposition, is a good example of how a charge could be leveled by the NKVD of someone's being both a counterrevolutionary Trotskyist and working for a hostile foreign power (Ol'berg arrived in the Soviet Union from Germany). In the months after the August show trial, this convergence of threats continued in more visible terms. On 29 September, for instance, the Politburo issued an order entitled "About the Relations to the Counterrevolutionary Trotskyist–Zinovievite Elements," which proclaimed that these enemies should be regarded as "intelligence agents, spies, subversives and wreckers of the fascist bourgeoisie in Europe."[39] The message was clear: domestic counterrevolutionaries were actively engaged in espionage and sabotage for foreign powers.

Why supporters of the former opposition were increasingly believed to be secretly working for foreign governments is difficult to know for certain, but the deteriorating international situation during 1936 and 1937 no doubt played an important role. On 25 October 1936, the Rome–Berlin Axis was formed, sealing the military and political alliance between Germany and Italy. One month later, Germany signed the anti-Comintern pact with Japan, a clear expression of their joint hostility toward the Communist International and the Soviet Union. The Spanish civil war between the Republican and Nationalist forces, ongoing since July 1936, had also already raised international tensions. The conflict risked becoming the flashpoint for world war. The Soviet Union provided significant material aid and military assistance to the Republican forces, and the regime attentively watched the situation unfold. However, the war in Spain also demonstrated the danger posed by foreign agents infiltrating a military, and Stalin received reports about a fifth column within the Republican armed forces. The Soviet trade representative in Spain, Artur Stashevskii, for instance, remarked in a letter from mid-December 1936 (forwarded to the Soviet leadership) that he was "convinced that provocation is all around and everywhere; there is a fascist organization among the higher command, which carries out sabotage and, of course, espionage."[40] The deputy chief of Soviet military intelligence also reported in February 1937 that unreliable officers were in the Republican army and were carrying out acts of sabotage. Apparently, to leave such "fascist elements" in the upper ranks could have "catastrophic consequences," and treason in the armed forces was already being blamed for lost territory.[41] Later, in March 1937, Georgii Dimitrov, head of the Communist International, recorded in his diary that Stalin had received two Spanish writers and discussed the ongoing civil war with them. Notably, according to Dimitrov, at this meeting, Stalin had commented that the general staff of the Republican forces was unreliable, remarking, "There has always been betrayal on the eve of an offensive by Republic[an] units."[42] With a supposed Trotskyist military organization recently exposed in his own Red Army, it is possible that Stalin was starting to think similarly about the reliability of his own armed forces.

Alongside the deteriorating international situation, Ezhov, as head of the NKVD, was without question a driving force behind why the perceived foreign threat grew in prominence over the second half of 1936 and the early months of 1937. We have already seen that Ezhov was a conspiracy theorist before his ascendance to the leadership of the NKVD. He believed the former opposition was engaged in various plots against the state on Trotsky's orders. However, Ezhov was also particularly sensitive to foreign connections and had already invested efforts in trying to safeguard the Soviet Union from espionage and subversion. He had been closely involved in checking Soviet citizens working abroad since 1934, and in 1936, the focus increasingly shifted toward uncovering espionage by foreigners living in the Soviet Union.[43] When Ezhov was finally in charge of the NKVD, he placed a higher priority on unmasking counterrevolutionaries and foreign agents than his predecessor had. Under Iagoda, much of the NKVD's resources had been increasingly used for policing the social order and nonpolitical crimes in the mid-1930s; this changed under Ezhov.[44] By early 1937, it is clear that Ezhov was seeking further evidence to connect an oppositionist conspiracy to hostile foreign governments. A second Moscow show trial held in January 1937 signaled the shift in the parameters of the imagined conspiracy.

The second Moscow show trial, this time the trial of the parallel anti-Soviet Trotskyite center, was held between 23 and 30 January 1937. The trial was staged as another lesson for the Soviet people about the danger to the state from the former political opposition and the need for widespread vigilance. The selected group of defendants included several leading industrial managers, and the trial reflected how the rolling wave of political violence after the first show trial had hit industry particularly hard.[45] Senior industry leaders arrested over the previous months, including the deputy people's commissar of heavy industry, Georgii Piatakov, and the first deputy people's commissar of light industry, Grigorii Sokol'nikov, were put on trial alongside fifteen others who also had fallen under suspicion during the investigation into the Zinoviev–Kamenev Counterrevolutionary Bloc. These people were not party outsiders. Unlike Zinoviev and Kamenev, they had not been isolated from the circles of power. More so than in the previous trial, the January show trial stressed the danger posed by double-dealers—that is, people in senior positions across the state who were in reality working for the enemy.[46] Moreover, at the same time that the imagined oppositionist conspiracy was rising up the party hierarchy, it was also evolving. The crux of the January trial was the charge that the defendants had formed a parallel Trotskyist center working alongside the Zinoviev–Kamenev Counterrevolutionary Bloc. This second center had not only prepared acts of terrorism, but wrecking was a more prominent accusation than in the previous trial. The regular stream of accidents and breakdowns plaguing Soviet industry gave surface credibility to charges of sabotage.

More importantly (certainly so for the future military purge), this second group of conspirators was said to have acted not only on Trotsky's orders but also those of the German and Japanese governments. Their goal was not merely to assassinate leading party figures but to overthrow the Soviet regime. Supposed connections had been made at the time of the first show trial between the ringleaders of the Zinoviev–Kamenev Counterrevolutionary Bloc and the German government, but the revelations of the January 1937 trial raised the stakes. This was not simply a case of being linked to fascist powers; rather, it was a case of working under their direction to undermine the Soviet state from within.[47] There is a marked difference between the first and second show trials in terms of the prominence of this imagined foreign connection. Because Stalin played such a central role in the behind-the-scenes management of the show trials, this could not have been done without his consent. Of course, it is impossible to know for certain if Stalin truly believed that former oppositionists were working with hostile foreign powers or if this was just another useful smear to use against his former political opponents. However, as we shall see, there is evidence that the perceived threat from foreign agents became a priority for Stalin in the first six months of 1937 and that he came to believe the Soviet Union's security was in danger. The second Moscow show trial signaled a change in the narrative of conspiracy that was driving forward the political violence of the Great Terror. The emphasis was moving away from domestic Trotskyist counterrevolution and toward espionage and subversion supposedly carried out by agents of fascism. Other indications of this shift were visible outside of the January trial. In early 1937, the NKVD began to compile registers of all foreign citizens living in the Soviet Union, with the aim of finding unaccounted individuals who might be potential spies.[48] As David Shearer notes, between October 1936 and February

1937, Ezhov oversaw the arrest of 2,116 people for their alleged participation in anti-Soviet groups or for working for foreign governments.[49] On 14 February, the NKVD emphasized the general threat posed by former oppositionists working with fascist states by calling attention to the "terrorist, diversionary and spy activity" of German Trotskyists supposedly carried out on the orders of the Gestapo.[50] Throughout January and February, Ezhov wrote to Stalin with reports about recently exposed Polish, Latvian, and German subversive organizations apparently operating on Soviet territory.[51] Importantly, this shift in the parameters of the political repression in the Communist Party during late 1936 and early 1937, with a refocusing of energy toward exposing foreign agents and combating espionage, directly shaped repression in the military. The foreign threat loomed much larger in early 1937; these were the perfect conditions for the Red Army to be pulled more deeply into the growing political violence.

A final point on the January 1937 show trial is that Tukhachevskii's name surfaced in the proceedings. Indeed, as part of his testimony to the court, Karl Radek recounted an episode where the now arrested former Trotskyist officer Putna had come to see him "with a request from Tukhachevskii" relating to a government task. Historians have often made much of this name dropping and have suggested that it was inserted by Stalin to incriminate Tukhachevskii.[52] At the same time, however, Radek went on to say that Tukhachevskii had no connection to the arrested men and that he was devoted to the party. In this sense, if Radek's comments were contrived and meant to be incriminating, they were clumsy and ambiguous. It is not hard to imagine that if Stalin really wanted to cast doubt over Tukhachevskii, he could have arranged this in a more direct way. That Tukhachevskii was mentioned by Radek was probably little more than because he had worked with Putna professionally. Yet Radek's comments might have attracted attention nonetheless. Even if not contrived by the regime, they provided another indirect association between Tukhachevskii and counterrevolution. Tukhachevskii had been indirectly linked to other counterrevolutionary groups in the past, and with political arrests steadily growing as more people were dragged into an imagined conspiracy, the name dropping would not have gone unnoticed.

As the second Moscow show trial went underway, there were several indications that the threat from foreign agents was becoming a more pressing issue for the Red Army specifically. Pavel Smirnov, for instance, wrote to Gamarnik in January about a soldier who had been arrested as a German agent after the supposed discovery of a Germany intelligence residency.[53] In the same month, I. M. Leplevskii, the head of the special department of the NKVD, notified Voroshilov that another subversive group had been discovered in the 16th Artillery Regiment in air defense, and eleven arrests had been made. This group had apparently been created by a German agent, who recruited German servicemen in the Red Army to carry out sabotage.[54] At the end of January, Ezhov sent Voroshilov a note about an ongoing investigation into a Trotskyist group that included several officers who had been arrested at an ammunition depot in November 1936. Ezhov reported that it had now been "fully established" that one was a German spy.[55] In this respect, Ezhov appears to have added a new charge of espionage against what had been previously identified as a straightforward Trotskyist group. He wrote to Voroshilov again on 9 March about another alleged German agent arrested in Leningrad who had served in the Red Army. Apparently this agent's task had been to steal military secrets from the Leningrad Military District.[56] Another alleged German spy was discovered in the same military district around the same time in the Artillery Academy. Notably, in March, Gamarnik and the head of the NKVD's special department noted that the number of counterrevolutionaries discovered in the Leningrad Military District, including foreign agents, had significantly increased.[57]

It is impossible to know for certain whether Ezhov believed that the Red Army had a serious espionage problem in early 1937, but the above cases suggest that the NKVD was at least alert to the threat. It would be surprising, however, if Ezhov had not suspected some level of army involvement in his vision of a vast conspiracy threatening the Soviet state. Not only had some of the arrested members of the former opposition made reference to a military plot just months before under interrogation, but also, at a time when the perceived threat from foreign subversives was becoming more pronounced in wider terms, the Red Army was an obvious place to start looking for a spy infiltration. As the previous chapters have shown, the Red Army had been judged as vulnerable to subversion ever since its formation in early 1918. Large foreign-backed "plots" had already been discovered in the ranks, particularly the supposed military specialist conspiracy revealed by Operation Vesna in 1930. The perceived espionage threat to the Red Army remained consistent throughout the 1930s as the international situation worsened. None of this would have escaped Ezhov's attention. At the NKVD conference in December 1936, Ezhov told his audience, "You well know about the aspirations of imperialist intelligence staffs to send their agents into our army, to organize diversion."[58] Moreover, the rumors from abroad that hinted at the existence of a secret connection between Germany and the Soviet military elite had never abated. Ezhov would be well aware that several senior officers, especially Tukhachevskii, were rumored to be ambitious for power. When he became head of the NKVD, Ezhov would have inherited thick files of compromising information and rumors collected by the political police over the past two decades relating to certain members of the high command. Because Ezhov was so intent on widening the scope of the counterrevolutionary conspiracy unmasked in 1936, the Red Army may well have been his next target.

In late 1936 and early 1937, further reports and rumors streamed into the Soviet Union concerning treachery inside the high command and the existence of a clandestine connection between the Red Army and the Nazis. In September and December 1936, for instance, the NKVD received information that Marshal Vasilii Bliukher, the head of the Special Red Banner Far Eastern Army, was apparently planning a coup.[59] In January 1937, *Pravda*'s correspondent in Berlin sent a letter to the paper's editor, Lev Mekhlis, about an alleged link between the Red Army high command and the Nazis. Tukhachevskii was named specifically.[60] Tukhachevskii had also recently been connected to an arrested Polish communist, Tomasz Dąbal', who worked at the Moscow institute of mechanization and electrification and who was arrested on 29 December 1936.[61] On 31 January 1937, Dąbal' confessed to being a member of the Polish Military Organization, a defunct subversive organization formed in 1914 that Ezhov was convinced was still active.[62] Indeed, Dąbal' confessed to having gathered information on the Red Army, and he claimed to have spoken with members of the high command, including Tukhachevskii.[63] Ezhov sent Dąbal's interrogation transcript to Stalin; it contained information about other supposed members of the Polish Military Organization.[64] In addition, Ezhov received a letter in January 1937 from the former head of the NKVD's foreign department, Artur Artuzov, containing information about sabotage apparently carried out by Tukhachevskii that had been obtained by Soviet agents abroad.[65] Finally, in March 1937, in a conversation with the Soviet ambassador, Vladimir Potcmkin, the French minister of war, Édouard Daladier, supposedly spoke about a possible German-sponsored coup in the Soviet Union that would make use of members of the Red Army high command. Apparently, after the coup, a new Soviet government would then ally with Germany against France.[66] Of course, it is possible that the German government was spreading these rumors in order to undermine Stalin's trust in his military.[67] It is also unclear how seriously the NKVD took the reports about disloyalty in the army and if they were regarded as disinformation. Even so, rumors about a connection between the high command and the Nazis were steadily accumulating, and it would be unusual if the NKVD did not increase their attention on the military elite, even as a precaution. Ezhov was more likely to accept rumors and disinformation as fact than his predecessor at the NKVD.[68] Moreover, at this time, the NKVD's foreign department planned to gather more material on senior military figures and pay closer attention to exposing fascist groups in the army.[69] It is perfectly possible that the steady stream of rumors about the high command in the early months of 1937 helped galvanize suspicions about the Red Army.

The plenum of the Central Committee held during February and March 1937 was a turning point in the Great Terror and gave new momentum to the political violence. This was no less so for the path of repression in the Red Army. In the months after the plenum, the military was subject to greater scrutiny to flush out any enemies still present in the ranks. Delayed by the suicide of Ordzhonikidze, the people's commissar of heavy industry (who, it appears, committed suicide after failing to save his colleagues from arrest[70]), the plenum was used by Stalin and other senior party leaders as a platform to highlight the serious threat posed by supporters of the former opposition and the mounting evidence of wrecking and sabotage in industry. Furthermore, the former leaders of the Right Deviation, Nikolai Bukharin and Alexei Rykov, were now fully pulled into the growing conspiracy theory. Both had already been incriminated by the coerced evidence given by the arrested former oppositionists in 1936, but Stalin had kept them in limbo. The other leading member of the Right Deviation, Mikhail Tomskii, committed suicide in August 1936 after being implicated with the Zinoviev–Kamenev Counterrevolutionary Bloc.[71] At the February–March plenum, however, Bukharin and Rykov were now accused of planning sabotage, espionage, and terrorist acts; having prior knowledge of the Kirov assassination; and plotting to overthrow the party.[72] Such accusations against senior party grandees represented another escalation in the political violence spreading throughout the party. Both Bukharin and Rykov were arrested in March.[73]

Voroshilov enthusiastically participated in the attack on Bukharin and Rykov at the February–March plenum. However, when the Red Army came up for discussion, he tried to downplay the danger of the enemy within. It is hard to believe that Voroshilov was being sincere. He, more than anyone else, was acutely aware of the Red Army's security failings in previous years. We have already seen that he repeatedly castigated weak vigilance in the officer corps for allowing enemies to go undetected. Nonetheless, he attempted to defend the army's record and its political reliability at the plenum. Voroshilov claimed, for example, that there was little to worry about from enemies in the Red Army and that the threat from Trotskyists was small: "In the army at this present time, happily, not that many enemies have been revealed." Moreover, in an attempt to bolster the case that the Red Army was politically reliable, Voroshilov argued that the party sent the "best of its cadres" to serve in the Red Army.[74] Voroshilov was not incorrect in pointing out what at this stage was still only a relatively small number of former Trotskyists arrested in the military. He produced figures showing that since the crackdown against the opposition began in the mid-1920s, 47,000 people had been discharged from leading military bodies, with 22,000 of these between 1934 and 1936. According to Voroshilov, only 5,000 of this number were clear oppositionists. Furthermore, these discharges had apparently been carried out with caution.[75] Voroshilov did concede that there were more enemies in the military still to be found, but the thrust of his speech was that the Red Army was protected and remained politically reliable. It had worked hard over the previous twenty years to remove subversive influences.[76] There was, of course, some room for improvement: Voroshilov pointed to the need to scrutinize people more effectively and to understand their personal lives on a deeper level to unmask potential enemies.[77] This was hardly a radical approach to safeguarding the Red Army from subversives. Voroshilov was offering the same solutions he had always done, which amounted to little more than asking for greater vigilance.

Voroshilov also tried to deflect responsibility for missing the Trotskyist military organization recently discovered in the Red Army by the NKVD. In doing so, he perhaps sensed that the connections between the arrested former Trotskyist officers and the Zinoviev–Kamenev Counterrevolutionary Bloc could develop into a more serious problem. Indeed, even though he was the head of the Red Army (and accountable for his troops), Voroshilov claimed that he was not fully responsible for the

Trotskyist military group's having gone undiscovered for so long, as no-body else had noticed anything suspicious or had alerted him with their concerns.[78] Voroshilov had his back against the wall and was protesting his innocence. There was little else he could do without admitting cul-pability. Notably, Voroshilov's speech at the plenum was confined to a discussion of the Red Army men already under arrest. Rather than look to the future and call for a purge of the ranks to find any other enemies, Voroshilov wanted to draw attention to the great efforts the army had already made in guaranteeing its security. With his repetition that the military contained the best cadres in the Soviet system, and in stressing the small number of dangerous enemies discharged or arrested in the ranks at present, Voroshilov did not strike a note of alarm.

Unfortunately for Voroshilov, not everyone was convinced by his performance at the plenum. Molotov certainly did not accept this de-fense of army loyalty, and in his speech, he called for a more thorough checking of the Red Army. Although Molotov did agree with Voroshilov that there were only "small signs" of sabotage, espionage, and Trotsky-ist activity in the army at this time, he argued that if the problem was "approached carefully," more enemies would be revealed: "If we have wreckers in all sectors of the economy, can we imagine that there are no wreckers in the military? It would be ridiculous. The military depart-ment is a very big deal, and its work will not be verified now, but later on, and it will be verified very closely."[79] Molotov's intervention is signif-icant; he would not have made these comments without Stalin's back-ing. It seems that Stalin did not accept Voroshilov's version of events. Molotov also put pressure on Gamarnik on 3 March, asking him to give more specific examples of failures in army political work. Molotov be-lieved that Gamarnik was being purposely evasive, commenting, "You have not criticized one concrete case."[80] Clearly, Stalin and Molotov had expected a fuller account of military weaknesses at the plenum—an ac-count that neither Voroshilov nor Gamarnik delivered. It is likely that the steadily growing number of former Trotskyists arrested in the Red Army from the summer of 1936 had undercut Voroshilov and Gamar-nik's defense of its reliability. Yet at the same time Molotov's remarks suggested a certain lack of urgency in verifying the Red Army. The mili-tary would be closely investigated, but not immediately; Molotov specif-ically noted this would be "later on." It seems that Stalin was acting with caution. Perhaps further evidence of counterrevolution in the army was needed before a more comprehensive (and likely destabilizing) verification was sanctioned. The Red Army was a vital institution to the Soviet state, especially in a time when the regime believed war was looming. Stalin may have wanted to avoid shaking it up until he deemed it absolutely necessary. Moreover, at least for the time being, wreckers and saboteurs in industry were probably considered to be a higher priority than the relatively few subversives currently discovered in the Red Army.

Stalin did not directly address the recent arrests in the Red Army at the February–March plenum. He did point to wider dangers, such as espionage and sabotage carried out by foreign fascist agents and Trotskyists, as well as the alleged connections between the two. That supporters of the former opposition were believed to be working with hostile foreign states was one of the central themes of the plenum. Stalin spoke about the danger from card-carrying party members who in reality were secretly working against the state.[81] The broader narrative driving forward the political violence had clearly evolved from its earlier focus on already ostracized former oppositionists in 1936 to encompass party figures in positions of responsibility, now revealed as double-dealers. Stalin delivered another warning about the ever-present threat of capitalist encirclement; he also claimed that foreign states continued to send agents to the Soviet Union who were preparing to undermine the state in wartime. As Oleg Khlevniuk has shown, Stalin seemed to be particularly concerned about a possible fifth column; he had underlined passages on a draft of Molotov's plenum speech that detailed how Trotsky's supporters would strike when the Soviet Union was engulfed in war.[82] Stalin raised this danger in his speech with a military reference: "In order to win a battle during war, this may require several corps of soldiers. But in order to thwart these gains at the front, all is needed are several spies somewhere on the staff of the army or even on the staff of the divisions, who are able to steal operative plans and give these to the enemy."[83] Stalin may well have only been speaking in general terms and making a point about the wider threat from spies and saboteurs to the Soviet state in wartime. However, the military reference is still telling. The Red Army was a place where spies and saboteurs could cause serious damage. There were few worse places for a fifth column to take root. Stalin surely understood this. Although there was still no urgent crisis in the Red Army in early 1937, and although the number of enemies arrested by the NKVD remained relatively small, Stalin wanted the ranks more carefully scrutinized, and the threat of a fifth column was clearly on his mind.

Stalin's arguments were reinforced by Ezhov, who spoke at the plenum about the dangers from spies and wreckers operating undetected in the country, and he complained that not enough was being done to find these enemies.[84] Indeed, Ezhov criticized the conduct of his predecessor, Iagoda, for orientating the NKVD too greatly toward policing the social order rather than concentrating on counterintelligence.[85] During the course of his speech, Ezhov outlined how enemies intended to undermine the regime by carrying out diversionary acts and sabotage in wartime, but he also mentioned a possible palace coup or there being a military plot in the higher ranks. Moreover, as he was speaking on this subject, Valerii Mezhlauk, who would soon be Ordzhonikidze's replacement in heavy industry, interjected that this idea was not unknown.[86] The idea of military plot as brought up by Ezhov was seemingly not especially surprising for some party members. We have already seen how a possible military plot had surfaced in the interrogation testimonies of former oppositionists arrested in 1936. However, Mezhlauk's interjection is particularly interesting. A potential military plot did not shock Mezhlauk, and other party figures perhaps felt the same. It is perfectly possible that rumors about a military conspiracy had begun spreading within party circles, and the reliability of the Red Army may have started to attract questions.

The February–March plenum had an instant impact on the approach the Red Army leadership was taking toward the problem of hidden enemies in the ranks. There is a sharp contrast between the speech that Voroshilov delivered at the plenum and a later speech he gave to a meeting of Red Army party members (*aktiv*) on 13 March. In this later speech, Voroshilov spoke with more concern about the threat to the army from hidden subversives, and he struck a tone much closer to Molotov's at the plenum. Voroshilov had no choice but to follow Stalin's lead. Just two days before his speech to the Red Army *aktiv* on 13 March, however, two senior officers were arrested on charges of wrecking, which would have only put further pressure on the increasingly embattled head of the Red Army. On 11 March, I. I. Garkavyi, the commander of the Urals Military District, and V. I. Vasilenko, his deputy were arrested.[87] Both had been implicated a month before when Stalin received a denunciation claiming that a wrecking group was operating in the engineering department of the Red Army. After an investigation by the NKVD, the aide to the head of the engineering troops in the Urals Military District, N. I. Velezhev, was arrested. This soon led to the incrimination of his superiors, Garkavyi and Vasilenko, but also the commander of the 65th Rifle Division, G. F. Gavriushenko, and several other officers.[88] Garkavyi's and Vasilenko's arrests were significant in that neither had been a supporter of the former opposition and both had connections to the military elite. Garkavyi, for instance, was an acquaintance of Iakir and Gamarnik. Notably, Stalin recalled at a military meeting a few months later in June (after the military-fascist plot had been exposed) that upon Garkavyi's arrest in March, he had been visited by Iakir, who apparently said, "I am guilty c.[omrade] Stalin. . . . I was close with him [Garkavyi], I did not expect that he was such a person. It's my fault."[89] The arrests in the Red Army were beginning to creep up the ranks, and Stalin was being kept well informed. For example, on 1 March, Ezhov reported to Stalin about the arrest of Major N. K. Malov, from the North Caucasus Military District, who supplied evidence to the NKVD about an anti-Soviet Trotskyist organization apparently led by several senior officers operating in the area. Further cases were sent to Stalin over the coming months as greater attention was turned on the Red Army.[90] It is likely that these new arrests in early 1937, particularly of Garkavyi and Vasilenko, helped push Voroshilov toward taking a more forthright stance over subversives in the Red Army. Yet it is without question that Molotov's insistence at the February–March plenum that the army would be carefully scrutinized in the future was a clear signal that Voroshilov needed to fall into line.

In his speech to the Red Army *aktiv* in mid-March, Voroshilov now spoke about how deeply fascist–Trotskyist bands had infiltrated into the Soviet Union, and he stressed the need for all officers and soldiers to keep an eye on one another.[91] This was a far more forthright speech than Voroshilov delivered at the February–March plenum; that the Red Army was presented as under threat from enemies was unmistakable. Indeed, for the first time, Voroshilov articulated the danger posed by foreign agents in clear terms. For instance, he mentioned a series of fires in the Far Eastern region that had resulted in a number of deaths and damage to machinery, remarking, "I am absolutely convinced that it is the work of Japanese spies, it is the work of Japanese agents."[92] Voroshilov also called attention to the large numbers of accidents in the Red Army that were apparently also the work of enemies; he wanted each incident carefully investigated.[93] However, most importantly, Voroshilov now argued that even though a number of former Trotskyists had been arrested in the ranks, this did not mean that the Red Army was no longer in danger: "We do not have the right to permit one enemy in the Workers' and Peasants' Red Army, we must not allow this. Not only should we not have a single enemy in the ranks of our party, but we should not accept one enemy in the army because the army should be utterly and completely clean."[94] Rather than argue that the Red Army was safe from enemies, as he had done just weeks before at the February–March plenum, Voroshilov now argued that not a single enemy was permissible. The Red Army needed to be "completely clean." Voroshilov did not propose specific ways army leaders might do this. He did little more than highlight poor levels of self-criticism and point the finger at the army party organizations, suggesting that Voroshilov still did not know how to resolve the problem of why enemies were going undiscovered in the ranks.[95] There was certainly no call for a mass purge. Even so, it is clear that Voroshilov had fallen into line. Since Molotov's intervention at the February–March plenum, he must have felt the pressure from above and was compelled to order army leaders to redouble their efforts in rooting out subversives. It was no longer possible to downplay the problem. Even though he gave no specific guidance about how to find the enemies supposedly still hidden in the ranks, rather than boast about how well the Red Army had done in keeping its house in order, it was now time for any dangerous subversives to be finally rooted out.

Voroshilov was not the only person to call for deeper scrutiny of the Red Army at this meeting of the *aktiv*. Budennyi, who had already argued in private that the officer corps needed closer inspection in 1936, echoed Voroshilov's remarks in proclaiming that it was impermissible that enemies were still inside the military. The Red Army was just too vital an institution to be compromised in such a way. Budennyi used part of his speech to call for deeper investigation of the military to find the conspirators he was convinced were still unmasked in the ranks. For Budennyi, the relatively small number of former Trotskyist officers arrested at the time of the first Moscow show trial was not the end of the matter: "It is not possible that it is one group, fifteen to twenty people, and no more. You know that in the first trial, the Trotskyist–Zinovievite trial, Mrachkovskii openly said that we have a direct order from Trotsky to plant groups in the RKKA."[96] Ivan Belov, commander of the Moscow Military District, spoke in similar terms to Budennyi:

> It is impossible to be so naive [to believe] that since the arrest of several of-
> ficers there are no more enemies in the ranks of the Workers' and Peasants'
> Red Army. . . . We should understand now more than ever that the Workers'
> and Peasants' Red Army is a very attractive object for all counterintelligence
> agents, and we should note that the group of arrested commanders, who
> were actively working, will have had some kind of nest, a nest that we have to
> open and help the organs of the People's Commissariat for Internal Affairs
> more actively in our future work than we are doing at the moment.[97]

Not only were supposed enemies still undiscovered in the army, but
also Belov made the danger from foreign agents clear. Moreover, at this
meeting of the *aktiv*, both Budennyi and Belov described the perceived
threat from hidden enemies in stronger terms than Voroshilov. It is
entirely possible that the two officers sensed an approaching round of
arrests now that the line toward the Red Army had become tougher at
the February–March plenum. It was important to display the necessary
signals that the dangers facing the Red Army were understood.

Not everyone, however, argued that subversives needed to be rooted
out from the ranks in such forthright terms. Fel'dman once again took
a softer approach. Although he did agree that insufficient vigilance was
to blame for giving the enemy the opportunity to infiltrate the ranks
and that army leaders should make greater efforts to study each individual officer carefully, Fel'dman remained consistent in arguing that
legality should be upheld in any investigation.[98] He pointed out that
since 1934, higher standards of evidence had resulted in declining arrest levels in the officer corps. Fel'dman emphasized the importance
of Voroshilov having gained the power to sanction arrests in the army
and how this had brought down wider arrest levels. Indeed, Fel'dman
saw a danger of a knee-jerk response to the more pronounced security
scare in the Red Army and a shift toward indiscriminate mass arrests
that were based on lists prepared ahead of time.[99] These concerns were
entirely justified. In less than six months, Stalin would sanction the first
of a series of mass operations, which targeted entire population cohorts
for arrest and exile and constituted the bulk of the violence of the Great
Terror. In March, however, there was no indication that mass arrests of
this type were just around the corner. In fact, some of Fel'dman's reser-
vations were not out of step with the NKVD. Ezhov had criticized mass
campaign-style policing as too blunt an instrument for finding genuine
foreign agents and counterrevolutionaries at the February–March ple-

num.[100] While Voroshilov, Budennyi, and Belov all called for a better scrutiny of the Red Army, there is little to suggest, at this stage, that this risked sliding into a mass military purge. The Red Army would face greater NKVD attention over the coming months, but it is likely that this was intended as a carefully controlled investigation to find out exactly how far the Trotskyist military organization extended in the ranks. This, of course, was not how things turned out. When the extent of the imagined military-fascist plot was finally revealed in May, panic quickly set in. A knee-jerk military purge was immediately launched in early June and was carried out with little restraint and a noticeable lack of central control.

Finally, Gamarnik's speech to the Red Army *aktiv* revealed most clearly the degree to which the military was believed to be internally compromised by enemies. In contrast to his speeches of previous years, Gamarnik now described the scale of the infiltration in much greater terms: "Comrades, the Japanese–German Trotskyist agents, spies, and wreckers are in a full range of our army organization, in the staffs, the institutions, the academies, the military-training institutions."[101] Evidently, the problem was understood as no longer just a small number of counterrevolutionary Trotskyist officers but rather foreign-backed agents operating across all military institutions. There is little sense that Gamarnik was now downplaying the perceived security threats facing the army. Like Voroshilov, he was in a position of responsibility and would similarly have had to fall into line after coming under pressure at the February–March plenum. Gamarnik, of course, may well have come to sincerely believe that the Red Army had a growing espionage problem, but it is also possible that he was simply being swept along by events and had no choice but to follow Stalin's lead. Gamarnik's claim that the infiltrated subversives in the Red Army were supported by hostile foreign governments corresponds with how espionage and subversion had become a growing priority for the NKVD. All foreign citizens living in the Soviet Union, for instance, had been placed under surveillance in early 1937 and those suspected of espionage deported. After the February–March plenum, the NKVD began to gather more information on suspected foreign agents, and a special registry was set up for all foreigners given Soviet citizenship since 1 January 1936. Instructions were also sent to local NKVD administrations that claimed that foreign agents inside the Soviet Union had set up networks primed to spark rebellion at the outbreak of war.[102] In short, in the first few months of 1937, it is clear that the regime's attentions were increasingly focused on the perceived threat of espionage and subversion. This danger was not exclusive to the Red Army, but Gamarnik's warning that the ranks had been infiltrated by foreign agents demonstrates that it could not escape being drawn into the evolving narrative of the Great Terror.

Another indication that espionage was becoming a bigger priority for the Red Army in early 1937 can be seen in the complaints about the security of secret documents at the March meeting of the *aktiv*. Gamarnik, for instance, criticized loose talk about the content of secret files and also noted that documents were being left open in public.[103] The chief of staff, Egorov, pointed to "the disappearance of a colossal number of critical documents" and commented that the army had rested on its laurels.[104] Another officer, B. I. Bazenkov, remarked, "There is not one month when in any department of the NKO [People's Commissariat for Defense] some kind of secret document is not lost."[105] The Red Army had always struggled with the security of secret documents, and there appears to have been at least one highly serious leak in recent months.[106] In November 1936, a Polish intelligence agent claimed that a group of Red Army men had apparently copied the mobilization plan for the western border regions, and the most senior officer had then fled to Poland. The same mobilization plan apparently later surfaced in the British press.[107] Whether this story is accurate or not, with increasing attention now being given to infiltrated foreign agents in the early months of 1937, further preventative measures were taken to counteract espionage in the army. Only days before the March meeting of the Red Army *aktiv,* Gamarnik signed a secret order regarding enemies working in the clerical and technical offices in a range of army staffs and institutions. Apparently secret documents were being handled by enemies, and this was going unchecked by the NKVD. Gamarnik ordered that all technical and clerical staff be checked within a one-month period, and those exposed as untrustworthy be discharged from the army.[108] On 20 March, Voroshilov also published a secret order concerning document security. This recounted an episode in which a secret military document had been left in a drawer in one of the rooms of the National Hotel on 3 February. An investigation had found that Pavel Dybenko, the commander of the Volga Military District, was responsible, and he received a reprimand. Voroshilov ordered a review of how documents were stored and noted that this case was not an isolated incident.[109]

The growing perceived threat from foreign subversives, however, was not the only problem for the Red Army. Any attempts in previous years toward improving its internal self-policing were still judged to have been inadequate. During his speech to the Red Army *aktiv*, Gamarnik returned to the familiar theme of poor vigilance and criticized persistent failings in recent efforts to root out dangerous enemies. In reference to the recent party purges, the *proverka* and *obmen*, for instance, he remarked:

> We have excluded many people from the party. Some of this group were excluded probably for nothing, for so-called passivity, insufficient activity, insufficient political preparedness, and so on. And regarding Trotskyists and Zinovievites, during the *obmen* and *proverka* of party documents, despite all the warnings of the TsK [Central Committee], we only excluded 300 people from all of the army. But the main thing is that after the *obmen* of party documents, after the issue of new party documents, 250 Trotskyists and Zinovievites were exposed and excluded from the party. Here are the characteristics of vigilance. For a long time, for almost a year, documents were checked and exchanged, and during this long period of work, only 300 enemies of the party were successfully exposed and excluded; after the *obmen*, 250 were exposed and excluded to whom party documents had been issued. Is this not evidence of insufficiency, of the belated vigilance of many of our party organizations and political organs? . . . Each of you understands that only one spy, penetrated in any staff of a division, corps, army, general staff, is able to cause enormous, incalculable disasters.[110]

Clearly there were still ongoing problems with vigilance in the Red Army. This time, however, the message was that dangerous enemies continued to be discovered in the ranks even after the lessons delivered by the *proverka* and *obmen*. As we have seen, Gamarnik had previously pointed to the party purges as a means of shedding light on the poor state of army self-policing. It had taken these purges to finally locate the dangerous enemies that the army was incapable of doing independently. Yet self-policing had not improved. Enemies were still apparently going unnoticed even as Stalin wanted better scrutiny of the Red Army.

Moreover, Gamarnik's comparison between the expulsion of political enemies from the party and people expelled for minor infractions (such as passivity) demonstrates that he was aware of the type of problems that had hindered the course of the *proverka* and *obmen* in the Red Army and in the party more broadly. As Arch Getty has shown, regional party leaders, who had often spent years building up systems of patronage in their local areas (so-called family circles), were reluctant to carry out either purge correctly as this might result in a loss of influence. Getty notes that local power groups were likely to have included former oppositionists who had managed to work their way to the top by the mid-1930s. These people should have certainly been expelled during the party purges, but this would inevitably weaken the family circles.[111] In this respect, there were strong self-interests at the regional party level toward undermining the *proverka* and *obmen* to preserve local autonomy and power. When ordered to cleanse their organizations, rather than focus on the more dangerous political enemies at the top of local networks, regional party leaders could turn their attention to supposed enemies lower down the hierarchy. Ordinary members were expelled from the party in large numbers for minor infractions such as passivity or poor political education. This technically fulfilled the order from above to root out enemies while at the same time preserving the family circles. As we have seen, there are indications that similar behaviors played out in the Red Army. A certain number of officers ordered unnecessary discharges for minor crimes and gave out reprimands en masse while people classified as more dangerous enemies were apparently going unnoticed. This behavior may have been part of a range of deliberate tactics aimed at satisfying ever increasing demands for vigilance while avoiding having to turn too much attention on a local military power network or small clique of powerful officers. Budennyi's complaint in his letter to Voroshilov from August 1936 that some officers were more interested in maintaining their own oligarchies than working for the good of the state is telling in this respect.[112] It is likely that, as in some regional party organizations, systems of patronage existed in parts of the Red Army. With some officers either looking out for their narrow individual interests or those of local cliques, Voroshilov's calls to raise vigilance could be purposely circumvented.

In a speech delivered in Leningrad at the end of March 1937, Gamarnik once again articulated the threat from foreign agents in clear terms:

> Didn't you know that each capitalist country has spies in other countries? Do the Germans not have their own counterintelligence agents, spies, and agents in France, Czechoslovakia, and a whole range of other countries, and the other way round? There is no capitalist country that would not practice espionage, wrecking, counterintelligence work in another capitalist country. These are the laws of capitalism. . . . And it is quite natural and understand-

able that if one capitalist country is sending agents and spies to another capitalist country, that it would be incomprehensible, strange, foolish, it would be naive if we did not think that each capitalist country is attempting to get agents, spies inside our country; it would be naive to think that each capitalist country does not have its own agents and spies inside our country.[113]

Gamarnik, moreover, mentioned the resolution from the recent February–March plenum of the Central Committee regarding wrecking and espionage within the People's Commissariats for Transport and Heavy Industry and how this also concerned the chemical industry and the Red Army. He noted that the People's Commissariat for Defense needed to report to the Soviet government and Central Committee about the espionage and sabotage threat within a month, adding ominously:

> The evidence of wrecking and espionage is not small. . . . We know that Trotsky gave a direct order from abroad to his agents to create a Trotskyist terrorist cell in the Workers' and Peasants' Red Army, and Hitler and Trotsky gave an order to organize subversive cells in the Workers' and Peasants' Red Army in peacetime, to prepare the defeat of the RKKA in the future approaching war.[114]

This was another clear message that Trotsky and Hitler were understood to be working in tandem and that one of their objectives was supposedly the subversion of the Red Army. A much broader security scare was erupting inside the military that had moved on from the narrow parameters of Trotskyism. Gamarnik had pointed to the espionage threat to the Red Army in previous years but had only ever emphasized its small scale. Circumstances had now changed. With pressure bearing down on the Red Army after the February–March plenum, and with Hitler and Trotsky now thought to be working closely together, the perceived threat from foreign agents had suddenly become more urgent. Indeed, the work needed to root out dangerous subversives across the Soviet state was far from over. In a speech delivered at the end of March to a meeting of NKVD cadres, for instance, Ezhov remarked:

> We are smashing the enemy, smashing him hard. We smashed the Trotskyists, smashed them hard. I shall not name any figures, but they are striking enough, we have annihilated not a few. We are smashing the SRs [Socialist Revolutionaries], we are smashing the German, Polish and Japanese secret

agents. That is not all but rather, as the saying has it, the first assault, as there are more of them.[115]

Ezhov would almost certainly urge his subordinates to focus on the Red Army as part of any future assaults on hidden enemies. Not only had Molotov called for more attention to be given to the Red Army at the February–March plenum, but this also was an obvious place to look for any subversives attempting to undermine the Soviet Union's strength. Indeed, increasing numbers of soldiers were arrested in the Far Eastern region on espionage charges from March 1937.[116] An NKVD directive published on 2 April warned about the dangers to the Red Army from foreign intelligence agencies and claimed that German espionage had increased in the Soviet Union. The infiltration of the Red Army was apparently a key goal of German agents, along with creating subversive cells in industry and preparing terrorist acts.[117] Just over a week later, on 13 April, in another NKVD circular, Ezhov delivered a warning about "Japanese–German agents" planning terrorist and diversionary acts. Alongside a range of countermeasures to be taken in various areas of the state apparatus, Ezhov wanted stronger surveillance of the military and new security measures, with special attention given to mechanized units and the air force.[118]

The NKVD, of course, was not alone in putting more pressure on the Red Army after the February–March plenum. As soon as Voroshilov and Gamarnik began to draw attention to the wider threat from foreign-backed subversives in March, an immediate impact was felt lower down the hierarchy. The army party organizations were now being instructed to seek out any masked enemies. For example, at a meeting of army party organizations in the Leningrad Military District at the end of March, the head of PUR, Pavel Smirnov, warned that enemies had gone undiscovered in the district and that there was a danger from Trotskyists, spies, and saboteurs.[119] Over the coming months, several articles appeared in the Red Army newspaper, *Krasnaia zvezda,* on the subject of spies and subversion.[120] Stalin also began to apply his own pressure. He made his distrust of the officer corps visible at the end of March, when the Politburo ordered that any senior officer who had been expelled from the party for political reasons was now to be discharged and sent to the economic commissariats.[121] This was an attempt to improve the reliability of the officer corps (which seemingly was valued more highly than the economic commissariats). Two weeks later, on 13 April,

Fel'dman was transferred from the head of the main administration of the Red Army to take the position as the deputy commander of the Moscow Military District.[122] Although this position remained a senior role, it suggests that Stalin believed that Fel'dman was not up to the job of overseeing army cadres and ruthlessly purging enemies from the ranks. We have already seen how Fel'dman showed a tendency to put up resistance to the baseless investigations launched by the NKVD, and it is unlikely that this escaped Stalin's attention. The transfer suggests that Stalin wanted someone compliant in his place now that the internal security of the Red Army was deemed to be a more urgent issue.

As more pressure was now bearing down on the Red Army, there are strong indications that the perceived threat from foreign agents was developing into a full-blown spy scare. Notably, on 21 April, the head of the air force, Iakov Alksnis, sent Voroshilov a report containing proposals to prevent wrecking and espionage.[123] Alksnis suggested several measures, such as tightening the fulfillment of orders to deprive spies and wreckers the chance to mask their activity and a careful scrutiny of people with access to secret documents.[124] In addition, people excluded from the party for political reasons should also be discharged from the army.[125] Alksnis's report was followed a day later by a similar report from the head of the navy, Vladimir Orlov, which also addressed saboteurs and spies. Orlov pointed to the need to check the commanding bodies, the central apparatus, and all industrial failures and look for evidence of wrecking. He wrote that this process was already underway in the navy and that forty-three discharges had already been sanctioned.[126] On the same day, another report was sent to Voroshilov from the army medical services that addressed these same security questions.[127] Voroshilov had clearly solicited these reports, demonstrating that the search for spies and wreckers was moving up his agenda. He had no choice but to follow the firmer line toward the Red Army set at the February–March plenum, and it appears that he was now laying the groundwork for serious countermeasures to be taken against infiltrated foreign agents specifically. Importantly, it was at this point that the first incriminating interrogation evidence emerged against Tukhachevskii and the other senior officers who would soon be executed for their supposed roles in a military-fascist plot. Yet rather than come from any line of investigation into the Red Army, these initial incriminations came from within the NKVD.

At the February–March plenum, Ezhov had accused his predecessor,

Iagoda, of showing poor leadership and had attacked his supporters still within the NKVD.[128] A resolution from the plenum entitled "Lessons of the Wrecking, Diversionary, and Espionage Activities of the Japanese–German–Trotskyist Agents" accused the previous NKVD leadership of having harbored criminal individuals who apparently had held back in the exposure of dangerous Trotskyists, despite already accumulated evidence.[129] After the plenum, Iagoda was expelled from the party and arrested. Having Iagoda purged from the party was just one part of Ezhov's consolidation of power in the NKVD. He carried out a wider purge of the NKVD after the February–March plenum, resulting in further arrests in early April.[130] These included M. I. Gai, the previous head of the NKVD's special department; G. E. Prokofiev, one of Iagoda's former deputies, who at the time of his arrest was the deputy people's commissar of communications; and the deputy of the special department, Z. I. Volovich.[131] That these men were targeted by Ezhov in 1937 is not too surprising. Ezhov had started bringing his own supporters into the NKVD when he became its head in September 1936, and Gai had already lost his position as head of the special department in November.[132] Moreover, Ezhov had claimed at a meeting of NKVD officers held between 19 and 21 March 1937 that Gai and Volovich were German spies.[133] Critically, during interrogations carried out at the end of April, Gai, Volovich, and Prokofiev all supplied incriminating evidence against the Red Army elite. They connected Tukhachevskii, Uborevich, Iakir, Kork, Eideman, and other senior officers with conspirators apparently around Iagoda, and there was talk of a planned coup and espionage activity.[134] This was the first time that directly incriminating testimony had been given against the members of the high command who would face military trial in June. From this point on, their names would feature frequently in the evidence supplied by other arrested officers. In a certain sense, it is understandable why it was the arrested NKVD men who finally delivered the first damning evidence against Tukhachevskii and the other senior officers. The political police had a long history of working up plots and trying to expose conspiracies in the ranks since the civil war. If Ezhov was trying to unearth evidence of a military conspiracy in the upper ranks—and one supported by fascist states—details of such a fantastic plot could be obtained from the arrested NKVD men. M. I. Gai, in particular, had been closely involved with the Red Army for a number of years. He had attended meetings of the Military Soviet and had repeatedly met with members of the high command. His testimony would carry weight. What this all means is that the evidence supplied by those who had worked for so long to protect the Red Army from subversion had, in the end, delivered the outlines of an imagined conspiracy that would cause enormous damage.

There are some indications that Ezhov had growing suspicions about Tukhachevskii even before he managed to get the incriminating evidence from the arrested NKVD men. A day before M. I. Gai gave his testimony, the Politburo canceled Tukhachevskii's trip to Britain to attend the coronation of King George VI. This was later publicized on the grounds of Tukhachevskii's ill health.[135] However, the true reason for the canceled trip can be seen in a message Ezhov sent to Stalin, Molotov, and Voroshilov on 21 April that contained a warning about a possible German terrorist attack against Tukhachevskii if he attended the coronation. There is nothing to suggest that this was anything more than a fabrication, and it seems in all likelihood that Ezhov used the story as a means of keeping Tukhachevskii inside the country.[136] Another suggestion that Ezhov was watching Tukhachevskii more closely can be seen even earlier, on 12 April, when he sent Voroshilov a report that contained details of a supposed connection between Tukhachevskii and the Japanese military attaché in Poland. Voroshilov noted on the report, "Reported. Decisions have been made to investigate."[137]

Stalin signaled his concerns about the reliability of the Red Army once again at the beginning of May, when the Politburo passed a resolution bringing single military and political command to an end and reinstating the powers of political commissars. This was a step backward to the arrangement that had existed during the civil war, when military specialists were judged to be unreliable and in need of close observation. It seems that the officer corps was beginning to test Stalin's capacity for restraint. Perhaps not unrelated to this decision were the arrests carried out by the NKVD of another group of senior officers at the end of April. This included N. G. Egorov, the head of the All-Russian Central Executive Committee military school; M. I. Alafuzo, head of the department of organization and mobilization at the academy of the general staff; and R. A. Peterson, the aide to the commander of the Kiev Military District.[138] Under arrest, and undoubtedly with NKVD coercion, Egorov and Peterson gave evidence about their role in a possible coup, and Peterson claimed he was a member of a "Right-counterrevolutionary organization."[139] Moreover, further evidence against Tukhachevskii and the senior officers already incriminated by the arrested NKVD men now surfaced. The case against Tukhachevskii and his alleged co-conspirators was steadily solidifying. On 6 May, a brigade commander, M. Ie. Medvedev, was arrested for being part of a counterrevolutionary group, and between 8 and 10 May, he gave evidence about his participation in a Trotskyist military organization that included Tukhachevskii, Fel'dman, Iakir, Putna, Primakov, and Kork.[140]

It is important to stress that Medvedev's evidence (like that received from the arrested NKVD men) was undoubtedly obtained using forced confessions, and it is not out of the question that Ezhov was looking to unmask some kind of military plot in the high command in the early months of 1937. We have already seen that Ezhov was acutely concerned about the threat to the Soviet Union from foreign subversives and how alleged connections between the former opposition and fascist states were openly publicized at the second Moscow show trial. After the February–March plenum, during which Stalin had stressed the dangers of sabotage and espionage carried out by fascist agents and Trotskyists, it is likely that the NKVD decided to expend more energy not only searching for any undiscovered enemies in the Red Army but also trying to make connections to the high command. As soon as he became head of the NKVD, Ezhov would have had open access to the many secret files previously put together on senior officers in the Red Army; he also would have been well aware of the persistent rumors about disloyalty, ambitions for power, and personal disputes in the military leadership. However, with a perceived spy threat becoming more prominent in the Red Army during March and April 1937, at the same time as even more rumors filtered into the Soviet Union suggesting that certain senior officers were disloyal and linked to the Nazis, Ezhov must have pushed harder in trying to piece together a more complex conspiracy than the one he had already unmasked among the former opposition. All members of the high command had spent extended periods in Germany training with the Reichswehr in the 1920s and early 1930s, and this put them in a vulnerable position. Established contacts with German military circles would look far more suspicious in 1937 in an atmosphere of increasing spy mania. For the conspiratorially minded Ezhov, all of this may have sparked more developed suspicions that a military plot existed in the high command that was connected to the already exposed oppositionist conspiracy. He could easily count on his subordinates to extract the necessary evidence from the arrested NKVD officers and from Medvedev. A confession—forced or not—was proof enough of wrongdoing. According to testimony from an NKVD interrogator given later in the 1950s, Ezhov and a colleague of his, Mikhail Frinovskii, ordered violence to be used against Medvedev to get him to give evidence about an extensive military plot.[141] In this respect, a broad perceived subversive threat to the Red Army that grew in prominence in March and April 1937, and one that had traveled far beyond the confines of Trotskyism, was the most likely factor behind the timing of when the first incriminating testimony emerged against Tukhachevskii and the other senior officers soon to be executed as military conspirators, beginning with the confessions extracted from the arrested NKVD men at the end of April.

The growing spy scare in the Red Army soon came to a head on 10 May, when Voroshilov sent a long report to Stalin and Molotov entitled, "Measures for the Exposure and the Prevention of Wrecking and Espionage in the RKKA."[142] In this report, Voroshilov described the serious spy infiltration now apparently facing the Red Army: "The wrecking and espionage activity of the Japanese–German–Trotskyist agents has touched (*zadela*) the Red Army. Acting on the instructions of intelligence agents of the imperialist states, the malicious enemies of the people—the Trotskyists and Zinovievites—have penetrated their vile designs into the Red Army and have already managed to inflict considerable damage in various domains of military construction." Voroshilov proposed a range of measures to combat infiltrated foreign agents. Along with the usual call for vigilance to be increased, he wanted officers to conduct widespread checks on political reliability, discipline, and military preparedness. Yearly appraisals were to be improved and formalism and irresponsibility stamped out. More attention would be given to investigating political pasts.[143] Voroshilov also called for a scrutiny of all officers in all areas of the Red army and navy. Those with access to secret documents were to be singled out for a more intensive checking. Accidents and "extraordinary incidents" would also be checked carefully to uncover evidence of wrecking or sabotage.[144] Alongside this range of proposals, Voroshilov commented on a culture of self-interest within the officer corps in criticizing "'familyness' (*semeistvennost'*), nepotism, injustice, helping on the one hand sycophants and unworthy people (and sometimes enemies) advance easily through the ranks and cause damage." Voroshilov argued that these behaviors were not only harmful but also produced discontent among loyal officers.[145] This was the clearest articulation yet of the existence of family circles in the officer corps that primarily served their own interests. Voroshilov's comments were similar to Budennyi's complaints about patronage groups in the officer corps in 1936 and can be set alongside earlier criticisms suggesting that some officers may have been deliberately circumventing the call to root out enemies in their commands. From the accusation that some officers were giving overly positive assessments of their units to the possibility that handing out excessive reprimands for minor crimes was a way to deflect attention, Voroshilov's comments provide more evidence that a certain number of officers closed ranks when ordered to search for hidden enemies in the Red Army. They were more interested in preserving their positions or networks of power, which only undermined military self-policing.

In short, Voroshilov's report showed clearly that a comprehensive verification of the Red Army was needed to combat an apparent infiltration by wreckers and foreign agents. The military was understood to have been heavily compromised by enemies who had already done serious damage. What had once been regarded as a relatively minor spy threat in previous years was now seen as having much greater proportions, and Voroshilov now made the threat a priority. It is not clear whether he did this reluctantly. Voroshilov had undoubtedly come under pressure at the February–March plenum on the issue of undiscovered enemies in the military, and he would have had little choice but to redouble his efforts from March onward. Voroshilov may well have been simply swept along by events, particularly the growing spy scare that gripped the state in the early months of 1937, and realized he had no choice but to follow Stalin's lead. Yet it is also entirely possible that Voroshilov came to sincerely believe that the ranks had been deeply compromised by foreign agents and that aggressive counteractions were needed. Either way, his 10 May report to Stalin and Molotov on foreign agents in the military represents the culmination of his renewed efforts to unmask more enemies in the Red Army.

Voroshilov's 10 May report coincided with the first action taken against Tukhachevskii and the other senior officers incriminated as members of the military-fascist plot. Up to this point, no action had been taken against the group despite the damaging evidence already collected by the NKVD in late April, suggesting that Stalin had been either unsure about the strength of the evidence or uncertain about how to next proceed. The day before Voroshilov sent his report about foreign agents to Stalin and Molotov, he requested sanction from the

Politburo for several transfers within the military elite. These received approval on 10 May and included the demotion of Tukhachevskii from deputy to the head of the Red Army to the lower position of commander of the Volga Military District. In doing so, it is possible that Voroshilov understood that he, of all people, needed to take some action in light of the evidence gathered by the NKVD incriminating Tukhachevskii as a military conspirator. This put him in a potentially difficult position. How could the head of the Red Army not have realized that his deputy was a spy? The extensive spy infiltration of the military outlined in his report of 10 May only raised the stakes further. The Red Army was reaching a crisis point in early May. Requesting that Tukhachevskii be transferred acted to distance Voroshilov from the incriminated officers but also provided a clear signal that he was taking the correct and decisive steps in defense of the Red Army.

Because the Politburo immediately approved the transfer, it appears that Stalin agreed that action now needed to be taken concerning Tukhachevskii's incrimination. That Voroshilov's report about a broad spy infiltration of the Red Army was sent to Stalin the very day that the Politburo considered and approved Tukhachevskii's transfer probably played a role in the decision. From Stalin's point of view, an infiltration of the army by foreign agents, as identified by Voroshilov, added further pressure to the reports that had already been coming in from the NKVD over the previous weeks about a military conspiracy in the high command. It may well have provided the final push he needed to sanction action against the incriminated senior officers.[146] Subsequently, after Tukhachevskii's demotion on 10 May, four days later, Kork was removed from the head of the Frunze Academy and immediately arrested. Kork initially denied the accusations of being a counterrevolutionary, but presumably under NKVD pressure, he confessed on 16 May about plans for a coup and how Tukhachevskii supposedly wanted to install a dictatorship. Notably, Kork also mentioned Tukhachevskii's close contact with the Reichswehr in the 1920s.[147] On 15 May, Fel'dman's appointment as deputy commander of the Moscow Military District was annulled, and he was also arrested. Under interrogation between 19 and 23 May, Fel'dman gave evidence about the existence of a Trotskyist military plot within the Red Army, which he claimed was headed by Tukhachevskii. He also named more than forty other officers and political workers.[148] Moreover, Putna (who was already under arrest) was interrogated again on 14 May as the military conspiracy was pieced together. He provided further incriminating material on Tukhachevskii.[149] Similarly Primakov, who had been imprisoned since 1936, supplied evidence against Iakir and on 21 May named Tukhachevskii and forty others as members of the military conspiracy, including Shaposhnikov, Dybenko, and Gamarnik.[150] Iakir was removed as commander of the Kiev Military District on 20 May and transferred to the Leningrad Military District; Uborevich faced similar treatment. He lost his position as commander of the Belorussian Military District and was transferred to the more remote Central Asian Military District.[151] On 22 May, Tukhachevskii, Iakir, Uborevich, and Eideman, head of Osoaviakhim, were all arrested. On 24 May, Tukhachevskii was expelled from the party on the grounds of "participation in an anti-Soviet, Trotskyist-rightist conspiratorial bloc" and having carried out espionage work for Germany (in the margins of this resolution, Budennyi had scrawled, "It's necessary to finish off this scum").[152] On 26 May, Tukhachevskii gave his own evidence under interrogation. With liberal use of violence from his interrogators (Tukhachevskii's interrogation transcript was later found to be blood spattered[153]), he confessed to his role in the conspiracy: "I headed a counterrevolutionary military plot, in which I fully acknowledge my guilt. The aim of the plot was the overthrow of the existing government by force of arms and the restoration of capitalism." Tukhachevskii also claimed that the military plot was connected to the Zinoviev–Kamenev Counterrevolutionary Bloc and to the Right Deviation, and that the plan was to seize power through a coup or spark revolts across the country that would undermine state security in a time of war. The next day, Tukhachevskii claimed that the military conspirators had carried out acts of sabotage and espionage, and he detailed his past connections with senior German military figures. On 29 May, Tukhachevskii admitted to being a "German intelligence agent."[154] By the end of May, all of the supposed ringleaders of the military-fascist plot were arrested and had admitted their guilt.

Stalin was closely involved throughout the investigation into the military-fascist plot. He regularly met with Ezhov between 21 and 28 May and received daily reports of the interrogations.[155] This supposed foreign-backed military plot closely aligned with his security priorities at this time. In the first half of 1937, Stalin appears to have been even more focused on the danger from foreign agents, particularly from Germany. He had already articulated what he saw as a threat to the Soviet state from foreign subversives at the February–March plenum, and in

May, he personally edited a long *Pravda* article that detailed the recruitment methods used by foreign intelligence agents. This article claimed that before World War I, German intelligence had a list of 47,000 people living in Russia, France, and Britain whom it could call upon to act as agents. The article pointed to the still-present danger from fascist agents and referred to a "continuous secret war" led by an "army of spies."[156] According to one historian, Stalin also told Voroshilov and Ezhov in May 1937 that the biggest danger was now the German intelligence service.[157] Moreover, at a meeting on 21 May, he declared that Soviet military intelligence had fallen into the "hands of the Germans" (military intelligence was particularly hit hard by large numbers of arrests beginning at the end of April).[158] Stalin was not wrong in suspecting that foreign intelligence agencies had become more active against the Soviet Union, but his concerns were exaggerated, and he misread the scale of the danger. Indeed, after the anti-Comintern pact was signed in November 1936, Germany and Japan did increase the scale of their joint military intelligence against the Soviet Union. This led to a formal agreement being signed on 11 May 1937 between Germany and Japan for the exchange of military intelligence on the Soviet Union.[159] It is entirely possible that the NKVD received reports about Germany and Japan's intention to carry out more intense espionage in 1936 and 1937, and this only inflamed broader concerns about foreign agents. Yet it also remains undeniable that the Soviet leaders exaggerated the scale of this threat.

With Stalin exhibiting deep concern about foreign agents in mid-1937, it is understandable why he took action against the Tukhachevskii group after their initial incriminations in late April and early May as military conspirators, particularly in light of the spy scare in the Red Army detailed in Voroshilov's 10 May report. What is curious is why he still hesitated even at this point. As we have seen, only Kork and Fel'dman were arrested immediately when Stalin decided to move against the incriminated officers. The other supposed military conspirators were first transferred before they were eventually arrested. Iakir's transfer from the Kiev Military District to the Leningrad Military District is the most unusual. Leningrad was a strategically important military district, and he remained in a position of responsibility despite his incrimination. It took twelve days for Tukhachevskii (the supposed leader of the plot) to be arrested after his transfer to the Volga Military District. These initial transfers and the large gaps before the final arrests strongly suggest a level of uncertainty from Stalin about how he should proceed. Certainly, there is little indication that the group of senior officers had been targeted for arrest for a long period of time or that there was a well-thought-out plan. Rather, the decision to move against the group appears to have been taken quickly and without a plan. One explanation for Stalin's hesitation is that he might not have been entirely convinced by the initial evidence against the group of officers obtained by the NKVD. Stalin perhaps needed to be more certain about the plot in the high command before he had a group of his most talented officers arrested. From Stalin's point of view, the broader spy infiltration of the Red Army detailed by Voroshilov was bad enough, but if the NKVD's evidence about a military conspiracy within the upper military elite stood up to scrutiny, it greatly raised the seriousness of the situation. This would mean that the Red Army had not only been infiltrated by foreign agents but they had managed to establish a conspiracy at the highest level. Stalin's response would need to be severe, and an extensive hunt for co-conspirators would cause huge upheaval inside the institution most vital for defense at a time when the Soviet leadership saw world war as increasingly likely. On this basis, in early May 1937, Stalin may have wanted further evidence of the alleged conspiracy in the high command. This meant that in the majority of cases, transfers were agreed as a precautionary measure (presumably to move the incriminated officers from their home support bases) while Stalin checked the evidence against the group of senior officers. He became closely involved in the NKVD's investigation, suggesting that he wanted to make certain of the reality of the charges himself.[160] Stalin had done this before in 1930 after Tukhachevskii's incrimination in Operation Vesna. There were reasons for Stalin to doubt Tukhachevskii's loyalty. His ambitions for influence in the Red Army were well known; he had been the subject of persisting rumors about his disloyalty throughout the 1920s and 1930s; and his name had already surfaced in several investigations into counterrevolutionary groups. At the same time, however, Stalin had dismissed the allegations against Tukhachevskii in 1930 after taking a closer look, and he may have wanted to take this cautious approach again in 1937, especially because the stakes were much higher in terms of future war. He met with Tukhachevskii on 13 May (after his transfer to the Volga Military District), and even though there is no record of the conversation, Stalin almost certainly would have questioned Tukhachevskii about the evidence against him.[161] This moment of hesitation on Stalin's part, however, did not last long. It seems that as soon as additional supporting material was obtained by the NKVD (probably beaten from Fel'dman, Kork, and other officers who had been immediately arrested), Stalin could not hesitate any longer. By the end of May, Stalin either now fully accepted that there was a military conspiracy in the high command, or he believed this to a great enough extent that it was too risky not to take any further action. How could he fight the approaching world war with an army he saw as infiltrated by foreign agents with a military conspiracy in the upper leadership? In this respect, it is possible that Stalin waited until the last moment until he was certain, but once he had sufficient evidence of a plot in the high command, taking no further action was impossible.

At the end of May, although not officially publicized, rumors about the arrests of some of the most senior officers in the Red Army had begun to filter down the army, which in turn sparked a new round of denunciations. Tukhachevskii was one of the most senior officers in the Red Army; he had a vast number of connections running through the ranks. More than anyone else, his name was a fertile source for denunciations.[162] This meant that the scale of the military plot began to expand almost immediately, and denunciations would be instrumental in providing momentum to the wave of arrests that hit the Red Army over the next two years. The NKVD also began to widen the line of its investigation. On 28 May, for instance, they compiled a list of people working in the artillery administration who had been incriminated during the investigation into the military-fascist plot. This totaled twenty-six officers, and Voroshilov gave the order to arrest.[163] The military plot instantly moved beyond the confines of the high command.

A final key victim drawn into the military-fascist plot was Gamarnik, who committed suicide on 31 May after being removed from his position the previous day. Gamarnik had been named by Primakov on 21 May as belonging to the conspiracy, but there is little indication that he was under any suspicion before this point. At the end of April, for instance, the Council for Labor and Defense was abolished and replaced by a defense committee under the Soviet government. This included, among others, Stalin, Ezhov, Molotov, Kaganovich, Voroshilov, and Gamarnik.[164] It is hard to see why Gamarnik would be extended membership to this exclusive defense committee if he was under any kind of suspicion, especially under suspicion of being a foreign agent. Moreover, there is little indication that Gamarnik disagreed or was becoming an obstacle to the rising political repression in the Red Army.

He continued to sanction the arrests of soldiers for political crimes into mid-May, just weeks before his death.[165] Unless Gamarnik's sanctioning of these arrests was insincere, that he continued to do so suggests that he raised no objections. What sealed his fate seems to have been his association with Iakir. This was mentioned specifically in the Politburo resolution of 30 May that removed Gamarnik from PUR. Indeed, the very day before his arrest, Iakir had visited Gamarnik in the morning.[166] It seems that as soon as Gamarnik was removed from his position, he realized there was no way out.

The Military Soviet met the day after Gamarnik's suicide in an extraordinary session between 1 and 4 June that was dominated by the news of the military-fascist plot.[167] In his opening speech, Voroshilov outlined the parameters of the conspiracy, to the shock of those assembled in the room. As Voroshilov detailed, the arrested officers were spies and wreckers working for Trotsky and foreign governments who had not left a single area of military industry or the Red Army unaffected by sabotage. The conspirators were said to have planned to undermine the army so it would be easily defeated in a future war. Notably, for some of the assembled officers, this was not only the first time they had heard about the evidence against the Tukhachevskii group, but alarmingly, a few discovered their own names in the interrogation transcripts that circulated around the room. Some were questioned about their links to the conspirators during the Military Soviet itself.[168] In sketching out the details of the military plot, Voroshilov regularly quoted from interrogation transcripts and pointed to other sources of evidence. Past disputes, such as the controversy over Tukhachevskii's radical armament plan in 1930, were now recast as evidence of wrecking.[169] In other cases (including cases where he might face questions of his own), Voroshilov downplayed the significance of old disputes. For example, he recounted the confrontation in his apartment in May 1936 when Tukhachevskii had accused Voroshilov and Budennyi of hoarding power within the Red Army. Voroshilov now argued that this clash was nothing but the "usual squabbles" between people who had worked together for a long time; seemingly the significance of events that could prompt questions about Voroshilov's own vigilance were underplayed.[170] Some people might rightly have wondered why Voroshilov did not recognize Tukhachevskii's dangerous ambitions for power in May 1936 or any time before. Voroshilov's main defense at the Military Soviet, in short, was to plead ignorance. He commented, for instance:

The people were so disguised that I have to be honest here and admit that I not only did not see counterrevolution in the actions of these people, but I simply did not have any idea. Of Tukhachevskii, I, as you well know, did not especially like, did not especially love. I had strained relations with him. I did not regard Tukhachevskii highly as a worker.[171]

Voroshilov was distancing himself from Tukhachevskii by stressing that they were not particularly close. This was true. The relationship between the two had been strained for years. Voroshilov must have known that he was in an awkward position after Tukhachevskii's arrest. He needed to avoid inviting questions about why he had not called attention to the suspicious conduct of his deputy, regardless of their poor working relationship. Even if he had harbored more doubts about Tukhachevskii's loyalty over the past few months, to bring these up now at the Military Soviet would have raised questions about his own vigilance. How could he have not noticed that his deputy was a German spy? If he had nagging suspicions, why was nothing done? Potentially, Voroshilov had a lot to answer for, and he played it safe. Rather than dwell on his own failures, he tried to spread the responsibility for having missed the military conspirators, remarking at one stage, "I have to declare just one more time that, from you sitting here, I did not once hear one signal."[172]

Other speakers at the Military Soviet likewise claimed ignorance about the arrested conspirators. Egorov, for instance, commented that "the party trusted them politically" and argued that there were no indications whatsoever that they were wreckers or spies.[173] Others took a different approach, arguing that suspicions had in fact been raised about Tukhachevskii before his arrest. Dybenko, the new commander of the Leningrad Military District, remarked that he had raised his concerns about Tukhachevskii in 1931 and had had doubts about him as early as 1923. According to Dybenko, Tukhachevskii had refused to sign a declaration condemning Trotsky that year. He also claimed that he had likewise raised suspicions about Uborevich and Iakir, but these were ignored.[174] Dybenko was doing his best to dispel any possible doubt he had not shown necessary vigilance. Voroshilov, however, did not accept his version of events and argued that Dybenko should have written to him with his suspicions.[175] It also seems that the arrests of some of the officers caused more surprise than others. Ivan Dubovoi, the commander of the Kharkov Military District (who would be arrested in August), remarked that he had believed Iakir to have been a loyal party member.

On this point Stalin agreed, noting that Iakir had been considered "one of the best commanders."[176] Interestingly, during the discussion of Iakir, the issue of regional power centers in military districts surfaced again. The deputy commander of the cavalry in the Belorussian Military District, Josef Apanasenko, remarked that Iakir had been at the top of an oligarchy (bat'kovshchina) in Ukraine. This was apparently an exclusive power group containing only Iakir's supporters and represents another indication that some officers had created their own fiefdoms inside the Red Army.[177]

Having glossed over his own responsibility for not noticing the formation of a military conspiracy under his watch, Voroshilov proposed a solution to the crisis. He wanted a purge of the Red Army, "to sweep out with an iron broom not only all this scum, but everything that recalls such an abomination. . . . It is necessary to purge the army literally up to the very last crack (shchelochek), the army should be clean, the army should be healthy."[178] This was the start of an extensive military purge aimed at rooting out the conspirators and foreign-backed subversives apparently hidden in the Red Army. It was a true moment of crisis. The Soviet leaders believed that hostile foreign powers had scored a direct attack, undermining not only the army's strength but also that of the wider state. In his speech to the Military Soviet, Stalin explicitly stated that the military plot was financed by the Nazis, and he repeatedly accused many of the arrested officers of being German spies. Stalin also presented the military-fascist plot as one part of a much broader conspiracy that connected the military conspirators to other high-profile traitors, including Bukharin, Iagoda, and Rykov.[179] As others had done, Stalin did not want to publicly admit to any prior suspicions he might have had about Tukhachevskii. Indeed, he remarked, "We did not think he was a bad soldier; I did not think he was a bad soldier."[180] As we have seen, it is likely that Stalin had some growing doubts about Tukhachevskii in the months before his arrest. Ezhov certainly did and would have communicated these to Stalin. However, nothing would be gained from admitting this at the Military Soviet. Moreover, if Stalin had spoken about any earlier suspicions, it would have undermined his old comrade, Voroshilov, who was already in a potentially difficult position. Stalin instead argued more generally and vaguely that the Red Army had been blinded by its successes.[181] He also pointed to wider intelligence failures and reiterated his belief that military intelligence was riddled with spies.[182] Stalin also raised the long-standing problem of making sure reliable officers were promoted, and he listed examples of people in command positions who had apparently turned out to be enemies.[183] The key part of his speech, however, was when Stalin encouraged denunciations from the ranks:

> I have to say that they signaled very poorly from the field. Badly. . . . They think that the center should know everything, see everything. No, the center does not see everything, nothing of the sort. The center sees only part; the rest is seen by the localities. It sends people, but it does not know these people 100 percent, you should check them. There is one way to test this—it is checking people at work, according to the results of their work.

Stalin wanted more denunciations "from the field"; he wanted more "signals" of enemy activity. Everyone needed to keep a closer eye on each other's conduct. The center could not be expected to do this alone. The slightest suspicion needed to be reported. Stalin even remarked that it would be enough if these reports contained only "5 percent truth."[184] He also raised this point during Egorov's speech, stressing the importance of denunciations from below, interjecting, "Not a single query, not a single letter from local people should remain without an answer."[185] Denunciations were to be a vital tool in combating the military plot. Stalin wanted the whole army to support the center in flushing out enemies in the ranks. This appeal to the wider army is one of the primary reasons that arrests stemming from the military-fascist plot exploded in the months after the June military trial.

A few days after the Military Soviet, Voroshilov reiterated many of the same points at a meeting of Red Army party members working in the Commissariat for Defense. The military conspiracy needed explaining to the broader rank and file, especially if they were to be mobilized in the hunt for enemies. At this meeting, Voroshilov made a reference to his earlier speech to the Red Army *aktiv* in March, remarking that at that time the army was in "last place" in terms of "revealed" enemies, but that over the course of three months, the picture had "sharply changed."[186] Voroshilov went on to describe the military conspirators. He claimed that Tukhachevskii had established a link with the Germans as early as 1925.[187] As for Iakir, his popularity within the Red Army was on show again when Voroshilov remarked that for many he was "a distinguished military worker" who had "sympathy among the Red Army masses." However, these qualities were apparently just a way that Iakir masked his criminality. Voroshilov similarly proclaimed that he had trusted both

Gamarnik and Eideman.[188] The main purpose of the speech, however, was to stress that enemies were still unexposed in the army.[189] In order to help mobilize the ranks toward searching out these enemies, Voroshilov emphasized a distinction between the younger loyal generation and the now corrupted command. The younger generation, with their apparent "healthy revolutionary fervor," were presented as models of correct behavior.[190] They would help flush out the traitors in the officer corps.

On 11 June, the military-fascist plot was finally publicized in *Pravda*, and Tukhachevskii, Iakir, Uborevich, Kork, Fel'dman, Eideman, Primakov, and Putna, the public faces of the imagined military conspiracy, all faced a closed military trial. They were executed the next day. Little is known of the military trial itself, but two senior officers, Belov and Budennyi, did record their impressions. On 14 July, Belov, now the commander of the Belorussian Military District, sent a report to Voroshilov with his thoughts on the process in which he described the behavior of each defendant in turn. According to Belov, during the trial, "Tukhachevskii tried to maintain his 'aristocratism' and his superiority over others, from the beautiful English suit, with an expensive thin tie, to how he held his head and the precision of expression." Belov remarked that Iakir tried to make an emotional appeal to the court "with several reminders about previous joint work and good relations with the majority of the members of the court." Uborevich was depicted as disheveled, wearing a suit without a tie; further, according to Belov, he had "lost his nerve more than the first two."[191] In contrast, Kork appeared confident and spoke more directly than the first three. Notably, at least from Belov's account, it seems that Fel'dman's earlier resistance to false evidence and groundless cases had completely collapsed. In Belov's words, he "chided his colleagues that they, like schoolchildren, were afraid to say things as they were, that they were often occupied with espionage, and here they want to turn this into legal communication with foreign officers."[192] It is highly likely that Fel'dman had been threatened or tortured into making these claims. Indeed, Belov's description of Eideman again suggests that torture was used in the interrogations. He looked "more miserable" than the others, had difficulty standing, and, as Belov noted, "babbled with a broken muffled spasmodic voice." Similarly, Putna was thin and showing signs of deafness. Yet despite the pressure that had clearly been applied to the officers, Belov was certain that they had not spoken the whole truth.[193] It seems that Budennyi felt the same. In his version of events, Tukhachevskii apparently tried to question some of the charges leveled against him and argued they did not correspond with reality. In the end, however, he eventually confessed.[194] Finally, on the day of the military trial, Voroshilov published a secret order regarding the promotion of loyal, talented officers and political workers throughout the Red Army. Voroshilov repeated Stalin's dictum that "every good organization is as strong as its cadres."[195] At the same time that a wave of discharges and arrests was about to hit the Red Army, replacements were already being anticipated.

6 | The Expansion of the Military Purge and the Mass Operations

After the executions of the ringleaders of the military-fascist plot in June 1937, there was an explosion in discharges and arrests in the Red Army as an increasing number of officers and soldiers were linked to the conspiracy. The executed officers had been some of the best-known servicemen in the Red Army, and this gave enormous potential for the imagined plot to spread through the ranks. Connections to the dead men ran all the way through the officer corps and down into the rank and file. Moreover, beyond the immediate chain of command, as we have seen, some senior officers appear to have maintained their own informal personal networks in the Red Army. That Iakir was at the head of a local power group in the Kiev Military District had been raised recently at the June Military Soviet. This might explain why a number of officers who had served under Iakir in the Kiev Military District were arrested just a month after the military trial.[1] In this way, the scale of the military-fascist plot expanded immediately, and the subordinates of the executed officers were some of the first to be arrested by the NKVD. PUR was also targeted by the NKVD early on, no doubt because of Gamarnik's suicide.[2] As the wave of arrests spread throughout the military districts from June, Stalin was kept closely informed.[3]

On 14 June, the Red Army newspaper *Krasnaia zvezda* called on the army party organizations attached to companies and regiments to help the NKVD flush out conspirators and subversives.[4] The army party organizations would prove central to the spread of the repression in the Red Army, approving the expulsions or arrests of military party members who, it was believed, had cases to answer. At the same time, Voroshilov and Ezhov attempted to solicit voluntary confessions of guilt from the troops. On 21 June, they published a joint order stressing the importance of finding the remaining enemies in the Red Army; they claimed that in several military districts, there were people with connections to the executed military conspirators who had not communicated this to the center. Voroshilov and Ezhov promised that if anyone associated with the traitors came forward, they would not be arrested or have criminal charges brought against them, and they might be able to remain in the army.[5] These promises, of course, were unlikely to be honored. Anyone naive enough to turn himself in was almost certainly arrested or discharged from the army (the special departments had already planned to launch investigations of anyone who handed himself in voluntarily). It is not surprising that very few soldiers took up Voroshilov and Ezhov's offer.[6]

However, denunciations from within the ranks played a critical role in pushing forward a wave of arrests after the June military trial.[7] These were driven by a variety of motives. Certainly, some Red Army men will have sincerely believed the reports printed in the Soviet press that their superiors—people they might have looked up to and who had been depicted as heroes of the Soviet Union—were in fact foreign agents.[8] For many, this would have been genuinely shocking news. Indeed, the Japanese military attaché stationed in Moscow at the start of the military purge recorded a sense of fear and distrust within the officer corps when the arrests began.[9] Servicemen who accepted the regime's portrayal of the military-fascist plot probably had little difficulty in sending in their own denunciations in hope of catching any still unmasked co-conspirators. However, a number of troops certainly would have taken advantage of the military plot for less patriotic reasons and denounced their fellow servicemen out of careerism, personal animosity, or malice.[10] As happened in other Soviet institutions during the Great Terror, rivalries and feuds at the ground level provided the substance for denunciations in a politically charged atmosphere. The networks of NKVD informers serving in military units would only have driven up the number of denunciations.

However, there is a sense that some Red Army men were disorientated after hearing the news of the military-fascist plot and felt that they no longer knew who could be trusted. For example, shortly after the military trial, Budennyi, now commander of the Moscow Military District, sent Voroshilov a report on 15 June containing some of the reactions within his military district to the news of the military plot. While Budennyi was happy with the general response, remarking that the executions of the fascist spies had met with the approval and satisfaction of the soldiers, there were some negative reactions.[11] Budennyi recorded some distrustful attitudes toward the regime. For example, one Red Army man had apparently remarked, "It is now impossible to believe any one of the leadership"; another commented, "Gamarnik shot himself, but he was a prominent and influential person, and to believe the others now is impossible."[12] Gamarnik's suicide in particular was a source of speculation for many soldiers. One historian has pointed to a dip in wider public morale after Gamarnik's death.[13] Budennyi, however, attributed any negative reactions to the military-fascist plot in the Moscow Military District to the influence of other enemies rather than representing a stronger cynicism toward the ruling elite.[14] However, galvanized distrust toward those in power is clearly evident in Budennyi's report, which pointed to the opinion among certain soldiers that any spies and wreckers were concentrated in the upper rather than the lower ranks.[15] This stronger distrust toward authority was similarly recorded by the NKVD in June. Even some workers in PUR were finding it difficult to answer questions from soldiers about the military-fascist plot. Rather than calm their suspicions, some political commissars agreed that it was difficult to trust anyone.[16]

There are strong indications that some soldiers were not just confused about whom they could trust after the unmasking of the military plot, but that the arrests had caused a panic. This can already be seen in the months before the June military trial. For example, Voroshilov received a report on 25 April from the commander of the Urals Military District, Boris Gorbachev (arrested in May), in which he detailed the condition of his district. Aside from describing a poorly prepared military district troubled by underfulfilled orders and overspending, all of which was apparently the result of deliberate sabotage, Gorbachev commented on the reactions of his soldiers to the apparent presence of wreckers in the Red Army, highlighting in particular

> frantic attempts to realize, open, and find the effects of sabotage in the most important areas. . . . Many workers in the district apparatus are full of fear of being made personally responsible for what is happening in the district. They show senselessness and excessive zeal; they make a lot of noise and try to protect themselves against an imaginary or real liability for their errors and mistakes.[17]

A level of panic had gripped the Urals Military District at least by April, and accusations of wrecking and sabotage had started to spread. People were showing "excessive zeal" and making frantic efforts to avoid coming under suspicion. It seems that accusations about sabotage had mushroomed in the district; some Red Army men were trying to insulate themselves from danger by preemptively incriminating others. Indeed, Gorbachev commented that the level of confusion was such that it was difficult to ascertain the true extent of wrecking in the district.[18] As to what sparked the panic, Gorbachev pointed to the arrests of the commander of the Urals Military District, I. I. Garkavyi, alongside his subordinates, V. I. Vasilenko and G. F. Gavriushchenko, in March, which marked an escalation in the repression within the military, as neither had been supporters of the former opposition.[19] With their district commander arrested at a time when the regime was publicly broadcasting the danger posed by wreckers and subversives, it is understandable that a confused and distrustful rank and file could start to turn on each other, especially when long-running problems in the military district could easily be interpreted as evidence of sabotage.

It is unlikely that the experience of the Urals Military District was isolated. Furthermore, because such a degree of panic had gripped the Urals Military District after the arrests of Garkavyi, Vasilenko, and Gavriushchenko, it is likely that after the executions of some of the most senior and well-known officers in the Red Army in June 1937, the wider rank and file were thrown into further disarray. At the Military Soviet of November 1937 (when the military purge was firmly underway), the commander of the Zabaikal Military District, M. D. Velikanov, spoke about the panic and distrust in his district, which he saw as a consequence of the increasing arrests in the army.[20] The impact of the military-fascist plot not only on the Red Army but also wider Soviet society should not be underestimated. The executions of the Tukhachevskii group were truly sensational. As David Brandenberger has commented, they "shattered public confidence in the Soviet system."[21] Privately, even Voroshilov appeared dejected. Shortly after the closed military trial, in a draft outline version of a speech intended for the June plenum of the Central Committee, Voroshilov had written that he believed the authority of the army was crippled and the high command undermined. These comments, for good reason, did not make it into the final version of his speech, but Voroshilov evidently was not celebrating the discovery of the military-fascist plot. Another line excised from the final speech makes this abundantly clear: "This [the military plot] means that our method of work, our whole system for running the army, and my work as People's Commissar, has utterly collapsed."[22] On this basis, Voroshilov appeared deeply affected by the military plot and feared it had severely undermined his authority. Even though he probably welcomed the removal of Tukhachevskii—he had been a potential rival for over a decade—the military plot was quickly becoming a far more serious problem than a handful of treacherous officers in the high command. The scale of the military conspiracy was rapidly expanding in June, and it is entirely possible that Voroshilov began to fear for his own position. It was impossible to say how far the search would go.

Moreover, there are indirect suggestions that Voroshilov may not have entirely accepted the basis of the military-fascist plot in the first place. Private doubts can be inferred from a letter he received from Bukharin, the former member of the Right Deviation who was arrested in February 1937 and executed after the third and final Moscow show trial in March 1938. It seems that Bukharin sent this undated letter to Voroshilov from prison at some point after the military-fascist plot was publicized.[23] In the letter, Bukharin expressed a sense of helplessness in the face of the widening political repression: "I am writing now and I am worried about a feeling of semireality (*polureal'nosti*), that it is a dream, a mirage, a madhouse, an hallucination? No, it is reality." Bukharin protested his innocence of any crime, but tellingly, he wanted to find out whether Voroshilov truly believed the conspiracies that were being uncovered across the state: "I wanted to ask one thing here: do you believe everything, sincerely?" Bukharin noted he had always "related so well" to Voroshilov, and he must have felt he could confide in him.[24] Presumably Bukharin hoped that Voroshilov might similarly question the supposed counterrevolutionary plots and might even try to intercede on his behalf. This was probably not an entirely unrealistic hope. We have seen how Voroshilov had shown some skepticism toward the methods used by the political police in the past, notably during the OGPU's handling of the Shakhty Affair in 1928 (at the time, he privately questioned whether the OGPU was fabricating the charges). Voroshilov was well aware that the political police could build cases on groundless accusations. He also appears to have been acutely affected by the military-fascist plot and took little pride in its discovery. In this sense, Bukharin was probably perceptive in trying to find an ally in Voroshilov. It cannot be completely discounted that even one of Stalin's closest allies had doubts about the level of truth behind the conspiracy theories that underpinned the violence of the Great Terror. However, even if doubts existed, ultimately Voroshilov had no choice but to fall into line.

The number of Red Army men discharged from the ranks on the basis of having committed political crimes in the immediate aftermath of the execution of the Tukhachevskii group can be seen in several sets of statistics. These figures demonstrate that the growth in arrests was not gradual but rather exploded after the military trial in June. It is clear that there was some growth in the number of discharges and arrests in the Red Army after the February–March plenum.[25] According to figures from PUR, from 1 January to 10 July 1937, there were 4,947 discharges from the army for political crimes, resulting in 1,217 arrests. However, 4,370 of these discharges were sanctioned after 1 April.[26] April was when the NKVD's investigation into the military-fascist plot was beginning to show real results, but it is not clear from this when the number of discharges and arrests truly began to accelerate. However, according to Vladimir Khaustov and Lennart Samuelson, even at the end of April, arrests in the Red Army were still at a relatively low level. During Stalin's speech to the extraordinary Military Soviet in early June, he placed the number of arrests strictly associated with the newly unmasked military-fascist plot at approximately 300 to 400.[27] It seems that noticeably larger numbers of arrests came only after the June military trial and when the military-fascist plot was finally publicized. During the nine days after the trial, for instance, another 980 senior officers were arrested as participants of the military conspiracy. At the plenum of the Central Committee at the end of June, Ezhov said that the number was now 1,100.[28] In August, at a meeting of political workers, the new head of PUR, Pavel Smirnov, noted that over the past few months, the total number of discharges from the army stood at approximately 10,000 and the number arrested was 1,217. This is consistent with the figures quoted by Ezhov at the June plenum.[29] Thus, although the Red Army certainly faced more official scrutiny from the February–March plenum, it was only when the military plot finally broke in June that significant acceleration was evident in the number of discharges and arrests. There was no rising tide of repression in the Red Army over the course of 1937. The spike in arrests from June suggests a knee-jerk reaction to the supposed military plot. It is also necessary to note that not all the discharges and arrests sanctioned over the course of 1937–1938 were strictly connected to the military-fascist plot. Recorded cases of crime increased during these years in general terms. Large numbers of soldiers were being discharged from the army for reasons outside of counterrevolutionary crime, such as being linked to a socially harmful element, having fought with White armies during the civil war, or for less serious issues such as drunkenness and hooliganism. It is understandable that the more intense scrutiny now placed on the Red Army by the NKVD and army party organizations, along with the noted surge in denunciations, drove up cases of general crime throughout the Red Army.[30]

At the PUR meeting in August 1937, Pavel Smirnov pressed the point that despite the large numbers of discharges from the Red Army, it was not yet fully purged. There was still a long way to go, as enemies apparently remained well masked.[31] However, Smirnov also highlighted the key role being played by denunciations in rooting out enemies, and this partly explains the sudden spike in discharges and arrests after the military trial. He remarked, "Hundreds and thousands of eyes are now looking at the troops for the intrigues of enemies. The troops and commanders are writing hundreds, thousands of letters about faults, failures. . . . Tens, hundreds of thousands of letters are now being received by the Secretariat; recently more than ten thousand were received."[32] Seemingly, there had been a massive increase in denunciations in recent weeks, not only revealing the forces on the ground level driving the violence in the Red Army but also suggesting that the military purge was beginning to gather a momentum of its own. Moreover, Stalin knew that some Red Army men were reacting with confusion and disorientation to the news of the military plot, and he seems to have been concerned about the party's image and authority. At this same PUR meeting, there was a revealing exchange between Stalin and a political commissar from the North Caucasus Military District, A. P. Prokofiev, on this question:

STALIN: And how have the soldiers related to the fact that they had commanders that they trusted, and then they were busted and arrested (*ikh khlopnuli, arrestovali*)? How did they react to that?

PROKOFIEV: As I reported, Com[rade] Stalin, at first in the ranks among an array of soldiers there were some doubts, and they expressed these doubts by saying that such people like Gamarnik and Iakir, whom the party trusted over a period of many years with high posts, had turned out to be enemies of the people, traitors of the party.

STALIN: Well, yes, the party was caught napping . . .

PROKOFIEV: Yes, the party was indeed caught napping.

STALIN: Are there instances where the party has lost its authority, where the military leadership has lost its authority? Do they say to hell with you, you send us someone today and then arrest him tomorrow. Let God sort it out and decide who's to be believed?[33]

The military purge continued into the second half of 1937, and soon even more senior officers were drawn into the military plot. Ivan Dubovoi, the commander of the Kharkov Military District, for instance, was arrested on 22 August. High-profile arrests like this allowed the process of incrimination by association to spread further throughout the Red Army. Someone as senior as Dubovoi had numerous associations and connections throughout the army hierarchy. Stalin also continued to be kept well informed about the number of military arrests, receiving regular reports from the new head of PUR, Lev Mekhlis, the former editor of *Pravda* who headed the organization from December 1937.[34] Voroshilov also kept up the pressure in driving the military purge onward. At the Military Soviet in November 1937, for instance, he declared that the purge was nowhere near complete and stressed that it must happen quickly. Notably, the military purge continued to be framed as a response to an infiltration of foreign agents. Voroshilov commented, "[Stalin] correctly says, and repeatedly draws our attention to, if the countries of the bourgeoisie are sending spies to each other, sending thousands of spies, then it would be ridiculous to think that they would not send hundreds and thousands of spies to us." According to Voroshilov, foreign governments had used people such as Tukhachevskii, Iakir, and Gamarnik to carry out their subversive designs—people whom he argued had never been true Bolsheviks or revolutionaries.[35] This remained the main lesson of the military purge.

However, at the same time that arrests and discharges spread throughout the Red Army, there were signs that the wider Great Terror was being reined in. Indeed, a resolution published by a plenum of the Central Committee in January 1938 criticized incorrect expulsions from the party based on false evidence.[36] This resolution was not a complete turnaround. Party members were still required to demonstrate vigilance in the face of the enemy, but drawing attention to incorrectly expelled party members was an attempt by the center to regain control over the surge of repression that had touched every sphere of the Soviet state in 1937.[37] Things were evidently getting out of hand. The resolution called for "slanderers" to be punished and a careful appeals process to be undertaken by party organizations.[38] This resolution can be easily criticized, however. Although the Central Committee acknowledged the large numbers of incorrect denunciations in January 1938, as Wendy Goldman notes, scapegoating supposed slanderers and careerists only added new categories of enemy to be sought out.[39] Nonetheless, the Soviet leaders evidently wanted to regain control over the Great Terror.

Shortly thereafter, matching efforts were made to reestablish central control over expulsions from the Red Army. On 23 February, Mekhlis sent a circular to all political administration organizations that noted:

> A range of party organizations have recently expelled from the party, often incorrectly, commanding officers and commissars from regiments, brigades, battalions, and other similar units; meanwhile, the question of their party membership should be handled with the knowledge and consent of the Political Directorate of the RKKA, working on an equal basis with the military department of the TsK VKP(b) [Central Committee].

Mekhlis reminded all army party organizations that material that "cast doubt on the advisability of party membership of commanding officers and commissars" should be sent to PUR. Moreover, the question of whether a Red Army man should be excluded from the party could only be considered after suitable permission had been gained from the center.[40]

There were further signs that the repression in the Red Army was being scaled down in March 1938. Ie. A. Shchadenko, deputy commissar of defense and head of the officer personnel section, sent Mekhlis a report on 9 March concerning complaints about incorrect discharges from the Red Army. In his report, Shchadenko noted, "Examination of the presented material on the removals from the RKKA from the command and other leading army bodies (*nachal'sostav*) shows that in the overwhelming majority the motive for removal is insufficiently grounded, and the incriminating material is unchecked."[41] Shchadenko then referenced the decision of the January plenum of the Central Committee that had criticized false allegations, and he argued that all discharges sanctioned in 1937 should be rechecked. Any individuals incorrectly discharged should be restored to the ranks.[42] Shchadenko did not specify, however, on what basis these people had been discharged. The degree to which those arrested for serious political crimes would be affected by the proposal is unknown. Nonetheless, Shchadenko's is another official admission that large numbers of Red Army men had been unjustly removed from the ranks during the course of the military purge.[43]

On 2 April 1938, Mekhlis delivered another report to a meeting of political workers that signaled a shift in tone in his description of the military plot. Apparently the military plot was now "defeated and destroyed," with only "fragments of various groups" remaining.[44] Although Mekhlis did warn the assembled political workers that it was still no time to be complacent (apparently PUR still contained enemies), it seems that he was trying to bring some sense of closure to the purge.[45] Mekhlis also raised the issue of incorrect expulsions from the party, referencing the earlier resolution from the January plenum of the Central Committee:

> The party commissions of PURKKA [Political Administration of the Red Army] looked at around one thousand appeals. Almost 50 percent of the excluded were readmitted. After the decision of the plenum of TsK VKP(b) [Central Committee], the stream of appeals to the party commissions of PURKKA increased—they were sent a new 2,081 declarations. Our sacred duty is to correct all the mistakes that happened at the time of the exclusions of communists from the party and to create a friendly environment for them for work.[46]

In accordance with the line set out by the January plenum resolution, Mekhlis blamed the large numbers of incorrect removals from the political administration in 1937 on enemies within the organization itself.[47] More strikingly, however, Mekhlis remarked, "They were not guilty when they were expelled from the party, but we were—the leaders of the political organs and commissars." Mekhlis called for any mistakes to be corrected.[48] As one historian has noted, Mekhlis went as far as to label some of the expulsions that had been sanctioned in 1938 as absurd.[49]

All of this, however, did not bring an immediate halt to the arrests in the Red Army. As we have seen, this was not Stalin's intention. He wanted greater control over the Great Terror—not, at this stage, an end to the hunt for enemies. When more senior officers were incriminated as supposed traitors, this gave a new burst of energy to the military purge, prompting new rounds of denunciations and new lines of investigation. For example, both Egorov, now first deputy people's commissar for defense, and Dybenko, commander of the Leningrad Military District, came under suspicion at the end of 1937. Dybenko was accused of being a German agent and having links to American spies.[50] At a military meeting at some point in the latter half of 1937, attended by Ezhov, Molotov, and Voroshilov, as well as several senior military figures, including Egorov and Dybenko, Stalin had shared his concerns about other anti-Soviet groups in the Red Army aside from the military-fascist plot. He referred to another possible group including Egorov, Dybenko, and Budennyi. According to Stalin, the three officers were not just a group of friends but were politically like-minded (*gruppirovka politicheskikh ed-inomyshlennikov*).[51] Apparently they had been unhappy with the state of the Red Army and harbored grudges about not being promoted fast enough. Stalin even suggested that the three men might have gone so far as to set themselves against the party. In the course of his speech, Stalin argued that loyalty and being closely aligned with the politics of the state were central to the Red Army's effectiveness. This was apparently a lesson from the civil war. Even though the White armies had had more military experience, the new Red Army had been politically loyal, which ensured victory. Stalin threatened to replace any officers who were in conflict with the politics of the party with new commanders, remarking, "They will probably be less capable than you at first, but they will be connected to the people and they will be much more useful than you, with your talents."[52]

The fates of Egorov and Dybenko were sealed shortly after. A Politburo decision in February 1938 accused Egorov of having prior knowledge of the military-fascist plot and having organized his own antiparty group. He was removed from his position, but it was suggested that he be given one final chance to command a smaller military district. Similarly, Dybenko was also removed from the Red Army in early 1938, and again it was suggested that he could still be put to work, this time in a civilian area.[53] However, both were soon arrested. Budennyi managed to avoid any further trouble after Stalin had mentioned his name alongside those of Egorov and Dybenko. It is possible that he was able to make a convincing case that his loyalty could not be questioned, or Stalin may have had second thoughts of his own. For whatever reason, clearly it was not just those outside of Stalin's immediate circle who were at risk of incrimination and arrest.[54] Other notable victims of the military purge in the high command included Marshal Vasilii Bliukher; the head of the air force, Iakov Alksnis; the head of military intelligence, Ian Berzin; the head of the Red Navy, Vladimir Orlov; and commander of the Caucasus Military District, Ivan Fedko.[55]

On 17 November 1938, Stalin finally called an end to the use of mass repression, signaling the close of the Great Terror.[56] Accordingly, Voroshilov repeated this message at the Military Soviet of the same month, where he reiterated the lessons of the military purge—namely, that the

Red Army had missed the conspirators in its midst. He also stressed the importance of politically reliable people serving in the ranks.[57] On the results of the military purge, Voroshilov remarked:

> Have we done everything to cleanse the ranks of the army from enemies of the people, of the enemy's spies (*lazutchikov*)? I think that not everything, but the main and most important [work] has already been done. The enemy has lost his eyes and ears in our ranks. But the ears and eyes, of course, are still somewhere, and they need to be found; otherwise they will bring enormous and serious harm to the country and to the Red Army.

Voroshilov also commented on the number of arrests in the Red Army, "I will not publish detailed figures here. They are fairly impressive. The *chistka* was carried out radically and comprehensively. . . . This stinking filth, unfortunately, did not leave one area, not one layer of our command and political staff, unpolluted, unmessed, not dirtied. Therefore, the quantity of those cleansed was high and very impressive."[58] Voroshilov claimed that the ranks were now trustworthy; he put the number of people purged at over 40,000.[59] There was still some work to do, but Voroshilov warned that any future search for enemies should be carried out carefully, cautioning that people should not "just shoot from the hip" (*ne prosto rubit' s plecha*).[60] Indeed, Voroshilov referred to the mistakes in the military purge when loyal people had been hastily discharged. He knew that the process had been chaotic and lacked control. Moreover, Voroshilov acknowledged that there would be difficulties in making sure that servicemen rapidly promoted into now vacated commanding positions received the help and guidance they needed.[61] Inexperienced officers quickly moved up the army hierarchy to replace their arrested superiors, but they often lacked the necessary skills. Voroshilov appeared to understand the difficultly of the task ahead. The military purge had not only caused a great deal of physical damage to the Red Army in terms of the sheer number of officers and soldiers discharged or arrested, but also valuable expertise had been lost.

In this respect, by the end of 1938, the repression in the Red Army was winding down. By early 1939, Lev Mekhlis was criticizing incorrect army expulsions and commenting that 50 percent of these were incorrect.[62] It is difficult to know the precise number of arrests stemming from the military-fascist plot across the entire Red Army. As Roger Reese has pointed out, officer recruitment eventually began to move faster than discharges.[63] In addition, a large number of arrests and discharges sanctioned between 1937 and 1938 were for crimes outside of the confines of the military plot, but were crimes that, all the same, were highlighted because of the intense pressure and scrutiny placed on the army during the Great Terror. The purge undeniably cost the Red Army dearly. Different sets of statistics have put the overall number of discharges of army leaders during the military purge at approximately 35,000, even if over 11,000 were eventually reinstated.[64] Concerning arrests, one set of figures records 4,474 arrests in 1937 and 5,426 in 1938.[65] Yet over 1,400 of those arrested were eventually returned to the ranks. In terms of expulsions from the party, Reese notes that 11,104 people were expelled in 1937 and 3,580 in 1938, with 7,202 later reinstated.[66] Despite the number of people eventually restored to the ranks, however, the true scale of the military purge is unknown. These figures only permit an understanding of the number of army leaders affected by the military purge, not the soldiers from the lower ranks. The total impact of the military purge on the entire Red Army was undoubtedly greater.

The Mass Operations

We have seen how repression in the Red Army followed the path of the wider Great Terror. As the regime targeted the former opposition in 1936, this was reflected in the Red Army in the arrest of the Trotskyist military center over the summer and autumn. When the imagined conspiracy depicting former oppositionists as terrorists evolved in early 1937 to encompass fascist agents and foreign subversives, this was likewise reflected in the army. Indeed, this was a crucial turning point in focusing the NKVD's attention toward the military in the months before the NKVD arrested the Tukhachevskii group. However, the course of repression in the Red Army during 1936–1938 did not just follow the path set down by the wider Great Terror. The unmasking of the military-fascist plot and the shocking news of the execution of the Tukhachevskii group created a sensation inside the Soviet Union; in addition, the start of the military purge represents a clear escalation in the wider political violence across the Soviet state. The execution of the Tukhachevskii group and the wave of arrests that hit the military over the summer of 1937 comprised a turning point. This was the first time that large numbers of people had been arrested or executed who had never been members of the former opposition and who had typically supported

Stalin.[67] In this way, the political violence of the Great Terror changed direction with the discovery of the military-fascist plot.

However, it is likely that the military purge had a bigger impact on the Great Terror beyond moving the political violence firmly beyond former oppositionist circles. The military purge can help explain why Stalin sanctioned the mass operations in the summer of 1937—a decision that finally pushed the Great Terror toward the ordinary Soviet population. The mass operations were large policing operations launched in the summer of 1937 and were brought to a halt in the autumn of 1938. These operations marked the high point of the Great Terror. Approximately 1.15 million people were sentenced by the NKVD as part of the mass operations, and 683,000 of this number were executed.[68] In this respect, when evidence of the mass operations was first published in the early 1990s, this made clear that ordinary people rather than party elites suffered the most during the Great Terror.[69] The first mass operation was launched on 30 July 1937 and targeted former kulaks and other anti-Soviet elements. Soon after, similar operations targeting a range of different population groups, including national minorities such as Poles, Germans, and Koreans, were ordered by the regime. As a result of the huge numbers of arrests and executions, Stalin's sanction of the mass operations in the summer of 1937 represented a significant acceleration in the scale of the Great Terror. It has been argued that the Great Terror only truly began with the mass operations.[70] However, even though the mass operations have received greater scholarly attention in recent years, Stalin's motivations in pushing the political violence of the Great Terror toward the Soviet population in the summer of 1937 remain contested. On the surface, it seems clear that the central purpose of the mass operations was to wipe out the threat posed by dangerous and unreliable population groups. Exactly why Stalin perceived these groups to be a threat to the Soviet Union, and why he decided to take action specifically in the summer of 1937, are disputed questions. Important documents concerning the preparations of the mass operations remain classified in the Russian archives, but nonetheless, two main interpretations have emerged: one sees the regime's concern that world war was approaching as the best explanation for why Stalin felt the need to internally secure his regime with mass operations, and the other argues that they were driven primarily by domestic political tensions.

The interpretation of the mass operations that emphasizes the approaching world war as the primary motivation for unleashing mass repression suggests that during the course of 1937, Stalin came to believe that various population groups, including kulaks recently returned from exile, criminals, religious believers, and a number of national minority groups, were potential members of a fifth column that could turn against the regime during a foreign invasion.[71] Fearing for the security of the regime in a future war, Stalin launched the mass operations, beginning in summer 1937, to neutralize this potential internal threat. In this respect, the mass operations were a prophylactic response to a perceived danger from supposedly dangerous population cohorts at a time when the regime believed that war was approaching. In this interpretation, the mass operations were carefully controlled and were only brought to an end after they had accomplished their goal of destroying any dangerous population bases. One historian has emphasized how the mass operations were representative of the Stalinist regime's high level of totalitarian control.[72] Moreover, the mass operations did not represent a stark change in the style of repression used by the regime. Similar large policing operations had been used during the collectivization and dekulakization campaigns of the early 1930s, as part of the social "cleansing" of Moscow and Leningrad, and also against juveniles and criminals as part of the NKVD's policing of the social order. Even though the use of mass operations came under fire in early 1937, and even received criticism from Ezhov as being too blunt an instrument,[73] just a few months later, in the summer, they were deployed again, and on a larger scale. In this respect, this interpretation of the mass operations sees concern about the internal security of the state in a future war as compelling Stalin to turn to mass operations once again.[74]

On the other hand, another prominent interpretation of the mass operations argues that they demonstrate the regime's lack of control over events on the ground in 1937, rather than representing the actions of an assured totalitarian regime.[75] Arch Getty, for instance, argues that Stalin ordered the mass operations as a means to secure the support of local party leaders who had become increasingly worried that they would lose their positions during planned elections to the Supreme Soviet in 1937. Importantly, this new legislative body was to be elected on an open franchise, creating fears among local party bosses that they might lose their positions as various "anti-Soviet elements" who had apparently become increasingly active during the year would soon be allowed to vote. After determined attempts, the local party leaders eventually convinced Stalin of the danger posed by a large pool of anti-Soviet elements in the summer of 1937, and Stalin then sanctioned a campaign of mass repression against these internal enemies. In contrast to the accounts of the mass operations that emphasize future war, Getty characterizes these as an irrational and chaotic strike against the Soviet population. The mass operations were neither long planned nor well prepared; further, they were prompted by a sudden fear within upper party circles that anti-Soviet elements would gain too great an influence during the elections for the Supreme Soviet.[76]

Yet neither explanation of the mass operations, whether emphasizing the external or internal threat, provides a definitive explanation for why Stalin sanctioned such radical repression in the summer of 1937. For instance, although it is certainly correct to highlight local party leaders' concerns about anti-Soviet elements in the run-up to the Supreme Soviet elections, this does not adequately explain why Stalin launched mass repression targeting specific national minority groups. The perceived threat of future war seems the most likely explanation for the repression of national minorities.[77] On the other hand, there are problems with the argument that the threat of war sparked the mass operations. When the first mass operation targeted against kulaks began at the end of July 1937, the Soviet Union was not in reality facing an immediate foreign threat. Japan invaded China in the same month, marking the beginning of the Sino-Japanese war, but this was not a pressing security threat for the Soviet Union. The Japanese armed forces were now entangled in China, which removed one potential military threat for the time being. In this sense, if the threat of war really was the primary catalyst of the mass operations, the timing is not adequately explained. As has been pointed out, why did Stalin not deploy the mass operations during 1938 in response to international events that posed a far greater security threat to the Soviet Union, such as Hitler's annexation of Austria?[78] We have seen how Stalin's tendency to misperceive the outside world and his concerns about the capitalist encirclement of the Soviet Union shaped his views about future war and foreign policy. Stalin had long believed that a war against the capitalist powers was inevitable. In the mid-1930s, Hitler's aggression in Europe, concern that the Spanish civil war might become a broader European conflict potentially endangering the Soviet Union, and the signing of the anti-Comintern pact between Germany and Japan in late 1936 no doubt sharpened security concerns stemming from the perceived external military threat. Indeed, Stalin highlighted the dangers to the state from hidden subversives during wartime at the February–March plenum in 1937. However, even if Stalin believed that war was more likely in 1937, why he turned to mass repression in the summer of that year specifically, and not earlier or later in the year, still requires a better explanation.

The military purge may hold the key to answering these questions. As we have seen, the significance of the military purge is not only in the high level of damage that was caused to the armed forces, but in how Stalin completely misperceived the danger. The military-fascist plot had no basis in reality. There was no fifth column in the army and no conspiracy in the high command, but the Red Army was purged nonetheless. There is much to suggest that Stalin truly believed that this action was unavoidable based on the evidence he received during the first half of 1937 about an apparent spy infiltration of the Red Army. The military plot was regarded as an extremely serious problem by the regime, and one requiring a swift and decisive response. It is not out of the question that the discovery of the military-fascist plot itself acted to shock Stalin into finally taking radical action against other population groups outside of the Red Army already labeled as suspicious, thus providing the trigger for the mass operations. It may have been the exposure of the military conspiracy that finally compelled Stalin to take serious action against subversives such as former kulaks and other supposed anti-Soviet elements that had been the object of so much concern for local party bosses in the first half of 1937, in view of the upcoming elections for the Supreme Soviet and then against national minorities over the coming months. Indeed, from the regime's point of view, the military-fascist plot was a stark demonstration of how the Soviet Union could be subverted by hostile foreign governments. If they had managed to establish a fifth column inside the Red Army, the regime surely feared that it would be a much easier task to infiltrate already discontented and unreliable population groups, such as former kulaks and criminals. How could Stalin be sure that the military plot was not just the tip of the iceberg? Even if foreign governments had not yet decided to recruit kulaks, Poles, or Germans living in the Soviet Union, could Stalin be certain that they would not try to do this more concertedly in the future, particularly after their success in infiltrating the Red Army? In this respect, like the military purge, it is possible that the decision to launch the mass operations was similarly taken at the last minute, lacked sufficient preparation, and was born of panic. The military purge heightened a sense of insecurity within ruling circles and may well have prompted Stalin to take more radical action to secure his regime and widen the circle of repression. Significantly, if the military purge did act as the trigger, the mass operations were launched primarily in response to a misperceived threat—one influenced by both domestic political tensions and the regime's perception of the external foreign threat, thus suggesting that the bulk of the Great Terror from the summer of 1937 lacked careful premeditation.

Evidence supporting this hypothesis can be seen from examining the events immediately after the start of the military purge. It is clear that from June 1937, the regime was making preparations for a crackdown on suspicious population groups with the justification that they were linked to foreign agents. For instance, on 17 June, Sergei Mironov, the head of the West Siberian NKVD, sent a report to Robert Eikhe, the head of the party in West Siberia, detailing that he had discovered a large Kadet-Monarchist and Socialist Revolutionary organization, which was apparently acting on the orders of Japanese intelligence agents. Mironov noted that branches of the organization were hidden in other cities across the region that planned to revolt against the regime.[79] As one historian has pointed out, what Mironov found particularly alarming was that this organization supposedly had a support base among kulaks and anti-Soviet elements in West Siberia. Mironov thus drew a direct connection between the activity of foreign agents and anti-Soviet elements resident in the population.[80] In response to this discovery, on 28 June, Stalin ordered the establishment of an extrajudicial troika in the region to execute the members of this supposed conspiracy.[81] It is not out of the question that the recent discovery of the military-fascist plot pushed NKVD operatives like Mironov toward trying to make links between already recognized domestic subversive groups and foreign agents. The military purge could thus be said to have transformed the scale and the targets of the Great Terror and was a decisive factor in pushing the violence toward the Soviet population. However, it is unlikely that Mironov was acting solely on his own initiative in making these wider connections. He would not be responding independently to the recent news of the military plot. During the summer of 1937, numerous articles appeared in the press on the subject of foreign espionage. Indeed, one of these was the *Pravda* article on foreign agents that Stalin personally edited in May, which claimed that spies were trying to recruit unreliable individuals from within the population.[82] Thus, in making his connections between foreign agents and domestic subversive groups, Mironov was likely responding to signals from above.

Further signals from above can be seen a week after Mironov's report during the June plenum of the Central Committee, convened between 23 and 29 June. There is no direct transcript for the plenum, but a summary of Ezhov's speech exists. According to this summary, Ezhov spoke about the existence of a widespread fascist anti-Soviet conspiracy within the Soviet Union that affected not only the military but also the party, the defense industry, transport, and agriculture. Ezhov ranked the various strands of this conspiracy in order of importance. The military-fascist plot appeared at the top of his list, followed by a plot exposed in the NKVD and eleven other substrands. Ezhov sketched out a vision of a wide-ranging conspiracy involving Rightists, Trotskyists, Socialist Revolutionaries, and Mensheviks, supported by Germany, Japan, and Poland and their respective intelligence services. These conspirators apparently planned to overthrow the regime by rising up during a foreign invasion and by leading a campaign of sabotage and terrorism. Importantly, Ezhov noted that these enemies were recruiting supporters among kulaks, White guards, criminals, and other subversive elements in the population.[83] As such, Ezhov was conceptualizing a much broader conspiracy than had been recently unmasked in the Red Army. Like Mironov, he was making further connections between suspicious groups in the population and foreign agents—and the scale of this imagined conspiracy was quickly growing.

Not long after, the regime took serious action against supposedly subversive groups in the population. One month after the June Military Soviet, which had called for a military purge, and just days after the June plenum during which Ezhov had described his vision of a broad conspiracy against the state, concrete preparations for the first mass operation began. On 3 July, Stalin sent a telegram to all regions calling for the registration of all former criminals and kulaks recently returned from exile, and the reestablishment of extrajudicial troikas to arrest and execute those deemed the most dangerous.[84] This was a call to begin mass repression against anti-Soviet elements. Stalin ordered estimates to be compiled of the number of formerly exiled kulaks and criminals in each region.[85] On 31 July, NKVD operational Order No. 00447 was sent to all regions; this formed the basis of the first mass operation. This was not just targeted at kulaks but also included a range of other anti-Soviet elements, including White guards, religious figures, and criminal elements. The order accused these groups of being the chief instigators of anti-Soviet crimes and sabotage. They needed to be eradicated once and for all.[86]

In this respect, there is a case to be made that the discovery of the military-fascist plot encouraged the NKVD to seek out other foreign-backed conspiracies in other Soviet institutions and among the ordinary population. After finding what it claimed was evidence of additional dangerous conspiracies, the launch of the mass operations began soon after. Indeed, it appears that it was only after the start of the military purge that Ezhov began visualizing a much broader conspiracy involving large numbers of population groups supposedly influenced by foreign powers. The military "conspirators" led by Tukhachevskii were accused of planning to make a move against the regime during a foreign invasion. The domestic base of dangerous anti-Soviet elements highlighted by the NKVD during June apparently planned the same thing. These were almost identical dangers, suggesting the military-fascist plot may have served as a model. Moreover, seeing the mass operations in the context of the military purge supports the argument that the external foreign threat from hostile governments is central to understanding the launch of the mass operations, but it demonstrates how this can be so even though there were no genuine and pressing international dangers facing the Soviet Union during the summer of 1937. What matters is not the real international events of the mid- to late 1930s (which only began to threaten the Soviet Union's security in 1938), but how the Soviet leaders perceived—or, more accurately, radically misperceived—foreign threats. The military-fascist plot was interpreted as a strike on the Soviet Union by Germany and Japan, despite its having little basis in reality. From the perspective of the party elite, they were under attack. The foreign threat appeared very real during the summer of 1937 despite the reality of events.

This interpretation of the military purge and the mass operations departs, however, from those who have highlighted the threat of war as the decisive factor behind the launch of mass repression in one crucial respect. It suggests that the mass operations were not a well-planned prophylactic cleansing of the Soviet Union in anticipation of future war. Stalin's response to the military-fascist plot, as we have seen, appears hesitant, last minute, and almost reluctant. He vacillated over the arrests of the Tukhachevskii group; he seems to have waited for more evidence of their guilt before sanctioning further action beyond transfers in mid-May. Launching a wave of repression inside the Red Army was not an action to be taken lightly, and Stalin presumably wanted to make sure that the case was credible. Yet when he received further evidence in late May with more detail of what the NKVD claimed was a conspiracy in the high command, in light of the already recognized infiltration of the wider Red Army by supposed foreign agents, Stalin faced little choice but to opt for a large purge. Because the military purge gives every indication of being a last-minute decision, it is reasonable to suggest that the mass operations stemmed from a similar impulse—perhaps even from a sense of panic. From the regime's point of view, if hostile governments had infiltrated the Red Army, where else could their agents be? In this respect, the military purge may have sparked the mass operations.

It must be noted, however, that there is some evidence that can be interpreted as the regime moving toward the use of mass repression before the start of the military purge, suggesting that the mass operations had a deeper level of planning in advance of the discovery of the military-fascist plot. The NKVD had already created organized and well-staffed operation sectors better suited to conducting mass repression in the outlying areas of the Soviet Union in April 1937. In the same month, the Politburo created an emergency council including Stalin, Ezhov, Molotov, Voroshilov, and Kaganovich that could make quick decisions and bypass formal Politburo procedure. The NKVD was also made directly responsible for combating "socially dangerous elements" in April, and its special board had its powers expanded.[87] The picture, however, is by no means clear. At the same time, as one historian has noted, the numbers of prison wardens were fixed at too low a level during May 1937; there were not enough camps to accommodate the future spike in the prison population. The procuracy was also putting pressure on the NKVD to try and curb its extrajudicial powers at this time, which does not suggest that the official sanction of an unprecedented level of such powers was just around the corner.[88] Most importantly, at the 1937 February–March plenum, Ezhov explicitly criticized the use of mass operations as an ineffective tool for finding the most dangerous hidden enemies because they were too geared toward policing the social order.[89] Finally, the bulk of the preparations for the kulak operation was rushed through in the weeks leading up its launch in August. None of this suggests that careful planning lay behind the mass operations.

It is of course possible that the Soviet leaders had been laying the groundwork for taking action against anti-Soviet elements on some level in April 1937 but at the same time they were unprepared for the enormous scale of the mass operations. If so, it is possible that the Soviet leaders' belief that a military plot had been discovered in the high command—alongside the certainty that foreign agents had infiltrated the wider Red Army—compelled a radicalization of these earlier measures. The regime had to quickly expand its penal system, reestablish extrajudicial troikas, and bring back mass policing campaigns—and do this within a matter of weeks. The timing of the exposure of the military-fascist plot, and how almost immediately after the NKVD began to sound the alarm about the large numbers of subversive groups within the population, suggests that they are linked. Facing a fifth column in the Red Army served to heighten the regime's fear that it was surrounded by unreliable population groups. Consequently, the mass campaign-style policing methods, rejected just months before, needed to be urgently reinstated. As such, the mass operations are unlikely to have been long planned but rather were a knee-jerk response to a misperceived internal danger.

However, this explanation of the mass operations does not entirely discount the explanations of the mass operations that focus on domestic factors. Notably, there is little to suggest that Stalin believed that the military-fascist plot extended beyond the Red Army. It does not seem that he feared that the arrested senior officers had large numbers of co-conspirators involved in the very same plot hidden in other institutions outside of the army. If Stalin had believed this, it seems strange that he did not order the first mass operation to target German and Japanese national minorities rather than kulaks and anti-Soviet elements. After all, the military-fascist plot was supposedly directed by Germany and Japan. Stalin did take some action against German nationals outside of the Red Army after the start of the military purge. On 20 July, he ordered the arrest of all Germans working in the defense, electrical, and chemical industries, along with German refugees. At the same time, the NKVD began targeting Soviet citizens who had been in contact with German nationals.[90] However, a dedicated mass operation against ethnic Germans living in the Soviet Union was not launched until February 1938.[91] Similarly, the Harbin mass operation, which looked to uncover Japanese agents, only began in late September 1937.[92]

Therefore, it is most likely that the perceived military plot in the Red Army was understood as being largely self-contained and confined to the military, but it compelled the Soviet leaders into finally taking action against other already recognized suspicious population groups. Kulaks were an obvious place to start. For the leadership, the military purge had highlighted how vulnerable the Soviet Union was to foreign infiltration, and former kulaks, as a group, were without question less loyal than serving military officers. As Arch Getty has emphasized, in the months before the start of the mass operations, the rhetoric within party circles about the threat posed by former kulaks and other anti-Soviet elements had reached to a fever pitch because of the planned elections for the Supreme Soviet. Fearing the loss of their positions, local party bosses tried to get Stalin to change his mind about the new voting procedures and sent in alarming reports about how counterrevolutionaries would gain influence in the elections.[93] The military-fascist plot perhaps explains why Stalin finally decided to heed the warnings of his subordinates during the summer, although he appears to have ignored these before. The discovery of a military conspiracy may have convinced Stalin that action did in fact need to be taken against the kulaks, who now represented an increasingly dangerous and unreliable population group at a time when it seemed clear that foreign governments were strengthening their efforts to undermine the Soviet Union. In this way, both the perceived external foreign threat and domestic political factors contributed to the mass operations, but the discovery of a fifth column in the Red Army compelled Stalin to act.

Finally, highlighting the possible connections between the military purge and the mass operations suggests that there was a direct line running through the earlier political repression within the Communist Party and the later mass repression of ordinary people during 1937–1938. It is unlikely that the military purge would have been launched without the earlier arrests of the former Trotskyist officers incriminated during the NKVD's investigation of the former political opposition preceding the first show trial in 1936. These particular arrests focused NKVD attentions more firmly on the Red Army and led to a concerted investigation into Trotskyist counterrevolution in the ranks. As detailed above, the scope of this investigation shifted in focus during early 1937 toward exposing ties between foreign agents and former Trotskyists in the military. This new line of investigation led to the unmasking of the military-fascist plot. As such, without the earlier political repression within the Communist Party that grew over the course of 1936 (and which itself stemmed from the Kirov assassination of December 1934), the military purge may never have happened. The right preconditions certainly existed for mass repression to erupt in the Soviet Union during the mid- to late 1930s, but without the trigger of the military purge, the mass operations might never have been launched in summer 1937.

Conclusion

During a series of interviews in the 1970s with writer Felix Chuev, Molotov spoke about the military purge and why, after all this time, he still believed it to have been necessary. Molotov's self-serving words of course must be treated with caution. Clearly he would look to portray the military purge in a way that excused him of having made a mistake. Yet Molotov's comments are a useful starting point in drawing together some of the central arguments of this book explaining why Stalin gutted his officer corps and purged the Red Army just years before the outbreak of World War II. As part of his interviews with Chuev, Molotov presented a rationale for the military purge that, on the surface, is similar to the broad argument put forward in this book. He argued that a real military conspiracy had been destroyed in 1937 and claimed that Tukhachevskii had been a dangerous Rightist working for the Nazis. Molotov stressed that it had been the correct decision to execute Tukhachevskii because he was disloyal and could not be counted on at the outset of war: "I consider Tukhachevsky a most dangerous conspirator in the military who was caught only at the last minute. Had he not been apprehended, the consequences could have been catastrophic."[1] Moreover, in explaining the purpose of the Great Terror, Molotov raised the danger posed by a fifth column:

> 1937 was necessary. Bear in mind that after the Revolution we slashed right and left; we scored victories, but tattered enemies of various stripes survived, and as we were faced by the growing danger of fascist aggression, they might have united. Thanks to 1937 there was no fifth column in our country during the war.[2]

For Molotov, if the Great Terror had not happened and the military purge not sanctioned, a fifth column would have had disastrous consequences for the Soviet Union. The stakes could not have been higher, and treachery in the Red Army might have caused the defeat of the Soviet Union in a war against Germany. Indeed, when commenting on Tukhachevskii and the other executed senior officers, Molotov insisted,

"The main thing, however, is at the decisive moment they could not be depended on."[3]

Even though Molotov's words cannot be taken at face value, they do have a degree of substance, as we have seen. The decisive factor in finally compelling Stalin to take action against the Red Army in the summer of 1937 was his misperception that it had been infiltrated by foreign agents at all levels, some of whom were supposedly operating in the high command. Although Stalin wavered at the last moment, choosing in the first instance to transfer the majority of the officers incriminated as the ringleaders of the military-fascist plot, when additional supporting material was obtained by the NKVD soon after, he sanctioned the remaining arrests. An extensive purge of the Red Army was now set into motion. From Stalin's point of view, the Red Army was facing a severe crisis, and mobilizing the ranks for a major purge was the only possible response. How could the Soviet Union fight the approaching war with an army that had been heavily infiltrated by foreign agents with a conspiracy of leading officers in the high command? Moreover, there is nothing to suggest that this spy scare in the military was cynically contrived. Stalin seems to have genuinely believed that foreign-backed enemies had infiltrated the ranks and managed to organize a conspiracy at the very heart of the Red Army.

In this respect, contrary to the majority of accounts, the Red Army was not purged in order to further consolidate Stalin's personal power. The military-fascist plot was not knowingly fabricated for the purpose of increasing Stalin's control over the army or as a means of removing a group of officers he believed one day might become an obstacle to his growing political dominance. The military purge was launched in reaction to a misperceived spy scare, and Stalin acted at the very last moment. There are no indications that the military purge was long planned or carefully premeditated. This was a last-minute response to a grossly exaggerated danger. Moreover, once unleashed, the military purge, like the wider Great Terror, soon reached an unforeseen scale. The rank and file responded to the regime's call to root out hidden conspirators with an explosion of denunciations. Thousands of baseless discharges and arrests followed that undermined military strength. It also appears that ordinary soldiers were panicked by the arrests of their superiors, which helped drive the surge in groundless denunciations as mutual trust broke down. Like the violence of the wider Great Terror, the regime was losing its grip in the Red Army and was forced to reestablish central control over the military purge in early 1938. In the mid-1970s, Molotov admitted that the military purge had spun out of control: "Did everyone who was charged or executed take part in the conspiracy hatched by Tukhachevsky? Some were certainly involved. Others might have been implicated by mistake. There could have been sympathizers among them. It was different with each individual."[4]

That the military-fascist plot was imaginary is of central importance in understanding the military purge. Stalin misinterpreted the danger from his army in 1937, with terrible consequences. However, the military conspiracy appeared very real in 1937. This misperception stemmed in part from the Bolsheviks' particular understanding of the international world and where they saw the position of the Soviet Union. Throughout the 1920s and 1930s, Stalin displayed acute concerns that foreign powers were attempting to undermine the Soviet Union and were actively preparing for war. He believed that foreign governments were forging secret alliances to make war on the Soviet Union. The capitalist encirclement of the Soviet Union was an accepted fact, and the perceived espionage threat only intensified as the international situation worsened in the 1930s. The false confessions beaten out of prisoners by the NKVD, and which described a host of fantastic counterrevolutionary crimes and acts of sabotage, supposedly carried out with the backing of foreign powers, provided the necessary proof to support such a conspiratorial worldview. By 1937, with Stalin's permission, the NKVD was searching for underground plots apparently hatched by an alliance of former oppositionists and foreign agents in all areas of the state. The Red Army, as one of the most valuable institutions in the Soviet Union, did not escape this scrutiny.

However, as this book has demonstrated, the military purge stemmed from much more than Stalin's tendency to misinterpret and exaggerate the scale of security threats and the broader spy mania that pervaded the 1930s. The uneasy nature of civil–military relations in the interwar Soviet Union was just as important. The Red Army had a long and specific history of being judged as vulnerable to subversion since its formation in early 1918. The Bolsheviks were never comfortable with the idea of maintaining a standing army; they had been forced to do so out of the need to win the civil war. From the very beginning, the new Red Army was fertile ground for imagined security scares and military conspiracies to take root. Over the course of the 1920s and 1930s, the Red Army was regarded as facing a real threat of infiltration from a range of subversive groups, including treacherous military specialists, the exiled White movement, foreign agents, and Trotskyists. The rank and file proved to be unreliable in times of domestic crisis (particularly during collectivization and dekulakization), and the high command was subject to persistent rumors that several senior officers were disloyal and working against the regime. Although the relative importance attached to these different perceived threats could alter (the danger posed by exiled Whites in the 1920s, for instance, was eclipsed by foreign agents and Trotskyists in the early 1930s), they were nearly always depicted as more dangerous than their reality.

This is not to say that the period between 1918 and 1937 saw a rising pressure on the army that forced Stalin to act. It is not true that a series of perceived security threats steadily culminated over twenty years, eventually reaching breaking point in 1937 and leading to a loss of trust in the Red Army. As we have seen, there were periods of both crisis and calm in the Red Army in the years before the military purge. Despite the range of threats supposedly arrayed against the Red Army, the 1920s were generally a time of relative stability, especially in comparison to the crisis years of the early 1930s, when the OGPU claimed to have discovered a major military specialist conspiracy as part of Operation Vesna at the same time as large numbers of rank-and-file soldiers were in uproar against collectivization. There would be no crises in the army on this sort of scale until the military-fascist plot of 1937, but this is not to say that the regime ever forgot how seriously the Red Army had been compromised in the early 1930s. Stalin certainly would never forget how an extensive "military plot," supposedly sponsored by foreign powers, had been unmasked in the upper levels of the Red Army in 1930–1931. This did not mean that the military purge was inevitable. Even though, in the aftermath of the crisis of the early 1930s, the army showed an alarming inability to police itself effectively, at a time when the espionage threat was believed to be increasing and the perceived danger from the former opposition was becoming a more pressing issue, it took a series of short-term triggers to make a military purge more likely. The first trigger was Kirov's murder in December 1934, which sharpened the political atmosphere; the Red Army could not help being pulled into the growing political violence now targeted against the former opposition. The second short-term trigger came in the summer of 1936, when, after the arrests associated with the Zinoviev–Kamenev Counterrevolutionary Bloc, the NKVD arrested the

Trotskyist military center, which focused attentions (notably those of Ezhov) more firmly on the Red Army. Finally, as the wider conspiratorial narrative that was driving the Great Terror began to shift in early 1937 and became ever more focused on foreign agents, the Red Army was left in a vulnerable position. The military had always been estimated to be susceptible to subversion, from the rank and file up to the high command, and the regime was now gripped by a growing spy mania. Although the security concerns about former Trotskyists in 1936 had little impact on the military elite, a spy scare was far more dangerous, especially considering the persistent rumors that still surrounded the high command concerning a secret connection to Germany and the contacts that many senior officers had forged with officers of the Reichswehr in the 1920s. The gulf between the perception and the reality of threat had become extensive by the middle of 1937. These were ideal conditions for a spy scare to erupt in the Red Army and for Ezhov and the NKVD to unmask the military-fascist plot. This final short-term trigger paved the way for a wide-reaching military purge.

The Great Terror, then, acted as the catalyst in finally bringing to a head a series of long-running security concerns that had shadowed the Red Army since 1918. In this sense, the key point is to see the deeper reality behind the rationale that Molotov put forward for the military purge in the 1970s. In mid-1937, Stalin was compelled to take action against the Red Army in response to what he believed to be a pressing danger from foreign agents. The twenty-year history of the Bolsheviks consistently seeing their armed forces as vulnerable to subversion was crucial in allowing such a large spy scare to develop in the military in the first place, and in giving this new danger credibility. The Great Terror alone was not enough to spark the military purge; nor were the longer-term security concerns that had trailed the Red Army since 1918. It was a combination of long-standing anxieties about the reliability of the military and the sudden eruption in political violence during the Great Terror that left the Red Army fatally exposed.

Although Stalin waited until the very last moment to take action to combat the military-fascist plot, there are some suggestions that he had suspicions about a possible conspiracy in the Red Army before May 1937. In the diary of Georgii Dimitrov, the head of the Communist International, an entry from 11 November 1937 (after the military purge had begun) recorded that Stalin had said the following about the former opposition:

> We were aware of certain facts as early as last year and were preparing to deal with them, but first we wanted to seize as many threads as possible. They were planning an action for the beginning of this year. Their resolve failed. *They were preparing in July to attack the Politburo at the Kremlin.* But they lost their nerve.[5]

That Stalin spoke about an attack on the Kremlin was no doubt a reference to the recently exposed military-fascist plot. Stalin, of course, will have wanted to portray himself as having anticipated this conspiracy in good time. He will have wanted to give the impression that he was in control of events and that he had taken timely action. Yet as we have seen, there is little indication that the military-fascist plot had been anticipated. Stalin's version of events, as relayed by Dimitrov, was unlikely little more than a face-saving effort. Stalin's vacillations about what to do with the incriminated senior officers in early May 1937 demonstrate this most clearly. His actions suggest a level of uncertainty about the truth in the military plot. Most of the officers were transferred in the first instance while Stalin seemingly checked the evidence for himself. This does not suggest that there was any kind of carefully coordinated or prearranged plan behind the arrest of the Tukhachevskii group.

However, Stalin's comments recorded by Dimitrov are still telling. They are a reminder that even if the nature or scale of the military-fascist plot came as a surprise, leaving Stalin undecided on the best course of action, it is likely that he did have some growing suspicions about the Red Army before this point. It is certain that these suspicions were more concrete in early 1937 when, at the February–March plenum, Molotov called for a closer verification of the military. Stalin's concerns about the reliability of the Red Army likewise will have stretched back to the early 1930s, when Operation Vesna appeared to show how deeply the military could be compromised by enemies and when the rank and file proved themselves to be unreliable in a crisis and susceptible to supposed kulak influences. It is possible that Stalin had some nagging doubts about the reliability of the Red Army earlier in the 1920s, when the OGPU insisted that the opposition (and Trotskyists in the military) were planning coup in November 1927. As we have seen, during the civil war, Stalin was suspicious of military specialists and questioned their loyalty to the new Bolshevik regime. In short, it can justifiably be said that Stalin was never able to put his full trust in his military. This put him in a difficult position as the regime came increasingly to rely on a powerful Red Army in the interwar period. However, it was probably only after the arrests of the group of former Trotskyist officers in mid-1936 that Stalin began to take any private concerns about the Red Army more seriously. When the NKVD connected the group of former Trotskyist officers, including Putna and Primakov, with the Zinoviev–Kamenev Counterrevolutionary Bloc in 1936, this was a decisive moment that paved the way for a fuller investigation of the military and best explains why Molotov called for a deeper scrutiny of the Red Army at the February–March plenum. Yet it remains unlikely that Stalin anticipated the military-fascist plot in the form it eventually took. There is nothing to suggest that he believed at any point before the first incriminating testimony against the Tukhachevskii group surfaced in April 1937 that some of his most senior officers were ringleaders in a military conspiracy. In this respect, even though it seems that Stalin's doubts about the Red Army did increase over the course of 1936 and into the early months of 1937 (and Ezhov played a crucial role in cultivating these concerns), the scale of the apparent spy infiltration of the army and the nature of the perceived conspiracy in the upper ranks, when these finally broke in May 1937, would have remained a deep shock. Stalin's hesitation in May 1937 does not suggest that he had carefully planned the military purge. These were the actions of an indecisive leader who, after years of nagging doubts about the Red Army, could no longer ignore his suspicions when facing such a serious crisis in the form of an extensive "military conspiracy."

Similarly, this book has also highlighted indirect evidence suggesting that Stalin resisted a destabilizing crackdown on the Red Army until it was absolutely necessary. The Red Army was not only an indispensible support of Stalin's personal power but also was vital for the defense of the Soviet Union. It makes sense that Stalin would want to avoid reducing its operational strength without good reason—the inevitable consequence of any extensive military purge. We have seen several examples of Stalin leaning toward restraint when dealing with the Red Army and of his ability to choose compromise solutions. For instance, despite his clear dislike and distrust of military specialists, Stalin accommodated large numbers in commanding positions during the 1920s and early 1930s even though the political police had serious doubts about whether they could be trusted. Like Lenin and Trotsky, Stalin knew that the Red Army could not do without the valuable expertise of the bourgeois officers. Indeed, he forged a working relationship with Tukhachevskii—the one person from the high command who attracted the most frequent rumors about his supposed disloyalty. Stalin recognized talent when he saw it, and he knew that Tukhachevskii was a key asset to the further development and modernization of the Red Army.

Stalin surely kept a close eye on the military elite, but until 1937 and the unmasking of the military-fascist plot, there was no strong case against them. Furthermore, Stalin was well briefed with political police reports detailing subversive activity carried out by various enemies inside the Red Army, but, as we have seen, he did not always agree with their threat assessments. Despite the efforts made by Menzhinskii for stronger repressive action to be taken against Trotskyists in the ranks in 1927 (going so far as to talk about a possible military coup), Stalin ruled that this was not necessary. He believed that Menzhinskii was overstating the danger, and he showed no compulsion in taking strong countermeasures against the Red Army at this point. Similarly, in 1930, when Operation Vesna incriminated Tukhachevskii, Stalin hesitated again; he needed more time to think over the best course of action. In the end, and after being closely involved with the investigation itself, he was convinced of Tukhachevskii's innocence. Stalin would not launch an attack on the high command on the basis of evidence he did not accept. Tukhachevskii remained valuable to the still-inexperienced Red Army and could not be removed without a more compelling reason. Stalin hesitated once again at the February–March 1937 plenum. Even though the NKVD had been discovering Trotskyists in the military at a growing rate since the summer of 1936, the careful scrutiny of the Red Army promised by Molotov at the plenum was to be delayed until an unspecified time in the future. Stalin seemingly wanted to proceed with caution, and knee-jerk reactions were to be avoided. However, when a spy scare erupted in the ranks in early May, at the same time as the NKVD was unmasking a "conspiracy" in the high command, Stalin was finally compelled into action. Even though there was one last moment of hesitation when Stalin wavered in transferring, rather than arresting, Tukhachevskii and the majority of the incriminated officers, by the end of May (and again after becoming involved in the NKVD's investigation), Stalin accepted that the Red Army was facing a severe crisis and that an extensive purge was the only option.

In this sense, the uneasy character of Soviet civil–military relations in the interwar period highlights how Stalin, the military leadership, and the political police held different positions toward security threats in the Red Army. Stalin had specific priorities as dictator. He needed to guarantee the security of the Soviet Union in the face of capitalist encirclement and the inevitable future war between communism and capitalism. The Red Army needed to be in a condition to fight and win a major conflict. In doing so, Stalin was forced to make compromises about whom to employ in senior military positions to maximize army expertise. Not everyone in the officer corps was a trusted Red commander, but from Stalin's point of view, this was something that could not be avoided. Yet Stalin's decision to compromise in this way clashed with the priorities of the political police, who were primarily focused on unmasking enemies in the ranks and guaranteeing the internal security of the army. From the early 1920s, the political police as an institution displayed the most acute concerns about the reliability of the Red Army. They were less accepting of officers with compromised pasts, particularly military specialists and former White officers. In the early 1930s, the OGPU continued to keep close watch over several former Trotskyist officers who had recanted their political pasts, even though some had been cleared by Voroshilov. When Ezhov assumed the leadership of the NKVD in 1936, he pushed harder than anyone else for a deeper scrutiny of the Red Army. It appears that Ezhov was looking to expose some kind of military conspiracy as early as mid-1936, and it is highly likely that he had more advanced suspicions about the high command before Stalin in the months leading up to the military purge. Although Stalin remains the central figure in sanctioning the military purge in 1937 after becoming convinced of the need to protect the Red Army from infiltrated enemies, Ezhov bears direct responsibility for fostering Stalin's concerns.

Voroshilov also had his own particular set of priorities as leader of the Red Army. Voroshilov was ultimately responsible for the political reliability and stability of the military, but he was a poor institutional leader. Rather than confront problems head on, Voroshilov stuck his head in the sand. He tended to downplay potential threats. This book has argued that Voroshilov behaved in this way not only in an effort to cover his own back and protect his position, but also because he did not actually have any credible solutions to the inefficiencies in army self-policing. More often than not, Voroshilov criticized poor vigilance in the officer corps and PUR rather than get to the root cause of why enemies consistently went undiscovered in the ranks. Indeed, as we have seen, there are numerous indications that some officers purposely avoided the task of locating dangerous enemies under their commands—

foreign agents and treacherous former oppositionists—and instead sanctioned high numbers of groundless discharges and reprimands. In this way, an officer had a better chance of avoiding attracting the attention of the political police and could still attempt to cultivate a reputation for vigilance. Moreover, the claims from senior officers, including Budennyi, that local power centers existed in the Red Army raises further questions about whether the hunt for enemies was being circumvented. It is likely that local power groups in the military districts closed ranks when the regime applied pressure to locate internal enemies. Crucially, it was Voroshilov's inability (or perhaps reluctance) to tackle the deeper problems preventing army self-policing from functioning properly that partly explains why the NKVD's view of Red Army vulnerability held sway in 1937. Voroshilov's leadership failures gave the NKVD greater freedom to act and undermined his frequent protests that the Red Army was in fact reliable. Through his inaction and unconvincing defenses of army reliability, Voroshilov only enhanced Ezhov's case that a deeper investigation of the military was necessary.

Even though this book has examined the military purge by consciously focusing on broader and evolving perceptions of the Red Army, rather than using the narrow framing of the Tukhachevskii Affair, the military purge cannot be understood without a consideration of his role. Tukhachevskii's name should certainly not be given to the military purge, but he, more than anyone else in the high command, managed to attract the most suspicion of being disloyal. The rumors about Tukhachevskii were so potent that his name was commonly used by the OGPU as part of their entrapment operations in the 1920s. Moreover, inside the Soviet Union, it seemed to be an almost unspoken assumption that Tukhachevskii was unreliable. His name had a tendency to surface during investigations into counterrevolutionary political groups, suggesting that the political police were keeping an eye on him. It is likely that any scrap of rumor or hearsay about Tukhachevskii would be placed in an expanding police file. Although there is nothing to suggest that Tukhachevskii entertained the idea of seizing power or was ever sympathetic to any opposition platform, he certainly had ambitions for power within the Red Army. He no doubt felt he was better placed to lead the army than Voroshilov. This does not mean that he actively conspired to have Voroshilov removed from the army leadership, even if it appeared that way to some of his colleagues. The military elite consisted of an awkward mixture of professional officers like Tukhachevskii and Stalin's political allies, such as Voroshilov and Budennyi, creating the conditions for conflict. Clashes about what role the cavalry should play in a modern army and the level of staff power in the late 1920s and early 1930s revealed fault lines within the military elite. Tukhachevskii was not always on the winning side of the argument, but when Japan invaded Manchuria in September 1931, Stalin endorsed his vision of a rapid mechanization of the Red Army, even though he must have known this would antagonize Tukhachevskii's critics. There is little doubt that the tense personal relationships within the army leadership helped give the military-fascist plot greater credibility on its exposure in 1937. Stalin knew that Tukhachevskii was ambitious and that he had a poor personal relationship with Voroshilov. Tukhachevskii's desire for more influence in the Red Army could be easily interpreted as ambition for political power when Stalin was confronted with the NKVD's claims about the military-fascist plot.

Finally, this book suggests that to understand the Great Terror, it is necessary to try and understand Stalin's worldview and how he subjectively defined the threats to the regime and his personal power. Stalin often misperceived the international world and held a skewed vision of the reliability of his own military. Crucially, he expected war but did not fully trust his means of defense. Stalin's misperception of threats led him to attack the Red Army in 1937 in response to what was an imaginary military conspiracy. Stalin acted from a position of weakness and perhaps even panic. This is not to say that there were no genuine foreign agents in the Red Army at this time, but the spy threat that peaked in 1937 was an extreme exaggeration of this danger. As leader of the Soviet Union, Stalin could build up the power of the Red Army to enormous levels in preparation for the inevitable war, but at the same time, he could easily undermine his strength by lashing out at misperceived conspiracies and plots within the ranks. Stalin's ability to build with one hand and destroy with the other defined the nature of his power, and his misperception of the threats surrounding him shaped his use of political violence.

Glossary

GPU—State Political Directorate (political police; predecessor of OGPU)

Komsomol—All-Union Leninist Youth League

Konarmiia—First Cavalry Army

MOTsR—Monarchist Union of Central Russia (fictional organization created by Operation Trust)

NEP—New Economic Policy

NKVD—People's Commissariat for Internal Affairs (Political Police)

Obmen partdokumentov—exchange of party documents

OGPU—Joint State Political Directorate (political police; predecessor of NKVD)

Osoaviakhim—Society to Assist Defense, Aviation, and Chemical Development (Soviet civil defense organization)

Proverka partdokumentov—verification of party documents

PUR—Political Administration of the Red Army

RKKA—Workers' and Peasants' Red Army

ROVS—Russian General Military Union (White émigré organization)

RVS—Revolutionary Military Council (military body attached to each unit enforcing party control)

RVSR—Revolutionary Military Council of the Republic (supreme military body, 1918–1934)

VChK (Cheka)—Extraordinary Commission to Combat Counterrevolution and Sabotage (political police; predecessor of GPU)

Notes

Introduction

1. Reese, "Impact of the Great Purge," 72.

2. See, e.g., Minakov, *Stalin i zagovor generalov*, 712; Pechenkin, *Gibel' voennoi elity*, 147, 166.

3. Overy and Wheatcroft, *Road to War*, 272–274.

4. "Delo o tak nazyvaemoi 'antisovetskoi trotskistskoi voennoi organizatsii' v krasnoi armii," 62–73.

5. From a large body of work, see, e.g., Wollenberg, *Red Army;* Schapiro, "Great Purge"; Armstrong, *Politics of Totalitarianism;* Erickson, *Soviet High Command;* O'Ballance, *Red Army;* Kolkowicz, *Soviet Military;* Mackintosh, *Juggernaut;* Blackstock, "Tukhachevsky Affair"; Conquest, *Great Terror;* Ulam, *Stalin;* Rapoport and Alexeev, *High Treason;* Tucker, *Stalin in Power;* Volkogonov, *Stalin;* Naveh, "Tukhachevsky"; Nichols, *Sacred Cause;* Ziemke, *Red Army.*

6. "The Purge of the Eight Russian Generals," *Manchester Guardian*, 3 July 1937, 16.

7. See Duranty's memoir, *USSR*, 222.

8. Davies, *Mission to Moscow*, 1:111. For more on Duranty's sympathies toward the Soviet Union, see Taylor, *Stalin's Apologist.*

9. See, e.g., "Many Doubts Rise in Russia on Guilt of Eight Generals," *New York Times*, 26 June 1937, 1.

10. Wollenberg, *Red Army*, 224.

11. See Erickson, *Soviet High Command*, 465; Conquest, *Great Terror*, 201–235; Ulam, *Stalin*, 457–458; Kolkowicz, *Soviet Military*, 56–59; Schapiro, "Great Purge," 71.

12. This argument can be seen in work published after Stalin's death. See, e.g., Petrov, *Partiinoe stroitel'stvo v sovetskoi armii i flote*, 298.

13. See, e.g., Conquest, *Great Terror*, 218–219.

14. For details on this version of the dossier story, see Lukes, "Tukhachevsky Affair," 508.

15. Beneš, *Memoirs*, 47. The same version of events was recounted by Churchill in *Second World War*, 1:258–259.

16. Volkogonov, *Stalin*, 319.

17. See, e.g., Alexandrov, *Tukhachevsky Affair*, 190. There are some particularly unconvincing accounts about why Stalin would purge the military that take the dossier story even further toward fiction. In one particularly dubious

version, several prominent officers, including Tukhachevskii, discovered that Stalin had secretly worked as an Okhrana agent before the October Revolution and decided to depose him. Apparently, in response, Stalin had the dossier fabricated to incriminate the officers before they made their move. There is, however, no reliable evidence that Stalin had ever been an Okhrana agent. For details, see Brackman, *Secret File of Joseph Stalin.*

18. Rigby, *Stalin Dictatorship,* 99. Khrushchev's explanation of the military purge blamed German intelligence for supplying the dossier of "evidence" against the high command that tricked Stalin. Thus, it was Stalin's suspicious personality, fueled by German intrigue, that led to the execution of the Soviet Union's military heroes. In this way, Khrushchev used the fabricated dossier story as a means to place responsibility for the military purge onto Stalin. This was in line with the thrust of postwar de-Stalinization, which looked to place blame for the violence of the Great Terror with Stalin rather than on the wider Soviet system.

19. The key memoir accounts are from political police defectors Walter Krivitskii and Aleksandr Orlov, and from the German intelligence agent Walter Shellenberg. For criticism of Krivitskii and Orlov, see Lenoe, "Did Stalin Kill Kirov, and Does It Matter?," 352–380; Getty, *Origins of the Great Purges,* 211–220. For criticism of Schellenberg and other memoir accounts relevant to the military purge, see "M. N. Tukhachevskii i 'voenno-fashistskii zagovor'" (1998), 3–6.

20. Lukes, "Tukhachevsky Affair," 505–529.

21. Anderson et al., *Voennyi sovet pri narodnom komissare oborony SSSR.* That the dossier was not used during the military trial has been known for a long time, but it did not lead to suspicions about its authenticity. See Conquest, *Great Terror,* 222–223.

22. The best-known example of this argument can be found in Conquest, *Great Terror.*

23. Getty, *Origins of the Great Purges,* 167.

24. Rittersporn, *Stalinist Simplifications,* 140.

25. Getty, *Origins of the Great Purges,* 168.

26. Reese, "Red Army and the Great Purges," 203. The distinction between *chistki* and the political repression of the Great Terror was first seen in Getty, *Origins of the Great Purges,* 38–57.

27. Reese, "Red Army and the Great Purges," 211.

28. Suvenirov, *Tragediia RKKA,* 45–59.

29. Ibid., 51.

30. For a study drawing heavily on the transcripts of the June 1937 Military Soviet, see Pechenkin, *Stalin i voennyi sovet;* Pechenkin, *Gibel' voennoi elity.*

31. See Anderson et al., *Voennyi sovet pri narodnom komissare oborony SSSR.*

32. For a comprehensive examination of how the military-fascist plot was put together by the political police, see Cherushev, *1937 god.* The argument that there was a genuine military conspiracy has been surprisingly persistent, particularly so in Russian popular books. Moreover, some more academic texts still maintain that a military plot was genuine, despite a lack of convincing evidence; see, e.g., Leskov, *Stalin i zagovor Tukhachevskogo.*

33. Kantor, *Voina i mir Mikhaila Tukhachevskogo;* Kantor, *Zakliataia druzhba.*

34. Reese, "Red Army and the Great Purges," 212.

35. See Pechenkin, *Gibel' voennoi elity,* 168. Kantor argues that Stalin "saw Tukhachevskii as an enemy of his system" and that he was loyal, but not unconditionally. According to Kantor, the connection between the Red Army and Germany was important in giving Stalin the opportunity to get rid of Tukhachevskii. See Kantor, *Zakliataia druzhba,* 295. Cherushev takes a similar line to Kantor's in *1937 god,* 570. For criticisms of Cherushev's argument, see Khaustov and Samuelson, *Stalin,* 16; Zdanovich, *Organy gosudarstvennoi bezopasnosti,* 32–33, 106.

36. Minakov, *1937.* Minakov's earlier work includes *Stalin i zagovor generalov; Za otvorotom marshalskoi shineli; Sovetskaia voennaia elita;* and *Stalin i ego marshal.*

37. The title of Minakov's latest book, *1937: zagovor byl!,* is a misnomer. Minakov does not argue that there was a genuine military plot or plans for a state coup, noting a lack of convincing evidence. Minakov instead concentrates on the supposed plot to unseat Voroshilov. For criticism of Minakov overestimating the significance of alliances in the army elite, see Khaustov and Samuelson, *Stalin,* 17. Much of Minakov's evidence for the alleged plans to remove Voroshilov include references to memoirs and sources dated from after the military-fascist plot had been exposed in 1937, such as the published transcript of the Military Soviet, which met in early June 1937 to discuss the military conspiracy. Minakov does not account for the likely possibility that those present at this meeting may have presented informal alliances within the military elite in a more conspiratorial light in view of the recently exposed military plot in the high command.

38. Reese's work on the military purge is the exception; see Reese, "Red Army and the Great Purges."

39. On terror being inherent in the Stalinist system, see Brzezinski, *Permanent Purge;* Friedrich and Brzezinski, *Totalitarian Dictatorship and Autocracy;* Arendt, *Origins of Totalitarianism.* Other historians writing during the Cold War, most notably Robert Conquest in *Great Terror,* blamed Stalin individually for the scale of the political violence during the 1930s and highlighted what he saw as defects in the dictator's personality. The view that Stalin was excessively paranoid and obsessed with power was popularized by Khrushchev during his Secret Speech of 1956; this greatly influenced Cold War historians. See Rigby, *Stalin Dictatorship.* For a more recent book that argues that Stalin's psychology was one of the prime causes of the Great Terror, see Tucker, *Stalin in Power.*

40. Fitzpatrick, *Cultural Revolution.* Fitzpatrick argues that during the 1920s, high levels of social mobility enabled ordinary workers and peasants to seize senior positions in the party and government. However, according to Fitzpatrick, this new elite was resistant to further revolutionary change, providing a foundation for a conservative Stalinist system.

41. See Fitzpatrick, *Everyday Stalinism;* Kotkin, *Magnetic Mountain.* For other work exploring popular responses to the Great Terror, see Davies, *Popular Opinion in Stalin's Russia;* Fitzpatrick, *Tear off the Masks!;* Thurston, *Life and Terror;* Goldman, *Terror and Democracy.*

42. Getty argued that the regime, frustrated by the resistance of regional

party leaders to follow orders, encouraged criticism from the party rank and file in 1937 in order to shake up entrenched local elites. This process, however, soon spiraled out of control when it became inseparable from rhetoric about "enemies of the people." See Getty, *Origins of the Great Purges.* For similar arguments, see Harris, *Great Urals;* Goldman, *Terror and Democracy.*

43. Rittersporn, *Stalinist Simplifications.*

44. Reese, in "Red Army and the Great Purges," is alone in having studied how the Red Army rank and file responded to the Great Terror.

45. See, e.g., Kosheleva, *Pis'ma I. V. Stalina V. M. Molotovu.*

46. van Ree, *Political Thought.* Getty's later work shows the strength of Marxist ideology within closed party circles; see Getty and Naumov, *Road to Terror.* See also Kotkin, *Stalin.*

47. Priestland, *Stalinism.*

48. Chase, *Enemies Within the Gates?;* Pons, *Stalin and the Inevitable War;* Pons and Romano, *Russia in the Age of Wars.*

49. Harris, "Encircled by Enemies." In contrast, Kuromiya, in *Voices of the Dead,* argues that Stalin initiated the Great Terror in response to a genuine threat from foreign agents, and as such, his perception of external dangers in 1937 was not completely misguided, if still exaggerated.

50. Hagenloh, *Stalin's Police,* 3.

51. For work covering the mass operations, see Hagenloh, *Stalin's Police;* Getty and Naumov, *Road to Terror;* Shearer, *Policing Stalin's Socialism;* Junge et al., *Stalinizm v sovetskoi provintsii;* Khlevniuk, *Master of the House.* Khlevniuk argues that the Great Terror only truly began with the initiation of the mass operations.

52. See Hagenloh, *Stalin's Police;* Shearer, *Policing Stalin's Socialism.* This view of the mass operations has given some renewed support to the idea that the Great Terror was carefully premeditated and orchestrated by Stalin, and used primarily to increase his power and control. This view is most explicit in works such as Courtois, *Black Book of Communism.* Gregory, in *Terror by Quota,* puts forward a case in a political-economic analysis that argues that Stalin initiated the Terror in order to increase and secure his power and control. A recent edited collection with a noticeable emphasis on the Terror as a premeditated act is Ilič, *Stalin's Terror.*

53. Getty, "Excesses Are Not Permitted."

54. Khlevniuk, in *Master of the House,* argues that Stalin launched the mass operations proactively from a position of strength and control, and that they are evidence of a dictator firmly in control of events.

Chapter 1. The Red Army in Civil War

1. Stone, "Russian Civil War," 16.

2. Swain, *Russia's Civil War,* 38–39.

3. Figes, *People's Tragedy,* 380.

4. Sanborn, *Drafting the Russian Nation,* 38–40; Erickson, *Soviet High Command,* 16. See also Wildman, *End of the Imperial Army.*

5. Reese, *Red Commanders*, 18. On the Red Guards, see Wade, *Red Guards and Workers' Militias.*

6. Erickson, "Origins of the Red Army," 232.

7. Benvenuti, *Bolsheviks and the Red Army*, 17.

8. The ideological basis for the support of a people's militia came primarily from the writings of Frederich Engels, who believed that a militia could be a democratizing force and a tool of social organization. See Neumann and von Hagen, "Engels and Marx," 277–278.

9. Another problem with a people's militia was that the majority of the Russian population were peasants. Critics of the plan argued that a militia would only work with a more reliable urban industrial population. See von Hagen, "Civil–Military Relations," 271.

10. Reese, *Soviet Military Experience*, 7.

11. Erickson, "Origins of the Red Army," 230–231.

12. Croll, "Mikhail Tukhachevsky," 59.

13. Benvenuti, *Bolsheviks and the Red Army*, 17.

14. Erickson, "Origins of the Red Army," 235.

15. Figes, "Red Army," 303; Erickson, "Origins of the Red Army," 241.

16. Brovkin, *Behind the Front Lines*, 15.

17. The Party of the Socialist Revolutionaries had split in October 1917 over support for the Bolsheviks. The Left Socialist Revolutionaries maintained an alliance with the Bolsheviks until the Treaty of Brest-Litovsk. The Socialist Revolutionaries took up arms against the Bolsheviks in summer 1918.

18. Figes, "Red Army," 303.

19. For an excellent survey of Russian civil–military relations from Peter the Great, see Taylor, *Politics and the Russian Army.*

20. Benvenuti, *Bolsheviks and the Red Army*, 38; Lenin, *Polnoe sobranie sochinenii*, 36:514–515.

21. Reese, *Soviet Military Experience*, 8.

22. Reese notes that at first recruitment for the Red Army was focused on the working class alone but it was quickly opened up to all who were willing to serve; *Soviet Military Experience*, 3; Benvenuti, *Bolsheviks and the Red Army*, 24.

23. Benvenuti, *Bolsheviks and the Red Army*, 25.

24. Ibid., 38; Erickson, *Soviet High Command*, 34–36.

25. Erickson, *Soviet High Command*, 56.

26. Benvenuti, *Bolsheviks and the Red Army*, 19.

27. Trotsky did actually prefer a militia system in the long term, but the immediacy of the civil war dictated a standing army.

28. Swain, *Russia's Civil War*, 27; Brovkin, *Behind the Front Lines*, 19.

29. Benvenuti, *Bolsheviks and the Red Army*, 25.

30. von Hagen, *Soldiers in the Proletarian Dictatorship*, 40. For corroborating figures, Main places the percentage of former imperial officers serving in the Red Army at 76 percent for 1918, 53 percent in 1919, and 42.5 percent in 1920, noting, however, that these figures are not complete. Main, "Red Army during the Russian Civil War," 806.

31. Kavtaradze, *Voennye spetsialisty na sluzhbe respubliki sovetov*, 224.

32. For such a complaint, see Rossiiskii gosudarstvennyi voennyi arkhiv (Russian State Military Archive [hereafter RGVA]), f. 9, op. 8, d. 70, l. 23.

33. Lenin, *Polnoe sobranie sochinenii*, 39:313.

34. Osipova, "Peasant Rebellions," 155–156.

35. Reese, *Red Commanders*, 19.

36. Ibid., 27.

37. Trotsky, *Military Writings and Speeches*, 1:10. A White intelligence report from 1921 gave a similar range of reasons for why military specialists would serve in the Red Army, covering those who had lost hope in the overthrow of the Bolsheviks, those who served to defend Russia rather than the Bolsheviks from invading foreign powers, and a small group of active anti-Soviet individuals. RGVA, f. 9, op. 28, d. 688, l. 195.

38. Trotsky, *Military Writings and Speeches*, 1:188.

39. Voitikov, *Otechestvennye spetssluzhby i krasnaia armiia*, 307.

40. Reese, *Soviet Military Experience*, 22.

41. Plekhanov and Plekhanov, *Zheleznyi Feliks*, 213.

42. Erickson, *Soviet High Command*, 41.

43. Murphy, *Russian Civil War*, 68.

44. Kvashonkin et al., *Bol'shevistskoe rukovodstvo. perepiska*, 85–86.

45. von Hagen, *Soldiers in the Proletarian Dictatorship*, 40. Benvenuti points to feeling within the party that military specialists were sabotaging the influence of the political commissars. Benvenuti, *Bolsheviks and the Red Army*, 68.

46. Trotsky, *Military Writings and Speeches*, 1:207.

47. Ziemke, *Red Army*, 36; Reese, *Red Commanders*, 81.

48. Croll, "Mikhail Tukhachevsky," 7–8, 137.

49. Tukhachevskii, *Izbrannye proizvedeniia*, 1:27.

50. Ibid., 1:28.

51. Ibid.

52. Zdanovich, *Organy gosudarstvennoi bezopasnosti*, 283.

53. Tukhachevskii, *Izbrannye proizvedeniia*, 1:98.

54. Lincoln, *Red Victory*, 408.

55. See Ziemke, *Red Army*, 38–39; Sanborn, *Drafting the Russian Nation*, 44.

56. Figes, *People's Tragedy*, 592; Swain, *Russia's Civil War*, 46.

57. For further examples of military specialist betrayals, see Erickson, *Soviet High Command*, 33; Petrov, *Partiinoe stroitel'stvo v sovetskoi armii i flote*, 68; Benvenuti, *Bolsheviks and the Red Army*, 31; Voitikov, *Otechestvennye spetssluzhby i krasnaia armiia*, 4, 346–347; RGVA, f. 9, op. 8, d. 147, l. 193.

58. Reese, *Red Commanders*, 33.

59. Butt, *Russian Civil War*, 104–106.

60. Plekhanov and Plekhanov, *F. E. Dzerzhinskii*, 130–132. There is additional background to the case concerning a debate on strategy between Vatsetis and the commander of the Eastern Front, Sergei Kamenev, in which the two disagreed about which White general—Denikin or Kolchak—represented the greatest threat to the Bolsheviks. Vatsetis believed that Denikin posed the greater threat in 1919, while Kamenev argued the opposite. Lenin backed Kamenev, and he replaced Vatsetis as commander in chief when the latter was

arrested. See Swain, *Russia's Civil War,* 107–109. It is, however, unlikely that this dispute was the sole reason for Vatsetis's arrest. Considering the high levels of entrenched suspicion about military specialists, it is likely that the political police exploited the opportunity created by the strategic dispute to arrest Vatsetis, whom they may have already suspected of disloyalty.

61. For an overview of the Vatsetis case, see Voitikov, *Trotskii i zagovor v krasnoi stavke,* 4–7. See also Swain, "Vatsetis."

62. To give an impression of the huge number of desertions in the civil war, Figes notes that from June 1919 to June 1920, the Central Committee recorded 2,638,000 deserters. Figes, "Red Army," 328.

63. Ibid., 326.

64. Erickson, *Soviet High Command,* 56.

65. Kvashonkin et al., *Bol'shevistskoe rukovodstvo. perepiska,* 58.

66. Service, *Trotsky,* 221.

67. Figes, *People's Tragedy,* 592.

68. Benvenuti, *Bolsheviks and the Red Army,* 80. Figes highlights articles in *Pravda* from November and December 1918, written by two political commissars hostile to Trotsky, describing military specialists as "autocrats" who make commissars "answer with their lives" if they disobeyed orders. Figes, *People's Tragedy,* 592.

69. Service, *Trotsky,* 221–224.

70. Sanborn, *Drafting the Russian Nation,* 50–51. Thatcher notes that Trotsky introduced the practice of decimation—that is, executing every tenth soldier in units refusing to fight. Thatcher, *Trotsky,* 101. Again, however, as with executions for desertion, it is unlikely this was strictly adhered to, instead being used as a threat.

71. See Voroshilov, *Stalin and the Red Army.*

72. Adams, *Bolsheviks in the Ukraine,* 46.

73. Stalin first met Voroshilov in Stockholm at the fourth Social Democratic Party Congress in 1906. Rayfield, *Stalin and His Hangmen,* 29, 39. The head of the Cavalry Army (*konarmiia*) and close ally of Voroshilov, Semen Budennyi, was also at Tsaritsyn.

74. Reese, *Red Commanders,* 34.

75. Stalin, *Works,* 4:120.

76. Kvashonkin et al., *Bol'shevistskoe rukovodstvo. perepiska,* 40.

77. Rossiiskii gosudarstvennyi arkhiv sotsial'no-politicheskoi istorii (Russian State Archive of Socio-Political History [hereafter RGASPI]), f. 558, op. 11, d. 5410, l. 1.

78. Benvenuti, *Bolsheviks and the Red Army,* 46.

79. RGASPI, f. 558, op. 11, d. 1139, l. 67.

80. Benvenuti, *Bolsheviks and the Red Army,* 47.

81. Ibid.

82. Trotsky, *Trotsky Papers,* 1:249.

83. RGASPI, f. 17, op. 109, d. 84, l. 36.

84. Benvenuti, *Bolsheviks and the Red Army,* 33.

85. Bevenuti points to an interview with Stalin published in *Izvestiia,* where

he gave the impression he was enthusiastic about the military specialists, commenting, "The appearance of a new corps of commanders consisting of officers promoted from the ranks who have practical experience in the imperialist war, and also enjoy the full confidence of the Red Army men." This was a public interview, and Stalin would no doubt want to avoid dissenting from the official line. Benvenuti, *Bolsheviks and the Red Army*, 50.

86. Latyshev, *Rassekrechennyi Lenin*, 277.

87. Kvashonkin et al., *Bol'shevistskoe rukovodstvo. perepiska*, 76.

88. Latyshev, *Rassekrechennyi Lenin*, 282.

89. RGASPI, f. 17, op. 109, d. 84, l. 1.

90. *Vos'moi s'ezd RKP(b), mart 1919 goda*, 19–20.

91. Ibid., 154.

92. Ibid., 146.

93. Ibid., 147.

94. Ziemke, *Red Army*, 84; Benvenuti, *Bolsheviks and the Red Army*, 101.

95. Benvenuti, *Bolsheviks and the Red Army*, 115; von Hagen, *Soldiers in the Proletarian Dictatorship*, 59.

96. von Hagen, *Soldiers in the Proletarian Dictatorship*, 59n98.

97. Stalin, *Sochineniia*, 4:249.

98. Benvenuti, *Bolsheviks and the Red Army*, 106–107.

99. Hagenloh, *Stalin's Police*, 26.

100. Kirmel', *Belogvardeiskie spetssluzhby v grazhdanskoi voine*, 198.

101. For a note on the Cheka having quelled a rebellion in the Red Army in Bryansk in March 1919, see RGVA, f. 6, op. 10, d. 112, l. 9.

102. Chebrikov, *Istoriia sovetskikh organov*, 24.

103. Vinogradov et al., *Arkhiv VChK*, 87.

104. Chebrikov, *Istoriia sovetskikh organov*, 36.

105. Leggett, *Cheka*, 97.

106. Ibid., 207.

107. For one extensive counterrevolutionary group discovered in the Red Army in summer 1921 and purges of the ranks carried out by Feliks Dzerzhinskii, see Plekhanov and Plekhanov, *Zheleznyi Feliks*, 193, 196.

108. Vinogradov et al., *Arkhiv VChK*, 128.

109. Kirmel', *Belogvardeiskie spetssluzhby v grazhdanskoi voine*, 202.

110. The national center was an underground organization supported by conservative and industrial interests. For the national center's supposed subversive activity against the Red Army, see Leggett, *Cheka*, 284–286.

111. Vinogradov et al., *Arkhiv VChK*, 131–133.

112. Plekhanov and Plekhanov, *F. E. Dzerzhinskii*, 133. For other examples of White agents discovered in the Red Army, see RGVA, f. 9, op. 28, d. 297, ll. 8–25; f. 9, op. 9, d. 229, l. 272.

113. For more on the Cheka's concerns about military specialists, see Voitikov, *Otechestvennye spetssluzhby i krasnaia armiia*, 173. For details of numerous plots uncovered in the Red Army, many of which resulted in the arrests of military specialists, see Chebrikov, *Istoriia sovetskikh organov*, 13–101. Tynchenko notes

that in autumn of 1919 there were mass arrests of military specialists at the time of the White offensive on Petrograd. Tynchenko, *Golgofa russkogo ofitsertva,* 71.

114. Leggett, *Cheka,* 114–115.

115. RGASPI, f. 17, op. 109, d. 90, l. 1.

116. Ibid. In this case, because the men were former Kolchak officers, Menzhinskii also wanted to check whether they were natives of Siberia. Because Kolchak had gathered his forces in Siberia, if a former White officer was a native, then he would be regarded with more suspicion.

117. Ibid. For more on the use of former Whites in the Red Army, see l. 2, and for concerns regarding the use of former Kolchak officers in Siberia, see l. 3.

118. Voitikov, *Otechestvennye spetssluzhby i krasnaia armiia,* 374.

119. Zdanovich notes that at the end of 1920, the special departments arrested eighty-nine former White officers, most on charges of counterrevolutionary activity. See Zdanovich, *Organy gosudarstvennoi bezopasnosti,* 341.

120. Voitikov, *Otechestvennye spetssluzhby i krasnaia armiia,* 293–295.

121. See, e.g., ibid., 71–77, 164, 289, 313, 362; Luzan, *Voennaia kontrrazvedka,* 6; RGVA, f. 9, op. 28, d. 287, ll. 46–47; d. 297, ll. 38–53. On Polish spy networks exposed in 1920, see Tumshis and Papchinskii, *1937 Bol'shaia chistka,* 18–19.

122. RGASPI, f. 588, op. 11, d. 5733, l. 3.

123. RGASPI, f. 588, op. 11, d. 5466, ll, 5–6.

124. Zdanovich, *Organy gosudarstvennoi bezopasnosti,* 535.

125. See Luzan, *Voennaia kontrrazvedka,* 18. For alleged cases of military specialists involved with foreign espionage and giving secret documents to Poland, see Zdanovich, *Organy gosudarstvennoi bezopasnosti,* 510–511. In mid-1919, the Cheka "exposed" an alleged espionage organization in the 1st Army, including Nikolai Tukhachevskii, the brother of Mikhail; see Kantor, *Voina i mir Mikhaila Tukhachevskogo,* 147–149. There were no consequences for Mikhail Tukhachevskii at this time.

126. Nation, *Black Earth, Red Star,* 32.

127. Voitikov, *Otechestvennye spetssluzhby i krasnaia armiia,* 396. See also Chebrikov, *Istoriia sovetskikh organov,* 16–17.

128. Lenin, *Polnoe sobranie sochinenii,* 37:111–125.

129. RGASPI, f. 588, op. 11, d. 1180, l. 38. In particular, see l. 45 for Stalin's claim that a White victory would be a victory for foreign powers.

130. Harris, "Intelligence and Threat Perception," 31.

131. Plekhanov and Plekhanov, *F. E. Dzerzhinskii,* 148–149.

132. Chebrikov, *Istoriia sovetskikh organov,* 21–23.

133. Brovkin, *Behind the Front Lines,* 28, 46–48.

134. For a discussion of the political police's vested interest in the counterrevolution, see Viola, "Popular Resistance," 53–55.

135. Brovkin, *Behind the Front Lines,* 325.

136. Figes, "Red Army," 302–303.

137. Brovkin, *Behind the Front Lines,* 87.

138. Osipova, "Peasant Rebellions," 155.

139. Brovkin highlights a mutiny at Nizhny Novgorod in October 1920 involv-

ing 7,000 soldiers; Brovkin, *Behind the Front Lines*, 56, 72–86, 147–148, 322. See also Figes, "Red Army," 308–326; Osipova, "Peasant Rebellions."

140. Figes, "Red Army," 326; Brovkin, *Behind the Front Lines*, 81.

141. RGASPI, f. 17, op. 109, d. 117, ll. 2–4.

142. von Hagen, *Soldiers in the Proletarian Dictatorship*, 76.

143. Voitikov, *Otechestvennye spetssluzhby i krasnaia armiia*, 357.

144. Murphy, *Russian Civil War*, 187–190.

145. Budennyi was one of Stalin's closest allies in the Red Army. The first RVS of the Konarmiia included Voroshilov, Budennyi, and Efim Shchadenko, and Stalin was even made an honorary cavalryman. Brown, "Communists and the Red Cavalry," 85–86.

146. At times Red Army troops did refuse to suppress revolts. Brovkin, *Behind the Front Lines*, 78.

147. Holquist, "To Count, to Extract, and to Exterminate," 131.

148. Ibid.

149. Erickson, *Soviet High Command*, 122.

150. Sakwa, *Soviet Communists in Power*, 104.

151. See, e.g., Tucker, *Stalin in Power*, 241.

152. Ziemke, *Red Army*, 118.

153. Ibid.

154. Reese, *Soviet Military Experience*, 47.

155. Brown, "Lenin, Stalin," 35.

156. Davies, *White Eagle, Red Star*, 212.

157. Raleigh, "Russian Civil War," 3:146.

158. Stone and Ponichtera, "Russo-Polish War," 41.

159. Brown, "Lenin, Stalin," 45.

160. Ibid.

161. Erickson, *Soviet High Command*, 97.

162. Brown, "Lenin, Stalin," 46.

163. "M. N. Tukhachevskii i 'voenno-fashistskii zagovor'" (1997), 219. Stalin did not accept this; he blamed the command and the poor condition of the forces attacking Warsaw. Minakov, *1937*, 46–47.

164. Erickson, *Soviet High Command*, 100. In March 1928, a critical article appeared in *Krasnaia zvezda* that questioned Tukhachevskii's leadership abilities and accused him of acting impulsively during the conflict; see Minakov, *Stalin i zagovor generalov*, 595, 611.

165. Ziemke, *Red Army*, 129.

166. Zdanovich, *Organy gosudarstvennoi bezopasnosti*, 284.

167. Tukhachevskii, *Izbrannye proizvedeniia*, 1:167.

168. Croll, "Mikhail Tukhachevsky," 229.

169. Samuelson rightly pointed out that Stalin and Tukhachevskii went on to work together productively after war with Poland. Samuelson, *Plans for Stalin's War Machine*, 208.

Chapter 2. The Red Army in Consolidation

1. Harrison and Markevich, "Russia's Home Front," 16.

2. Harrison, *Russian Way of War,* 124.

3. Erickson, *Soviet High Command,* 191. Reese notes that in autumn 1921, 43.4 percent of officers had no formal military education. Reese, *Red Commanders,* 62.

4. Kavtaradze, *Voennye spetsialisty na sluzhbe respubliki sovetov,* 224; Harrison, *Russian Way of War,* 122.

5. RGVA, f. 33987, op. 3, d. 186, l. 71.

6. Kudriashov et al., *Krasnaia armiia v 1920-e,* 149. Zdanovich has shown that one of the main motives for discharges in the *chistka* was political unreliability and that the military specialists were not seen to share the "spirit" (*dukhe*) of the Red Army. Zdanovich, *Organy gosudarstvennoi bezopasnosti,* 348.

7. Quoted in Andrew and Gordievsky, *KGB,* 68; Lenin, *Polnoe sobranie sochinenii,* 44:5.

8. Ershov et al., "Ofitsery i komanduiushchie," 74.

9. For different political views among the Whites, see Stukov, "Dokumenty spetssluzhb svidetel'stvuiut," 117–129.

10. Not all Whites chose to join ROVS, and there were a number of competing unaligned organizations, such as the terrorist organization the Brotherhood of Russian Truth. See Robinson, *White Russian Army in Exile,* 132–133.

11. Ibid., 112.

12. Ibid., 134; Goldin, *Rossiiskaia voennaia emigratsiia i sovetskie spetssluzhby,* 412.

13. Ershov et al., "Ofitsery i komanduiushchie," 83.

14. Zdanovich, *Organy gosudarstvennoi bezopasnosti,* 62.

15. Goldin, *Rossiiskaia voennaia emigratsiia i sovetskie spetssluzhby,* 45. See also Lenin, *Polnoe sobranie sochinenii,* 40:115. In March 1922, an order was given to strengthen the political police's informant networks in the Red Army because the level of their activity had been judged to be inadequate. Chebrikov, *Istoriia sovetskikh organov,* 143.

16. Zolotarev, *Russkaia voennaia emigratsiia,* vol. 1, bk. 2, 87–89.

17. Zdanovich, *Organy gosudarstvennoi bezopasnosti,* 377.

18. RGVA, f. 33987, op. 3, d. 186, ll. 34–35; Kudriashov et al., *Krasnaia armiia v 1920-e,* 86.

19. Tynchenko, *Golgofa russkogo ofitsertva,* 109; RGVA, f. 37837, op. 21, d. 10, l. 1; f. 9, op. 29, d. 10, ll. 208–210.

20. Tynchenko, *Golgofa russkogo ofitsertva,* 17.

21. Former Whites who had worked for counterintelligence or other punitive institutions were excluded from amnesty. Zdanovich, *Organy gosudarstvennoi bezopasnosti,* 344–345.

22. Ibid., 347.

23. Zolotarev, *Russkaia voennaia emigratsiia,* 3:69.

24. Kol'tiukov, *Russkaia voennaia emigratsiia,* 4:803–804.

25. Ibid., 4:815–817. For similar material about Wrangel's espionage activity, see 4:803–804.

26. RGASPI, f. 74, op. 2, d. 49, l. 54.

27. Zdanovich, *Organy gosudarstvennoi bezopasnosti,* 343, 347.

28. RGVA, f. 33987, op. 2, d. 174, l. 40.

29. Plekhanov and Plekhanov, *Zheleznyi Feliks,* 214.

30. Goldin, *Rossiiskaia voennaia emigratsiia i sovetskie spetssluzhby,* 212–213.

31. Kol'tiukov, *Russkaia voennaia emigratsiia,* 5:80. See also Goldin, *Rossiiskaia voennaia emigratsiia i sovetskie spetssluzhby,* 409, 430.

32. Robinson, *White Russian Army in Exile,* 137; Goldin, *Armiia v izgnanii,* 59.

33. RGASPI, f. 588, op. 11, d. 71, l. 2.

34. Lenoe, "Fear, Loathing, Conspiracy," 198–199; Khaustov et al., *Lubianka: Stalin i VChK-GPU-OGPU-NKVD,* 137.

35. Khaustov et al., *Lubianka: Stalin i VChK-GPU-OGPU-NKVD,* 133.

36. For the 1927 war scare, see Di Biagio, "Moscow."

37. Khaustov et al., *Lubianka: Stalin i VChK-GPU-OGPU-NKVD,* 133–134.

38. Ershov and Shinkaruk, "Rossiiskaia voennaia emigratsiia," 2:109; Stukov, "Dokumenty spetssluzhb svidetel'stvuiut," 124.

39. Goldin, *Rossiiskaia voennaia emigratsiia i sovetskie spetssluzhby,* 187, 432. According to Goldin, Kutepov was one of the main targets of the political police at the end of the 1920s. See also Ershov and Shinkaruk, "Rossiiskaia voennaia emigratsiia," 2:110.

40. RGVA, f. 33988, op. 3c, d. 69, l. 16.

41. Anderson et al., *Reforma v krasnoi armii,* 1:69.

42. Zdanovich, *Organy gosudarstvennoi bezopasnosti,* 334.

43. Kudriashov et al., *Krasnaia armiia v 1920-e,* 57, 72, 76.

44. Fedotoff-White, *Growth of the Red Army,* 305. Gusev repeated many of his criticisms from the Plenum in a book published in 1925, 180. See also Ziemke, *Red Army,* 133.

45. Diakov and Bushueva, *Fashistskii mech kovalsia v SSSR,* 258.

46. Kudriashov et al., *Krasnaia armiia v 1920-e,* 68. Despite acknowledging this error, Gusev still maintained that the command was dominated by military specialists and that the Revolutionary Military Council was doing nothing about it. See RGASPI, f. 82, op. 2, d. 799, ll. 15–29.

47. Voroshilov, *Stat'i i rechi,* 152.

48. Ibid., 149. For details on the New Economic Policy and the economic reforms of the 1920s, see chapter 3.

49. Ibid., 150.

50. Ibid., 154. For similar optimistic appraisals of the Red Army from Voroshilov, see *Stat'i i rechi,* 15–16, 41, 57, 144; Zdanovich, *Organy gosudarstvennoi bezopasnosti,* 332.

51. Zdanovich points to a report from the end of 1927. See Zdanovich, *Organy gosudarstvennoi bezopasnosti,* 383.

52. Goldin, *Rossiiskaia voennaia emigratsiia i sovetskie spetssluzhby,* 192–193. The GPU became the Ob'edinennoe gosudarstvennoe politicheskoe upravlenie (Joint State Political Directorate [OGPU]) in 1923.

53. Ibid., 454.

54. Goldin, *Rossiiskaia voennaia emigratsiia i sovetskie spetssluzhby,* 108–109.

55. Shearer, *Policing Stalin's Socialism*, 96.

56. Khaustov et al., *Lubianka: Stalin i VChK-GPU-OGPU-NKVD*, 11–15.

57. Plekhanov and Plekhanov, *Zheleznyi Feliks*, 199.

58. Khaustov et al., *Lubianka: Stalin i VChK-GPU-OGPU-NKVD*, 37–38, 64–65.

59. In November 1927, Stalin made it clear during a discussion with a foreign delegation that the revolution was still under threat and that the GPU was the first line of defense. See Khaustov et al., *Lubianka: Stalin i VChK-GPU-OGPU-NKVD*, 143–144. For Stalin's defense of the GPU, see 27.

60. Shearer, *Policing Stalin's Socialism*, 136; Chebrikov, *Istoriia sovetskikh organov*, 137.

61. Shlapentokh, *Counter-Revolution in Revolution;* Figes, *People's Tragedy*, 357–358.

62. Minakov, *Stalin i zagovor generalov*, 71.

63. Ibid., 77.

64. There were other candidates for the role of the Russian Bonaparte. For instance, Sergei Kamenev, Budennyi, and Trotsky were also rumored to be untrustworthy at different times, though to a lesser degree and at a lower exposure than Tukhachevskii; see Minakov, *Stalin i zagovor generalov*, 82–85.

65. Minakov, *Stalin i zagovor generalov*, 89, 93.

66. For more about the growth of the Russian Bonaparte rumors and von Lampe, see Minakov, *Stalin i zagovor generalov*, 71–98.

67. Quoted in ibid., 72.

68. Kol'tiukov, *Russkaia voennaia emigratsiia*, 5:421–422.

69. "M. N. Tukhachevskii i 'voenno-fashistskii zagovor'" (1997), 244.

70. Zdanovich, *Organy gosudarstvennoi bezopasnosti*, 282–283.

71. Ibid., 285. For more on the political police's attempts to find out more about Tukhachevskii's views, see "M. N. Tukhachevskii i 'voenno-fashistskii zagovor'" (1997), 244.

72. For details on both operations, see Goldin, *Rossiiskaia voennaia emigratsiia i sovetskie spetssluzhby*, 188–189.

73. "M. N. Tukhachevskii i 'voenno-fashistskii zagovor'" (1997), 229.

74. Goldin, *Rossiiskaia voennaia emigratsiia i sovetskie spetssluzhby*, 327–331.

75. "M. N. Tukhachevskii i 'voenno-fashistskii zagovor'" (1997), 231–232.

76. Ibid., 230.

77. Goldin, *Rossiiskaia voennaia emigratsiia i sovetskie spetssluzhby*, 337.

78. "M. N. Tukhachevskii i 'voenno-fashistskii zagovor'" (1997), 233.

79. Robinson, *White Russian Army in Exile*, 138–141. Tukhachevskii's name was officially withdrawn from the operation at the beginning of 1924; however, the political police continued to use it. See "M. N. Tukhachevskii i 'voenno-fashistskii zagovor'" (1997), 236–237.

80. "M. N. Tukhachevskii i 'voenno-fashistskii zagovor'" (1997), 235.

81. Zdanovich, *Organy gosudarstvennoi bezopasnosti*, 630.

82. Robinson, *White Russian Army in Exile*, 140–141.

83. Minakov, *Stalin i zagovor generalov*, 580.

84. Harris, "Intelligence and Threat Perception," 35. For more on the regime's fear of war in the 1920s and the perceived foreign threat, see in particular Velikanova, *Popular Perceptions*.

85. See Harris, "Encircled by Enemies"; Goldin, *Rossiiskaia voennaia emigratsiia i sovetskie spetssluzhby.*

86. Sanborn, *Drafting the Russian Nation,* 128. For further details of the political police's concerns about the security of secret military documents, see Zdanovich, *Organy gosudarstvennoi bezopasnosti,* 483–524.

87. Viktorov, *Bez grifa "sekretno,"* 62; Tynchenko, *Golgofa russkogo ofitsertva,* 100; "Pol'skii shpionazh na Ukraine—Delo general Belavina," *Krasnaia zvezda,* 27 May 1925, 4.

88. "Delo kontrrevoliutsionnoi i shpionskoi organizatsii," *Krasnaia zvezda,* 22 March 1925, 1. For another example of alleged Polish spy operations with links to former officers, Whites, and serving members of the Red Army, see "Shpionskaia rabota pol'skikh diplomatov s SSSR," *Krasnaia zvezda,* 3 April 1925, 1.

89. Some military specialists had been "exposed" as working for British and Finnish intelligence in November 1926; see Viktorov, *Bez grifa "sekretno,"* 66. For the case of a Latvian agent, see RGVA, f. 4, op. 14, d. 84, l. 111.

90. Zdanovich, *Organy gosudarstvennoi bezopasnosti,* 606–613.

91. Ibid., 493.

92. Chebrikov, *Istoriia sovetskikh organov,* 167–168. The Whites and foreign governments were often believed to be secretly working together to gather information on the Red Army. See Khaustov et al., *Lubianka: Stalin i VChK-GPU-OGPU-NKVD,* 139–141.

93. Zdanovich, *Organy gosudarstvennoi bezopasnosti,* 74–75; Goldin, *Rossiiskaia voennaia emigratsiia i sovetskie spetssluzhby,* 268.

94. RGVA, f. 4, op. 14, d. 70, l. 1.

95. Ibid., ll. 14–15. The report gave further examples of Red Army men allegedly working for Latvian, Polish, and Estonian intelligence.

96. Ibid., l. 1.

97. For separate statistics on the relatively small scale of the espionage threat, see RGVA, f. 4, op. 14, d. 81, l. 6.

98. Stalin aired these views in an interview published in *Pravda* in May 1920. See RGASPI, f. 588, op. 11, d. 1180, ll. 53, 60.

99. This point has been made in numerous works, including May, *Knowing One's Enemies;* Gorodetsky, "Formulation of Soviet Foreign Policy"; Reiber, "Stalin as Foreign Policy-Maker"; Harris, "Encircled by Enemies"; Harris, "Intelligence and Threat Perception." On the threat of war and war scares in the 1920s, see in particular Velikanova, *Popular Perceptions.*

100. Zolotarev, *Russkaia voennaia emigratsiia,* vol. 1, bk. 2, 129. For British support of Kutepov, see Goldin, *Rossiiskaia voennaia emigratsiia i sovetskie spetssluzhby,* 413. For American negotiations and Polish agreements with Monarchist groups, known to the Soviets through Operation Trust, see Zdanovich, *Organy gosudarstvennoi bezopasnosti,* 632.

101. Goldin, *Rossiiskaia voennaia emigratsiia i sovetskie spetssluzhby,* 272.

102. Harris, "Intelligence and Threat Perception," 36; Stone, "Prospect of War?," 804.

103. Zdanovich, *Organy gosudarstvennoi bezopasnosti,* 283–286.

104. Steiner, *Lights That Failed,* 170–171.

105. Harris, "Encircled by Enemies," 518–519.

106. Velikanova, *Popular Perceptions,* 28.

107. Pozniakov, "Enemy at the Gates," 218.

108. Harris, "Encircled by Enemies," 517.

109. RGASPI, f. 558, op. 11, d. 71, l. 29.

110. Nekrich, *Pariahs, Partners, Predators,* 5.

111. Stoecker, *Forging Stalin's Army,* 77.

112. Samuelson points to Germany's wish to avoid joint construction ventures and investments. It was the failure of the collaboration and the Bolshevik realization that they needed to industrialize independently, rather than the pressure of the worsening international situation, that entailed a move toward independent military rearmament; see Samuelson, *Plans for Stalin's War Machine,* 32–34. As Erickson notes, there was a shift in the type of collaboration between Germany and the Soviet Union in 1925, with less emphasis placed on the production of war matériel in the Soviet Union and greater emphasis on testing equipment and training personnel. This shift brought the Red Army and the Reichswehr into closer contact. Erickson, *Soviet High Command,* 248.

113. In a July 1929 letter to Stalin, the Soviet ambassador in Berlin, Nikolai Krestinskii, notes that the Germans had friendly relations with Uborevich; see Kantor, *Zakliataia druzhba,* 108.

114. RGASPI, f. 74, op. 2, d. 19, l. 110.

115. Nekrich, *Pariahs, Partners, Predators,* 13, 30, 36–37.

116. Document reproduced in Zdanovich, *Organy gosudarstvennoi bezopasnosti,* 643–648.

117. Nekrich, *Pariahs, Partners, Predators,* 47.

118. Kantor, *Zakliataia druzhba,* 119.

119. See the interrogation transcript from September 1946 of the German military attaché, General-Major Karl Spalcke, in Khristoforov et al., *Tainy diplomatii Tret'ego reikha,* 698.

120. RGVA, f. 33987, op. 3, d. 295, l. 75.

121. Ibid., l. 77.

122. Stoecker, *Forging Stalin's Army,* 81.

123. Kantor, *Zakliataia druzhba,* 176. For a request instructing information to be collected in Germany from military intelligence, see RGVA, f. 4, op. 14, d. 393, l. 140.

124. An example of the close personal relations that were struck up between the Soviet and German officers comes from the German military attaché, General-Major Karl Spalcke, who claimed under interrogation after World War II that he had been on good terms with Iakir, who apparently had given him a cigarette case. See Khristoforov et al., *Tainy diplomatii Tret'ego reikha,* 700.

125. For a brief overview of the NEP, see Davies, "Changing Economic Systems," 8–13.

126. For a discussion of Trotsky's views in the early 1920s, see Service, *Trotsky,* 349–357.

127. Reiman, "Trotsky and the Struggle for 'Lenin's Heritage,'" 47.

128. Service, *Trotsky,* 284.

129. Harrison, *Russian Way of War,* 125.

130. Erickson, *Soviet High Command,* 164–165.

131. Ibid., 168.

132. Ibid., 171.

133. Zdanovich, *Organy gosudarstvennoi bezopasnosti,* 287, 323.

134. Hincks, "Support for the Opposition," 143; Erickson, *Soviet High Command,* 165. Von Hagen notes that in an address to the Moscow Garrison, Antonov-Ovseenko said that the military cells "were solidly behind Trotsky." According to von Hagen, this is probably an exaggeration on Antonov-Ovseenko's part, but he does not doubt that the opposition got a fair hearing in Moscow and Petrograd. See von Hagen, *Soldiers in the Proletarian Dictatorship,* 200. During the 1937 February–March plenum of the Central Committee, Voroshilov confirmed that the Moscow garrison had supported Trotsky. "M. N. Tukhachevskii i 'voenno-fashistskii zagovor'" (1997), 154.

135. Kariaeva et al., *Partiino-politicheskaia rabota v krasnoi armii: dokumenty 1921–1929 gg.,* 184.

136. The Bolsheviks had a tradition of sending internal critics abroad. Lenin had previously sidelined Alexandra Kollontai into a diplomatic role because of her opposition to the general line.

137. von Hagen, *Soldiers in the Proletarian Dictatorship,* 254.

138. For more detail on the emergence of the Trotskyist opposition and the growing divides in the party in the early 1920s, see Priestland, *Stalinism,* 133–189.

139. von Hagen, *Soldiers in the Proletarian Dictatorship,* 252–255.

140. RGVA, f. 33988, op. 3, d. 69, l. 133. "Lessons of October" was an attack on Zinoviev and Kamenev for their opposition to Lenin's push to seize power in 1917.

141. RGASPI, f. 74, op. 2, d. 51, l. 21.

142. Ibid., l. 24.

143. Ibid., ll. 23–24.

144. RGVA, f. 33987, op. 3, d. 227, ll. 190–191. The report does mention that it is not comprehensive, and a few military districts are absent from the figures. It is also worth noting that PUR was concerned about individuals wavering between loyalty to the party and going over to the opposition; see RGVA, f. 9, op. 26, d. 446, ll. 12–25.

145. RGASPI, f. 74, op. 2, d. 51, l. 11.

146. Ibid., l. 6.

147. RGVA, f. 33987, op. 3, d. 186, ll. 1–18. Voroshilov had also described the Red Army as a "very complex and delicate instrument" the year before in June at a joint plenum of the Central Committee and Central Control Commission; see RGASPI, f. 74, op. 2, d. 49, l. 17.

148. See, e.g., RGVA, f. 33988, op. 3, d. 106, l. 2.

149. Zdanovich, *Organy gosudarstvennoi bezopasnosti,* 323.

150. See ibid., 288–203, Minakov, *Stalin i zagovor generalov,* 449–459.

151. Zdanovich, *Organy gosudarstvennoi bezopasnosti,* 289.

152. Quoted in ibid., 290. That Antonov-Ovseenko made this threat to the

Central Committee has been in circulation for a long time; see Deutscher, *Prophet Unarmed,* 117.

153. Zdanovich, *Organy gosudarstvennoi bezopasnosti,* 289.

154. Zdanovich details that under interrogation, Dvorzhets admitted to agitating within the Kremlin military organizations. Apparently, Dvorzhets said he had been acting on Trotsky's orders. It is easy to see how agitating at the Kremlin could be interpreted by the political police as preparing the grounds for a coup. Zdanovich, *Organy gosudarstvennoi bezopasnosti,* 292–293.

155. See Reiman, *Birth of Stalinism,* 124–126.

156. Fel'shtinskii and Cherniavskii, *Lev Trotskii,* 238, 267–268; Zdanovich, *Organy gosudarstvennoi bezopasnosti,* 320–322; Suvenirov, *Tragediia RKKA,* 86; Kotkin, *Stalin,* 644n246.

157. Reiman, *Birth of Stalinism,* 124.

158. Ibid., 125. Some questions have been raised over the reliability of the documents published in *Birth of Stalinism.* These documents were held in the German Ministry of Foreign Affairs and had been secretly copied by German intelligence agents. This has led to questions regarding their authenticity; see Koppers, "On the Use of Forged Documents." However, as we have seen, the OGPU had already raised concerns about a possible oppositionist military group and a potential military coup before Menzhinskii's November 1927 letter. Moreover, according to Fedotoff-White, in 1927, Nikolai Bukharin, then editor of *Pravda,* also believed that oppositionist groups in the army were planning a rebellion. Fedotoff-White, *Growth of the Red Army,* 253. The contents of Menzhinskii's November letter correspond with increasing concerns about a military coup in 1927.

159. See PUR report for October 1927, RGVA, f. 33987, op. 3, d. 227, l. 24, 89. A report for December had similar conclusions; see l. 24.

160. Ibid., l. 10.

161. Reiman, *Birth of Stalinism,* 127.

162. RGASPI, f. 74, op. 2, d. 49, ll. 53–54.

163. Voroshilov, *Stat'i i rechi,* 151.

164. See Zdanovich, *Organy gosudarstvennoi bezopasnosti,* 315.

165. RGASPI, f. 74, op. 2, d. 49, l. 17. At a joint plenum of the Central Committee and Central Control Commission in July 1926, Voroshilov replied to Zinoviev's criticisms by saying that Zinoviev had "lost his head."

166. Getty, *Practicing Stalinism,* 170–178. Also see Wheatcroft, "Agency and Terror."

167. Zdanovich, *Organy gosudarstvennoi bezopasnosti,* 322–324. According to Zdanovich, the only charge that stuck was Trotskyist activity.

168. RGVA, f. 4, op. 14, d. 74, ll. 11–12, 19.

169. Mozokhin, *Pravo na repressii,* 87. For a detailed study of Soviet crime and justice and the conflict between legal and extrajudicial methods, see Solomon, *Soviet Criminal Justice.*

170. RGASPI, f. 74, op. 2, d. 38, l. 35.

171. Ibid., l. 33.

172. RGASPI, f. 74, op. 21, d. 42, l. 9.

173. Ibid., l. 91.
174. Ibid.
175. UK National Archives, Public Record Office, KV 2/2404. According to Vinokurov, Putna did have an intelligence role in Japan and Germany. Vinokurov, *Istoriia voennoi diplomatii*, 2:14, 27.
176. Maiskii, *Vospominaniia sovetskogo posla*, 1:273.
177. RGVA, f. 33987, op. 3, d. 302, l. 51.
178. Ibid., l. 53.
179. Bradley, *Civil War in Russia*, 51.
180. RGASPI, f. 558, op. 11, d. 36, l. 17.
181. Stone, *Hammer and Rifle*, 226.
182. van Ree, *Political Thought*, 114–115.

Chapter 3. Reorganization and Crisis in the Red Army

1. Stone, *Hammer and Rifle*, 40.
2. For a discussion of the Red Army's struggle to secure funds and the trade-off in spending between the army and the defense industry, see Stone, *Hammer and Rifle*, 18–42.
3. Figes, *People's Tragedy*, 653.
4. The Stalinist contingent in the Red Army had previously been strengthened in March 1924 when Frunze, at the time deputy people's commissar, created a new RVSR, which included a number of Stalin's allies, including Andrei Bubnov, Budennyi, Unshlikht, and Ordzhonikidze. See Erickson, *Soviet High Command*, 171.
5. Frunze's death has been the subject of some speculation about whether it was arranged by Stalin. For a short discussion, see Erickson, *Soviet High Command*, 199–200. However, it seems unlikely that Stalin would want Frunze murdered. His promotion to the army leadership had strengthened Stalin's position in the military in the first place. If for whatever reason Stalin decided to install his old comrade Voroshilov as the head of the army, having Frunze sidelined into another position would have been much more straightforward than arranging a murder. Stalin had not achieved full control over the Communist Party in the mid-1920s, and having Frunze killed would have been too risky to his own position.
6. Chaney, *Zhukov*, 24. See also Ken, *Mobilizatsionnoe planirovanie*, 130–131.
7. Stone, "Tukhachevsky in Leningrad," 1367. Not all agree with this characterization of Voroshilov. Ken has argued that many accounts of Voroshilov's poor military knowledge are exaggerations and that he was smarter than his detractors make out. Ken notes that individuals, such as Zhukov and Khrushchev, had a personal motive in criticizing Voroshilov. Ken, *Mobilizatsionnoe planirovanie*, 312. Even if accounts of Voroshilov's military abilities were exaggerated by some for political or personal reasons, it does not necessarily mean that he was a capable head of the Red Army, especially in comparison to Tukhachevskii.
8. Pechenkin, *Gibel' voennoi elity*, 21–22.

9. See Main, "Red Army and the Soviet Military."

10. Stone, "Tukhachevsky in Leningrad," 1368. This division was reduced to a two-way split in 1926, when the inspectorate was incorporated in the main administration of the Red Army. This still did not give Tukhachevskii the authority he wanted invested in the staff, however.

11. Samuelson, *Plans for Stalin's War Machine,* 45.

12. Ibid., 37.

13. Minakov, *Stalin i ego marshal,* 357.

14. Ibid.

15. Samuelson, *Plans for Stalin's War Machine,* 55.

16. Anderson et al., *Reforma v krasnoi armii,* 2:43–44.

17. Ibid., 2:173.

18. Quoted in Samuelson, *Plans for Stalin's War Machine,* 59. Samuelson does not explain why the letter remained unsent.

19. Quoted in Stone, "Tukhachevsky in Leningrad," 1369.

20. Ibid. For more on the tensions between Tukhachevskii, Egorov, and Dybenko, see Kantor, *Voina i mir Mikhaila Tukhachevskogo,* 44. In 1929, for instance, Egorov criticized Tukhachevskii's conduct during the war against Poland in his book *L'vov—Varshava. 1920 g. vzaimodeistvie frontov.*

21. Stone, "Tukhachevsky in Leningrad," 1369–1370.

22. Ibid., 1372–1375.

23. Anfilov, "Semen Mikhailovich Budenny," 60.

24. As early as 1922, Tukhachevskii had given a lecture on the decline of the cavalry and the rise of mechanized units; see Naveh, *In Pursuit of Military Excellence,* 177.

25. Reese, *Red Commanders,* 89; Ken, *Mobilizatsionnoe planirovanie,* 29–30.

26. In the late 1920s and early 1930s, Uborevich should be regarded as close to Tukhachevskii in terms of ideas about army reform, especially mechanization. Because Uborevich supported Tukhachevskii in this sense, he has often been regarded as part of a Tukhachevskii group. However, some historians have argued that Uborevich was also close to Stalin and that he should be considered as a member of his clique. Uborevich's rise through the army hierarchy was certainly rapid, which suggests that he had Stalin's trust. In 1929, for instance, Uborevich was given the responsible position of director of armaments. In this respect, power groups within the Red Army are difficult to distinguish and were not always clear-cut. Uborevich may well have been close to Tukhachevskii in terms of ideas about army reform, but Stalin also may have considered him a loyal party officer. See Reese, *Red Commanders,* 81; Minakov, *Sovetskaia voennaia elita 20-kh godov,* 245; Ken, *Mobilizatsionnoe planirovanie,* 89n94.

27. Quoted in Kantor, *Voina i mir Mikhaila Tukhachevskogo,* 303.

28. Samuelson, *Plans for Stalin's War Machine,* 145.

29. RGVA, f. 33987, op. 3, d. 174, l. 43.

30. Ibid., l. 42.

31. Ibid., ll. 44, 46.

32. Stoecker notes that Egorov and Dybenko also defended the cavalry. Stoecker, *Forging Stalin's Army,* 155.

33. RGVA, f. 33987, op. 3, d. 174, l. 47.

34. Stoecker, *Forging Stalin's Army*, 18.

35. RGASPI, f. 558, op. 11, d. 726, ll. 56–57.

36. Simonov, "Strengthen the Defence," 1358–1359.

37. Stone, *Hammer and Rifle*, 1, 20.

38. Sokolov, "Before Stalinism," 44; Davies, "Planning for Mobilization," 119.

39. Samuelson, *Plans for Stalin's War Machine*, 40–41.

40. Harris, "Encircled by Enemies," 521. Velikanova notes that Stalin received conflicting information about the threat of war in 1927, including alarmist reports from the OGPU and military intelligence, as well as reports from Soviet diplomats who did not see such a threat. Velikanova, *Popular Perceptions*, 52, 78.

41. Harris, "Encircled by Enemies," 521.

42. Ibid.

43. Samuelson, *Plans for Stalin's War Machine*, 36.

44. Stone, *Hammer and Rifle*, 62–63.

45. Shearer, *Industry, State, and Society*, 8.

46. Davies, "Industry."

47. For a brief summary see Stone, *Hammer and Rifle*, 109–111.

48. Harrison and Davies, "Soviet Military–Economic Effort," 369.

49. Stone, *Hammer and Rifle*, 91.

50. Ibid., 163–164.

51. Samuelson, *Plans for Stalin's War Machine*, 92–94.

52. Davies, "Planning for Mobilization," 120.

53. Stoecker, *Forging Stalin's Army*, 43.

54. Stone, *Hammer and Rifle*, 163; Samuelson, *Plans for Stalin's War Machine*, 97.

55. Samuelson, *Plans for Stalin's War Machine*, 99.

56. RGASPI, f. 558, op. 11, d. 447, l. 9.

57. Quoted in Samuelson, *Plans for Stalin's War Machine*, 110.

58. Kvashonkin et al., *Bol'shevistskoe rukovodstvo. perepiska*, 113.

59. Stone, *Hammer and Rifle*, 164.

60. RGASPI, f. 558, op. 11, d. 446, l. 66.

61. In a letter to Ordzhonikidze in 1936, Uborevich wrote that during his time as director of armaments, he had been under tremendous pressure and had made many mistakes. His underperformance in this role no doubt contributed to his being replaced by Tukhachevskii. See Minakov, *Stalin i zagovor generalov*, 100.

62. Samuelson, *Plans for Stalin's War Machine*, 86–89.

63. Ibid., 118.

64. Haslam, *Soviet Union*, 25.

65. Davies, *Crisis and Progress*, 113.

66. Ibid., 115; Stone, *Hammer and Rifle*, 190–191.

67. Stone, *Hammer and Rifle*, 184.

68. RGASPI, f. 588, op. 11, d. 447, l. 2.

69. Davies and Wheatcroft, "Agriculture," 113.

70. Davies, *Socialist Offensive*, 18.

71. Ibid., 39.

72. Viola, *Tragedy of the Soviet Countryside*, 57.

73. The resistance of the peasantry to collectivization has been examined by many scholars, including Fitzpatrick, *Stalin's Peasants;* Viola, *Peasant Rebels Under Stalin.*

74. Reese, "Red Army Opposition"; Tarkhova, *Krasnaia armiia.*

75. Anderson et al., *Reforma v krasnoi armii,* 2:49; RGASPI, f. 74, op. 2, d. 23, l. 99. See Tarkhova, *Krasnaia armiia,* 86, for corroborating figures for 1926.

76. Erickson, *Soviet High Command,* 179–181.

77. Zdanovich, *Organy gosudarstvennoi bezopasnosti,* 447.

78. Plekhanov and Plekhanov, *Zheleznyi Feliks,* 199.

79. Zdanovich, *Organy gosudarstvennoi bezpasnosti,* 446.

80. Tarkhova, *Krasnaia armiia,* 116.

81. For the September 1925 law, see Velikanova, *Popular Perceptions,* 99.

82. RGVA, f. 33988, op. 2, d. 528, l. 52. For more on the Red Army's reaction to taxes, see RGVA, f. 9, op. 29, d. 27, l. 62.

83. Plekhanov and Plekhanov, *Zheleznyi Feliks,* 200–201.

84. RGVA, f. 33988, op. 2, d. 528, l. 111; Velikanova, *Popular Perceptions,* 101.

85. Velikanova, *Popular Perceptions,* 101.

86. RGVA, f. 33988, op. 2, d. 528, l. 111.

87. RGVA, f. 9, op. 29, d. 27, l. 62. The peasant mood was not just a reflection of dissatisfaction with grain requisitions but also encompassed dissatisfaction with livelihoods in the villages, bread prices, the supply of industrial goods to the villages, agricultural taxes, and market relations; see Tarkhova, *Krasnaia armiia,* 258.

88. Tarkhova notes that before 1928, religious belief in the Red Army was seen as a bigger problem than the soldiers' dissatisfaction with the regime's approach to the countryside. Tarkhova, *Krasnaia armiia,* 94.

89. Tukhachevskii, *Izbrannye proizvedeniia,* 2:167.

90. Davies, *Socialist Offensive,* 260.

91. Khlevniuk, *Politbiuro,* 23.

92. Stone, *Hammer and Rifle,* 11.

93. Voroshilov went against Stalin on another issue in 1927, a time when there was still some chance of open discussion in the Soviet leadership. See Khlevniuk, *Master of the House,* 3.

94. Tarkhova, *Krasnaia armiia,* 104. The military procuracy also recorded growing discontent; see RGVA, f. 4, op. 14, d. 70, l. 5.

95. Tarkhova, *Krasnaia armiia,* 95. For comments on the growth in the peasant mood in the Leningrad, Moscow, Ukrainian, and Volga military districts in 1928, see RGVA, f. 33987, op. 3, d. 258, ll. 46–53.

96. RGVA, f. 9, op. 26, d. 446, l. 131.

97. RGASPI, f. 74, op. 2, d. 49, l. 116.

98. Ibid., ll. 137–138.

99. Tarkhova, *Krasnaia armiia,* 327, 357.

100. Ibid., 358.

101. RGVA, f. 33987, op. 3, d. 258, l. 47.

102. Tarkhova, *Krasnaia armiia,* 98.

103. PUR report quoted in Viola, *Tragedy of the Soviet Countryside*, 89.

104. RGVA, f. 33987, op. 3, d. 258, l. 46.

105. See, e.g., RGVA f. 33987, op. 3, d. 258, l. 49; Tarkhova, *Krasnaia armiia*, 97–99.

106. RGVA, f. 33987, op. 3, d. 258, l. 7.

107. Ibid., l. 53. For letters from the Moscow Military District from 1932, see RGASPI, f. 82, op. 2, d. 799, ll. 88–90.

108. See document in Plekhanov, *VChK-OGPU v gody novoi ekonomicheskoi politiki*, 636.

109. Tarkhova, *Krasnaia armiia*, 208. Suvenirov provides figures for discharges from the army for the period 1 November 1929 to 31 October 1930, noting that 4,473 individuals were discharged from the cadre units and 5,600 from the territorial units. Suvenirov, "Narkomat oborony i NKVD v predvoennye gody," 26.

110. Tarkhova, *Krasnaia armiia*, 209–219.

111. Ibid., 206.

112. It is important to note that the use of mass discharges was not a new tactic unique to the Red Army. Although the purge of the Red Army is suggestive of how serious the regime estimated the peasant mood, Hagenloh has shown that policing in the late 1920s, in general terms, was increasingly moving toward managing population cohorts rather than investigating individual cases. As such, the purge of the Red Army did not represent an entirely new approach for tackling social unrest. This should also be seen in terms of the evolving nature of policing in broader terms. Hagenloh, *Stalin's Police*, 48–146.

113. Tarkhova, *Krasnaia armiia*, 114. PUR did attribute kulak influence to some of the discontent in the rank and file, but they had faith in soldiers' ability to withstand this. Tarkhova, *Krasnaia armiia*, 111.

114. RGVA, f. 33987, op. 3, d. 293, l. 23. For optimistic appraisals from PUR, see Tarkhova, *Krasnaia armiia*, 104.

115. Tarkhova, *Krasnaia armiia*, 125.

116. Ibid., 124–126. See also Suvenirov, *Tragediia RKKA*, 61.

117. Reese, "Red Army Opposition," 42.

118. Tarkhova, *Krasnaia armiia*, 127.

119. RGVA, f. 9, op. 29, d. 29, l. 18.

120. Kariaeva et al., *Partiino-politicheskaia rabota v krasnoi armii: dokumenty, iiul 1929 g.–mai 1941 g.*, 46.

121. Tarkhova, *Krasnaia armiia*, 126.

122. Ibid., 131.

123. Ibid., 204.

124. Viola, *Tragedy of the Soviet Countryside*, 244; Reese, "Red Army Opposition, 33.

125. Zdanovich, *Organy gosudarstvennoi bezopasnosti*, 314. Zdanovich notes that this figure is incomplete and is missing the number of discharges for the second half of 1931, 314n134. It is also important that this figure includes discharges that continued into 1933 even after stability had been regained in the Red Army in 1932. These additional, and not unrelated, discharges, continuing in 1933, will be discussed in more detail in the next chapter. At the very least,

however, over 10,000 (and likely many more) soldiers were discharged from the ranks by 1932.

126. For an example of criticism of PUR from the OGPU for what it saw as its inability to control the peasant mood, see Tarkhova, *Krasnaia armiia*, 115–116.

127. Voroshilov, *Stat'i i rechi*, 442.

128. Estimates vary on the total number of military specialists discharged and arrested during Operation Vesna. The number is typically placed at approximately 3,000. Iaroslav Tynchenko, however, has revised the figure upward, to a possible 10,000, in his study on the operation. Tynchenko, *Golgofa russkogo ofitserstva*, 3. As Zdanovich notes, many of the arrested military specialists were freed a few years later when the scare passed and often went into administrative or teaching positions, though not command positions. See Zdanovich, "Byvshie morskie," 115.

129. Tynchenko, *Golgofa russkogo ofitserstva*, 29–30, 100–101; Suvenirov, *Tragediia RKKA*, 46.

130. Zdanovich, *Organy gosudarstvennoi bezopasnosti*, 381–382.

131. See Fitzpatrick, *Cultural Revolution*.

132. Tynchenko, *Golgofa russkogo ofitserstva*, 104–105.

133. Ibid., 23. For more on the arrested lecturers in Leningrad, the so-called Academy Affair, see Alferov et al., *Akademicheskoe delo 1929–1931 gg.*

134. RGVA, f. 33987, op. 3, d. 293, l. 220. This document is undated; however, Zdanovich points to an OO OGPU report sent to Stalin on 14 September 1930 from the Central Archive of the Federal Security Service of the Russian Federation that detailed wrecking in exactly these areas, in the same order as they appear on the document. It is likely the same document. See Zdanovich, *Organy gosudarstvennoi bezopasnosti*, 415.

135. RGVA, f. 33987, op. 3, d. 293, l. 226. For more on wrecking in the Red Army blamed on former White officers, see Zdanovich, *Organy gosudarstvennoi bezopasnosti*, 674.

136. On repression in industry in general at this time, see Shearer, *Industry, State, and Society*, 187–203; Stone, *Hammer and Rifle*, 64–84; Zdanovich, *Organy gosudarstvennoi bezopasnosti*, 409–439. Tynchenko notes that between November 1929 and February 1930, almost all members of the artillery inspectorate, administration, and scientific committee were arrested. During February and March 1930, nearly all members of the military topographic department were imprisoned. Tynchenko, *Golgofa russkogo ofitserstva*, 105–107.

137. Zdanovich, *Organy gosudarstvennoi bezopasnosti*, 348.

138. Plekhanov, *VChK-OGPU v gody novoi ekonomicheskoi politiki*, 325.

139. Zdanovich, *Organy gosudarstvennoi bezopasnosti*, 385–386.

140. Ibid., 386–387. Zdanovich does not note the date that this additional intelligence was received by the OGPU.

141. Ibid., 387.

142. Ibid., 388–389.

143. According to Tynchenko, the first arrest of the operation occurred on 27 January 1930 on a charge of being a member of a monarchist organization. Tynchenko, *Golgofa russkogo ofitserstva*, 105.

144. Ibid., 29, 114.
145. Tumshis and Papchinskii, *1937 Bol'shaia chistka*, 212.
146. Lazarev and Mil'bakh, "Politicheskie repressii," 101–102.
147. Artizov et al., *Reabilitatsiia*, 2:598.
148. "M. N. Tukhachevskii i 'voenno-fashistskii zagovor'" (1997), 247.
149. Minakov, *Stalin i ego marshal*, 107.
150. "M. N. Tukhachevskii i 'voenno-fashistskii zagovor'" (1997), 249–250.
151. Khaustov et al., *Lubianka: Stalin i VChK-GPU-OGPU-NKVD*, 277–279.
152. Zdanovich, *Organy gosudarstvennoi bezopasnosti*, 395.
153. RGASPI, f. 558, op. 11, d. 778, l. 38.
154. Khlevniuk argues that Stalin must have consequently suspected that the entire case was an OGPU fabrication. Khlevniuk, *Politbiuro*, 37. However, it is just as possible that Stalin did not discount the possibility of Tukhachevskii's guilt, and he hesitated to allow time for more evidence to emerge.
155. RGASPI, f. 558, op. 11, d. 778, l. 34.
156. Ibid.
157. Kosheleva, *Pis'ma I. V. Stalina V. M. Molotovu*, 231. Boris Shaposhnikov was also implicated as a member of a supposed Moscow counterrevolutionary center. However, in a face-to-face confrontation in March 1931, with the participation of Stalin, Molotov, Voroshilov, and Ordzhonikidze, the charges were also dismissed. See "M. N. Tukhachevskii i 'voenno-fashistskii zagovor'" (1997), 250.
158. Kosheleva, *Pis'ma I. V. Stalina V. M. Molotovu*, 209. Zdanovich also points to a Politburo order of 15 March 1930 on the subject of a possible Polish invasion. Zdanovich, *Organy gosudarstvennoi bezopasnosti*, 67.
159. Chebrikov, *Istoriia sovetskikh organov*, 230.
160. For instance, Ken notes that in January 1931, Voroshilov sent Stalin letters from two arrested officers, Verkhovskii and Bergavinov. Voroshilov's commentary notes that Bergavinov's letter gave a "brilliant and damning characterization" of Tukhachevskii. See Ken, *Mobilizatsionnoe planirovanie*, 132.
161. Zdanovich, *Organy gosudarstvennoi bezopasnosti*, 390. See also Khaustov et al., *Lubianka: Stalin i VChK-GPU-OGPU-NKVD*, 262.
162. Zdanovich, *Organy gosudarstvennoi bezopasnosti*, 390–391.
163. Zdanovich notes that a few leaders of the OGPU questioned the idea of an all-Union military plot and raised doubts about the links between the different counterrevolutionary military groups. However, they were soon removed from their positions by the Politburo, suggesting that Stalin firmly rejected these doubts. Zdanovich, *Organy gosudarstvennoi bezopasnosti*, 393.
164. Tynchenko, *Golgofa russkogo ofitserstva*, 238.
165. See the interrogation of a military specialist, a certain Akhdverov, from 7 January 1931, published in Tynchenko, *Golgofa russkogo ofitserstva*, 421. That "enemies" would take advantage of peasant discontent was already understood to be true before the launch of Operation Vesna. For instance, supposed links between kulaks and the White émigrés had been established at the outset of forced grain requisitions in the North-Caucasus Military District in 1927. See RGVA, f. 4, op. 14, d. 70, l. 32.
166. Such concerns can be seen in OGPU materials of the late 1920s and early

1930s. For an example, see a letter from the head of the OGPU to all police heads and heads of special departments in the military districts, reproduced in Zdanovich, *Organy gosudarstvennoi bezopasnosti*, 668–669.

167. After Stalin had proclaimed that Tukhachevskii and a number of other senior officers were in fact not counterrevolutionaries in 1930, one of Iagoda's rivals, Efim Evdokimov, along with two other senior OGPU operatives, accused Iagoda and Balitskii of having exaggerated the whole case against the high command. See Tumshis and Papchinskii, *1937 Bol'shaia chistka*, 213.

168. Tynchenko argues that Operation Vesna was a precursor for the military purge in 1937 but does not analyze the similarities between the two. Tynchenko, *Golgofa russkogo ofitserstva*.

Chapter 4. The Red Army and the Communist Party, 1930–1936

1. Combining Tynchenko's estimate for the number of discharges during Operation Vesna with the number of discharges of "socially harmful" and "alien elements" noted in the previous chapter, the total number is in excess of 47,000 people. Tynchenko, *Golgofa russkogo ofitserstva*.

2. Mil'bakh, "Repression in the Red Army," 58–59; Mil'bakh, *Osobaia Krasnoznamennaia Dal'nevostochnaia armiia*, 9.

3. Haslam, *Soviet Union*, 9, 25; Harris, "Encircled by Enemies," 525; Best, "Imperial Japan," 58–62.

4. Stone, *Hammer and Rifle*, 195–209.

5. Lenin, *Imperialism*.

6. RGASPI, f. 588, op. 11, d. 185, ll 15–36. For similar intelligence received by Stalin in December 1931, see ll. 1–9.

7. Harris notes this in his discussion of these documents. Harris, "Encircled by Enemies," 535–536.

8. Ibid., 527–528.

9. Nekrich, *Pariahs, Partners, Predators*, 40–41.

10. Robinson, *White Russian Army in Exile*, 144–150; Sudoplatov, *Special Tasks*, 91. For OGPU plans to kidnap Kutepov, see Goldin, *Armiia v izgnanii*, 77.

11. Robinson, *White Russian Army in Exile*, 157; Goldin, *Armiia v izgnanii*, 119.

12. RGVA, f. 37837, op. 21, d. 39, l. 378.

13. For a discussion of Soviet intelligence and intelligence in general, see Harris, "Encircled by Enemies"; Andrew and Elkner, "Stalin and Foreign Intelligence"; Ferris, "Intelligence."

14. For instance, in November 1932, the OGPU notified Stalin about the arrest of a group of twenty-five spies in the Far East that had supposedly been organized by the Japanese general staff. RGVA, f. 4, op. 19, d. 13, l. 2.

15. See, e.g., RGVA f. 37837, op. 21, d. 10, l. 366; op. 19, d. 19, l. 29; op. 9, d. 42, l. 45.

16. Zdanovich, *Organy gosudarstvennoi bezopasnosti*, 502–507; RGVA, f. 37837, op. 10, d. 20, l. 22.

17. Getty, *Practicing Stalinism*, 39.

18. RGVA, f. 9, op. 29, d. 10, l. 341. For another case of soldiers supposedly working as Latvian spies from September 1934, see RGVA, f. 37837, op. 21, d. 39, l. 46.

19. RGVA, f. 9, op. 29, d. 14, l. 592. For another Japanese spy case in the army from March 1934, see RGVA, f. 37837, op. 21, d. 63, l. 59. For Soviet interception of Japanese intelligence in the 1930s, see Shinin, "Deiatel'nost' dal'nevostochnykh organov," 233.

20. Zdanovich, *Organy gosudarstvennoi bezopasnosti*, 521.

21. RGVA, f. 33987, op. 3, d. 615, l. 70.

22. Zdanovich, *Organy gosudarstvennoi bezopasnosti*, 77. For examples of Polish espionage cases in the army in 1932–1934, see RGVA, f. 37837, op. 21, d. 39, l. 360; d. 52, l. 53; d. 39, ll. 324–325.

23. Zdanovich, *Organy gosudarstvennoi bezopasnosti*, 76.

24. RGVA, f. 9, op. 29, d. 178, ll. 2–3.

25. Ibid., l. 4.

26. Ibid., l. 10. For German espionage groups, see ibid., l. 25; f. 37837, op. 21, d. 52, l. 44.

27. RGVA, f. 9, op. 29, d. 178, l. 4.

28. Plekhanov and Plekhanov, *Zheleznyi Feliks*, 204.

29. RGVA, f. 4, op. 14, d. 1414, ll. 2–4. According to this same document, in 1933, seventeen other Finnish spy groups were also discovered.

30. Document reproduced in Zdanovich, *Organy gosudarstvennoi bezopasnosti*, 682–684.

31. Khaustov et al., *Lubianka: Stalin i VChK-GPU-OGPU-NKVD*, 424–425.

32. See NKVD report noted by Denningkhaus, *V teni "Bolshogo Brata,"* 572.

33. Khaustov, "Repressii protiv sovetskikh nemtsev," 75–76; Shearer, *Policing Stalin's Socialism*, 215.

34. Khaustov et al., *Lubianka: Stalin i VChK-GPU-OGPU-NKVD*, 460–463.

35. RGVA, f. 37837, op. 10, d. 76, l. 55.

36. Ibid.

37. Ibid., l. 52.

38. For examples of transfers from the border regions to interior districts because of doubts about reliability or the individual having a connection abroad, see RGVA, f. 37837, op. 21, d. 40, ll. 226, 231, 318.

39. RGVA, f. 37837, op. 9, d. 42, l. 65.

40. This argument follows that raised by Getty in 1985 in *Origins of the Great Purges* concerning so-called family circles in the Communist Party that stuck together to preserve their own networks of power and resist orders from above to carry out internal purges.

41. RGASPI, f. 74, op. 2, d. 19, l. 63.

42. Voroshilov, *Stat'i i rechi*, 573–576.

43. See Getty, *Origins of the Great Purges*, 38–58.

44. For individual examples of expulsions from the party in the 1933 *chistka*, see RGVA, f. 37837, op. 21, d. 55, ll. 125–325; op. 9, d. 42, l. 145.

45. In the first instance, individuals excluded from the army party organizations appear not to have been also discharged from the Red Army. However,

in October 1933, Anton Bulin and Fel'dman wrote to Voroshilov suggesting that people that had been excluded from the party for being "class aliens," for keeping their pasts secret (e.g., having previous service in the White armies), and for being "double-dealers," "careerists," and morally degenerate, and those obstructing military preparation and discipline should be discharged from the army as well. This suggestion was adopted in October, and a corresponding resolution was sent to all districts. See RGVA, f. 37837, op. 21, d. 21, ll. 16–18.

46. Voroshilov, *Stat'i i rechi*, 611.

47. RGASPI, f. 74, op. 2, d. 23, l. 94. The 1933 *chistka* was conducted in 60 percent of army party organizations. See l. 101.

48. RGVA, f. 9, op. 29, d. 178, ll. 27–28; f. 37837, op. 21, d. 39, l. 345; RGVA, f. 37837, op. 21, d. 39, l. 360.

49. Document published in Zdanovich, *Organy gosudarstvennoi bezopasnosti*, 697.

50. RGVA, f. 9, op. 29, d. 178, ll. 27–28.

51. Ibid., l. 3.

52. See a letter from Dobroditskii, deputy head of OO OGPU, to Fel'dman from January 1935. RGVA, f. 37837, op. 21, d. 63, l. 17.

53. Suvenirov, *Tragediia RKKA*, 49.

54. Shearer, *Policing Stalin's Socialism*, 136–137.

55. Khaustov et al., *Lubianka: Stalin i VChK-GPU-OGPU-NKVD*, 275.

56. RGVA contains many examples of cases of counterrevolutionary crime in the Red Army discovered by the OGPU in the first half of the 1930s. See, e.g., RGVA, f. 37837, op. 19, d. 29, ll. 28, 32, 229, 249; op. 21, d. 10, ll. 239–502; d. 39, ll. 72, 289, 392; d. 52, ll. 25–228; op. 10, d. 26, l. 35; op. 9, d. 42, ll. 20–21, 136.

57. For examples of commissions throughout 1933–1935, see RGVA, f. 37837, op. 10, d. 23, ll. 2–103; d. 20, ll. 28–88, 199–207, 265–271.

58. RGVA, f. 37837, op. 21, d. 21, l. 9.

59. RGVA, f. 37837, op. 10, d. 26, l. 37. In this particular case, the OO OGPU also acknowledged the mistake; see l. 49.

60. RGVA, f. 37837, op. 10, d. 23, l. 107.

61. Davies et al., *Stalin–Kaganovich Correspondence*, 246.

62. Ibid., 248.

63. Khaustov, "Inostrantsy i sovetskie grazhdane," 216.

64. Davies et al., *Stalin–Kaganovich Correspondence*, 248.

65. RGASPI, f. 558, op. 11, d. 50, l. 46.

66. Davies et al., *Stalin–Kaganovich Correspondence*, 252.

67. RGASPI, f. 588, op. 11, d. 84, l. 57.

68. Khaustov et al., *Lubianka: Stalin i VChK-GPU-OGPU-NKVD*, 477–547; RGASPI, f. 558, op. 11, d. 51, l. 22.

69. RGASPI, f. 558, op. 11, d. 186, ll. 79–81.

70. Document reproduced in Zdanovich, *Organy gosudarstvennoi bezopasnosti*, 700.

71. Ibid., 326.

72. Getty and Naumov, *Road to Terror*, 52–58.

73. For a discussion, see Davies, "Syrtsov–Lominadze Affair."

74. Anderson et al., *Stenogrammy zasedannii Politbiuro TsK RKP(b)*, 3:211.

75. Khlevniuk, *Master of the House,* 26.

76. Despite the votes against him, Uborevich was promoted as a candidate member of the Central Committee in the Sixteenth Party Congress; see Anderson et al., *Stenogrammy zasedannii Politbiuro TsK RKP(b),* 3:275n139.

77. Ibid., 282.

78. Khlevniuk, *Master of the House,* 28.

79. After the investigation, Eismont and the other members of the group were expelled from the party as punishment for their antiparty conversations and received three years in labor camps. See Getty and Naumov, *Road to Terror,* 101.

80. Ibid., 76.

81. Anderson et al., *Stenogrammy zasedannii Politbiuro TsK RKP(b),* 3:568, 3: 650–651.

82. Minakov, *Sovetskaia voennaia elita 20-kh godov,* 296n802.

83. "M. N. Tukhachevskii i 'voenno-fashistskii zagovor'" (1997), 252; "M. N. Tukhachevskii i 'voenno-fashistskii zagovor'" (1998), 7–9.

84. Minakov, *Stalin i zagovor generalov,* 672.

85. RGVA, f. 9, op. 29, d. 178, l. 55. For a small number of cases of Trotskyist agitation in the army in 1930–1934, see RGVA, f. 9, op. 29, d. 16, l. 1; f. 37837, op. 10, d. 20, ll. 131–132; op. 21, d. 52, ll. 46, 48; d. 39, l. 32.

86. Gorlov, *Sovershenno sekretno,* 233.

87. Quoted in Zdanovich, *Organy gosudarstvennoi bezopasnosti,* 325.

88. Ibid., 325–326.

89. Ibid., 326.

90. Getty, *Origins of the Great Purges,* 120.

91. "Delo o tak nazyvaemoi 'antisovetskoi trotskistskoi voennoi organizatsii' v krasnoi armii," 44.

92. RGVA, f. 37837, op. 10, d. 32, l. 60.

93. Haslam, *Soviet Union,* 27.

94. Lenoe, "Fear, Loathing, Conspiracy," 195.

95. Getty and Naumov, *Road to Terror,* 141.

96. See, e.g., Conquest, *Great Terror,* 72–96.

97. For a comprehensive collection on the Kirov murder, see Lenoe, *Kirov Murder.*

98. Lenoe, "Fear, Loathing, Conspiracy," 196.

99. Ibid., 196, 202–205.

100. Ibid., 196.

101. Getty and Naumov, *Road to Terror,* 147.

102. Ibid., 147–150; Lenoe, "Fear, Loathing, Conspiracy," 207.

103. Getty and Naumov, *Yezhov,* 140.

104. Suvenirov, *Tragediia RKKA,* 27. See, e.g., RGVA, f. 37837, op. 10, d. 26, l. 289.

105. For a case from the Belorussian Military District, see RGVA, f. 37837, op. 10, d. 26, ll. 194–196.

106. Bobylev et al., *Voennyi sovet pri narodnom komissare oborony SSSR, dekabr' 1934 g.,* 123.

107. Ibid., 125.

108. Ibid., 121.

109. Ibid.

110. Ibid., 247.

111. Ibid., 252.

112. Ibid., 349–351.

113. Ibid., 352.

114. Ibid.

115. Ibid., 360–362.

116. Ibid., 366.

117. Maiolo, *Cry Havoc*, 52.

118. Roberts, "Fascist War Threat," 149.

119. Pozniakov, "Enemy at the Gates," 223.

120. Ziemke, *Red Army*, 195.

121. Khaustov and Samuelson, *Stalin*, 93.

122. Getty and Naumov, *Road to Terror*, 156.

123. RGVA, f. 9, op. 29, d. 281, l. 144. For individual examples of such counterrevolutionary crimes, see RGVA, f. 37837, op. 21, d. 82, ll. 7–49; d. 63, l. 47; d. 64, ll. 82, 145, 181–206, 391; d. 80, ll. 64, 106, 163, 180, 212, 394; f. 4, op. 14, d. 1413, ll. 12–13; op. 10, d. 76, l. 345; d. 32, l. 247. Before the Kirov murder, arrests for counterrevolutionary crimes (not convictions) had in fact been falling in the Red Army, declining from 2,811 cases in 1932 to 2,390 in 1933. See RGVA, f. 9, op. 29, d. 178, l. 3.

124. RGVA, f. 4, op. 14, d. 1684, ll. 33–36.

125. According to the chief military procurator, in 1927–1928, there were 16,059 convictions in the army; in 1928–1929, this fell to 11,123. See RGVA, f. 9, op. 29, d. 281, l. 144. On declining arrests in the officer corps between 1934 and 1936, see Fel'dman's comments in March 1937 to a meeting of the Red Army *aktiv*: RGVA, f. 4, op. 14, d. 1820, l. 558.

126. See Afanas'ev et al., *Istoriia Stalinskogo Gulag*, 1:248–251. The number of counterrevolutionary crimes processed through military tribunals also declined over the course of 1935, suggesting that the Kirov murder led to a spike in cases early in the year that then petered out; see 252.

127. Suvenirov, *Tragediia RKKA*, 62; Suvenirov, "Narkomat oborony i NKVD v predvoennye gody," 27; Khaustov et al., *Lubianka: Stalin i VChK-GPU-OGPU-NKVD*, 524; RGVA, f. 4, op. 14, d. 1820, l. 558.

128. Getty and Naumov, *Road to Terror*, 121–123.

129. Shearer, *Policing Stalin's Socialism*, 94–129; Hagenloh, *Stalin's Police*, 149–157.

130. For Gai's interrogation transcript, see RGASPI, f. 671, op. 1, d. 142, l. 94.

131. Cherushev, *1937 god*, 75–78.

132. RGASPI, f. 671, op. 1, d. 142, l. 102.

133. Minakov, *Stalin i ego marshal*, 96.

134. RGVA, f. 4, op. 14, d. 1684, ll. 33–36. For examples of cases of Trotskyist agitation in 1935, see RGVA, f. 37837, op. 21, d. 39, l. 32; d. 63, ll. 223–226, 256, 356–357, 458, 633; d. 64, ll. 21, 355, 417; d. 80, ll. 126, 164, 219, 238, 355; d. 94,

ll. 6, 209, 270, 307, 324, 338–339. For Trotskyist double-dealers highlighted by the military procuracy, see f. 4, op. 14, d. 1366, ll. 12, 62.

135. RGVA, f. 37837, op. 21, d. 107, ll. 14, 16.

136. RGVA, 37837, op. 10, d. 32, l. 404.

137. Ibid., l. 381.

138. See the following articles in *Krasnaia zvezda:* "Bditel'nost' prezhde vsego," 5 January 1935, 1; "Eshche vishe bditel'nost'," 20 June 1935, 1; "V khode proverki partiinikh dokumentov," 17 October 1935, 1.

139. RGVA, f. 33987, op. 3, d. 872, l. 85. For examples of individual expulsions, see RGVA, f. 37837, op. 21, d. 64, l. 257; f. 9, op. 29, d. 231, ll. 17–19, 68–72.

140. Getty, *Origins of the Great Purges,* 82.

141. RGVA, f. 33987, op. 3, d. 872, l. 85. For cases of espionage in the Red Army during 1935 investigated by the NKVD, see RGVA, f. 37837, op. 21, d. 63, ll. 18, 45–46, 59, 198–201, 678–679; d. 80, ll. 161, 269, 373.

142. RGVA, f. 9, op. 29, d. 15, l. 39.

143. Ibid.

144. Getty and Naumov, *Road to Terror,* 200–201.

145. Chase, *Enemies Within the Gates?,* 103.

146. Morris, "Polish Terror," 757–758; Hagenloh, *Stalin's Police,* 233.

147. Jansen and Petrov, *Stalin's Loyal Executioner,* 40. See also Chase, *Enemies Within the Gates?,* 102–145.

148. Khaustov, "Inostrantsy i sovetskie grazhdane," 224.

149. Bobylev et al., *Voennyi sovet pri narodnom komissare oborony SSSR, dekabr' 1935 g.,* 56.

150. Ibid., 57–58.

151. Ibid., 130–131.

152. Gailit did not mention the reasons for the discharges he was complaining about and whether these were for less serious reasons such as drunkenness or for being a kulak, or even a political enemy. However, because Gailit also argued that reeducation and support should be used more extensively, it is unlikely that the discharges he referred to were for serious political crimes or espionage. They were more likely for low-level crimes where reeducation was a possible remedy.

153. Getty, *Origins of the Great Purges,* 58–91.

154. RGVA, f. 33987, op. 3, d. 872, l. 85.

155. "M. N. Tukhachevskii i 'voenno-fashistskii zagovor'" (1997), 166.

156. Harris, "Encircled by Enemies," 541; Harrison and Davies, "Soviet Military–Economic Effort," 371; Khlevniuk, *Master of the House,* 173.

157. Getty and Naumov, *Yezhov,* 184–186; Chase, *Enemies Within the Gates?,* 134.

158. Khaustov et al., *Lubianka: Stalin i VChK-GPU-OGPU-NKVD,* 738–741.

159. RGVA, f. 9, op. 29, d. 263, l. 42.

160. RGVA, f. 9, op. 29, d. 281, l. 19.

161. RGVA, f. 9, op. 29, d. 263, l. 42.

162. Ibid., l. 81.

163. Ibid., l. 83.

164. RGVA, f. 37837, op. 21, d. 107, l. 3. Fel'dman details that in 1933, approxi-

mately 10,000 individuals were discharged from commanding bodies and 7,500 in 1934. Another set of approximately corresponding statistics notes that 8,463 people from commanding bodies were discharged in 1935, falling to 5,634 for 1936; see l. 14. Also see a report from the then head of PUR, Pavel Smirnov, to Voroshilov from December 1937, detailing discharges within PUR and showing 978 discharges in 1935 and 716 in 1936. According to this report, in contrast to the situation in the army commanding bodies, PUR actually saw falling levels of those discharged for political crimes, declining from 301 in 1935 to 250 in 1936; see RGVA, f. 33987, op. 3, d. 992, l. 209. For similar general trends, see Mozokhin, *Pravo na repressii* (2011), 449, 455.

165. RGVA, f. 4, op. 14, d. 1684, l. 89. For a further corroborating report of this trend until September 1936, also from Ulrikh, see l. 107. Ulrikh also noted that counterrevolutionary crime and agitation fell between the first nine months of 1935 and the matching period in 1936, from 1,158 cases to 416; see l. 108.

166. RGVA, f. 37837, op. 21, d. 107, ll. 14–16. This report details that in 1935, commanding bodies discharged 268 people for Trotskyism; this increased to 337 in 1936. For approximate corroborating figures showing the same increase in cases of Trotskyism in the military, see l. 16. For sample cases, see RGVA, f. 9, op. 29, d. 291, l. 108.

167. In the first half of 1936, for instance, the NKVD sent directives to the localities calling for greater efforts to root out Trotskyists. Starkov, "Narkom Ezhov," 26.

168. Lukes, "Tukhachevsky Affair," 507.

169. RGVA, f. 4, op. 19, d. 16, l. 57.

170. Samuelson, "Wartime Perspective," 210.

171. RGVA, f. 4, op. 19, d. 16, l. 171.

172. Kantor, *Zakliataia druzhba*, 253.

173. Maiskii, *Dnevnik diplomata*, 1:100.

174. *Documents on German Foreign Policy,* 2:338. For Tukhachevskii's comments, relayed by F. von Twardowski, see 2:81–83. For similar remarks from Egorov, see 2:352. For Voroshilov's similar comments to H. von Dirksen and R. Nadolny, see *Documents on German Foreign Policy,* 1:422.

175. Suvenirov, *Tragediia RKKA*, 54.

176. "M. N. Tukhachevskii i 'voenno-fashistskii zagovor'" (1998), 11.

177. Minakov, *1937*, 247.

178. RGASPI, f. 558, op. 11, d. 188, l. 119.

179. Danilov, "Sovershenstvovanie sistemy," 78.

180. *XVII s'ezd Vsesoiuzno kommunisticheskoi partii (b),* 226; Naveh, *In Pursuit of Military Excellence,* 199n.

181. Zhuravlev et al., *Vlast' i oppozitsiia,* 161. Voroshilov confirmed this story in June 1937; see Anderson et al., *Voennyi sovet pri narodnom komissare oborony SSSR,* 76. Tukhachevskii had not been the only person to speak out of turn in Voroshilov's apartment in May. Gamarnik and Iakir were also supposedly on poor terms with Voroshilov at this time.

182. Naveh, *In Pursuit of Military Excellence,* 199n62.

183. RGVA, f. 4, op. 19, d. 18, l. 18.

184. Ibid., l. 58.

185. Getty and Naumov, *Road to Terror*, 247; Chase, *Enemies Within the Gates?*, 134–135.

186. Getty and Naumov, *Road to Terror*, 248.

187. Getty and Naumov, *Yezhov*, 154.

188. Getty and Naumov, *Road to Terror*, 248.

189. Ibid., 247–260.

190. For the letter, see ibid., 250–251.

191. Ibid., 257.

192. Cherushev, *1937 god*, 101; Mil'bakh, *Osobaia Krasnoznamennaia Dal'nevo-stochnaia armiia*, 29.

193. Khaustov et al., *Lubianka: Stalin i VChK-GPU-OGPU-NKVD*, 765.

194. Cherushev, *1937 god*, 96. The NKVD probably had little trouble putting a case together against someone like Shmidt. Not only did he have incriminating Trotskyist affiliations but he also had already been flagged as a poor commander. In early 1935, an officer from the Kiev Military District had complained to Voroshilov that Shmidt lacked vigilance in his selection of subordinates, which apparently had led to a range of kulaks, crooks, speculators, and former White officers acquiring top positions. According to this officer, Shmidt had done nothing about this: "Going by theft, drunkenness, and accidents, Shmidt's unit comes first, and obviously, not only in the Kiev Garrison, but in the whole district." RGVA, f. 9, op. 29, d. 283, ll. 22–23.

195. For details of Dreitser's arrest, see Khaustov et al., *Lubianka: Stalin i VChK-GPU-OGPU-NKVD*, 764.

196. RGVA, f. 33987, op. 3, d. 872, l. 76. In his letter, Artuzov displays a surprisingly lenient attitude to the whole case: he requests that Putna's wife and son be given material aid of 500 rubles a month and that an appropriate school be found for her son. Artuzov's comments also reveal that he was not yet convinced about the case against Putna and that he was keeping an open mind: "Com[rade] N. R. PUTNA gave me the impression of not being dedicated to the Trotskyist-Zinovievite business of PUTNA in any case, if the latter was indeed involved with them." See ll. 77–78.

197. Getty, *Practicing Stalinism*, 40.

198. RGVA, f. 4, op. 19, d. 16, l. 268.

199. UK National Archives, Public Record Office, KV 2/404: 52a.

200. See RGVA, f. 4, op. 19, d. 16, l. 298, for Primakov's wife's letter of appeal about her husband's innocence and noting his disappearance on 14 August.

201. RGASPI, f. 74, op. 2, d. 37, l. 107.

202. RGASPI, f. 74, op. 21, d. 42, l. 91.

203. "Delo o tak nazyvaemoi 'antisovetskoi trotskistskoi voennoi organizatsii' v krasnoi armii," 43. Primakov was expelled from the Military Soviet along with Turovskii in late September; see RGVA, f. 4, op. 19, d. 18, l. 99.

204. RGVA, f. 9, op. 29, d. 260, l. 60.

Chapter 5. The Military Purge

1. Arrests in the Red Army on charges of Trotskyism continued during 1936 on the same pattern of previous years; not all were connected to the new Trotskyist military organization. For instance, see a report about the arrest of a group of four Trotskyists in the Belorussian Military District in August 1936 that was not connected to the conspiracy stemming from the Zinoviev–Kamenev Counterrevolutionary Bloc. RGVA, f. 33987, op. 3, d. 872, ll. 24–26.

2. RGVA, f. 4, op. 19, d. 16, l. 265.

3. Ibid., l. 262.

4. Getty and Naumov, *Road to Terror,* 276.

5. Ibid., 248.

6. Khlevnyuk, "Economic Officials in the Great Terror."

7. Getty, *Origins of the Great Purges,* 132.

8. Getty and Naumov, *Yezhov,* 187.

9. Ibid., 216.

10. Letter reproduced in Jansen and Petrov, *"Stalinskii pitomets,"* 251.

11. RGVA, f. 37837, op. 22, d. 1, l. 178.

12. Goldman, *Inventing the Enemy.* See also Figes, *Whisperers.*

13. RGVA, f. 9, op. 29, d. 285, ll. 22; 232–242.

14. Khaustov and Samuelson, *Stalin,* 108.

15. RGASPI, f. 558, op. 11, d. 93, l. 43.

16. Khaustov and Samuelson, *Stalin,* 108. For other army arrests in December 1936 and January 1937, see Khaustov and Samuelson, *Stalin,* 108.

17. Kniaz'kov et al., *Voennyi sovet pri narodnom komissare oborony SSSR, oktiabr' 1936 g.,* 418–419.

18. Ibid., 327.

19. Ibid., 354.

20. Ibid., 377.

21. Ibid., 418–422.

22. RGVA, f. 37837, op. 21, d. 107, l. 14. Although political arrests were increasing in the Red Army, one report indicates that arrests for counterrevolutionary agitation halved between 1935 and 1936 in the command and leading army bodies. In addition, a separate report from the then head of PUR, Pavel Smirnov, sent to Voroshilov from 27 December 1937, shows that the number of discharges of political workers for either political reasons or belonging to the Trotskyist opposition actually fell between 1935 and 1936, from 301 to 250. PUR thus seemed to be the exception to the rising political arrests that occurred in 1936. See RGVA, f. 33987, op. 3, d. 992, l. 209.

23. RGVA, f. 37837, op. 21, d. 99, l. 57; Cherushev, *1937 god,* 70, 97.

24. RGVA, f. 37837, op. 21, d. 109, l. 87.

25. Rogovin, *1937,* 414.

26. For example, see a petition from Fel'dman to Voroshilov from 14 November about keeping an officer accused of Trotskyist agitation in the army: RGVA, f. 37837, op. 21, d. 99, l. 91. For another similar case from 19 November, see RGVA, f. 37837, op. 21, 109, l. 191. On 14 December, Fel'dman examined

another case brought by M. I. Gai for a discharge on the basis of Trotskyist agitation. Fel'dman requested that the man be kept in the army and that PUR should help him "improve himself" and become a good officer. In this case, Voroshilov agreed. See RGVA, f. 37837, op. 21, d. 94, ll. 311–312. In December, Fel'dman petitioned Voroshilov about an academy student who was linked to Primakov, Shmidt, and Ziuk and requested that he be allowed to work within Osoaviakhim in a remote area rather than be demobilized to the reserves. See RGVA, f. 37837, op. 21, d. 94, l. 375. In a letter to Voroshilov on 9 January 1937, Fel'dman agreed with an indictment against an army man for anti-Soviet agitation, but he argued that the man's background and his appraisals were good and that he was not a "hopeless commander." In Fel'dman's opinion, he needed support in order to improve himself. See RGVA, f. 37837, op. 21, d. 109, l. 126. On 19 March 1937, Fel'dman wrote to Gamarnik about a colonel whose brother had been arrested as a spy. Fel'dman argued that the colonel said he had no knowledge of the espionage charge and that he found this explanation convincing. Fel'dman asked whether the colonel could be transferred to another position in the army and perhaps be kept in the party. See RGVA, f. 37837, op. 21, d. 99, l. 160.

27. RGVA, f. 37837, op. 21, d. 100, l. 570, 537.

28. Ibid., l. 570.

29. Ibid., l. 563.

30. Ibid., l. 565.

31. Document reproduced in Jansen and Petrov, *"Stalinskii pitomets,"* 269.

32. RGVA, f. 4, op. 19, d. 18, l. 179.

33. Ibid., l. 176.

34. RGASPI, f. 558, op. 11, d. 90, l. 47.

35. Minakov, *1937,* 236.

36. This is Minakov's interpretation; see ibid., 236–237.

37. RGASPI, f. 558, op. 11, d. 93, l. 1.

38. RGASPI, f. 588, op. 11, d. 779, l. 101.

39. Khaustov and Samuelson, *Stalin,* 93.

40. Document reproduced in Radosh, *Spain Betrayed,* 92.

41. Ibid., 131.

42. Dimitrov, *Diary,* 60.

43. For more on Ezhov's concerns about foreign agents, see Getty and Naumov, *Yezhov,* 182–184; Hagenloh, *Stalin's Police,* 230.

44. As Hagenloh notes, however, this was not a complete reorientation of the NKVD, which was still forced to deal with nonpolitical crimes on some level. See Hagenloh, *Stalin's Police,* 234–235.

45. Khlevnyuk, "Economic Officials in the Great Terror," 40.

46. Chase, "Stalin as Producer," 241.

47. Ibid., 238–239.

48. Shearer, *Policing Stalin's Socialism,* 316.

49. Ibid., 320.

50. Okhotin and Roginskii, "Iz istorii 'nemtskoi operatsii,'" 40.

51. Khaustov et al., *Lubianka: Stalin i glavnoe upravlenie gosbezopasnosti NKVD*, 41–44, 52–54, 92–94.

52. See Conquest, *Great Terror,* 212. Erickson argued that Radek's testimony was a "substantial hint that a move against the military was being contemplated." Erickson, *Soviet High Command*, 451.

53. RGVA, f. 37837, op. 21, d. 99, l. 16.

54. RGVA, f. 33987, op. 3, d. 851, ll. 39–40.

55. Ibid., l. 50.

56. Ibid., l. 134.

57. Mil'bakh, Grigorian, and Chernavskii, *Politicheskie repressii komandno-nachal'stvuiushchego sostava*, 22, 82–83.

58. Document reproduced in Jansen and Petrov, *"Stalinskii pitomets,"* 269.

59. "M. N. Tukhachevskii i 'voenno-fashistskii zagovor'" (1998), 10.

60. "Delo o tak nazyvaemoi 'antisovetskoi trotskistskoi voennoi organizatsii' v krasnoi armii," 61.

61. Khaustov et al., *Lubianka: Stalin i glavnoe upravlenie gosbezopasnosti NKVD*, 43–44.

62. On Ezhov's view of the Polish Military Organization, see Morris, "Polish Terror," 756–757.

63. Details of Tukhachevskii's incrimination by Dąbal' can be found in Kantor, *Voina i mir Mikhaila Tukhachevskogo*, 366.

64. Khaustov et al., *Lubianka: Stalin i glavnoe upravlenie gosbezopasnosti NKVD*, 43–44.

65. "M. N. Tukhachevskii i 'voenno-fashistskii zagovor'" (1993), 255.

66. Artizov et al., *Reabilitatsiia*, 2:601.

67. For more on possible German disinformation attempts, see "M. N. Tukhachevskii i 'voenno-fashistskii zagovor'" (1998), 15–20.

68. According to the testimony of a former member of the NKVD's foreign department, provided in 1939, when Iagoda was the head of the NKVD, he once received material from Germany suggesting that a "military party" existed in the Red Army. However, he quickly realized that this was Soviet disinformation that had been returned from a double agent. In 1937, when Ezhov was sent this same information, he apparently requested that it be investigated, arguing that a Trotskyist organization was undoubtedly operating inside the Red Army. Artizov et al., *Reabilitatsiia*, 2:600.

69. "M. N. Tukhachevskii i 'voenno-fashistskii zagovor'" (1997), 255.

70. Khlevniuk, *Master of the House*, 165.

71. See Getty and Naumov, *Road to Terror,* 324.

72. Ibid., 367–369.

73. Interestingly, Iakir was one of the few party members who voted for the death penalty for Bukharin and Rykov. This vote is difficult to square with the common explanation of the military purge claiming that certain members of the military elite were unhappy with the rising political repression during 1937, which was partly why Stalin had them executed. For Iakir's vote, see Getty and Naumov, *Road to Terror,* 412–413.

74. "M. N. Tukhachevskii i 'voenno-fashistskii zagovor'" (1997), 153.

75. Ibid., 165.

76. Ibid., 153.

77. Ibid., 165.

78. Ibid., 171.

79. For Molotov's comments to the February–March plenum, see "Delo o tak nazyvaemoi 'antisovetskoi trotskistskoi voennoi organizatsii' v krasnoi armii," 45.

80. RGASPI, f. 558, op. 11, d. 18, l. 105.

81. "Materialy fevral'skogo-martovskogo plenuma TsK VKP(b) 1937 goda" (1995), 3–10.

82. Khlevniuk, *Master of the House,* 175.

83. "Materialy fevral'skogo-martovskogo plenuma TsK VKP(b) 1937 goda" (1995), 13–14.

84. Danilov et al., *Tragediia sovetskoi derevni,* vol. 5, bk. 1, 162–164.

85. "Materialy fevral'skogo-martovskogo plenuma TsK VKP(b) 1937 goda" (1994), 15–16.

86. "Materialy fevral'skogo-martovskogo plenuma TsK VKP(b) 1937 goda" (1992), 10.

87. Cherushev, *1937 god,* 100, 163.

88. Khaustov and Samuelson, *Stalin,* 110.

89. Anderson et al., *Voennyi sovet pri narodnom komissare oborony SSSR,* 150. See also Cherushev, *1937 god,* 125.

90. Khaustov and Samuelson, *Stalin,* 109–111.

91. RGASPI, f. 74, op. 2, d. 117, ll. 42, 47.

92. Ibid., l. 51.

93. Ibid., ll. 51–53.

94. Ibid., l. 58.

95. Ibid., ll. 95–97.

96. RGVA, f. 4, op. 14, d. 1820, ll. 448–449.

97. Ibid., l. 485.

98. Ibid., ll. 547–551.

99. Ibid., ll. 558–559.

100. "Materialy fevral'skogo-martovskogo plenuma TsK VKP(b) 1937 goda" (1994), 15–16.

101. RGVA, f. 9, op. 29, d. 319, l. 2.

102. Hagenloh, *Stalin's Police,* 233–234; Khlevniuk, *Master of the House,* 180.

103. RGVA, f. 9, op. 29, d. 319, l. 6.

104. RGVA, f. 4, op. 14, d. 1820, l. 170.

105. Ibid., l. 247.

106. On document security in the Red Army, see Zdanovich, *Organy gosudarst-vennoi bezopasnosti,* 483–524.

107. Durachinski and Sakharov, *Sovetsko-pol'skie otnosheniia,* 67–68.

108. RGVA, f. 4, op. 15, d. 12, l. 16.

109. Ibid., l. 28.

110. RGVA, f. 9, op. 29, d. 319, l. 4.

111. Getty and Naumov, *Road to Terror,* 204–205; Getty, *Origins of the Great Purges.*

112. RGVA, f. 4, op. 19, d. 16, l. 265.

113. RGVA, f. 9, op. 29, d. 319, ll. 73–74.

114. Ibid., ll. 75, 84.

115. Quoted in McLoughlin, "Mass Operations," 122.

116. Mil'bakh, *Osobaia Krasnoznamennaia Dal'nevostochnaia armiia,* 34, 38–39.

117. Okhotin and Roginskii, "Iz istorii 'nemtskoi operatsii,'" 41.

118. Tumshis and Papchinskii, *1937 Bol'shaia chistka,* 451–454.

119. Mil'bakh, Grigorian, and Chernavskii, *Politicheskie repressii komandno-nachal'stvuiushchego sostava,* 124–125.

120. See the following *Krasnaia zvezda* articles: "Fashistsko-trotskistskii zagovor v Valensii," 28 March 1937; "Podrobnosti shpionskoi raboty fashistskoi organizatsii v madride," 20 April 1937; "Iaponskaia razvedka v russko-iaponskoi voine," 23 April 1937; "Avstro-germanskii shpionazh pered mirovoi voinoi," 24 April 1937; "Aktivnaia maskirovka," 28 April 1937; "Set' shpionazha i provokatsii fashistskoi germanii," 14 May 1937; "Germanskaia shpionazh v ispanii," 28 May 1937. Moreover, a *Pravda* article published on 28 April called on the Red Army to tackle "internal enemies" and to "master politics." See Conquest, *Great Terror,* 193.

121. Khlevniuk, *Master of the House,* 180.

122. Pechenkin, *Gibel' voennoi elity,* 28–29.

123. RGVA, f. 33987, op. 3, d. 965, l. 88.

124. Ibid., ll. 90, 97.

125. Ibid., l. 98.

126. Ibid., l. 101.

127. Ibid., l. 110.

128. Getty and Naumov, *Road to Terror,* 422.

129. Ibid., 422–425.

130. Ibid., 280.

131. Ibid., 433, 436; For more details on the NKVD purge, see Jansen and Petrov, *Stalin's Loyal Executioner,* 60–62.

132. Shearer, *Policing Stalin's Socialism,* 293.

133. Jansen and Petrov, *Stalin's Loyal Executioner,* 61.

134. Artizov et al., *Reabilitatsiia,* 2:602.

135. Erickson, *Soviet High Command,* 459.

136. "Delo o tak nazyvaemoi 'antisovetskoi trotskistskoi voennoi organizatsii' v krasnoi armii," 45.

137. See Artizov et al., *Reabilitatsiia,* 2:601. Today this document is understood as disinformation by Japanese intelligence. See "M. N. Tukhachevskii i 'voenno-fashistskii zagovor'" (1998), 33.

138. Suvenirov, *Tragediia RKKA,* 158; Cherushev, *1937 god,* 128, 331.

139. Cherushev, *1937 god,* 331. Peterson had a run-in with the NKVD two years before when he was fired from the head of the Kremlin Guard in mid-1935 after the discovery of so-called enemies working in the Kremlin staff. The NKVD thus already had incriminating material on him. See Lenoe, "Fear, Loathing, Conspiracy," 207.

140. Khaustov and Samuelson, *Stalin,* 115.

141. Artizov et al., *Reabilitatsiia,* 2:94.

142. RGVA, f. 33987, op. 3, d. 965, l. 65.

143. Ibid.

144. Ibid., ll. 65, 72, 81.

145. Ibid., l. 65.

146. It is possible that Stalin had ordered Voroshilov to include Tukhachevskii's transfer in his 9 May letter to the Politburo in the first place. This would mean that his decision to transfer Tukhachevskii was not overly influenced by receiving Voroshilov's report on foreign agents sent the following day. At the same time, however, it is possible that Stalin was already aware of the content of the report that Voroshilov was compiling before he received the final product. In this sense, the underlying spy scare in the Red Army may still have provided a catalyst for Tukhachevskii's transfer. Indeed Stalin and Voroshilov were close allies, and it would be surprising if they did not share important information about a widespread spy infiltration of the military before Voroshilov had written up his final report. Without documents showing the precise timeline of events, it is impossible to understand this series of events for certain. It remains likely, however, that Voroshilov's final May report had a significant impact on the steps taken by the regime against the officers incriminated in the military-fascist plot.

147. "M. N. Tukhachevskii i 'voenno-fashistskii zagovor'" (1997), 182; Kantor, *Voina i mir,* 373.

148. "Delo o tak nazyvaemoi 'antisovetskoi trotskistskoi voennoi organizatsii' v krasnoi armii," 49. For a transcript of the interrogation, see Khaustov et al., *Lubianka: Stalin i VChK-GPU-OGPU-NKVD,* 170–176.

149. In addition, on 13 May, Ezhov received a report from his subordinates containing more material on Tukhachevskii. This included the incriminating "evidence" against Tukhachevskii that had been extracted from Kakurin and Troitskii during Operation Vesna in 1930, along with a note claiming that Tukhachevskii apparently dreamed "more about being a Marshal at the command of Germany than the Soviet government." "M. N. Tukhachevskii i 'voenno-fashistskii zagovor'" (1997), 255.

150. "Delo o tak nazyvaemoi 'antisovetskoi trotskistskoi voennoi organizatsii' v krasnoi armii," 48.

151. Ibid., 48–49.

152. Getty and Naumov, *Road to Terror,* 448. Tukhachevskii was also expelled from the Military Soviet alongside Eideman and the officers E. F. Appoga, N. A. Efimov, and R. V. Longva, who had also been incriminated in the military plot. See Pechenkin, *Gibel' voennoi elity,* 41.

153. Getty, "Politics of Repression Revisited," 41.

154. Kantor, *Voina i mir,* 377–381.

155. Ibid.; "Delo o tak nazyvaemoi 'antisovetskoi trotskistskoi voennoi organizatsii' v krasnoi armii," 51.

156. RGASPI, f. 558, op. 11, d. 203, ll. 62–88.

157. Vinogradov, "Tret'ia reforma," 2:93.

158. Document reproduced in Jansen and Petrov, *"Stalinskii pitomets,"* 291; Khaustov and Samuelson, *Stalin,* 199–120.

159. Kuromiya and Mamoulia, "Anti-Russian and Anti-Soviet Subversion," 1426–1427.

160. In a letter Primakov sent to Ezhov on 8 May, after nine months of denying his participation in the military conspiracy, he finally relented and confessed his "guilt." However, Primakov indicated that Stalin had been involved during his investigation. It seems that Stalin had some involvement with the investigation into the military conspiracy from at least early May. See "M. N. Tukhachevskii i 'voenno-fashistskii zagovor'" (1997), 180–181.

161. "Delo o tak nazyvaemoi 'antisovetskoi trotskistskoi voennoi organizatsii' v krasnoi armii," 49–50.

162. RGVA, f. 37837, op. 21, d. 100, l. 110; op. 10, d. 90, l. 86; op. 21, d. 100, ll. 112–113, 121–193, 591; op. 22, d. 1, ll. 1, 27, 131, 133.

163. "Delo o tak nazyvaemoi 'antisovetskoi trotskistskoi voennoi organizatsii' v krasnoi armii," 58. For the many other senior officers discharged from the army and arrested in May, see Cherushev, *1937 god,* 143–145.

164. Jansen and Petrov, *Stalin's Loyal Executioner,* 72.

165. RGVA, f. 37837, op. 21, d. 109, l. 327.

166. RGVA, f. 9, op. 29, d. 313, l. 1; "Delo o tak nazyvaemoi 'antisovetskoi trotskistskoi voennoi organizatsii' v krasnoi armii," 52.

167. In an early list of attendees for the June Military Soviet (which has been dated between 21 and 22 May), Iakir, Uborevich, and Tukhachevskii were actually included as being invited. Additional incriminating testimony against the three was extracted from Primakov, Kork, and Fel'dman at around this time, but either there was still some confusion or no firm decision had been made about what to do with the three after their transfers earlier in the month. This implies that Stalin was undecided about what to do with the incriminated officers and that there had never been a long-term plan to gut the high command. See Anderson et al., *Voennyi sovet pri narodnom komissare oborony SSSR,* 29–34. Moreover, another senior officer, M. V. Sangurskii, deputy commander of the Special Red Banner Far Eastern Army, was initially included in the lineup of the ringleaders of the military-fascist plot. On 7 June, his name appeared alongside those of Tukhachevskii and other senior officers in an order published by the People's Commissariat of Defense. However, shortly after, Sangurskii's name disappeared, and he never made the final lineup for the closed military trial. It has been noted that Sangurskii refused to give false testimony and could not be relied on for the upcoming military trial. See Mil'bakh, *Osobaia Krasnoznamennaia Dal'nevostochnaia armiia,* 45–46.

168. Cherushev, *1937 god,* 139.

169. Anderson et al., *Voennyi sovet pri narodnom komissare oborony SSSR,* 66–70.

170. Ibid., 76.

171. Ibid., 74–75.

172. Ibid., 76.

173. Ibid., 320.

174. Ibid., 81.
175. Ibid., 84.
176. Ibid., 148. Stalin repeated this opinion later in the meeting; see 256.
177. Ibid., 146.
178. Ibid., 77.
179. Ibid., 128–131.
180. Ibid., 133.
181. Ibid., 136.
182. Ibid., 136–137.
183. Ibid., 140.
184. Ibid., 137.
185. Ibid., 320.
186. RGASPI, f. 74, op. 2, d. 118, l. 3.
187. Ibid., ll. 8, 50.
188. Ibid., ll. 9, 63.
189. Ibid., l. 30.
190. Ibid., l. 62.
191. RGVA, f. 33987, op. 3, d. 955, l. 97.
192. Ibid., l. 98.
193. Ibid., ll. 98–99.
194. Khaustov and Samuelson, *Stalin*, 118.
195. RGVA, f. 4, op. 15, d. 13, l. 191.

Chapter 6. The Expansion of the Military Purge and the Mass Operations

1. Khaustov and Samuelson, *Stalin*, 189–190.
2. Ibid., 206.
3. Ibid., 194–195.
4. Reese, *Stalin's Reluctant Soldiers*, 138.
5. RGVA, f. 4, op. 15, d. 13, l. 196.
6. Khaustov and Samuelson, *Stalin*, 192–193.
7. For denunciations after the military trial and going into July see, RGVA, f. 37837, op. 10, d. 90, ll. 209, 301; d. 91, l. 25; op. 21, d. 100, ll. 116, 161, 210, 388, 390–391, 451; f. 9, op. 29, d. 320, l. 181.
8. For one example, see Figes, *Whisperers*, 272.
9. RGASPI, f. 558, op. 11, d. 188, l. 124.
10. Mil'bakh records examples of what seem to be personally motivated denunciations in the Far East Region. Mil'bakh, *Osobaia Krasnoznamennaia Dal'nevostochnaia armiia*, 43.
11. RGVA, f. 33987, op. 3, d. 1023, l. 40.
12. Ibid.
13. RGVA, f. 37837, op. 10, d. 90, l. 212; Brandenberger, *Propaganda State in Crisis*, 185–186.
14. RGVA, f. 33987, op. 3, d. 1023, l. 41.
15. Ibid.

16. Khaustov and Samuelson, *Stalin*, 194. See also Davies, "Us Against Them," 79.

17. RGVA, f. 33987, op. 3, d. 955, l. 16.

18. Ibid.

19. Ibid., ll. 24–26.

20. Kniaz'kov et al., *Voennyi sovet pri narodnom komissare oborony SSSR: noiabr' 1937 g.*, 119.

21. Brandenberger, *Propaganda State in Crisis*, 185–197. Also see Pechenkin, *Gibel' voennoi elity*, 147.

22. Quoted in Brandenberger, *Propaganda State in Crisis*, 190.

23. Bukharin's letter makes reference to remarks Voroshilov had made about Sergei Kamenev, the former chief of staff, who died on 25 August 1936 and was posthumously included as a member of the military-fascist plot after its discovery. Bukharin describes the accusation that Kamenev had been a conspirator as "monstrously vile." See RGVA f. 4, op. 19, d. 16, l. 275.

24. Ibid.

25. In a set of statistics on discharges from commanding bodies on the charge of counterrevolutionary Trotskyism in the second quarter of 1937 (from the February–March plenum until 1 June), the number totals 3,387. The point at which the pace of discharges accelerated is not specified in these figures, however. See Anderson et al., *Voennyi sovet pri narodnom komissare oborony SSSR*, 4. However, it is clear that there was growth in the number of discharges after the February–March plenum. Between 1 January and 1 March, there were only 125 discharges from leading army bodies. See RGVA, f. 37837, op. 21, d. 107, l. 16.

26. RGVA, f. 9, op. 29, d. 340, l. 429; f. 37837, op. 21, d. 107, l. 14.

27. Khaustov and Samuelson, *Stalin*, 113; Anderson et al., *Voennyi sovet pri narodnom komissare oborony SSSR*, 134.

28. "Delo o tak nazyvaemoi 'antisovetskoi trotskistskoi voennoi organizatsii' v krasnoi armii," 57.

29. RGVA, f. 9, op. 29, d. 318, l. 11. According to another set of figures, from June to November 1937, a total of 15,140 commanders and political commissars were discharged from the army; see Kniaz'kov et al., *Voennyi sovet pri narodnom komissare oborony SSSR: noiabr' 1937 g.*, 5.

30. Larger numbers of crimes were recorded across the board in the Red Army in 1937 in comparison to 1936; see RGVA, f. 9, op. 29, d. 383, l. 73.

31. RGVA, f. 9, op. 29, d. 318, l. 11.

32. Ibid., l. 22.

33. Ibid., l. 90. Brandenberger quotes the same exchange between Stalin and Prokofiev, and his translation is used here; Brandenberger, *Propaganda State in Crisis*, 191.

34. See, e.g., RGVA, 33987, op. 3, d. 1085, ll. 1–6, 35, 57, 99, 133, 323; f. 9, op. 29, d. 358, ll. 5–6, 10, 21–22, 37, 49, 72, 196. Also see similar reports compiled by a senior political commissar, Kuznetsov, ll. 94, 118, 140, 176. Pavel Smirnov served six months as head of the political administration before being replaced by Mekhlis in December 1937. Mekhlis also became deputy people's commissar for defense. Smirnov then served as head of the navy until his arrest in June 1938.

35. Kniaz'kov et al., *Voennyi sovet pri narodnom komissare oborony SSSR: noiabr' 1937 g.*, 24, 324–325.

36. Getty and Naumov, *Road to Terror*, 493.

37. Ibid., 496.

38. Goldman, *Inventing the Enemy*, 251.

39. Ibid., 262–264.

40. RGVA, f. 33987, op. 3, d. 1085, l. 49.

41. Ibid., l. 70.

42. Ibid.

43. For more detail on the broader moves to curtail repression, see Getty and Naumov, *Road to Terror*, 528.

44. RGVA, f. 33987, op. 3, d. 1085, l. 101.

45. Ibid., l. 104.

46. Ibid., l. 116.

47. Ibid.

48. Ibid.

49. Reese, *Stalin's Reluctant Soldiers*, 137–138.

50. "Delo o tak nazyvaemoi 'antisovetskoi trotskistskoi voennoi organizatsii' v krasnoi armii," 56. Ezhov received information in May 1937 concerning Dybenko's supposed support of Trotsky, and Vitalii Primakov incrimated him just before the June 1937 military trial.

51. RGASPI, f. 558, op. 11, d. 1120, l. 104.

52. Ibid., ll. 103–109.

53. Getty and Naumov, *Road to Terror*, 521–523; Khaustov and Samuelson, *Stalin*, 216.

54. Budennyi was also incriminated by I. P. Apanasenko, the commander of the Central Asian Military District, in a denunciation sent in early February 1938. According to Apanasenko, Budennyi had been close to Iakir and Uborevich. Further incriminating information about Budennyi came from Apanasenko later in November. However, this "evidence" was either not convincing or Stalin may have personally intervened to save Budennyi, as no arrest followed. See Pechenkin, *Gibel' voennoi elity*, 126, 134.

55. For a fuller list, see "Delo o tak nazyvaemoi 'antisovetskoi trotskistskoi voennoi organizatsii' v krasnoi armii," 59–60.

56. Shearer, *Policing Stalin's Socialism*, 368.

57. Bobylev et al., *Voennyi sovet pri narodnom komissare oborony SSSR, 1938, 1940 gg.: dokumenty i materialy*, 236.

58. Ibid.

59. Ibid.

60. Ibid., 238.

61. Ibid.

62. Reese, *Stalin's Reluctant Soldiers*, 146.

63. Ibid., 135.

64. Different totals include 33,460, 36,761 and 38,352. See "M. N. Tukhachevskii i 'voenno-fashistskii zagovor'" (1998), 113–117. According to Reese, between 1937 and May 1940, 34,301 leaders from the Red army, navy, and air

force were discharged, but 11,596 of these were eventually reinstated. Reese, *Stalin's Reluctant Soldiers*, 75, 210.

65. "M. N. Tukhachevskii i 'voenno-fashistskii zagovor'" (1998), 114. Reese has the same number of arrests for 1937 but lists 5,032 for 1938. Reese, *Stalin's Reluctant Soldiers*, 143.

66. Reese, *Stalin's Reluctant Soldiers*, 143. For another discussion of these figures, see Pechenkin, *Gibel' voennoi elity*, 148–156. Pechenkin details that from 1 March 1937 to 1 March 1938, 22,260 people were discharged from the army, 14,140 for political reasons.

67. Getty and Naumov, *Road to Terror*, 447.

68. Hagenloh, *Stalin's Police*, 3. For the national operations, see Shcherbakova, *Nakazannyi narod;* Morris, "Polish Terror."

69. Details of the first mass operation were first published in *Trud* in 1992.

70. Khlevniuk, *Master of the House*, 167.

71. Khlevniuk, "Objectives of the Great Terror," 158–176; Khlevniuk, *Master of the House*. See also Kuromiya, *Voices of the Dead;* Kuromiya, "Accounting for the Great Terror."

72. See Khlevniuk, *Master of the House*, esp. 201–202.

73. "Materialy fevral'skogo-martovskogo plenuma TsK VKP(b) 1937 goda" (1994), 15–16.

74. See Shearer, "Crime and Social Disorder"; Shearer, *Policing Stalin's Socialism;* Hagenloh, "Socially Harmful Elements"; Hagenloh, *Stalin's Police*.

75. Getty, "Excesses are not permitted," 113–138.

76. Getty and Naumov, *Road to Terror*, 444–490; Getty, "Excesses are not permitted," 117, 127. For another account of the mass operations (one that downplays the threat of war), see Junge and Binner, *Kak terror stal bol'shim*.

77. Shearer emphasizes this point. See Shearer, *Policing Stalin's Socialism*, 298.

78. Getty emphasizes this point in "Pre-election Fever," 218.

79. Khaustov and Samuelson, *Stalin*, 332–335.

80. Hagenloh, *Stalin's Police*, 245.

81. See Danilov et al., *Tragediia sovetskoi derevni*, vol. 5, bk. 1, 258.

82. RGASPI, f. 588, op. 11, d. 203, l. 62.

83. Danilov et al., *Tragediia sovetskoi derevni*, vol. 5, bk. 1, 306–308.

84. Ibid., 258.

85. Hagenloh, *Stalin's Police*, 245–246.

86. For Order No. 00447, see Danilov et al., *Tragediia sovetskoi derevni*, vol. 5, bk. 1, 330–337.

87. Shearer, *Policing Stalin's Socialism*, 328–329.

88. Rittersporn, "Terror and Soviet Legality," 182–183.

89. "Materialy fevral'skogo-martovskogo plenuma TsK VKP(b) 1937 goda" (1994), 15–16.

90. Okhotin and Roginskii, "Iz istorii 'nemtskoi operatsii,'" 37–38.

91. Ibid., 52.

92. Shearer, *Policing Stalin's Socialism*, 349.

93. Getty, "Excesses are not permitted," 126; Getty, "Pre-election Fever," 228–230.

Conclusion

1. Chuev, *Molotov Remembers,* 280.
2. Ibid., 254.
3. Ibid.
4. Ibid., 280.
5. Dimitrov, *Diary,* 70; Getty and Naumov, *Road to Terror,* 446.

Bibliography

Archival Sources

Rossiiskii gosudarstvennyi voennyi arkhiv (Russian State Military Archive [RGVA])

Fond, opis', delo
f. 4, op. 10, d. 32; 76
f. 4, op. 15, d. 12; 13
f. 4, op. 14, d. 70; 74; 81; 84; 145; 393; 1366; 1413; 1414; 1684; 1820
f. 4, op. 19, d. 13; 16; 18
f. 6, op. 10, d. 112
f. 9, op. 8, d. 70; 147
f. 9, op. 9, d. 229
f. 9, op. 26, d. 446
f. 9, op. 28, d. 287; 297; 688
f. 9, op. 29, d. 10; 14; 15; 16; 27; 29; 178; 231; 260; 263; 281; 283; 291; 313; 318; 319; 320; 340; 358
f. 33987, op. 2, d. 174
f. 33987, op. 3, d. 174; 186; 227; 258; 293; 295; 302; 615; 851; 872; 965; 992; 995; 1023; 1085
f. 33988, op. 2, d. 528
f. 33988, op. 3, d. 69; 106
f. 33988, op. 3c, d. 69
f. 37837, op. 9, d. 42
f. 37837, op. 10, d. 20; 23; 26; 32; 76; 90; 91
f. 37837, op. 11, d. 120
f. 37837, op. 19, d. 19; 29
f. 37837, op. 21, d. 10; 21; 39; 40; 52; 55; 63; 64; 80; 82; 94; 99; 100; 107; 109
f. 37837, op. 22, d. 1
Rossiiskii gosudarstvennyi arkhiv sotsial'no-politicheskoi istorii (Russian State Archive of Socio-Political History [RGASPI])

Fond, opis,' delo
f. 17, op. 109, d. 84; 90; 117
f. 74, op. 2, d. 19; 23; 37; 38; 49; 51; 117; 118
f. 74, op. 21, d. 42
f. 82, op. 2, d. 799
f. 588, op. 11, d. 18; 36; 50; 51; 71; 90; 93; 185; 186; 188; 203; 446; 447; 726; 778; 1120; 1139; 1180; 5410; 5466; 5733
f. 671, op. 1, d. 142

UK National Archives
   National Archives, Public Record Office, KV 2/404 (Witovt Kazimirovich
      PUTNA)

Newspapers

   Krasnaia zvezda
   Manchester Guardian
   New York Times

Works Cited

Adams, Arthur. *Bolsheviks in the Ukraine: The Second Campaign, 1918–1919.* New
   Haven, CT: Yale University Press, 1963.
Afanas'ev, Iu. N., et al., eds. *Istoriia Stalinskogo Gulag: konets 1920-kh-pervaia
   polovina 1950-kh godov; sobranie dokumentov v semi tomakh.* 7 vols. Moscow:
   Rosspen, 2004–2005.
Alexandrov, Victor. *The Tukhachevsky Affair.* London: Macdonald, 1963.
Alferov, Zh. I., et al., eds. *Akademicheskoe delo 1929–1931 gg: dokumenty i materialy
   sledstvennogo dela, sfabrikovannogo OGPU,* 2 vols. Saint Petersburg: Biblioteka
   Rossiiskoi akademiia nauk, 1993–1998.
Anderson, K. M., et al., eds. *Reforma v krasnoi armii: dokumenty i materialy 1923–
   1928 gg.* 2 vols. Moscow: Letnii sad, 2006.
———. *Stenogrammy zasedannii Politbiuro TsK RKP(b)—VKP(b) 1923–1938 gg.* 3
   vols. Moscow: Rosspen, 2007.
———. *Voennyi sovet pri narodnom komissare oborony SSSR: 1–4 iiunia 1937 goda:
   dokumenty i materialy.* Moscow: Rosspen, 2008.
Andrew, Christopher, and Julie Elkner. "Stalin and Foreign Intelligence." *Total-
   itarian Movements and Political Religions* 4, no. 1 (2003): 69–94.
Andrew, Christopher, and Oleg Gordievsky. *KGB: The Inside Story of Its Foreign
   Operations from Lenin to Gorbachev.* London: Hodder & Stoughton, 1990.
Anfilov, Viktor. "Semen Mikhailovich Budenny." In *Stalin's Generals,* edited by
   Harold Shukman, 57–66. London: Weidenfeld & Nicolson, 1993.
Arendt, Hannah. *The Origins of Totalitarianism.* London: Allen & Unwin, 1958.
Armstrong, John A. *The Politics of Totalitarianism: The Communist Party of the Soviet
   Union from 1934 to the Present.* New York: Random House, 1961.
Artizov, A., et al., eds. *Reabilitatsiia: kak eto bylo.* 3 vols. Moscow: Mezhdunarodnyi
   fond "Demokratiia," 2003.
Beneš, Eduard. *Memoirs of Dr. Eduard Beneš: From Munich to New War and New
   Victory.* London: Allen & Unwin, 1954.
Benvenuti, Francesco. *The Bolsheviks and the Red Army, 1918–1922.* Cambridge:
   Cambridge University Press, 1988.
Best, Anthony. "Imperial Japan." In *The Origins of World War Two: The Debate*

Continues, edited by Robert Boyce and Joseph Maiolo, 52–69. Basingstoke: Palgrave, 2003.

Blackstock, Paul W. "The Tukhachevsky Affair." *Russian Review* 28 (1969): 171–190.

Bobylev, P. N., et al., eds. *Voennyi sovet pri narodnom komissare oborony SSSR, dekabr' 1934 g.: dokumenty i materialy.* Moscow: Rosspen, 2007.

———. *Voennyi sovet pri narodnom komissare oborony SSSR, dekabr 1935 g.: dokumenty i materialy.* Moscow: Rosspen, 2008.

———. *Voennyi sovet pri narodnom komissare oborony SSSR, 1938, 1940 gg.: dokumenty i materialy.* Moscow: Rosspen, 2006.

Brackman, Roman. *The Secret File of Joseph Stalin: A Hidden Life.* London: Frank Cass, 2001.

Bradley, J. F. N. *Civil War in Russia, 1917–1920.* London: B. T. Batsford, 1975.

Brandenberger, David. *Propaganda State in Crisis: Soviet Ideology, Indoctrination, and Terror under Stalin, 1927–1941.* New Haven, CT: Yale University Press, 2012.

Brovkin, Vladimir. *Behind the Front Lines of the Civil War: Political Parties and Social Movements in Russia, 1918–1922.* Princeton, NJ: Princeton University Press, 1994.

Brown, Stephen. "Communists and the Red Cavalry: The Political Education of the Konarmiia in the Russian Civil War, 1918–1920." *Slavonic and East European Review* 74, no. 1 (1995): 82–99.

———. "Lenin, Stalin, and the Failure of the Red Army in the Soviet–Polish War of 1920." *War and Society* 14, no. 2 (1996): 35–47.

Brzezinski, Zbigniew. *The Permanent Purge: Politics in Soviet Totalitarianism.* Cambridge, MA: Harvard University Press, 1956.

Butt, V. P., ed. *The Russian Civil War: Documents from the Soviet Archives.* Basingstoke: Macmillan, 1996.

Chaney, Otto Preston. *Zhukov.* Norman: University of Oklahoma Press, 1996.

Chase, William. *Enemies Within the Gates? The Comintern and the Stalinist Repression, 1934–1939.* New Haven, CT: Yale University Press, 2002.

———. "Stalin as Producer: The Moscow Show Trials and the Construction of Mortal Threats." In *Stalin: A New History,* edited by Sarah Davies and James Harris, 226–248. Cambridge: Cambridge University Press, 2005.

Chebrikov, Viktor. *Istoriia sovetskikh organov gosudarstvennoi bezopasnosti: uchebnik.* Moscow: KGB, 1977.

Cherushev, Nikolai. *1937 god, byl li zagovor voennykh?* Moscow: Veche, 2007.

Chuev, Feliks. *Molotov Remembers: Inside Kremlin Politics—Conversations with Feliks Chuev.* Chicago: I. R. Dee, 1993.

Churchill, Winston. *The Second World War.* 6 vols. London: Cassell, 1949.

Conquest, Robert. *Great Terror: Stalin's Purge of the Thirties.* London: Macmillan, 1973.

Courtois, Stéphane, ed. *The Black Book of Communism: Crimes, Terror, Repression.* Cambridge, MA: Harvard University Press, 1999.

Croll, Neil Harvey. "Mikhail Tukhachevsky in the Russian Civil War." PhD thesis, University of Glasgow, 2002.

Danilov, V. "Sovershenstvovanie sistemy tsentral'nikh organov voennogo rukovodstva v 1929–1939 gg." *Voenno-istoricheskii zhurnal* 6 (1982): 74–70.

Danilov, V., et al., ed. *Tragediia sovetskoi derevni: kollektivizatsiia i raskulachivanie: dokumenty i materialy v 5 tomakh, 1927–1939.* 5 vols. Moscow: Rossiiskaia politicheskaia entsiklopediia, 1999–2006.

Davies, Joseph E. *Mission to Moscow.* 2 vols. London: Gollancz, 1942.

Davies, Norman. *White Eagle, Red Star: The Polish–Soviet War, 1919–1920.* London: Macdonald, 1972.

Davies, R. W. "Changing Economic Systems: An Overview." In Davies, Harrison, and Wheatcroft, *Economic Transformation of the Soviet Union,* 1–23.

———. *Crisis and Progress in the Soviet Economy, 1931–1933.* Basingstoke: Macmillan, 1996.

———. "Industry." In Davies, Harrison, and Wheatcroft, *Economic Transformation of the Soviet Union,* 131–157.

———. "Planning for Mobilisation: The 1930s." In *Guns and Rubles: The Defence Industry in the Stalinist State,* edited by Mark Harrison, 118–155. New Haven, CT: Yale University, Sheridan Books, 2008.

———. *The Socialist Offensive: The Collectivisation of Soviet Agriculture, 1929–1930.* London: Macmillan, 1980.

———. "The Syrtsov–Lominadze Affair." *Soviet Studies* 33, no. 1 (1981): 29–50.

Davies, R. W., Mark Harrison, and S. G. Wheatcroft, eds. *The Economic Transformation of the Soviet Union, 1913–1945.* Cambridge: Cambridge University Press, 1994.

Davies, R. W., and Stephen Wheatcroft. "Agriculture." In Davies, Harrison, and Wheatcroft, *Economic Transformation of the Soviet Union,* 106–130.

Davies, R. W., et al., eds. *The Stalin–Kaganovich Correspondence, 1931–36.* New Haven, CT: Yale University Press, 2003.

Davies, Sarah. *Popular Opinion in Stalin's Russia: Terror, Propaganda, and Dissent, 1934–1941.* Cambridge: Cambridge University Press, 1997.

———. "'Us Against Them': Social Identity in Russia, 1934–41." *Russian Review* 56, no. 1 (1997): 70–89.

"Delo o tak nazyvaemoi 'antisovetskoi trotskistskoi voennoi organizatsii' v krasnoi armii." *Izvestiia TsK* 4 (1989): 42–73.

Denningkhaus, Viktor. *V teni "Bolshogo Brata": Zapadnye natsionalnye menshinstva v SSSR (1917–1938 gg.).* Moscow: Rosspen, 2011.

Deutscher, Isaac. *The Prophet Unarmed: Trotsky, 1921–1929.* London: Oxford University Press, 1960.

Diakov, Iu. L., and T. S. Bushueva. *Fashistskii mech kovalsia v SSSR: krasnaia armiia i reikhsver: tainoe sotrudnichestvo, 1922–1933: neizvestnye dokumenty.* Moscow: Sovetskaia Rossiia, 1992.

Di Biagio, Anna. "Moscow, the Comintern, and the War Scare, 1926–28." In Pons and Romano, *Russia in the Age of Wars,* 83–103.

Dimitrov, Georgi. *The Diary of Georgi Dimitrov, 1933–1949.* Edited by Ivo Banac. New Haven, CT: Yale University Press, 2003.

Documents on German Foreign Policy, 1918–1945. Series C (1933–1937): The Third

Reich: First Phase, vol. 1, *January 1930–October 14, 1933.* London: H.M.S.O., 1957; vol. 2, *October 14, 1933—June 13, 1934.* London: H.M.S.O., 1959.

Durachinski, E., and A. N. Sakharov, eds. *Sovetsko-pol'skie otnosheniia v politich-eskikh usloviiakh Evropi 30-kh godov XX stoletiia.* Moscow: Nauka, 2001.

Duranty, Walter. *USSR: The Story of Soviet Russia.* Melbourne: Hamish Hamilton, 1945.

Erickson, John. "Origins of the Red Army." In *Revolutionary Russia,* edited by Richard Pipes, 224–259. Cambridge, MA: Harvard University Press, 1968.

———. *The Soviet High Command: A Military–Political History, 1918–1941.* London: Macmillan, 1962.

Ershov, V. F., and I. S. Shinkaruk. "Rossiiskaia voennaia emigratsiia i ee pechat' v 1920–1939 gg." In *Ocherki antibol'shevistskoi emigratsii, 1920–1940-kh gg.,* edited by S. S. Ippolitov, 2:96–166. 4 vols. Moscow: Izdatel'stvo ippolitova, 2002.

Ershov, V. F., et al. "Ofitsery i komanduiushchie." In *Russkie bez otechestva: ocherki antibol'shevistskoi emigratsii 20–40-kh godov,* edited by S. V. Karpenko et al., 122–176. Moscow: Rossiiskii gosudarstvennyi gumanitarnyi universitet, 2000.

Fedotoff-White, Dmitri. *The Growth of the Red Army.* Princeton, NJ: Princeton University Press, 1944.

Fel'shtinskii, Iurii, and Georgii Cherniavskii. *Lev Trotskii. Kniga tret'ia. Oppozitsioner, 1923–1929 gg.* Moscow: Tsentrpoligraf, 2012.

Ferris, John. "Intelligence." In *The Origins of World War Two: The Debate Continues,* edited by Robert Boyce and Joseph Maiolo, 308–329. Basingstoke: Palgrave, 2003.

Figes, Orlando. *A People's Tragedy: The Russian Revolution, 1891–1924.* London: Bodley Head, 2014.

———. "The Red Army and Mass Mobilisation during the Russian Civil War, 1918–1920." In *Warfare in Europe, 1919–1938,* edited by Geoffrey Jensen, 297–340. Aldershot: Ashgate, 2008.

———. *The Whisperers.* London: Penguin, 2008.

Fitzpatrick, Sheila. *Everyday Stalinism: Ordinary Life in Extraordinary Times—Soviet Russia in the 1930s.* New York: Oxford University Press, 1990.

———. *Stalin's Peasants: Resistance and Survival in the Russian Village after Collectivization.* New York: Oxford University Press, 1994.

———. *Tear Off the Masks! Identity and Imposture in Twentieth-Century Russia.* Princeton, NJ: Princeton University Press, 2005.

Fitzpatrick, Sheila, ed. *Cultural Revolution in Russia, 1928–1931.* Bloomington: Indiana University Press, 1978.

Friedrich, Carl, and Zbigniew Brzezinski. *Totalitarian Dictatorship and Autocracy.* Cambridge, MA: Harvard University Press, 1956.

Getty, J. Arch. "'Excesses Are Not Permitted': Mass Terror and Stalinist Governance in the Late 1930s." *Russian Review* 61, no. 1 (2002): 113–138.

———. *Origins of the Great Purges: The Soviet Communist Party Reconsidered, 1933–1938.* Cambridge: Cambridge University Press, 1991.

———. "The Politics of Repression Revisited." In *Stalinist Terror: New Perspectives*, edited by J. Arch Getty and Roberta T. Manning, 40–64. Cambridge: Cambridge University Press, 1993.

———. *Practicing Stalinism: Bolsheviks, Boyars, and the Persistence of Tradition*. New Haven, CT: Yale University Press, 2013.

———. "Pre-election Fever: The Origins of the 1937 Mass Operations." In *The Anatomy of Terror: Political Violence under Stalin*, edited by James Harris, 216–235. Oxford: Oxford University Press, 2013.

Getty, J. Arch, and Oleg Naumov. *Yezhov: The Rise of Stalin's "Iron Fist."* New Haven, CT: Yale University Press, 2008.

Getty, J. Arch, and Oleg Naumov, eds. *The Road to Terror: Stalin and the Self-Destruction of the Bolsheviks, 1932–1939*. New Haven, CT: Yale University Press, 1999.

Goldin, Vladislav. *Armiia v izgnanii stranitsy istorii russkogo obshche-voinskogo soiuza*. Arkhangelsk: Solti, 2002.

———. *Rossiiskaia voennaia emigratsiia i sovetskie spetssluzhby v 20-e godu XX veka*. Saint Petersburg: Poltorak, 2010.

Goldman, Wendy Z. *Inventing the Enemy: Denunciation and Terror in Stalin's Russia*. Cambridge: Cambridge University Press, 2011.

———. *Terror and Democracy in the Age of Stalin: The Social Dynamics of Repression*. Cambridge: Cambridge University Press, 2007.

Gorlov, Sergei. *Sovershenno sekretno: Moskva–Berlin, 1920–1933: voenno-politicheskie otnosheniia mezhdu SSSR i Germaniei*. Moscow: IVI RAN, 1999.

Gorodetsky, Gabriel. "The Formulation of Soviet Foreign Policy: Ideology and *Realpolik*." In *Soviet Foreign Policy, 1917–1991: A Retrospective*, edited by Gabriel Gorodetsky, 30–44. London: Frank Cass, 1994.

Gregory, Paul. *Terror by Quota: State Security from Lenin to Stalin (An Archival Study)*. New Haven, CT: Yale University Press, 2009.

Hagenloh, Paul. "Socially Harmful Elements and the Great Terror." In *Stalinism: New Directions*, edited by Sheila Fitzpatrick, 286–308. London: Routledge, 2000.

———. *Stalin's Police: Public Order and Mass Repression in the USSR, 1926–1941*. Baltimore, MD: Woodrow Wilson Center Press, 2009.

Harris, James. "Encircled by Enemies: Stalin's Perceptions of the Capitalist World, 1918–1941." *Journal of Strategic Studies* 30, no. 3 (2007): 513–545.

———. *The Great Urals: Regionalism and the Evolution of the Soviet System*. Ithaca, NY: Cornell University Press, 1999.

———. "Intelligence and Threat Perception: Defending the Revolution, 1917–1937." In *The Anatomy of Terror: Political Violence under Stalin*, edited by James Harris, 29–43. Oxford: Oxford University Press, 2013.

Harrison, Mark, and R. W. Davies. "The Soviet Military–Economic Effort During the Second Five-Year Plan (1933–1937)." *Europe–Asia Studies* 49, no. 3 (1997): 369–406.

Harrison, Mark, and Andrei Markevich. "Russia's Home Front, 1914–1922: The Economy." CAGE Online Working Paper Series. http://dx.doi.org/10.2139/ssrn.2001002.

Harrison, R. W. *The Russian Way of War: Operational Art, 1904–1940.* Lawrence: University Press of Kansas, 2001.

Haslam, Jonathan. *The Soviet Union and the Threat from the East, 1933–41: Moscow, Tokyo, and the Prelude to the Pacific War.* Basingstoke: Macmillan, 1992.

Hincks, D. "Support for the Opposition in Moscow in the Party Discussion of 1923–1924." *Soviet Studies* 44. no. 1 (1992): 137–151.

Holquist, Peter. "To Count, to Extract, and to Exterminate: Populations Statistics and Population Politics in Late Imperial and Soviet Russia." In *A State of Nations: Empire and Nation-Making in the Age of Lenin and Stalin,* edited by Ronald Grigor Suny and Terry Martin, 111–144. Oxford: Oxford University Press, 2001.

Ilič, Melanie, ed. *Stalin's Terror: Revisited.* Basingstoke: Palgrave Macmillan, 2006.

Jansen, Marc, and Nikita Petrov. *"Stalinskii pitomets"—Nikolai Ezhov.* Moscow: Rosspen, 2008.

———. *Stalin's Loyal Executioner: People's Commissar Nikolai Ezhov, 1895–1940.* Stanford, CA: Hoover Institution Press, 2002.

Junge, Marc, and Rolf Binner. *Kak terror stal bol'shim: sekretnyi prikaz no. 00447 i tekhnologiia ego ispolneniia.* Moscow: Airo-XX, 2003.

Junge, Marc, et al., eds. *Stalinizm v sovetskoi provintsii: 1937–1938 gg.: massovaia operatsiia na osnove prikaz No. 00447.* Moscow: Rossiiskaia politicheskaia entsiklopedia, 2009.

Kantor, Iuliia. *Voina i mir Mikhaila Tukhachevskogo.* Moscow: Ogonek, 2005.

———. *Zakliataia druzhba: sekretnoe sotrudnichestvo SSSR i Germanii v 1920–1930-e gody.* Saint Petersburg: Piter, 2009.

Kariaeva, T. F., et al., eds. *Partiino-politicheskaia rabota v krasnoi armii: dokumenty 1921–1929 gg.* Moscow: Voennoe izdatel'stvo Ministerstva oborony SSSR, 1981.

———. *Partiino-politicheskaia rabota v krasnoi armii: dokumenty, iiul 1929 g.–mai 1941 g.* Moscow: Voennoe izdatel'stvo Ministerstva oborony, 1985.

Kavtaradze, A. G. *Voennye spetsialisty na sluzhbe respubliki sovetov, 1917–1920 gg.* Moscow: Nauka, 1988.

Ken, Oleg. *Mobilizatsionnoe planirovanie i politicheskie resheniia, konets 1920— seredina 1930-kh godov.* Saint Petersburg: Evropeiskii universitet S. Peterburga, 2002.

Khaustov, Vladimir, and Lennart Samuelson. *Stalin, NKVD i repressii 1936–1938 gg.* Moscow: Rosspen, 2010.

Khaustov, Vladimir, et al., eds. *Lubianka: Stalin i glavnoe upravlenie gosbezopasnosti NKVD, 1937–1938.* Moscow: Mezhdunarodnyi fond "Demokratiia," 2004.

———. *Lubianka: Stalin i VChK-GPU-OGPU-NKVD, ianvar' 1922-dekabr' 1936.* Moscow: Mezhdunarodnyi fond "Demokratiia," 2003.

Khaustov, Vladimir. "Inostrantsy i sovetskie grazhdane inostrannogo proiskhozhdeniia—potentsial'nye 'agenty burzhuaznykh razvedok.'" In *Istoricheskie chteniia na Lubianke, 1997–2007,* edited by Aleksandr Zdanovich et al., 219–227. Moscow: Kuchkovo Pole, 2008.

———. "Repressii protiv sovetskikh nemtsev do nachala massovoi operatsii 1937 g." In *Nakazannyi narod: po materialam konferentsii "Repressii protiv rossiiskikh nemtsev v Sovetskom Soiuze v kontekste sovetskoi natsional'noi politiki,"* edited by I. L. Shcherbakova, 35–75. Moscow: Zven'ia, 1999.

Khlevniuk, Oleg. *Master of the House: Stalin and His Inner Circle.* New Haven, CT: Yale University Press, 2009.

———. "The Objectives of the Great Terror, 1937–1938." In *Soviet History, 1917–53: Essays in Honour of R. W. Davies,* edited by Julian Cooper et al., 158–176. Basingstoke: Macmillan, 1995.

———. *Politbiuro: mekhanizmy politicheskoi vlasti v 1930-e gody.* Moscow: Rosspen, 2001.

Khlevnyuk, Oleg. "Economic Officials in the Great Terror, 1936–38." In *Stalin's Terror Revisited,* edited by Melanie Ilič, 38–67. Basingstoke: Palgrave Macmillan, 2006.

Khristoforov, V. S., et al., eds. *Tainy diplomatii Tret'ego reikha: germanskie diplomaty, rukovoditeli zarubezhnykh voennykh missii, voennye i politseiskie attashe v sovetskom plenu, dokumenty iz sledstvennykh del, 1944–1955.* Moscow: Mezhdunarodnyi fond "Demokratiia," 2011.

Kirmel', N. S. *Belogvardeiskie spetssluzhby v grazhdanskoi voine, 1918–1922 gg.* Moscow: Kuchkovo Pole, 2008.

Kniaz'kov, A. S., et al., eds. *Voennyi sovet pri narodnom komissare oborony SSSR, oktiabr' 1936 g.: dokumenty i materialy.* Moscow: Rosspen, 2009.

———. *Voennyi sovet pri narodnom komissare oborony SSSR: noiabr' 1937 g.: dokumenty i materialy.* Moscow: Rosspen, 2006.

Kolkowicz, Roman. *The Soviet Military and the Communist Party.* Princeton, NJ: Princeton University Press, 1967.

Kol'tiukov, A. A., et al., eds. *Russkaia voennaia emigratsiia 20-kh-40-kh godov: dokumenty i materialy,* 5 vols. Moscow: RGGU, 2007–2010.

Koppers, André A. "On the Use of Forged Documents: 'Die russischen Geheimdokumente,' 1925–1929." *Jahrbücher für Geschichte Osteuropas* 37, no. 2 (1989): 264–269.

Kosheleva, L., et al., eds. *Pis'ma I. V. Stalina V. M. Molotovu: 1925–1936 gg.: sbornik dokumentov.* Moscow: Rossiia molodaia, 1995.

Kotkin, Stephen. *Magnetic Mountain: Stalinism as Civilization.* Berkeley: University of California Press, 1995.

———. *Stalin.* Volume 1, *Paradoxes of Power, 1878–1928,* London: Allen Lane, 2014.

Kudriashov, Sergei, ed. *Krasnaia armiia v 1920-e.* Moscow: Vestnik arkhiva Prezidenta Rossiiskoi Federatsii, 2007.

Kuromiya, Hiroaki. "Accounting for the Great Terror." *Jahrbücher für Geschichte Osteuropas* 53, no. 1 (2005): 86–100.

———. *Voices of the Dead: Stalin's Great Terror in the 1930s.* New Haven, CT: Yale University Press, 2007.

Kuromiya, Hiroaki, and Georges Mamoulia. "Anti-Russian and Anti-Soviet Subversion: The Caucasian–Japanese Nexus, 1904–1945." *Europe–Asia Studies* 61, no. 8 (2009): 1414–1440.

Kvashonkin, A. V., ed. *Sovetskoe rukovodstvo perepiska, 1928–1941.* Moscow: Rosspen, 1999.

Kvashonkin, A. V., et al., eds. *Bol'shevistskoe rukovodstvo. perepiska, 1912–1927.* Moscow: Rosspen, 1996.

Latyshev, A. G. *Rassekrechennyi Lenin.* Moscow: Izdatel'stvo MART, 1996.

Lazarev, S. Ie., and V. S. Mil'bakh. "Politicheskie repressii v voennykh aka-demiiakh Leningrada v 1930–1938 gg." *Noveishaia istorii Rossii* 2 (2012): 100–113.

Leggett, George. *The Cheka: Lenin's Political Police: The All-Russian Extraordinary Commission for Combating Counter-revolution and Sabotage (December 1917 to February 1922).* Oxford: Clarendon, 1981.

Lenin, Vladimir. *Imperialism: The Highest Stage of Capitalism—A Popular Outline.* London: Pluto Press, 1996.

———. *Polnoe sobranie sochinenii.* 55 vols. Moscow: Gosudarstvennoe izdatel'stvo politicheskoi literatury, 1941–1968.

Lenoe, Matthew. "Did Stalin Kill Kirov, and Does It Matter?" *Journal of Modern History* 74, no. 2 (2002): 352–380.

———. "Fear, Loathing, Conspiracy and the Kirov Murder as Impetus for the Terror." In *The Anatomy of Terror: Political Violence under Stalin,* edited by James Harris, 195–215. Oxford: Oxford University Press, 2013.

———. *The Kirov Murder and Soviet History.* New Haven, CT: Yale University Press, 2010.

Leskov, Valentin. *Stalin i zagovor Tukhachevskogo.* Moscow: Veche, 2003.

Lincoln, Bruce. *Red Victory: A History of the Russian Civil War.* London: Simon & Schuster, 1991.

Lukes, Igor. "The Tukhachevsky Affair and President Edvard Beneš." *Diplomacy and Statecraft* 7, no. 3 (1996): 505–529.

Luzan, N. N. *Voennaia kontrrazvedka: tainaia voina.* Moscow: Kuchkovo Pole, 2010.

Mackintosh, Malcolm. *Juggernaut: A History of the Soviet Armed Forces.* London: Secker & Warburg, 1967.

Main, Steven. "The Red Army and the Soviet Military and Political Leadership in the Late 1920s: The Case of 'Inner-Army Opposition of 1928.'" *Europe–Asia Studies* 47, no. 2 (1995): 337–355.

———. "The Red Army during the Russian Civil War, 1918–1920: The Main Results of the August 1920 Military Census." *Journal of Slavic Military Studies* 7, no. 4 (1994): 800–808.

Maiolo, Joseph. *Cry Havoc: The Arms Race and the Second World War, 1931–1941.* London: John Murray, 2010.

Maiskii, Ivan. *Dnevnik diplomata: London 1934–1943: v dvukh knigakh.* 2 vols. Moscow: Nauka, 2006.

———. *Vospominaniia sovetskogo posla.* 3 vols. Moscow: Nauka, 1964.

"Materialy fevral'skogo-martovskogo plenuma TsK VKP(b) 1937 goda." *Voprosy istorii* 3 (1995): 3–14.

"Materialy fevral'skogo-martovskogo plenuma TsK VKP(b) 1937 goda." *Voprosy istorii* 4–5 (1992): 3–56.

"Materialy fevral'skogo-martovskogo plenuma TsK VKP(b) 1937 goda." *Voprosy istorii* 10 (1994): 3–27.

May, Ernest R., ed. *Knowing One's Enemies: Intelligence Assessment before the Two World Wars*. Princeton, NJ: Princeton University Press, 1984.

McLoughlin, Barry. "Mass Operations of the NKVD, 1937–8: A Survey." In *Stalin's Terror*, edited by Barry McLoughlin and Kevin McDermott, 118–152. Basingstoke: Palgrave Macmillan, 2002.

Mil'bakh, V. S. *Osobaia Krasnoznamennaia Dal'nevostochnaia armiia (Krasnoznamennyi Dal'nevostochnyi front). Politicheskie repressii komandno-nachal'stvuiushchego sostava, 1937–1938 gg.* Saint Petersburg: Izd-vo S.-Peterburskogo Universiteta, 2007.

———. "Repression in the Red Army in the Far East." *Journal of Slavic Military Studies* 16, no. 4 (2003): 58–130.

Mil'bakh, V. S., A. M. Grigorian, and A. N. Chernavskii. *Politicheskie repressii komandno-nachal'stvuiushchego sostava, 1937–1938: Leningradskii voennyi okrug.* Saint Petersburg: Izd-vo S.-Peterburskogo Universiteta, 2013.

Minakov, Sergei. *1937: zagovor byl!* Moscow: Iauza; Eksmo, 2010.

———. *Sovetskaia voennaia elita 20-kh godov: sostav, evoliutsiia, sotsiokul'turnye osobennosti i politicheskaia rol'.* Orel: Orelizdat, 2000.

———. *Stalin i ego marshal.* Moscow: Iauza; Eksmo, 2004.

———. *Stalin i zagovor generalov.* Moscow: Eksmo, 2005.

———. *Za otvorotom marshalskoi shineli.* Orel: Orelizdat, 1999.

"M. N. Tukhachevskii i 'voenno-fashistskii zagovor.'" *Voenno-istoricheskii arkhiv* 1 (1997): 149–255.

"M. N. Tukhachevskii i 'voenno-fashistskii zagovor.'" *Voenno-istoricheskii arkhiv* 2 (1998): 3–123.

Morris, James. "The Polish Terror: Spy Mania and Ethnic Cleansing in the Great Terror." *Europe–Asia Studies* 56, no. 5 (2004): 751–766.

Mozokhin, Oleg. *Pravo na repressii: vnesudebnye polnomochiia organov gosudarstvennoi bezopasnosti, 1918–1953.* Moscow: Kuchkovo Pole, 2006.

———. *Pravo na repressii: vnesudebnye polnomochiia organov gosudarstvennoi bezopasnosti: statisticheskie svedeniia o deiatel'nosti VChK-OGPU-NKVD-MGB SSSR (1918–1953).* Moscow: Kuchkovo Pole, 2011.

Murphy, Brian. *The Russian Civil War: Primary Sources.* Basingstoke: Macmillan, 2000.

Nation, R. Craig. *Black Earth, Red Star: A History of Soviet Security Policy, 1917–1991.* Ithaca, NY: Cornell University Press, 1992.

Neumann, Sigmund, and Mark von Hagen. "Engels and Marx on Revolution, War, and the Army in Society." In *Makers of Modern Strategy: From Machiavelli to the Nuclear Age*, edited by Peter Paret et al., 262–280. Princeton, NJ: Princeton University Press, 1986.

Naveh, Shimon. *In Pursuit of Military Excellence: The Evolution of Operational Theory.* London: Frank Cass, 1997.

———. "Tukhachevsky." In *Stalin's Generals*, edited by Harold Shukman, 255–274. London: Weidenfeld & Nicolson, 1993.

Nekrich, Aleksandr. *Pariahs, Partners, Predators: German-Soviet Relations, 1922–1941.* New York: Columbia University Press, 1997.

Nichols, Thomas M. *The Sacred Cause: Civil–Military Conflict over Soviet National Security, 1917–1992.* London: Cornell University Press, 1993.

O'Ballance, Edgar. *The Red Army.* London: Faber & Faber, 1964.

Okhotin, N., and A. Roginskii. "Iz istorii 'nemtskoi operatsii' NKVD 1937–1938 gg." In *Nakazannyi narod: po materialam konferentsii "Repressii protiv rossiiskikh nemtsev v Sovetskom Soiuze v kontekste sovetskoi natsional'noi politiki,"* edited by I. L. Shcherbakova, 35–74. Moscow: Zven'ia, 1999.

Osipova, Taisia. "Peasant Rebellions: Origin, Scope, Dynamics, and Consequences." In *The Bolsheviks in Russian Society: The Revolution and the Civil Wars,* edited by Vladimir Brovkin, 154–176. New Haven, CT: Yale University Press, 1997.

Overy, Richard, and Andrew Wheatcroft. *The Road to War.* Vintage Books: London, 2009.

Pechenkin, Aleksandr. *Gibel' voennoi elity, 1937–1938 gg.* Moscow: VZFEI, 2011.

———. *Stalin i voennyi sovet.* Moscow: Vserossiiskii zaochnyi finansovo-ekonomicheskii institut, 2007.

Petrov, Iuri. *Partiinoe stroitel'stvo v sovetskoi armii i flote, 1918–1961.* Moscow: Voenizdat, 1964.

Plekhanov, A. A., and A. M. Plekhanov. *Zheleznyi Feliks: belye piatna v biografii chekista.* Moscow: OLMA-Media grupp 2010.

Plekhanov, A. A., and A. M. Plekhanov, eds. *F. E. Dzerzhinskii—predsedatel' VChK—OGPU, 1917–1926.* Moscow: MFD; Materik, 2007.

Plekhanov, A. M. *VChK-OGPU v gody novoi ekonomicheskoi politiki, 1921–1928.* Moscow: Kuchkovo Pole, 2006.

Pons, Silvio. *Stalin and the Inevitable War, 1936–1941.* London: Frank Cass, 2002.

Pons, Silvio, and Andrea Romano, eds. *Russia in the Age of Wars, 1914–1945.* Milan: Feltrinelli, 2000.

Pozniakov, Vladimir. "The Enemy at the Gates: Soviet Military Intelligence in the Inter-war Period and its Forecasts of Future War, 1921–1941." In Pons and Romano, *Russia in the Age of Wars,* 215–234.

Priestland, David. *Stalinism and the Politics of Mobilisation: Ideas, Power, and Terror in Inter-war Russia.* Oxford: Oxford University Press, 2007.

Radosh, Ronald, et al., eds. *Spain Betrayed: The Soviet Union in the Spanish Civil War.* New Haven, CT: Yale University Press, 2001.

Raleigh, Donald J. "Russian Civil War, 1917–1922." In *The Cambridge History of Russia,* edited by Ronald Grigor Suny, 3:140–167. 3 vols. Cambridge: Cambridge University Press, 1996.

Rapoport, Vitaly, and Iuri Alexeev. *High Treason: Essays on the History of the Red Army, 1918–1938.* Durham, NC: Duke University Press, 1985.

Rayfield, Donald. *Stalin and His Hangmen.* Viking: London, 2004.

Reese, Roger. "The Impact of the Great Purge on the Red Army: Wrestling with Hard Numbers." *Soviet and Post-Soviet Review* 19, no. 1–3 (1992): 71–90.

———. "The Red Army and the Great Purges." In *Stalinist Terror: New Perspectives,* edited by J. Arch Getty and Roberta T. Manning, 198–214. Cambridge: Cambridge University Press, 1993.

————. *Red Commanders: A Social History of the Soviet Army Officer Corps, 1918–1991*. Lawrence: University Press of Kansas, 2005.

————. "Red Army Opposition to Forced Collectivization, 1929–1930: The Army Wavers." *Slavic Review* 55, no. 1 (1996): 24–45.

————. *The Soviet Military Experience: A History of the Soviet Army, 1917–1991*. London: Routledge, 2000.

————. *Stalin's Reluctant Soldiers: A Social History of the Red Army, 1925–1941*. Lawrence: University Press of Kansas, 1996.

Reiber, Alfred J. "Stalin as Foreign Policy-Maker: Avoiding War, 1927–1953." In *Stalin: A New History*, edited by Sarah Davies and James Harris, 140–158. Cambridge: Cambridge University Press, 2005.

Reiman, Michel. *The Birth of Stalinism: The USSR on the Eve of the "Second Revolution."* Bloomington: Indiana University Press, 1987.

————. "Trotsky and the Struggle for 'Lenin's Heritage.'" In *The Trotsky Reappraisal*, edited by Terry Brotherstone and Paul Dukes, 41–52. Edinburgh: Edinburgh University Press, 1992.

Rigby, T. H., ed. *The Stalin Dictatorship: Khrushchev's "Secret Speech" and Other Documents*. Sydney: Sydney University Press, 1968.

Rittersporn, Gábor. *Stalinist Simplifications and Soviet Complications: Social Tensions and Political Conflicts in the USSR, 1933–1953*. Chur, Reading: Harwood, 1991.

————. "Terror and Soviet Legality: Police vs. Judiciary, 1933–1940." In *The Anatomy of Terror: Political Violence under Stalin*, edited by James Harris, 176–190. Oxford: Oxford University Press, 2013.

Roberts, Geoffrey. "The Fascist War Threat and Soviet Politics in the 1930s." In Pons and Romano, *Russia in the Age of Wars*, 147–158.

Robinson, Paul. *The White Russian Army in Exile*. Oxford: Oxford University Press, 2002.

Rogovin, Vadim. *1937: Stalin's Year of Terror*. Oak Park, MI: Mehring Books, 1998.

Sakwa, Richard. *Soviet Communists in Power: A Study of Moscow during the Civil War, 1918–21*. Basingstoke: Macmillan, 1988.

Samuelson, Lennart. *Plans for Stalin's War Machine: Tukhachevskii and Military Economic Planning, 1925–1941*. Basingstoke: Macmillan, 2000.

————. "Wartime Perspective and Economic Planning: Tukhachevsky and the Military-Industrial Complex, 1925–37." In Pons and Romano, *Russia in the Age of Wars*, 187–214.

Sanborn, Joshua. *Drafting the Russian Nation: Military Conscription, Total War, and Mass Politics, 1905–1925*. Dekalb: Northern Illinois University Press, 2003.

Schapiro, Leonard. "The Great Purge." In *The Soviet Army*, edited by B. H. Liddell Hart, 65–72. London: Weidenfeld & Nicolson, 1957.

Service, Robert. *Trotsky: A Biography*. Cambridge, MA: Belknap Press of Harvard University Press, 2009.

Shcherbakova, I. L., ed. *Nakazannyi narod: po materialam konferentsii "Repressii protiv rossiiskikh nemtsev v Sovetskom Soiuze v kontekste sovetskoi natsional'noi politiki."* Moscow: Zven'ia, 1999.

Shearer, David R. "Crime and Social Disorder in Stalin's Russia: A Reassessment of the Great Retreat and the Origins of the Mass Repression." *Cahiers du Monde russe* 39, no. 1–2 (1998): 119–148.

———. *Industry, State, and Society in Stalin's Russia, 1926–1934*. Ithaca, NY: Cornell University Press, 1996.

———. *Policing Stalin's Socialism: Repression and Social Order in the Soviet Union, 1924–1953*. New Haven, CT: Yale University Press, 2009.

Shinin, O. V. "Deiatel'nost' dal'nevostochnykh organov gosudarstvennoi bezopasnosti po dobyvaniiu informatsii o politicheskom, voennom i ekonomicheskom polozhenii prigranichnykh gosudarstv v mezhvoennye gody (1922–1941)." In *Istoricheskie chteniia na lubianke, 1997–2007*, edited by A. A. Zdanovich et al., 228–241. Moscow: Kuchkovo Pole, 2008.

Shlapentokh, Dmitry. *The Counter-revolution in Revolution: Image of Thermidor and Napoleon at the Time of the Russian Revolution and Civil War*. Basingstoke: Macmillan, 1999.

Simonov, Nikolai. "'Strengthen the Defence of the Land of Soviets': The 1927 'War Alarm' and Its Consequences." *Europe–Asia Studies* 48, no. 8 (1996): 1355–1364.

Sokolov, Andrei. "Before Stalinism: The Early 1920s." In *Guns and Rubles: The Defence Industry in the Stalinist State*, edited by Mark Harrison, 31–49. New Haven, CT: Yale University, Sheridan Books, 2008.

Solomon, Peter. *Soviet Criminal Justice under Stalin*. Cambridge: Cambridge University Press, 1996.

Stalin, Josef. *Sochineniia*. 13 vols. Moscow: Gosudarstvennoe izdatel'stvo politicheskoi literatury, 1947–1951.

———. *Works*. 13 vols. Moscow: Foreign Languages Publishing House, 1952–1955.

Starkov, Boris. "Narkom Ezhov." In *Stalinist Terror: New Perspectives*, edited by J. Arch Getty and Robert T. Manning, 21–39. Cambridge: Cambridge University Press, 1993.

Steiner, Zara. *The Lights That Failed: European International History, 1919–1933*. Oxford: Oxford University Press, 2005.

Stoecker, Sally. *Forging Stalin's Army: Marshal Tukhachevsky and the Politics of Military Innovation*. Boulder, CO: Westview Press, 1998.

Stone, David. *Hammer and Rifle: The Militarization of the Soviet Union, 1926–1933*. Lawrence: University Press of Kansas, 2000.

———. "The Prospect of War? Lev Trotskii, the Soviet Army, and the German Revolution in 1923." *International History Review* 25, no. 4 (2003): 799–817.

———. "The Russian Civil War, 1917–1921." In *The Military History of the Soviet Union*, edited by R. Higham and F. W. Kagan, 13–34. New York: Palgrave, 2002.

———. "Tukhachevsky in Leningrad: Military Politics and Exile, 1928–1931." *Europe–Asia Studies* 48, no. 8 (1996): 1365–1386.

Stone, David, and Robert Ponichtera. "The Russo-Polish War." In *The Military History of the Soviet Union*, edited by R. Higham and F. W. Kagan, 35–50. New York: Palgrave, 2002.

Stukov, B. G. "Dokumenty spetssluzhb svidetel'stvuiut. Rossiiskaia politicheskaia emigratsiia v mezhvoennyi period (1920–1930-e gg.)." In *Istoricheskie chteniia na lubianke, 1997–2007*, edited by A. A. Zdanovich et al., 117–129. Moscow: Kuchkovo Pole, 2008.

Sudoplatov, Pavel. *Special Tasks: The Memoirs of an Unwanted Witness—A Soviet Spymaster.* London: Little, Brown, 1994.

Suvenirov, Oleg. "Narkomat oborony i NKVD v predvoennye gody." *Voprosy istorii* 6 (1991): 26–35.

———. *Tragediia RKKA, 1937–1938.* Moscow: Terra, 1998.

Swain, Geoffrey. *Russia's Civil War.* Charleston, SC: Tempus, 2000.

———. "Vatsetis: The Enigma of the Red Army's First Commander." *Revolutionary Russia* 16, no. 1 (2003): 68–86.

Tarkhova, Nonna. *Krasnaia armiia i stalinskaia kollektivizatsiia, 1928–1933 gg.* Moscow: Rosspen, 2010.

Taylor, Brian D. *Politics and the Russian Army: Civil–Military Relations, 1689–2000.* Cambridge: Cambridge University Press, 2003.

Taylor, Sally J. *Stalin's Apologist: Walter Duranty, the* New York Times*'s Man in Moscow.* Oxford: Oxford University Press, 1990.

Thatcher, Ian. *Trotsky.* London: Routledge, 2002.

Thurston, Robert. *Life and Terror in Stalin's Russia, 1934–1941.* New Haven, CT: Yale University Press, 1996.

Trotsky, Leon. *The Military Writings and Speeches of Leon Trotsky.* Vol. 1, *1918: How the Revolution Armed.* London: New Park, 1979.

———. *The Trotsky Papers, 1917–1922.* 2 vols. Edited by Jan Meijer. The Hague: Mouton, 1964–1971.

Tucker, Robert C. *Stalin in Power: The Revolution from Above, 1928–1941.* New York: Norton, 1990.

Tukhachevskii, Mikhail. *Izbrannye proizvedeniia.* 2 vols. Edited by G. I. Oskin and P. P. Chernushkov. Moscow: Voenizdat, 1964.

Tumshis, Mikhail, and Aleksandr Papchinskii. *1937 Bol'shaia chistka: NKVD protiv Cheka.* Moscow: Eksmo, 2009.

Tynchenko, Iaroslav. *Golgofa russkogo ofitserstva v SSSR, 1930–1931 gody.* Moscow: Moskovskii obshchestvennyi nauchnyi fond, 2000.

Ulam, Adam. *Stalin: The Man and His Era.* New York: Viking Press, 1974.

van Ree, Erik. *The Political Thought of Joseph Stalin: A Study in 20th Century Revolutionary Patriotism.* Richmond: Routledge Curzon, 2002.

Velikanova, Olga. *Popular Perceptions of Soviet Politics in the 1920s: Disenchantment of the Dreamers.* Basingstoke: Palgrave Macmillan, 2013.

Viktorov, Boris. *Bez grifa "sekretno": zapiski voennogo prokurora.* Moscow: Iurid. litra, 1990.

Vinogradov, V. K. "Tret'ia reforma organov bezopasnosti (1934–1941)." In *Trudy Obshchestva izucheniia istorii otechestvennykh spetssluzhb*, edited by V. K. Bylinin et al., 2:76–96. 4 vols. Moscow: Kuchkovo Pole, 2006.

Vinogradov, V. K., et al., eds. *Arkhiv VChK: sbornik dokumentov.* Moscow: Kuchkovo Pole, 2007.

Vinokurov, V. I. *Istoriia voennoi diplomatii: voennaia diplomatiia mezhdu pervoi i vtoroi mirovymi voinami.* 4 vols. Moscow: Inzhener, 2010.

Viola, Lynne. *Peasant Rebels Under Stalin: Collectivization and the Culture of Peasant Resistance.* New York: Oxford University Press, 1996.

———. "Popular Resistance in the Stalinist 1930s: Soliloquy of a Devil's Advocate." *Kritika: Explorations in Russian and Eurasian History* 1, no. 1 (2000): 45–69.

Viola, Lynne, et al., eds. *The Tragedy of the Soviet Countryside.* Vol. 1, *The War against the Peasantry, 1927–1930.* New Haven, CT: Yale University Press, 2005.

Voitikov, S. S. *Otechestvennye spetssluzhby i krasnaia armiia, 1917–1921.* Moscow: Veche, 2010.

———. *Trotskii i zagovor v krasnoi stavke.* Moscow: Veche, 2009.

Volkogonov, Dmitri. *Stalin: Triumph and Tragedy.* London: Weidenfeld & Nicolson, 1991.

von Hagen, Mark. "Civil–Military Relations and the Evolution of the Soviet Socialist State." *Slavic Review* 50, no. 2 (1991): 268–276.

———. *Soldiers in the Proletarian Dictatorship: The Red Army and the Soviet Socialist State, 1917–1930.* Ithaca, NY: Cornell University Press, 1990.

Voroshilov, Kliment. *Stalin and the Red Army.* Moscow: Foreign Languages Publishing House, 1941.

———. *Stat'i i rechi.* Moscow: Partizdat, 1937.

Vos'moi s'ezd RKP(b), mart 1919 goda: protokoly. Moscow: Gospolitizdat, 1919.

Wade, Rex. *Red Guards and Workers' Militias in the Russian Revolution.* Palo Alto, CA: Stanford University Press, 1984.

Wheatcroft, Stephen. "Agency and Terror: Evdokimov and the Mass Killing in Stalin's Great Terror." *Australian Journal of Politics and History* 53, no. 1 (2007): 20–43.

Wildman, Allan. *The End of the Imperial Army.* 2 vols. Princeton, NJ: Princeton University Press, 1987.

Wollenberg, Erich. *The Red Army.* London: Secker & Warburg, 1938.

XVII s'ezd Vsesoiuzno kommunisticheskoi partii (b), 26 ianvaria—10 fevralia 1934 g.: stenograficheskii otchet. Moscow: Partizdat, 1923.

Zdanovich, Aleksandr. "Byvshie morskie ofitsery kak ob'ekt operativnogo vozdeistviia organov VChK-OGPU (1918–1931)." In *Istoricheskie chtenia na Lubianke, 1997–2007,* edited by Aleksandr Zdanovich et al., 102–116. Moscow: Kuchkovo Pole, 2008.

———. *Organy gosudarstvennoi bezopasnosti i krasnaia armiia.* Moscow: Kuchkovo Pole, 2008.

Zhuravlev, V. V., et al., eds. *Vlast' i oppozitsiia: rossiiskii politicheskii protsess XX stoletiia.* Moscow: Rossiiskaia politicheskaia entsiklopediia, 1995.

Ziemke, Earl F. *The Red Army, 1918–1941: From Vanguard of World Revolution to US Ally.* London: Frank Cass, 2004.

Zolotarev, V. A., et al., eds. *Russkaia voennaia emigratsiia 20-kh-40-kh godov: dokumenty i materialy.* 5 vols. Moscow: Geia and Triada-f, 1998–2002.

Index